An Educational
Resource Published
by the Society of
Wine Educators

SOCIETY
of WINE
EDUCATORS

D1710094

CERTIFIED
SPECIALIST
OF WINE

**STUDY GUIDE
2022**

The Society of Wine Educators (SWE) is a membership-based nonprofit organization focused on providing wine and spirits education along with the conferral of several certifications. The Society is internationally recognized and its programs are highly regarded for both their quality and relevance to the industry.

The mission of the Society of Wine Educators is to set the standard for quality and responsible wine and spirits education and professional certification.

With its diverse programs, SWE is unique among other educational programs in the wine and spirits field. Each year, the Society presents an annual conference with over 50 educational sessions and significant opportunities for professional interaction. Education and networking are further enhanced through symposiums, the Society's newsletter, and robust social media efforts.

SWE offers four professional credentials for those seeking to certify their wine and spirits knowledge, including the Certified Specialist of Wine (CSW), the Certified Specialist of Spirits (CSS), the Certified Wine Educator (CWE), and the Certified Spirits Educator (CSE). In addition, the Hospitality/Beverage Specialist Certificate is available, offered both as a self-study guide and an online class.

SWE members include the following types of individuals:
- Educators offering classes and tastings
- Instructors in public and private colleges, universities, and hospitality schools
- Importers, distributors, and producers
- Retailers, restaurateurs, and hoteliers
- Industry consultants
- Sommeliers, wine stewards, bartenders, and mixologists
- Culinary and hospitality school students
- Wine industry media professionals
- Wine enthusiasts

For more information about the Society's educational and membership programs, please contact us.

Society of Wine Educators
Telephone: (202) 408-8777
Website: www.societyofwineeducators.org

ACKNOWLEDGMENTS

This Certified Specialist of Wine Study Guide is based on previous editions, and the Society greatly appreciates the efforts of those who contributed to earlier versions.

SWE also extends its thanks to the following authors for their extensive contributions to specific chapters:
- Marian Baldy, PhD, CWE: "The Sensory Evaluation of Wine"
- Edward M. Korry, CSS, CWE: "Wine Etiquette and Service," "Food and Wine Pairing," and "Responsible Beverage Alcohol Service"

The Society is also grateful to the following people and organizations for their generosity in providing SWE with permission to use their figures and images throughout this publication:
- International Riesling Foundation (Riesling flavor profile)
- William Lembeck, CWE (maps)
- Lodi Winegrape Commission ("Lodi Rules Sustainable Winegrowing Certified Green Seal" logo)
- USDA National Organic Program (NOP logo)
- Verband Deutscher Qualitäts und Prädikatsweingüter (VDP logo)
- Mick Stephenson – mickstephenson.photoshelter.com ("Two-year-old and six-year-old Cabernet Sauvignon" photo)
- Genta_hgr Photography (photo of Koshu grapes)
- Vbecart Photography (photo of Marselan grapes)

INTRODUCTION

Despite the simple conversion from fruit to fermented beverage, wine is an extremely complex product. The diversity of grape varieties, viticultural practices, and winemaking techniques results in a broad array of divergent wine styles in the marketplace. As the wine industry continues to grow, diversify, and become global in scope, an understanding of the ever-changing world of wine becomes increasingly necessary to succeed in the field.

The Certified Specialist of Wine (CSW) credential meets this need by providing wine professionals with a solid foundation of knowledge that will prepare them to build or enhance their careers. In addition, earning the CSW certification publicly acknowledges that the holder has successfully acquired this knowledge.

The knowledge base needed to pass the CSW Exam is contained in this Study Guide, and all CSW Exam questions are drawn exclusively from it. However, many questions on the examination will require the candidate to interpret this information or to use multiple pieces of data together in order to come to a conclusion. Candidates are expected to read the CSW Study Guide in its entirety in preparing for the exam, as exam questions may be based on any of the information contained herein.

MAPS

The maps included in this Study Guide are available electronically on the membership portal of the SWE website. Candidates are encouraged to access these maps electronically and are granted permission to download copies of the maps for personal use. The maps are considered an integral part of the material in this Study Guide, and candidates should expect that information from the maps will be included on the CSW Exam.

RESOURCES FOR CSW CANDIDATES

The Society of Wine Educators offers many resources for CSW students and exam candidates, including the following:

Webinars: Monthly SWEbinars, available at no charge and to the public, covering CSW- and CSS-related topics. For more information, including the schedule, see the SWEbinar webpage at SWE's blog, http://winewitandwisdomswe.com/.

The Insider's Guide to the CSW Exam: Offered at least once a month, this SWEbinar will cover all aspects of the CSW, including what the test covers, how difficult the test is, what types of questions to expect, the resources available to students, and how long SWE recommends for study before sitting for the exam. Find the latest schedule for the Insider's Guide to the CSW Exam on our SWEbinar webpage: http://winewitandwisdomswe.com/swebinars-2/swebinar-schedule/.

Online Prep Classes: Several times a year, SWE offers instructor-led online prep classes covering the CSW Study Guide. These classes are offered free of charge for professional members of SWE who hold a current CSW Exam attendance credit. For more information, contact Jane Nickles at jnickles@societyofwineeducators.org.

Workbook: A workbook designed to accompany this Study Guide is available for purchase through Amazon.com. For other purchase options, please contact SWE's Home Office.

Study Guide Updates: To assist all members of the adult beverage industry so that they may keep current with the ever-changing world of wine and spirits, SWE maintains "Study Guide Updates" pages for both the CSW and CSS Study Guides. Any changes that occur in the regulatory landscape, or elsewhere, that affect the information in the Study Guides will be updated on these pages. To access our Study Guide Updates page, see http://winewitandwisdomswe.com/study-guide-updates/.

eBook: Our CSW Study Guide is available as an eBook on both Amazon and iTunes.

CSW Exams: The CSW Exam consists of 100 multiple-choice questions, with all question content drawn exclusively from the CSW Study Guide. Candidates are provided with one (1) hour in which to complete the exam. CSW Exams are available most days of the year throughout the world, by appointment, at Pearson VUE Testing Centers, as well as via at-home, online proctored exams through ProctorU. To find a Pearson VUE Center near you, use the search function on SWE's landing page at the Pearson VUE website: http://www.pearsonvue.com/societyofwineeducators/.

Exams based on the 2022 version of the CSW Study Guide will be available at Pearson VUE Testing Centers and via ProctorU through December 30, 2024.

ORGANIZATION OF THE CSW STUDY GUIDE

The CSW Study Guide is organized into four units, each consisting of multiple chapters:

Unit One – Wine Defined: This unit comprises two chapters covering information about the chemical composition of wine and provides information concerning the most common wine faults that reduce the quality of wines, whether they have been poorly made or have become contaminated.

Unit Two – Viticulture and Enology: This unit covers grape growing and winemaking and provides a summary of the characteristics of the world's most successful wine grapes. Specialized branches of winemaking, such as organic, dessert, fortified, and sparkling wines, are covered here as well.

Unit Three – Wine Labels, Laws, and Regions: This is the largest section of the Study Guide, and it includes a detailed discussion of the wine regions of the world. The unit begins with an introduction to the world wine industry, with an emphasis on the European Union. Subsequent chapters of this unit provide detailed information on the primary winegrowing countries and regions of the world, including geography, climate, significant grape varieties, and wine laws.

Unit Four – Wine Consumption and Service: This unit begins with a discussion of the sensory perception of wine from a physiological point of view. The procedures for setting up a formal wine tasting, the etiquette of wine service, the pairing of food and wine, and a short overview of the health issues surrounding wine and alcohol are covered as well.

Additional Resources: Following the four main units, the appendixes contain a glossary of wine terms, a bibliography, a supplementary reading list, a wine aroma checklist, and the SWE Logical Tasting Rationale.

TABLE OF CONTENTS

SOCIETY
of WINE
EDUCATORS

WINE DEFINED

UNIT ONE

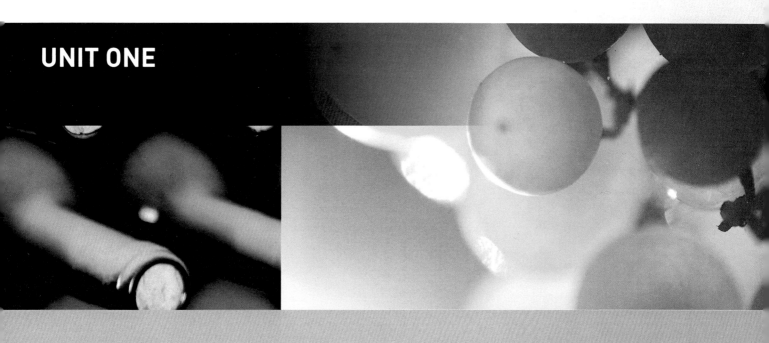

UNIT ONE WINE DEFINED

WINE COMPOSITION AND CHEMISTRY

CHAPTER ONE

LEARNING OBJECTIVES

After studying this chapter, the candidate should be able to:

• Recognize the main categories of chemical compounds in wine.
• Identify the approximate concentrations of the major components of wine.
• Describe the specific types of alcohols, acids, and sugars that are most prominent in wine.
• Discuss the types of phenolic compounds that are important in wine.

Wine is the fermented product of grapes. Although beverages such as strawberry wine and rice wine are produced with other raw materials, the unmodified term in the United States legally refers to a beverage made from grapes. Of all the types of fruit in the world, grapes have the most valued combination of fermentable sugars, significant acidity, desirable flavors, and liquid content to make a complex beverage like wine.

From the scientist's point of view, wine is a complex blend of chemicals that collectively give the liquid its visual, olfactory, and tactile characteristics. Many chemical compounds found in wine originate in the grapes themselves and remain in the liquid from the wine press to the bottle. Others are created during the fermentation process through the action of yeast cells. Still others occur along the way in purely chemical reactions when molecules interact, break apart, and recombine as new compounds.

Many of these chemical reactions continue to expand and evolve over time. As a consequence, the concentrations of some compounds increase as a wine ages, while others decrease with time,

resulting in a wine's ever-changing character. While some wines become more complex and desirable with time, others begin to fade soon after bottling. However, the truth remains that with sufficient time, nearly all wines are overcome by undesirable components as the chemical reactions reach their final stages.

The major components of wine include the following:
• Water
• Alcohol
• Acid
• Sugar
• Phenolic compounds

Various impurities such as bacteria may also be present in wine, but modern winemaking techniques usually reduce the amount of any unintended components to a negligible level. Other compounds, such as yeast or proteins, may be present in very small concentrations in some wines, particularly those that have undergone extensive aging in contact with yeast cells.

WINE COMPONENTS

WATER

Wine is typically 80–90% water. The water in wine is primarily from the grapes themselves, although small amounts of water may be added incidentally during winemaking. Although an uncommon practice, in some situations the winemaker will intentionally add water to dilute grape juice or wine when potential alcohol, actual alcohol, or phenolic compounds are beyond desired levels.

ALCOHOL

After water, the most prevalent ingredient in wine is alcohol, which is usually 10–15% of the volume, although there are certainly many examples of wines that contain more or less than this average amount. *Ethyl alcohol*, also referred to as *ethanol*, is the primary result of alcoholic fermentation and the main alcohol component of wine. Other types of alcohol that occur in smaller amounts include *glycerol* and *methyl alcohol* (or *methanol*), as well as a group of compounds known as *fusel alcohols* (*fusel oils*) or *higher alcohols*.

Alcohol is the intoxicating element in wine and is what distinguishes wine from grape juice. Ethanol is a volatile compound, which means that it evaporates easily. When it does, it carries the wine's aromas to the nose.

Alcohol content is one element that contributes to the mouth-filling, tactile sensation of a wine as it rests on the palate; this sensation is often referred to as a wine's "weight" or "body." Wines with higher levels of alcohol tend to be heavier in weight than wines with lower levels of alcohol, all other things being equal. High levels of alcohol can also result in slow, thick-appearing "tears" or "legs" in the glass after the wine is swirled.

Figure 1–1: Wine diamonds

ACID

Water and alcohol are essential to wine, but it is the other components that make each wine unique. A variety of acids, especially in white wines, give the wine much of its structure, balance, and thirst-quenching refreshment. Acids usually make up between 0.5% and 0.75% of a wine's volume.

The principal acids in wine include the following:

- *Tartaric acid*
  Tartaric acid is the most prevalent of the acids found in both grapes and wine. It is also the strongest in terms of pH. Tartaric acid also has a unique propensity to form solid crystals at low temperatures. These crystals are known as tartrates, or "wine diamonds" if found in wine. Once tartaric acid takes this form, it will not redissolve into the liquid, and the wine will become noticeably less acidic. Tartrate crystals are not considered a defect in most wines; however, the formation of tartrates in bottled wine can be avoided or minimized via the winemaking process of cold stabilization (see chapter five).

- *Malic acid*
  Malic acid is a sharp-tasting acid frequently associated with green apples. Underripe grapes and cool-climate grapes are typically high in malic acid. However, the level of malic acid decreases during the ripening phase of the grapes on the vine. Wines made from overripe grapes or grapes grown in hot climates tend to have relatively low levels of this acid. High levels of malic acid can be assuaged using the winemaking technique known as *malolactic fermentation*.

- *Citric acid*
  Citric acid is not usually considered to be a normal component of grapes, as it exists in such minute quantities that specialized equipment is required to measure it. Therefore, it has no sensory impact on the majority of wines. However, citric acid is sometimes added to increase the total acidity in a wine, although its distinctive citrus fruit flavor makes it generally unsuitable for quality wines.

- *Lactic acid*
  Lactic acid is not found in grapes; rather, it is created in wine by lactic acid bacteria, which convert malic acid into lactic acid in the optional winemaking process known as malolactic fermentation. As lactic acid is less intensely acidic than malic acid, wines that undergo malolactic fermentation tend to be softer and smoother in mouthfeel than those that do not. The by-products of malolactic fermentation also provide wine with

a creamy texture and, in some cases, a "buttery" aroma. Lactic acid is also created during primary fermentation, albeit in very small amounts.

- *Acetic acid*
  Acetic acid is the acid found in most types of vinegar. A low level of acetic acid is typically created during fermentation. Unlike the other acids discussed above, acetic acid is volatile, so it readily evaporates and joins the aromas of the wine, adding to the complexity of a wine's bouquet, particularly in red wines. However, higher concentrations, typically the result of a chemical reaction between ethanol and oxygen caused by harmful (to wine) bacteria called *acetobacter*, can be unpleasant and may make a wine undrinkable.

- *Succinic acid*
  Succinic acid is a minor component in grapes and a by-product of normal alcoholic fermentation. Succinic acid has a sharp, slightly bitter, slightly salty flavor.

GRAPE ACIDS	FERMENTATION ACIDS
Tartaric Acid	Lactic Acid
Malic Acid	Acetic Acid
(Citric Acid)	Succinic Acid
(Succinic Acid)	

Total Acidity and pH

Two numbers are used to describe the acidity level of a wine. One is for *total acidity* (TA), which is the volume of all the acids in a wine. In general, more acid equates to a more acidic taste. However, TA includes several different acids, some of which are stronger than others. For that reason, a second measurement, *pH*, is also used.

The pH level of a wine represents the combined chemical strength of the acids present. Wine usually measures between 2.9 and 3.9 on the logarithmic pH scale. A *lower* pH indicates a *stronger* acid content. Thus, a wine with a pH of 2.9 will be more acidic than a wine with a pH of 3.4. To get a complete picture of a wine's acidity, you need to know both its TA and pH. However, winemakers place particular emphasis on pH, as it gives an indication of stability and plays a role in determining sulfur additions.

SUGAR

Grapes typically contain 15% to 28% sugar at harvest. More specifically, the grapes contain roughly equal amounts of two sugars:
- Glucose
- Fructose

Glucose and fructose are both highly fermentable monosaccharides, commonly known as "simple sugars." During fermentation, given the right conditions, yeast converts these sugars into ethanol, turning grape juice into wine. If the yeast is both able to and allowed to finish the job, the wine will be fermented to dryness. However, even dry wines contain a trace amount of sugar, as grapes actually contain tiny quantities of unfermentable sugars. These unfermentable sugars generally remain in concentrations below one's ability to detect them.

Wines that have less sugar than a person can taste are described as *dry*. However, many wines do have detectable sugar. This is generally because the fermentation was stopped, through winemaker intervention or by natural causes, before all of the sugar was converted to alcohol. Depending on the amount of residual (remaining) sugar, the wines may be called *off-dry* (sometimes referred to as *medium dry*), *medium sweet*, or *sweet*. Residual sugar can add weight and viscosity to a wine, and as such—particularly in the case of sweet wines—can influence the mouthfeel, body, and texture of a wine.

The presence of sugar after fermentation adds a new dimension to the taste of a wine, which may be desirable or not, depending on the situation. Some of the world's most renowned dessert wines are extremely sweet, even up to 24% or more residual sugar. In other cases, a small amount of sweetness is used to balance high acidity in a wine, or vice versa. In some lower-quality wines, sweetness may be used to hide the wine's minor flaws.

The production of sweet wines will be covered in more detail in chapter 5.

PHENOLIC COMPOUNDS

Phenolic compounds (also known as *phenolics*, *polyphenolics*, or *polyphenols*) are a large category of various molecules that are present in many wines. Phenolics occur in wine in minute quantities, yet they can have a major impact on the sensory profile of a wine.

Phenolics include the following:
- *Anthocyanins*
  Anthocyanins are compounds that give red wine its color, which in fact ranges from blue to purple to red. The color of a red wine is influenced by both the amount of anthocyanins and the acidity level of the wine; more acidic wines appear redder in hue, while less acidic ones appear bluer.

- *Flavonols*
  These yellow pigments are found in white wines. Flavonols (sometimes called *flavones*) increase in grapes with increased exposure to sunlight; therefore, white wines from sunnier climates tend to have a more golden color than white wines from cooler (or cloudier) climates.

- *Tannins*
  Tannins are astringent, bitter compounds found in the skins, seeds, and stems of grapes. They are also found in oak and oak barrels. These compounds form part of the structure, or "backbone," of big red wines. Tannins are a natural preservative and help to protect red wines from oxidation during the aging process. When present in a young wine, tannins are easily recognizable by the textural, drying sensation they create in the mouth.

- *Vanillin*
  Vanillin is an aromatic phenolic compound in oak that imparts a vanilla scent to barrel-aged wines. While vanilla aromas are often associated with American oak, the amount of vanillin present in the wood varies according to several factors—including the level of seasoning used in the preparation of the barrel and the age and size of the barrel—as well as species of oak. In general, the level of vanillin increases (as compared to raw oak) with light to medium toast levels and may decrease with the use of heavier levels of toast.

- *Resveratrol*
  A compound in wine believed to have several beneficial health effects in humans, resveratrol is discussed in more detail in chapter 22.

The phenolics of a grape are concentrated primarily in its skin and seeds. Because of this, red wines, which are fermented in contact with the grape solids, are much richer in phenolic compounds than white wines.

Over time, some phenolic compounds, particularly tannins and pigments, tend to polymerize, or combine into longer molecule chains. These chains may eventually become too heavy to stay suspended in the liquid and may drop out of the solution as sediment. This development has a major impact on the flavor of the wine and is one of the main results of the aging process. In many cases, the production of sediment in a properly-aged red wine renders a wine lighter in color and less astringent. However, it should be noted that new research indicates that polymerized tannins can possibly continue to alter in structure and may eventually break down during extended aging; thus it may be impossible to predict how the tannins in a well-aged wine will be perceived by the taster.

OTHER COMPONENTS
- *Aldehydes*
  Aldehydes are oxidized alcohols that are formed when wine is exposed to air. Some wines such as Sherry and Madeira are made using techniques that encourage the formation of aldehydes, but any wine will take on an oxidized or "maderized" character if it has been exposed to excessive oxygen during production or storage. Wines may also become oxidized after being open too long or exposed to heat. The most common aldehyde in wine is *acetaldehyde*, which is formed by the oxidation of ethanol. Acetaldehyde contributes to the distinctive aroma of fino Sherry.

- ***Esters***

  Esters are molecules that result from the joining of an acid and an alcohol. They represent the largest group of odiferous compounds found in wine. Most are desirable at low concentrations, but some are considered off-odors when found in high enough concentrations. One of the most common esters in wine is *ethyl acetate*, the ester of acetic acid and ethanol. At low concentrations, ethyl acetate imparts a fruity, flowery aroma; however, at high concentrations, it may impart the faulty aromas of nail polish remover, varnish, or glue.

- ***Dissolved gases***

  Dissolved gases are inevitably present in any liquid, although they are not necessarily present in significant concentrations. In wine, dissolved oxygen promotes many chemical reactions through the process known as *oxidation*. While this may be beneficial to some wines, it can also be damaging. Thus, winemakers try to avoid air exposure and often add sulfur during the winemaking process in order to absorb any free oxygen molecules before these molecules have the opportunity to harm the wine.

  Another dissolved gas routinely found in wine is carbon dioxide (CO_2). This gas is what gives sparkling wine its bubbles. Carbon dioxide is a natural by-product of fermentation. Small amounts are present even in still wines, and some winemakers leave enough carbon dioxide in their wines to create a bit of petillance (slight bubbling under the surface) when the wine is poured. The CO_2 in wine keeps a wine feeling fresh and lively in the mouth and promotes the release of the wine's aromatic compounds.

- ***Sulfites***

  Sulfites are a class of chemicals that are based on the element sulfur. Sulfur is an important preservative that is widely used to keep wines stable after fermentation. Sulfur is also produced in minute quantities as a natural by-product of fermentation. Therefore, all wines contain at least trace amounts of sulfites even if no sulfur is added during winemaking. As sulfur is an antioxidant and an antibacterial agent, producing wine without the addition of sulfur is very challenging. Some people are extremely sensitive to sulfur and can have negative reactions to it. Therefore, wines destined for interstate commerce in the United States that contain more than 10 parts per million (ppm) of sulfur dioxide are required to display the "Contains Sulfites" warning on the label.

WINE FAULTS

CHAPTER TWO

LEARNING OBJECTIVES

After studying this chapter, the candidate should be able to:

- Recall the main terminology associated with wine faults.
- Describe the source and effect of cork taint.
- Discuss the impact of sulfur compounds on wine.
- Recognize which odors are acceptable and under which conditions.

Much of the flavor and, hopefully, the enjoyment of wine is due to its unique aromas. A wine's distinct scent is derived from many possible sources, including the grapes themselves, fermentation processes, aging, oxidation, or contact with oak.

With careful winemaking, most of the aromas that occur in wine will be pleasant and desirable, but winemaking errors, improper storage, or, in some cases, simple bad luck can introduce unpleasant aromas into a wine. The ability to recognize these wine faults is a crucial element of wine appreciation.

This chapter lists some of the faulty aromas occasionally found in wine. In some cases, these aromas are acceptable or even welcome in low concentrations, but they are considered faults at higher concentrations.

FAULTS IN WINE

2,4,6-TRICHLOROANISOLE (TCA)

One of the biggest concerns in terms of wine quality control is the incidence of a musty, moldy odor—similar to that of a dank basement—occasionally found in wine. Wines showing this aroma are often referred to as being *corked* or as having *cork taint*, although it is now known that infected corks are not the only source of this fault.

The culprit is a mold that can grow on and in the bark of the cork oak tree, on the winemaking implements, or even in the winery itself. This mold readily interacts with other compounds to generate the chemical 2,4,6-trichloroanisole, also known as TCA. If the TCA leaches out of a cork and into the wine, or if it is present in the wine from other sources, the wine may display an overtly unpleasant odor. In milder cases, the wine will taste muted or seem less flavorful as a result of the spoilage, although it is not harmful to ingest.

TCA is highly persistent. If it saturates any part of a winery's environment (barrels, cardboard boxes, or even the winery's walls), it can even be transferred into wines that are sealed with screw caps or artificial corks. Thankfully, recent technological breakthroughs have shown promise, and some cork producers are predicting the eradication of cork taint in the next few years. In the meantime, while most industry experts agree that the incidence of cork taint has fallen in recent years, an exact figure has not been agreed upon. Current reports of cork taint vary widely, from a low of 1% to a high of 8% of the bottles produced each year.

TCA has an extremely low recognition threshold, meaning that it can be noticeable at relatively low concentrations. While some people cannot smell TCA at all, most can detect it at concentrations of 2 to 7 parts per trillion. Once identified, the aroma is unmistakable. However, many consumers have not been taught to identify the odor and simply find an infected wine to be somewhere between uninteresting and undrinkable, potentially dismissing the entire output of a producer, region, or grape variety as unpleasant.

ODORS RESULTING FROM SULFUR COMPOUNDS

As explained, sulfur is a common and often necessary preservative addition to wine. In excess, or combined with other chemicals, however, sulfur can produce some strong off-odors:

- **Sulfur dioxide (SO_2)**
  Wines with overly high concentrations of SO_2 will possess an acrid smell, similar to that of burnt matches. Sulfur dioxide may also cause an unpleasant "burning" sensation in the throat and nose. The sensory effects of SO_2 are directly related to pH. The more acidic the wine, the more pronounced the sulfur dioxide will be.

- **Hydrogen sulfide (H_2S)**
  When a sulfur-rich wine sits too long in the complete absence of oxygen, it may develop the odor of rotten eggs. This happens most often when a barrel or tank of wine rests for a long time with a large amount of yeast sediment in the bottom. It has also been reported as a potential problem for wines closed with screw caps, most of which, unlike corks, are impervious to oxygen.

- **Mercaptan**
  In some circumstances, *ethyl mercaptan* may form as a combination of sulfur and ethanol. This results in a very unpleasant odor, sometimes described as smelling like garlic or onions. Mercaptan is the odor added to odorless natural gas to help people detect a leak. Although it can be confused with hydrogen sulfide, this defect is very serious and is less remediable than are those encountered with the other two sulfur compounds.

ODORS RESULTING FROM THE ACTION OF BACTERIA

Although most bacteria cannot survive in the highly acidic environment that is wine, the major exceptions are lactic bacteria and acetobacter. These bacteria can wreak havoc in wine if allowed to flourish. Lactic bacteria are responsible for malolactic fermentation, intentional or otherwise, and acetobacter can convert alcohol into acetic acid. Such bacteria attack various chemical compounds in the wine—changing the composition of the wine and sometimes producing carbon dioxide or some other gas (a potentially disastrous situation in a sealed bottle)—and frequently produce unpleasant odors.

Typical bacteria-related off-odors include the following:

- *Acetic acid:* The odor of vinegar. The term "volatile acidity" may be used in reference to a wine with a decided aroma of white vinegar caused by acetic acid. The term *ascensence* may be used to refer to a fault evidenced in a wine with discernible volatile acidity accompanied by a high level of ethyl acetate (discussed below).
- *Butyric acid:* The odor of rancid butter or spoiled cheese.
- *Lactic acid:* A smell described as being like sauerkraut or a goat.
- *Ethyl acetate:* The odor of fingernail polish remover or model airplane glue. This common ester is formed through a reaction of ethanol and acetic acid.
- *Geranium fault:* An odor resembling crushed geranium leaves (which can be overwhelming); normally caused by the metabolism of sorbic acid (derived from potassium sorbate, a preservative) via lactic acid bacteria (as used for malolactic fermentation)

ODORS RESULTING FROM OTHER CAUSES

Additional off-odors are described as the following:

- *Brett:* Short for *Brettanomyces*, "Brett" is a member of the yeast family and can infect a winery and some or all of the wines made there. Brett causes a "sweaty" or "horsy" odor, or it may simply deaden the primary flavors in a wine. Other common descriptors for Brett include "Band-Aid–like" or "medicinal." Some people find Brett in small quantities to be acceptable, while others consider its presence to be a fault at any level.
- *Green:* The odor of leaves, usually resulting from the use of immature (underripe) grapes.
- *Oxidized:* Oxygen from the air will physically dissolve in wine that has been exposed to air. This oxygen then reacts with some of the phenolic compounds in the wine. The resulting chemical oxidative reaction may create acetaldehyde. While the nutty, caramelized character of oxidation is an aroma classically associated with fino Sherry, when it is present in wines that are not intentionally oxidized, those wines have a pronounced lack of fruit character. Browning may also occur.
- *Maderized:* A cooked or baked odor, resulting from excessive heating or oxidization. This is generally considered to be a fault; however, it is an acceptable characteristic in wines such as Madeira that are deliberately heated.
- *Moldy:* The odor of mold resulting from the use of moldy grapes or moldy barrels.
- *Rubbery:* The odor of rubber, sometimes associated with very low-acid wines or excess sulfur.
- *Stagnant:* A stale water odor.
- *Stemmy:* The bitter, green odor of grape stems.

- *Wet cardboard:* A papery chemical odor, frequently associated with cork taint or the misuse of filter pads or filtering materials.
- *Yeasty or leesy:* A pronounced odor of yeast that may develop if dead yeast cells remain in contact with the wine too long, although this is normal and acceptable in sparkling wines and some other wines that are intentionally aged "on the lees."
- *Reduction or reductive:* A term that refers to a smell of rotten eggs, garlic, struck matches, cabbage, or burnt rubber. It is not an accurate term to describe the actual chemical process that creates these odors, but it is commonly used. These odors occur in what is known as reductive conditions: conditions that lack oxygen.

Depending on the source of the odor, it may be limited to a specific bottle, or it may be rampant through an entire batch of wine. Modern winemaking techniques permit many of these issues to be addressed if they are identified at the winery, but many of the problems may not be detected right away. Regardless of the cause, it is important for wine professionals to be able to recognize these odors in order to appropriately evaluate a given glass of wine.

CERTIFIED
SPECIALIST
OF WINE

VITICULTURE
AND ENOLOGY

UNIT TWO

GRAPE VARIETIES

CHAPTER THREE

LEARNING OBJECTIVES

After studying this chapter, the candidate should be able to:

- State the differences between *Vitis vinifera* and other vine species.
- Discuss hybrids, crossings, and clones.
- Describe the primary characteristics of the classic international white grape varieties.
- Describe the primary characteristics of the classic international red grape varieties.

Grapes are an extremely diverse agricultural product. A few other crops, such as apples and tomatoes, may have as wide-ranging a selection of cultivars and varieties as wine grapes, but in no other instance are so many different varieties grown commercially. Diversity even exists within the grape varieties themselves, as certain varieties of grapes are well-known to show radically different characteristics when grown in different soils, climates, and viticultural configurations.

GRAPEVINE SPECIES AND VARIETIES

As a vine, grapes belong to the genus *Vitis*. Within the *Vitis* genus, there are a few dozen different species of grapes. However, only one, *Vitis vinifera*, is used on a widespread basis in commercial winemaking. It is believed that vinifera vines developed in the Caucasus Mountains region between Europe and Asia and spread, largely due to human intervention, across southern Europe, into the Middle East, and eventually around the world.

As the habitat of vinifera vines expanded to encompass most of the temperate Western world, differences developed among the grapevines growing in disparate areas, due partly to natural evolution and partly to the encouragement given to certain strains of vines over others by early grape growers. Eventually, the differences became distinct enough that they could be identified as discrete subspecies, in the same way domesticated wolves over millennia became the vast array of dog breeds. The vine subspecies are more commonly called *grape varieties*, and thousands of them are recorded. Many are quite familiar to wine consumers, such as Sauvignon Blanc and Merlot, while others are known only among growers in obscure regions.

Beyond vinifera, there are several grape species native to North America that are also important to the wine industry, although not necessarily for wine production. One such example—*Vitis labrusca*—while commercially important, is primarily appreciated for its sweet, flavorful grapes that are used for fresh consumption or unfermented grape juice. Labrusca grapevines were found growing wild in America during the colonial period and were cultivated for winemaking, but these grapes were found to have extremely high acidity and a characteristic flavor component—often described as a *foxy* character—that, while pleasant in fresh grapes, is generally less desirable in wine.

One notable advantage that native North American vines have over vinifera is their natural resistance to the aphid-like insect phylloxera, which ravaged European vineyards in the nineteenth century and continues to wreak havoc worldwide. Attempts were made to breed vinifera with native North American vines to create phylloxera-resistant hybrid wine grapes, but the results were less successful than expected. However, growers soon discovered that the vinifera part of the vine, known as the *scion*, could be grafted onto the trunk, or rootstock, of North American vines to achieve a phylloxera-resistant plant. These days, *Vitis labrusca* rootstocks are still used for grafting, as are several other native North American vine species such as *Vitis riparia, Vitis aestivalis,* and *Vitis rupestris.*

TERMINOLOGY

Some terms that relate to vine types include the following:

- **Species**
  A species is a scientific grouping of plants or animals that are genetically similar, have broad characteristics in common, and can produce viable offspring through sexual reproduction. Grapevine species include vinifera and labrusca.

- **Variety**
  A variety is a subspecies. In winegrowing, a variety is an identifiable group of vines of the same species that share many characteristics of appearance, flavor, and growth. For example, Chardonnay and Syrah are varieties of vinifera.

- **Cross or crossing**
  A cross is the offspring of sexual reproduction between different subspecies within the same species. An example is Cabernet Sauvignon, which has been shown to be a cross between Cabernet Franc and Sauvignon Blanc.

- **Clone**
  In commercial viticulture, virtually all grape varieties are reproduced via *vegetative propagation*. This typically involves a cutting or offshoot from a single parent vine that is encouraged to sprout roots and produce a new plant. Initially, this new plant could be considered identical to the parent, at least in theory. However, with time it will likely develop some unique characteristics as it adapts to its new environment. If the new vine shows consistent distinctions (from its parent or other vines)—such as being slightly more vigorous or showing more aromatic intensity—it may be determined to be a

new clone. Clones are therefore slightly different from their parent, but not so unique as to be classified as a new variety. Pinot Noir is an example of a grape variety that is available in hundreds of clonal variations (although not all are viticulturally significant). Some clones of Pinot Noir are identified via a number (such as *115* or *447*), while others have acquired specific names such as the *Pommard, Dijon,* and *Wädenswil* clones.

- **Mutation**
  A *mutation* is a grape that has—via successive adaptation—developed characteristics distinct enough from its parent (or other plants) to be considered a separate variety. For example, Pinot Blanc and Pinot Gris are color mutations of Pinot Noir and are considered commercially distinct grape varieties.

- **Hybrid**
  A hybrid is the result of sexual reproduction between two closely related but different species, such as *Vitis vinifera* and *Vitis labrusca*. Many hybrid grape varieties have been developed over the years in an attempt to create a grape that could withstand the ravages of powdery mildew, phylloxera, cold weather, humidity, or other such challenges. Hybrids generally struggle to develop adequate levels of tannin and can be exceedingly acidic. For these reasons, hybrids are not universally accepted for use in commercial wine. However, some are consumer favorites, even in areas where vinifera thrives. Hybrids are normally not fertile, but they may still be propagated indefinitely through cuttings. Seyval Blanc, Vidal Blanc, and Baco Noir are among the more well-known and widely grown hybrids.

INTERNATIONAL VERSUS INDIGENOUS

Among the thousands of recognized grape varieties, most are relatively unknown. For example, few consumers have ever heard of Airén despite the fact that it is one of the most widely grown white wine grapes in the world. Perhaps this is because it is grown primarily in central Spain, whose wines are just beginning to be discovered by international consumers, or because it is so often distilled into brandy.

Among the several dozen or so grape varieties that have become well-known on an international scale, most became famous as the result of a single great wine produced in a specific area. Examples of this include Cabernet Sauvignon and Merlot from Bordeaux, as well as Pinot Noir and Chardonnay from Burgundy.

Other grape varieties have been found to thrive in a wide range of growing conditions and are currently grown throughout the wine-producing world. Informally referred to as "international varieties," these grapes have the potential to be successful in many different areas. For example, Cabernet Sauvignon is now planted in nearly every major wine region in the world—particularly so in Bordeaux, Napa, Chile, and Australia; but including many other areas as well—and can produce wines with the unmistakable varietal character of Cabernet Sauvignon in most of them.

Among the thousands of other important grape varieties, many have either not been widely transplanted in areas beyond their native home or have been tried in other growing areas with unimpressive results to date. Such grapes, when planted in their native area, are often referred to as *traditional*, *native*, or *indigenous*. The term *autochthonous*, a more technical term, typically refers to indigenous grapes that are the result of natural cross-breeding or natural mutation in a specific area.

Whatever the term that is used—whether *traditional*, *native*, or *indigenous*—these labels are meant to imply grapes that are grown primarily in one place, have a long history in the area, and have throughout their development adjusted extremely well to local conditions. It is believed that such grapes reach their highest quality under specific conditions that may be impossible to duplicate away from their native area. Nebbiolo is a good example; it is an indigenous grape quite famous for producing fine wines in northwest Italy, but it is rarely planted in the rest of the world.

The line between international and indigenous varieties is an arbitrary one; however, the grapes profiled below are some of the most widely planted of the vinifera varieties.

Figure 3–1: Chardonnay grapes in a harvest tub

WHITE GRAPE VARIETIES

Grapes and wines that do not have any red or purple pigmentation are typically called "white," even though they are almost always some shade of yellow or green. (Be careful not to confuse the color of "green" grapes with the term "green grapes," which usually refers to underripe grapes rather than to their actual color.)

CHARDONNAY

Chardonnay is among the world's most popular white grape varieties, with wide recognition among consumers. It is considered relatively easy to grow and as such, is planted in nearly every major wine-producing area in the world.

The variety is thought to be indigenous to the Burgundy region of France, and many consider it to produce its highest expression when planted in the area's limestone soils. It is also important in nearby Champagne for the region's classic sparkling wines. Hoping to replicate the outstanding wines of Burgundy and Champagne, winegrowers around the world have planted Chardonnay and, in some cooler climates, have produced similarly styled wines.

However, Chardonnay can show markedly distinctive characteristics depending on the climate. Chardonnay planted in warmer climates will generally have ripe, tropical fruit flavors and will produce wines with high alcohol and considerable body. In contrast, grapes grown in cooler climates will tend to have citrus flavors and green fruit aromas and will produce wines with crisp acidity and a light to medium body.

Chardonnay is among the white grape varieties that are most likely to benefit from interaction with wood and is often aged in new oak barrels to allow it to take on flavors from the oak. Oak-aged Chardonnay is often considered to be quite age-worthy and likely to improve with time in the bottle. Many topflight white Burgundies, for example, can continue to evolve toward a more complex and flavorful wine for a decade or more.

However, there are also many examples of Chardonnay that are unaged, as well as those that are briefly aged in used barrels (which impart little, if any, oak flavor) or in stainless steel tanks.

While Chardonnay is rarely made into a truly sweet wine, it is not unusual for winemakers to leave a minimally detectable amount of residual sugar in the wine to round out the body and appeal to a certain type of consumer.

Chardonnay Profile

Well-known examples: cool climate versions include white Burgundy, Champagne, Oregon, and the coastal areas of California; warmer climate versions include the inland areas of California and Australia

Top-producing countries: France, United States, Australia

Characteristic aromas: green apple, melon, pears (cool climate); tropical fruit (warm climate); butter (malolactic fermentation); vanilla, butterscotch, caramel, toast (oak-aged)

Acidity: medium to high

Alcohol: medium to high

CHENIN BLANC

Chenin Blanc is among the most versatile of all grape varieties. It can produce world-class wines at all sweetness levels, from dry to very sweet, in either still or sparkling versions. Chenin Blanc is known for its high level of acidity, especially when grown in cool-climate vineyards, making it ideal as a base for sparkling wines. In still wines, a little residual sugar is often used to take the edge off the sharp acidity; taken to its extreme, this results in superb late-harvest dessert wines, sometimes with the added influence of botrytis. These sweet Chenin Blancs can last for decades.

Beyond its home in the Loire Valley, Chenin Blanc has been adopted by the winegrowers of South Africa, where it is still sometimes called Steen. Chenin Blanc is the most widely planted grape variety in South Africa, representing 18% of all plantings. In fact, there is twice as much Chenin Blanc in South Africa as there is in France. Significant plantings are also found in California's Central Valley. These wide plantings show Chenin Blanc's adaptability to climate, as it thrives in some of the warmest regions of the winemaking world, as well as in the very cool, continental climate of the Loire.

Chenin Blanc Profile
Well-known examples: Vouvray, Savennières, Saumur
Top-producing countries: South Africa, France, United States
Characteristic aromas: green apple, yellow pear, melon, green plum, citrus, almond, white flowers, chamomile tea; honey and quince (aged)
Acidity: medium-plus to high
Alcohol: medium to high

MUSCAT

Muscat is an ancient grape variety that has been carried to nearly every wine region of the world. It is used primarily to produce sweet wines. Muscat's ability to produce a range of sweet wines has made it very popular with consumers in recent years, propelling the grape to double-digit growth in the US market. Muscat is also capable of producing excellent dry wines, although these are less well-known than the sweet versions.

Having mutated many times, Muscat forms a family of several related varieties, of which the most prevalent and well-known members are Muscat Blanc à Petits Grains ("white Muscat with small berries"), Muscat of Alexandria, and Muscat Ottonel. Muscat Blanc à Petits Grains is generally considered to be of a higher quality than the others, but all Muscats share a characteristic powerful floral aroma and, often, the scent of fresh white grapes in the finished wine. This grape seems to perform best in warm-to-hot climates, although the Ottonel variety does well in cool climates.

Dessert Muscats are produced in many countries; well-known examples include several *vins doux naturels* from southern France, Rutherglen Muscats from Australia, and Moscatels from the south of Spain. Perhaps the best-known Muscat-based wine is the wildly popular, slightly sparkling, moderately sweet Moscato d'Asti of northwestern Italy.

Muscat Profile
Well-known examples: southern France, northern Italy, Australia
Top-producing countries: Italy, France, Chile, Australia
Characteristic aromas: musk, honey, orange blossom, floral, apricot, table grapes
Acidity: low to medium
Alcohol: medium to high

Figure 3–2: Pinot Gris grapes on the King Estate

PINOT GRIGIO/PINOT GRIS

Pinot Grigio and Pinot Gris are two well-known names for the same grape variety, which developed as a mutation of Pinot Noir in the Burgundy area of France. Both mean "gray Pinot," in reference to the grape's dusky or lightly pink-colored skin. The Pinot Gris of France became the Pinot Grigio of Italy when it was planted in Italy centuries ago.

Although the two names are technically synonymous, each has become associated with a particular style of wine. While the French term, Pinot Gris, is used to identify the type of wine produced in the Alsace region of France, it is also frequently used in Oregon, which has had success with this variety since its introduction in the mid-1960s. This style of cool-climate Pinot Gris has medium-plus acidity, medium to full body, neutral aromas displaying an apple-, pear-, or almond-like character, and sometimes a moderate amount of residual sugar. This is also the style generally found in Germany, where the grape is called *Ruländer* or *Grauburgunder*.

Pinot Grigio is the more recognizable name among consumers, having become a popular Chardonnay alternative after it was introduced into the US market from northeastern Italy in the late 1970s. Its popularity led to significant new plantings of the variety in California and Australia, as well as more expansive planting in Italy. Pinot Grigios from the warmer regions of California and Australia typically display medium-minus acidity and higher alcohol than those grown in the cooler regions of Alto Adige and the Veneto of Italy. Wines labeled Pinot Grigio are normally dry and are often neutral and unoaked, although some versions can be aromatic and lees-aged.

Pinot Grigio/Pinot Gris Profile

Well-known examples: northeastern Italy, Alsace, Oregon

Top-producing countries: Italy, United States, Germany, France, Australia

Characteristic aromas: apple, lemon, melon, peach, minerals, almond

Acidity: low to high

Alcohol: medium

RIESLING

Riesling is indigenous to Germany and, because of its ability to withstand cold weather, is one of the few quality grapes that can be grown there and in other regions with similarly marginal climates. Riesling's intense floral aroma profile varies a bit with climate and growing conditions and easily reflects variations in *terroir*. Nevertheless, its highly aromatic style and unique "petrol" scent make it an easy variety to recognize in just about any guise.

Riesling wines cover the full spectrum of sweetness levels. In recent years, dry Rieslings have become more common and are highly regarded in many cases. However, many commercial Rieslings are made in the off-dry or medium-sweet range. These wines often have low levels of alcohol; some are as low as 7% or 8% abv (alcohol by volume). Riesling also produces luscious dessert wines from late-harvest or botrytis-affected grapes.

An outstanding characteristic of Riesling is its naturally high acidity, which the grape is able to retain even with increasing levels of ripeness. In finished wines, this high acidity is often balanced with some residual sugar, both of which have a preservative effect. As a result, Rieslings are among the most long-lived of white wines, both in the bottle and after opening. Oak aging is rare.

It should be noted that there are grapes the world over that use the word *Riesling* as part of their name, but many of these are unrelated to true Riesling. For example, in the United States, *White Riesling* is the only synonym for true Riesling, while *Missouri Riesling* is an indigenous American grape and, thus, a completely different variety.

Riesling Profile

Well-known examples: Mosel, Rheingau, Rheinhessen, and Pfalz in Germany; Alsace in France; Clare and Eden Valleys in Australia; Finger Lakes in New York; Washington State

Top-producing countries: Germany, Australia, France, United States

Characteristic aromas: lime, peach, nectarine, apricot, honeysuckle, wet stone, petrol/kerosene (depending upon ripeness and bottle age); baking spices (well-aged)

Acidity: high to very high

Alcohol: very low to high

SAUVIGNON BLANC

Like Chardonnay, Sauvignon Blanc is native to France, where it achieved its reputation in the Loire Valley and Bordeaux. From France, it was taken to most overseas wine regions and prospered in many of them, especially in the cooler zones. Sauvignon Blanc acts as a true barometer of soil, site, and viticultural practices and can produce many different styles of wine, depending on where it is grown and how it is handled in the winery.

Sauvignon Blanc has a particular affinity for New Zealand, where it produces wines with distinct herbal character and fruit-forward flavors of grapefruit and tropical fruit. Beginning in the 1980s, this style of wine was eagerly embraced by the market, establishing a strong reputation for New Zealand Sauvignon Blanc. Today, other regions are producing wines that mirror this highly aromatic, zesty style.

Oak-aged Sauvignon Blanc is another popular style. While white Bordeaux is often aged in older oak, a more pronounced style of oaked Sauvignon Blanc was created by California winemaker Robert Mondavi in the 1960s. Called "Fumé Blanc" for marketing purposes, the wine became an instant hit. In the United States, *Fumé Blanc* is an approved synonym for *Sauvignon Blanc*, and the two terms are legally interchangeable.

Table wines made using Sauvignon Blanc are usually quite high in acidity and are almost always dry. Due to its naturally high acidity, the juice of these grapes is often blended with that of low-acid grapes, such as

Sémillon, as is done in Bordeaux. Sauvignon Blanc also plays a role in the classic sweet dessert wines of the Bordeaux area, including Sauternes.

Sauvignon Blanc Profile
Well-known examples: Sancerre, Pouilly-Fumé, white Bordeaux, Fumé Blanc, New Zealand
Top-producing countries: France, New Zealand, Chile, United States, South Africa
Characteristic aromas: grass, hay, grapefruit, green pepper (cool climate); asparagus, melon (warm climate); flint (Loire); gooseberry (New Zealand); toast, smoke (oak-aged)
Acidity: medium-plus to high
Alcohol: medium

OTHER IMPORTANT WHITE VARIETIES

Sémillon is perhaps best-known as a blending partner rather than a stand-alone varietal. Sémillon is often paired with Sauvignon Blanc, as is done in Bordeaux and Bordeaux-influenced blends. In Australia, it is often blended with Chardonnay. On its own, it has a distinct waxy or oily character on the palate and typically shows aromas of citrus (lemon, yellow grapefruit), flowers (honeysuckle, lemon blossom) and tree fruit (peach, pear, or green apple). When slightly underripe, Sémillon may display herbal notes reminiscent of Sauvignon Blanc. The Hunter Valley in Australia is one region well-known for producing 100% varietal wines from Semillon. (Note: Outside of France, the grape is typically spelled without the accent over the *e*.)

Viognier would have been considered an indigenous variety not many years ago, as very little of it was found outside of the Northern Rhône Valley in France. However, it has quietly been gaining devotees around the world and, since the mid-1980s, has been widely planted in Australia, California, South America, Texas, and the East Coast of the United States. Viognier's admirers appreciate its rich, viscous, full-bodied heft and potent aromas of flowers, peach, and tangerine.

Pinot Blanc is a descendant of Pinot Noir, having mutated from Pinot Gris. White it may not be the best-known grape in any particular region, Pinot Blanc is grown in quite a few places in Europe and beyond. The majority of it can be found in Italy, where it is called *Pinot Bianco*, and in Germany and Austria, where it is known as *Weissburgunder*. It is also one of the main grapes of Alsace. Pinot Blanc is similar in many ways to Pinot Gris, and depending on the specific clone and the growing conditions, the two can be difficult to tell apart. However, Pinot Blanc is generally lighter on the palate and more exotic in its aromas than Pinot Gris.

Gewürztraminer is one of the most aromatic of the white grape varieties, with a unique perfume of flowers, spice, lychee, and rose. It is not a major variety in any region, but its pronounced flavors have endeared it to a cadre of consumers, and there are small plantings of it in most countries. It was first recorded in the Italian Alps, but it is probably most prominent today in Alsace. (Note: Outside of Germany and Austria, the grape is often spelled without the umlaut over the *u*.)

Trebbiano Toscano is a commercially important grape variety. This neutral white grape is principally associated with Italy, where it is the most common variety used for white wines as well as for commercial balsamic vinegar. In France, where it is known as *Ugni Blanc*, it is grown in considerable quantities and used for the production of brandy, including cognac. Small amounts of Trebbiano Toscano/Ugni Blanc are grown in several other countries as well.

Other significant white grapes include the following:
- *Argentina:* Torrontés Riojano
- *Austria:* Grüner Veltliner
- *France:* Aligoté, Marsanne, Roussanne
- *Germany:* Müller-Thurgau, Silvaner
- *Greece:* Assyrtiko, Moschofilero, Rhoditis
- *Hungary:* Furmint
- *Italy:* Cortese, Garganega, Glera, Verdicchio, Vermentino, Vernaccia
- *Portugal:* Alvarinho, Arinto, Fernão Pires, Loureiro
- *Spain:* Albariño, Godello, Macabeo/Viura, Palomino, Parellada, Pedro Ximénez, Verdejo, Xarel-lo
- *Switzerland:* Chasselas

RED GRAPE VARIETIES

Grapes with red or purple pigmentation in their skins are called "red" or, sometimes, "black" grapes, regardless of their exact color, which may run from bluish to garnet to coal black when fully ripe. Following are some of the red grapes that are most commonly found in wine around the world.

CABERNET FRANC

Cabernet Franc is perhaps best known as the blending partner of Cabernet Sauvignon and Merlot in the famous reds of Bordeaux and similar blends produced elsewhere. Not surprisingly, given that Cabernet Sauvignon is its offspring (crossed with Sauvignon Blanc), its red fruit and herbal flavors are complementary with the flavors of Cabernet Sauvignon.

Cabernet Franc is less commonly bottled as a varietal wine, but it is a mainstay in some cooler regions that have trouble ripening Cabernet Sauvignon. Several regions in France's Loire Valley, such as Chinon and Bourgueil, as well as some parts of California and the eastern United States, produce wines dominated by Cabernet Franc. In these areas, it is sometimes used for rosé wines as well.

Cabernet Franc Profile
Well-known examples: red Bordeaux, Loire Valley, northeast Italy, New York State, California
Top-producing countries: France, Italy, United States
Characteristic aromas: cranberry, strawberry, tobacco, mushroom, bell pepper, tea (cool climate); raspberry, violet (warm climate)
Acidity: medium to high
Tannin: light to medium
Alcohol: medium

Figure 3–3: Cabernet Sauvignon at harvest

CABERNET SAUVIGNON

Cabernet Sauvignon is one of the world's most respected and widely grown wine grape varieties. Cabernet's reputation comes from a combination of consistency, reliability, depth of flavor, and its ability to develop complex flavors over a long, graceful aging period. Much of this can be attributed to its high tannin levels, which are often bolstered even further by maturation in new oak barrels.

Cabernet Sauvignon originated in Bordeaux and is an important ingredient in the traditionally blended red wines of the region. Bordeaux wines made from a majority of Cabernet Sauvignon came to be recognized as some of the best wines of France, and therefore of the world, in the mid-nineteenth century. Thus, it is not surprising that this vine was brought to new vineyards far and wide for experimentation. It turned out to be one of the most successful of the traveling vines, not only surviving but also thriving in diverse growing conditions.

As a result, there is more Cabernet Sauvignon planted than any other quality wine grape in the world. A late-blooming variety, Cabernet Sauvignon is not particularly well suited to areas that have early winters, and in fact, it requires sufficient heat and sun exposure to fully ripen. Conversely, it is quite at home in regions much hotter than Bordeaux, and is a leading variety in California's Napa Valley. Because of the warmer growing conditions, as well as different winemaking priorities, Napa "Cabs" are usually higher in alcohol, lower in acidity, and more fruit-forward than the typical Bordeaux.

In addition to being bottled as a varietal wine, Cabernet Sauvignon often finds its way into red wine blends. Mimicking the classic wines of Bordeaux, it may be blended with Merlot, Malbec, or Cabernet Franc; in Australia, Cabernet Sauvignon is often blended with Shiraz (Syrah).

Cabernet Sauvignon Profile

Well-known examples: red Bordeaux, Napa, Washington State

Top-producing countries: France, Chile, United States, Australia

Characteristic aromas: black currant, black cherry, eucalyptus, mint, bell pepper (cool climate); dark chocolate, cedar, vanilla, tobacco (aged in new oak); coffee, caramel, cigar box (well-aged)

Acidity: medium to high

Tannin: high

Alcohol: high

GRENACHE

Grenache is an important grape variety, but it is not often bottled by itself. Instead, it typically appears in blends such as G-S-M (Grenache-Syrah-Mourvèdre) for added color, acidity, and complexity. Grenache thrives in hot, dry conditions where it develops considerable sugar and, therefore, high alcohol.

The variety grows in abundance in the South of France, but it did not originate there. It was recorded earlier in both Spain, where it is called Garnacha and is equally abundant, and on the Italian island of Sardinia, where it is known as Cannonau, although it is not clear which region had it first. Grenache is also planted in Australia, where it is made into both varietal wines and blends, and is increasingly grown in California and Washington State.

Old-vine Grenache is highly prized for its concentration of flavor. Grenache is often made into distinctive rosés, and it may be used to make sweet fortified wines. Grenache-based wines tend to oxidize quickly, picking up a salmon or somewhat orange tinge as well as a rusticity noticeable in the wine's aroma or bouquet.

Grenache Profile

Well-known examples: southern Rhône, Priorat, Rioja, Navarra, Australia

Top-producing countries: France, Spain

Characteristic aromas: strawberry, sour cherry, flowers, black pepper, cranberry

Acidity: low to medium

Tannin: low to medium

Alcohol: high

MERLOT

Merlot and Cabernet Sauvignon have a lot in common in terms of style and aromas. Some Merlot is even every bit as powerful as a Cabernet Sauvignon, but Merlot, in general, tends to be a little less intense, less tannic, and less alcoholic—and it has lighter, brighter fruit flavors.

Like Cabernet Sauvignon, Merlot was first noted as a distinct variety in Bordeaux, and the two grapes are normally blended together in Bordeaux reds. Often, particularly on the Right Bank, Merlot represents the majority of the blend. Merlot and Cabernet Sauvignon complement each other because their aromas are similar but not identical, giving the combination a much richer array of flavors. For this reason, these varieties are frequently blended in many wine regions, even in varietally labeled wines that are dominated by one or the other. They also complement each other viticulturally, as Merlot ripens early and Cabernet ripens late, thus mitigating the risk of damage from extreme weather at either end of the growing season. Merlot is one of the most popular red wines among consumers and is successfully grown in almost every wine-producing country in the world.

Merlot Profile

Well-known examples: red Bordeaux, Napa, Washington State

Top-producing countries: France, United States, Spain, Italy, Chile

Characteristic aromas: blueberry, plum, black cherry, mint, coffee, chocolate

Acidity: medium

Tannin: medium

Alcohol: medium to high

PINOT NOIR

While the true origin of Pinot Noir has been the subject of much debate, it is generally considered to be native to Burgundy, France. To many wine lovers, Burgundy is the standard for perfection in Pinot Noir. Pinot Noir is a unique red grape that is able to thrive and ripen in cool climates, and for this reason, many of the moderate- and cool-climate wine regions in the world have at least experimented with Pinot Noir. Oregon, New Zealand, and the cooler regions of California have had the greatest success.

The ability to produce flavorful grapes in cool conditions also makes Pinot Noir a natural choice for use in sparkling wines. Worldwide, a substantial proportion of Pinot Noir goes into sparkling wine production—including in France, where more Pinot Noir is planted in the Champagne region than in Burgundy. Its affinity for cool climates also makes it popular in Germany, where, known as Spätburgunder, it is the most widely planted red grape variety.

Pinot Noir is characterized by low to moderate tannin, high levels of acidity, and pale to medium color. Its aromas when young include berry (raspberries, strawberries), cherry, and red flowers. As it matures, it may take on earthy and rustic characteristics that are described as "forest floor," "leather," or "mushroom."

As a variety, Pinot Noir is genetically unstable and highly prone to mutation, as evidenced by the large number of clones that have been cataloged. Some of these genetic mutations have become popular grape varieties in their own rights, such as Pinot Gris, Pinot Blanc, and Pinot Meunier.

Pinot Noir Profile
Well-known examples: red Burgundy, Champagne, New Zealand, Oregon, California
Top-producing countries: France, United States, Germany
Characteristic aromas: cherry, raspberry, strawberry, earth, violet, lilac, sandalwood, mushroom
Acidity: medium to high
Tannin: low to medium
Alcohol: medium

SYRAH/SHIRAZ

Syrah is a well-known grape of southern France, but it is perhaps just as well-known under its alternative name, Shiraz. In addition to its status as the leading grape of Australia, Syrah/Shiraz is widely planted and gaining popularity in California's Central Coast region, Washington State, South Africa, and Argentina.

There are numerous styles of Syrah. As a stand-alone varietal wine, it can be inky, dark-flavored, and tannic, with some examples rivaling top Cabernet Sauvignons in price and reputation. It is also used to produce dry, full-bodied rosés full of bright flavors. Like Cabernet, it is often blended with other grape varieties. In southern France, Syrah is often blended with an assortment of locally grown varieties, often including Grenache and Mourvèdre, to create some of the region's unique wines, such as Châteauneuf-du-Pape. In Australia, it is often part of a Grenache-Syrah-Mourvèdre blend or a Cabernet Sauvignon–based blend.

Syrah/Shiraz Profile
Well-known examples: Rhône Valley, Australia, Paso Robles
Top-producing countries: France, Australia, United States
Characteristic aromas: blackberry, tar, leather, anise, rosemary, black pepper, smoke, lavender, forest floor, earth, dried fruits; smoked meats (well-aged)
Acidity: low to medium
Tannin: high
Alcohol: high

Figure 3–4: Shiraz grapes growing in the Yarra Valley

OTHER IMPORTANT RED VARIETIES

Zinfandel is perhaps best known for its success in California, where it is often used to produce densely pigmented, high-alcohol, spicy red wines. These full-bodied wines generally possess jammy fruit character with notes of raspberry, blackberry, and raisin. Zinfandel is also made into delightful dry rosé, although many consumers still equate Zinfandel with the widely distributed, sweet, blush-style wine known as White Zinfandel.

Zinfandel's long lineage has been a subject of much debate. In 1994, it was determined by Dr. Carole Meredith and her research team at UC Davis that Zinfandel is genetically identical to both Italy's Primitivo and Croatia's Tribidrag grape varieties. The European Union (EU) has recognized *Zinfandel* as a legal synonym for *Primitivo*; however, citing a lack of evidence, the US Alcohol and Tobacco Tax and Trade Bureau (TTB) has not.

Sangiovese is the backbone of Chianti and other Tuscan wines in Italy. While traditionally used in a blend, as of 1996 Chianti producers have the option of producing Chianti with 100% Sangiovese. As a result, Sangiovese is increasingly seen as a stand-alone varietal. However, Sangiovese's tradition as a blending partner continues in the wines of Italy (where it is often blended with traditional grapes such as Colorino and Canaiolo Nero) and elsewhere, where it may be blended with nontraditional partners such as Syrah, Merlot, and Cabernet Sauvignon. Sangiovese-based wines are often noted for moderate-to-high levels of acidity and earthy aromas accompanied by flavors of orange zest and sour cherry.

Nebbiolo is the sole ingredient in some of Italy's most highly respected wines, particularly Barolo, Barbaresco, and others produced in the northwest region of Piedmont. Nebbiolo is used in other regions of Italy as well, in 100% varietal wines and some blends. Its unique flavors and aromas are often described as "tar and roses" and as cherry, blackberry, and licorice. Nebbiolo produces long-lived, highly tannic wines that benefit from oak and bottle aging.

Tempranillo, the leading red grape of Spain, often produces wines dominated by leather, tobacco, and chalky dust flavors, although much of this is attributable to traditional winemaking. The grape itself shows aromas of strawberry, red cherry, currant, and spice. In Rioja, Tempranillo is generally blended with Mazuelo and other red grapes. However, more recently, 100% Tempranillo wines have become a bit more common. As Tinta Roriz or Aragonêz, Tempranillo is a significant grape in Portugal. Outside the Iberian Peninsula, Tempranillo has been discovered by many American producers, especially in California and, to a lesser extent, Texas and Oregon.

Malbec is a relatively minor French grape mainly known for being a minor component in some red Bordeaux blends and as the main ingredient in the "black wine" of Cahors. Yet it has achieved stardom in Argentina, where the climate and soil seem to bring out the best this grape has to offer. Malbec produces wines that are deeply colored—often inky black—and have corresponding flavors of blackberry and plum. Much of the world's Malbec is found in Argentina and southwestern France, but small amounts are also grown in the Loire Valley, California, Washington State, Oregon, and Chile.

Gamay (technically known as "Gamay Noir à Jus Blanc") is primarily known for producing the low-tannin, fruit-forward red wines of Beaujolais. These wines, traditionally made at least partially through carbonic maceration, tend to show aromas of red cherry, strawberry, banana, and red candy. However, Gamay has a more serious side and is capable of producing rich, age-worthy wines redolent of fruit (raspberry, cranberry, currant), flowers (violets, lilacs), spice (black pepper), savory green herbs, and earth (wet stones).

Gamay is also planted in the Mâconnais, the Loire Valley, and Switzerland. In these regions it is primarily used as a single variety; however, it is sometimes blended with Pinot Noir and sometimes made into rosé. Until the early 2000s, Gamay grown in California was the subject of some confusion and debate. Grapes formerly known as "Napa Gamay" or "Gamay Beaujolais" have now been determined to be unrelated to true Gamay, and these terms are no longer permitted to be used on wine labels. These days, however, small amounts of Gamay Noir à Jus Blanc are planted in California.

Alicante Bouschet is a red grape variety with a unique difference—it is a *teinturier*, meaning that it has red flesh in addition to red skin. The grape, a cross of Petit Bouschet and Grenache, was first cultivated by the family of French grower Henri Bouschet in 1866. From that point up until the end of the 1900s, Alicante Bouschet became one of the most widely-planted vinifera grapes in both Europe and North America. In more recent times its popularity has waned, but it is still planted throughout Spain, southern Portugal, parts of southern France, Australia, and central California. Due to its red-colored flesh and thick skins, the grape is often used in blends in order to add body and color intensity to red and rosé wines; however, it is certainly possible to find excellent examples of varietal wines produced from Alicante Bouschet. In Spain, the grape is referred to as *Garnacha Tintorera*.

Other significant red grapes include the following:
- *Chile:* Carmenère
- *France:* Carignan, Cinsaut (Cinsault), Meunier (Pinot Meunier), Mourvèdre
- *Germany/Austria:* Blauer Portugieser, Blaufränkisch, Zweigelt
- *Greece:* Agiorgitiko, Mavrodaphne, Xinomavro
- *Italy:* Aglianico, Barbera, Corvina, Dolcetto, Montepulciano, Negroamaro, Nero d'Avola
- *Portugal:* Touriga Franca, Touriga Nacional
- *South Africa:* Pinotage
- *Spain:* Monastrell (Mourvèdre)
- *United States:* Petite Sirah
- *Uruguay:* Tannat

VITICULTURE

CHAPTER FOUR

LEARNING OBJECTIVES

After studying this chapter, the candidate should be able to:

- Describe the physical structure of a grapevine.
- Explain the annual life cycle and metabolic processes of the vine.
- Identify the factors that affect the amount of sugar and acid in grapes.
- Recognize the elements that make up the concept of terroir.
- Recall the effects of vine diseases, pests, and botrytis.
- Understand how viticultural practices such as organic, biodynamic, and sustainable differ from those of mainstream viticulture and from each other.

Globally, grapevines cover nearly 19 million acres (7.7 million ha) and produce more than 70 million tons of fruit annually, making grapes the world's most important fruit crop. Of this output, 70% goes into wine; the rest is used for table grapes, grape juice, or raisins.

Viticulture is the term used for the branch of agriculture that specifically deals with the intentional cultivation of grapevines. Viticulture is an art that has been practiced for millennia. When grapes are grown specifically to make wine, as opposed to juice or for use as table grapes, viticulture is sometimes called *winegrowing*. Today, winegrowing runs the gamut from tiny plots tended by a single farmer using ancient farming methods to vast tracts tended by a small army of trained viticulturists using high-technology equipment and machinery.

THE GRAPEVINE

PHYSICAL STRUCTURE

The vine, as cultivated, consists of a single *trunk* that connects its underground root system to the aboveground structure of branches, shoots, and leaves. The roots continue to grow and spread throughout the lifetime of the vine, eventually creating an elaborate network far larger than the visible plant, capable of pulling water and nutrients from soil deep below the surface. The trunk thickens slowly with time, growing from a slender stick to a gnarled, tree-like pillar after many years.

From the trunk, a well-maintained vine will usually have one or two branches, sometimes called *arms*. These start as *spurs* that develop into young, thin *canes*. During annual pruning, most canes are removed. However, those that are retained from season to season will eventually form thicker arms known as *cordons*. Most trunks are encouraged to have one or two arms, but in some vineyards the vines may be allowed to grow in a more complex arrangement with four or more limbs. Without intervention, the vine would quickly develop an unruly tangle of multiple canes, which is why pruning and training are important. The vine's arms support the leaves and grape bunches that grow seasonally. This entire portion of the vine, including the fruit, is referred to as the *canopy*.

Grapes, like all fruits, are seed repositories. The skin and pulp of the grape are designed to protect the seed from damage and nourish it while it matures. The green skin provides camouflage, and the pulp is so acidic that it dissuades consumption. As the seed approaches maturity, the skin develops an attractive red or gold coloring, while the pulp becomes increasingly sweet and juicy, encouraging birds or other animals to eat the grapes or carry them away, thereby spreading the seeds. When the pulp is near its maximum sweetness and the seeds are mature, the grapes are said to be ripe.

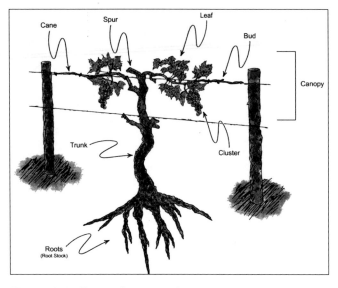

Figure 4-1: Parts of a grapevine

THE LIFE CYCLE

In nature, grapes propagate by producing seeds, but in commercial viticulture, this method is considered too unpredictable and tedious. A seed represents a genetically unique entity, drawing traits from both of its parents but with infinite, unpredictable variations possible. Furthermore, growing a plant from seed takes a long time and has a high failure rate.

One commercially viable method of grapevine propagation is cloning. The grower can choose a healthy grapevine that is known to have desirable characteristics, cut off a short length of a young cane, place it in water where it will start to grow roots, and then plant it in the vineyard. This new plant will be a *clone* of the vine from which it was cut, genetically identical, and with the same desirable characteristics. This method is more efficient than planting seeds and produces more consistent results.

An alternative to using rooted cuttings is *field grafting*. This is a method that may be used, for example, if there is an existing vineyard that is currently growing an undesired variety of grapes. As long as the vine's *rootstock* (the major root system) is healthy, the grower can remove its existing branches, make a small incision in the trunk, and insert an unrooted cutting from a desirable vine. The rootstock will heal at the wound site, and the cutting will begin to grow as if it had been planted in the ground, except that it will already have access to an extensive root network.

A newly planted or grafted vine will produce grapes during its first or second season, but these clusters of grapes are usually considered substandard in quality and removed in order to allow the vine to focus its energies on trunk and shoot development. The first crop of grapes to be used for wine is normally harvested in the third year, which is sometimes called "third leaf." While there is some debate about when a vine begins producing quality fruit, a common assertion is that it takes an average of six years before a grapevine develops to the point where its fruit is at its optimal quality level. It will then continue to produce its best grape crops for a decade or more.

After about twenty years, the vine becomes less vigorous, producing fewer grape clusters and fewer leaves. However, the *quality* of the grapes often continues to improve after vines are twenty years old, and grapes from these vines can be made into outstanding "old vine" wines. The term *old vine* is not widely regulated, but many vines given this designation are fifty years old or older. Some grapevines are still producing small amounts of quality grapes at more than a hundred years old.

THE ANNUAL GROWTH CYCLE

Winegrowing is most successful in temperate climates. Generally, the ideal regions fall between 30° and 50° latitude in both the Northern Hemisphere and the Southern Hemisphere, where the change of seasons brings long, warm-to-hot days in summer, and short, cool-to-cold days in winter.

The winter dormancy period, when the vines conserve their energy for the following spring, establishes an annual cycle of growth that culminates with the harvest of ripe grapes in the fall. It is important to remember, however, that the seasons are reversed between the Northern and Southern Hemispheres, so harvests in the two hemispheres take place roughly six months apart.

The cycle begins with the emergence of new greenery in the spring. The first sign of this process—which starts when the ground temperatures begin to rise above 50°F (10°C)—is *weeping*. Weeping occurs as the sap begins to flow upward from the trunk and out to the tips of the canes. This should only last a day or two, and soon thereafter, tiny shoots called buds emerge from the nodes in the vine's branches. This is known as *bud break*, and it is the first critical event leading toward the success or failure of the year's vintage. Bud break can be a hazardous time, especially in cooler climates, because the new growth is quite vulnerable to temperature extremes, and a late frost can do serious damage to the vines at this stage.

Figure 4-2: Bud break

As the shoots grow and strengthen, they begin to produce leaves. Until this point, the plant is drawing upon carbohydrate reserves stored in the vine from the previous year, and growth is slow. Once the leaves develop, however, photosynthesis can begin, and the plants can take in new energy directly from the sun and accelerate the pace of additional growth.

Flowering, the next critical phase, takes place 40 to 80 days after bud break. Clusters of tiny flowers appear at intervals along the shoots. Each flower that is fertilized will become the foundation for a grape. Vinifera grapevines are self-pollinating, so bees or other insects are not necessary for fertilization. Instead, the breeze blows the pollen from one part of the plant to another, or to neighboring vines, and the flower is fertilized to create a grape berry.

Warm, dry weather is ideal during flowering. Rainy or windy conditions at this time can prevent the pollen from reaching its destination within the flowers, resulting in fewer viable grapes and therefore a smaller crop. This transition from flower to berry (grapes are sometimes referred to as *berries*, especially when immature) is called *berry set* or *fruit set*.

A malady known as *coulure* ("shatter" in English) can cause poor fruit set, with many flowers failing to become fully developed berries. Another condition, *millerandage* (abnormal fruit set), sometimes caused by bad weather during flowering, results in grape bunches that have a high proportion of small seedless berries mixed in with the normal, larger, seed-bearing grapes.

After fruit set, the grape berries grow from tiny dots to their eventual mature size of approximately one-half to three-quarters of an inch in diameter over the next three months or so. They are initially small, hard, dull green in color, high in acid, and low in sugar. The berries grow slowly for about a month and a half, at which point a major change in their development takes place. This short but important event is known as *veraison*.

Veraison signals a sudden acceleration toward maturation. It is most noticeable in red grapes, which begin to take on color at this time. White grapes also change in appearance—often remaining green but becoming translucent—or transitioning to yellow or gold. After veraison, the grapes continue to mature, soften, and enlarge. Inside the berries, sugar is being stored, acidity levels are falling, and the seeds are developing.

Harvest generally takes place a month and a half to two months after veraison, when the grapes are ripe in terms of both sugar levels (*physical maturity*) and *phenolic maturity*. Phenolic maturity refers to the level and character of certain phenolic compounds in the grape, including tannins and other compounds that enhance the color, flavor, and aromas of the resulting wine. Sugar concentration and phenolic ripening occur together over the summer, but not necessarily at the same rate. Sometimes the grapes will develop an acceptable level of sugar before the flavors and phenolics—particularly color and tannins—fully emerge, while at other times the situation is reversed.

The time period from bud break to harvest is normally around 140 to 160 days; however, under certain circumstances it can be as short as 110 days or as long as 200 days.

The time period from bud break to harvest is normally around 140 to 160 days but can be as short as 110 days or as long as 200. Harvest begins in early fall with the earliest-ripening grape varieties in the warmest regions, and it may continue into late fall and even early winter in the coolest regions, where grapes need more time to fully ripen.

Cold nights in autumn signal the vine to go into a dormant state in order to protect itself from damage over the winter. The vine will drop its leaves and withdraw sap from the branches and shoots, moving it into the trunk and roots, where there is less likelihood of injury from freezing. Once the vine enters dormancy, growers will conduct winter pruning, removing most of the year's growth in an attempt to keep the vine at a manageable size and ensure an appropriate yield the following year.

Figure 4-3: Veraison

THE VINE'S METABOLIC PROCESSES

There are several fundamental processes of grapevine metabolism that have a direct impact on wine quality, and that should be understood by wine professionals. These include photosynthesis, respiration, transpiration, and translocation.

Photosynthesis: This is a process common to all green plants in which sunlight is used by the chlorophyll-containing (green) parts of a plant, primarily the leaves, to convert carbon dioxide and water into sugar. These sugars are the basic building blocks of most materials found in the vine. In grapevines and many other plants, some of this sugar is stored in the fruit. The rate of sugar production, and thus the rate at which the grapes are filled with sugar, is directly related to the amount of photosynthesis that takes place. Photosynthesis depends primarily on two things: sunshine and temperature.

Photosynthesis only occurs when the sun is shining, and it slows at temperatures less than 50°F (10°C) or greater than 95°F (35°C). Optimal sugar production takes place on sunny days with temperatures between 70°F and 85°F (20–30°C).

Ideal conditions for photosynthesis during the growing season include the following:
- *Warm days:* Photosynthesis slows down both when it is very hot and when it is chilly or cold.
- *Long days:* As photosynthesis can only occur when the sun is shining, the more hours of daylight, the more sugar is produced. This is an advantage for locations farther from the equator, which have longer days during the summertime.
- *Clear days:* When clouds block the sun, less energy is available for photosynthesis. Some will still occur, but sugar production will be reduced. Hours of fog or overcast skies during the day mean less sugar.
- *Minimal shading:* If many of a vine's leaves are shaded by other leaves, they will conduct very little photosynthesis. In an overgrown, bushy grapevine, fewer than half of the leaves might actually be receiving direct sunlight; the leaves that are not in the sun are ineffective at performing photosynthesis.
- *Southern aspect (or northern aspect in the Southern Hemisphere):* If the ground on which the vineyard sits is on a hillside slope that faces the sun, the plants will receive more direct sunlight. This is particularly significant in regions far from the equator, where the sun's rays arrive at a lower angle.

Respiration: Respiration occurs as the plant breaks down sugar and related carbohydrates, releasing their energy for use by the plant for activities such as root and leaf growth. However, during veraison and at other times when sugar is unavailable, the vine shifts from metabolizing sugar to metabolizing malic acid (as well as trace amounts of other compounds) for energy. Early in their development, grapes are full of malic acid, but later on, as respiration starts to utilize this acid, the acid level in the grapes will be much lower. If the level drops too low, the wine's flavor may be affected, and other problems may develop.

Respiration is a continuous process that occurs throughout the growing season, but its rate is affected by temperature. For every 18°F increase in temperature, the rate of respiration doubles. The warmer it is, the faster the plant respires, and the quicker the acid level drops as the vine uses its acid for energy. For this reason, cool nights are usually beneficial for the ripening of grapes, as this will minimize the acid loss during a time when photosynthesis is not taking place.

Some of the world's premier winegrowing regions experience a large diurnal (daily) temperature range with warm-to-hot afternoons but cool-to-cold nights; such weather conditions allow for maximum photosynthesis and enable the grapes to retain sufficient natural acidity.

Based on these considerations, the best conditions for producing grapes that are rich in sugar and still maintain a significant amount of natural acidity are warm—but not hot—cloudless days and cool nights in a well-groomed vineyard that slopes downward, facing the sun.

Transpiration: Transpiration is the process by which water evaporates through openings on the underside of the leaves known as *stomata*. Transpiration is analogous to perspiration in animals and serves to cool the vine. The rate of transpiration is closely linked to the weather. It is highest under sunny, hot, windy, and dry conditions, and it is lowest under cloudy, cool, still, and humid conditions. The stomata will close if not enough water is brought in through the roots to meet the transpirational demand.

Because these openings also control the intake of carbon dioxide, a shutdown of transpiration will also stop photosynthetic activity.

Translocation: A final metabolic process is translocation, the process by which materials are moved from one area of the plant to another. Sugars, for example, are moved from the leaves, where they are made, to the growing shoot tips, roots, or trunk, where they are needed for energy. Sugars not needed for energy may be directed to the grape clusters, or stored in the woody portions of the trunk and root system for future use.

TERROIR

Beyond grape variety and viticultural practices, the combined natural aspects of a vineyard, such as climate, soil, sunlight, and water, can have a major impact on the overall character and quality of a wine. The French term for this, *terroir*, has been adopted throughout the wine community. This section describes some of the elements that make up terroir.

CLIMATE AND WEATHER

There are several mechanisms by which weather affects viticulture, changing the way vines grow and grapes ripen. Weather is the most changeable and uncontrollable of the variables that go into making wine and is often the biggest factor that causes one vintage to be different from the next.

It is important to distinguish between climate and weather, as they are not the same thing. *Weather* is the actual meteorological conditions experienced, whereas *climate* is the historical average weather of a place. Climate is what is expected in the long term, and weather is what is forecast in the short term and is what actually occurs.

It is the annual differences in weather that cause the variations in grapes and wine from year to year. In a region with a dry climate, the odds are that, on any day randomly chosen in the future, it will not rain. However, every once in a while, rainy weather will develop. A vineyard site is selected based on its climate, but the weather may or may not cooperate in a particular year.

The term *climate* is a general one, and is often modified by the prefixes *macro-*, *meso-*, and *micro-*. *Macroclimate* refers to the conditions of the overall region, and is roughly synonymous with *climate*. For instance, the effects of the Cascade rain shadow on the Yakima Valley AVA is an example of macroclimate. The term *mesoclimate* refers to what happens to a specific portion of the region, such as an entire vineyard. For instance, the mesoclimate of the Copeland Vineyard, a warm region with as little as 6 inches (15 cm) of rainfall a year located within the Yakima Valley AVA, is greatly influenced by its location on a south-facing slope some 1,300 feet (400 m) above sea level. The term *microclimate* refers to the climate of a small portion of a vineyard, such as a few rows. Finally, the term *canopy microclimate* is used to refer to the environment within and directly surrounding a single vine's canopy (or, at most, a small section of a single row).

The distinction between micro- and mesoclimates is important because these small differences in climate can account for significant differences in the resulting fruit, despite the fact that the vines were grown within the same macroclimate.

Below are some of the climatic and weather features that have the greatest effect on viticulture.

TEMPERATURE

As described above, the temperature in a vineyard has a great effect on the sugar–acid balance in grapes and helps to determine the quality of the resulting wine. A poor sugar–acid balance is usually the result of high temperatures. The impact of cold temperatures can also be significant, for example, at the very beginning of the growing season, when a late frost can endanger young shoot growth, or late in the season, when an early frost can damage an unharvested crop. Temperatures in the winter dormancy period are not normally a concern, unless it gets cold enough to freeze the ground several feet down and cause winterkill. These parameters define the limits of viticulture between the equator and the poles.

PRECIPITATION

Vines need about 20–30 inches (51–76 cm) of water annually, which they can receive through rainfall, irrigation, or a combination of the two. As long as irrigation is not prohibited by regional wine law and water is available, vineyards do not require rain. Otherwise, a moderate amount of precipitation is needed during the growing season, as well as over the winter to replenish the groundwater. Rain is particularly unwelcome during harvest, when the water swells the berries and dilutes their sugar content. In some regions, hail is not unusual in the summer. Hail can wipe out an entire crop if it strikes a vineyard after veraison.

HUMIDITY

High humidity makes for perfect conditions for the growth of fungus and mold, which can degrade the quality of grapes and may create the need for fungicides.

FOG

Frequent fogs can be good or bad. They reduce temperatures and sunlight in the vineyard, which may be beneficial in hotter climates but is not useful in cooler ones. Fog also raises the humidity, but if it is burned off by the sun in the late morning, as is often the case, it is not harmful. In some cases, fog creates the ideal conditions for the development of the *Botrytis cinerea* fungus, which is desired for the production of certain dessert wines.

WIND

Wind can also have a favorable or negative effect on a vineyard. Wind can interfere with the flowering and pollination process, thereby impacting the vine's ability to develop healthy fruit. High winds anytime during the season can put significant strain on the vines, which is why windbreaks are used in some locations. In regions subject to high-velocity winds, such as southern France with its mistral winds, the winds dictate the methods for trellising and pruning. However, some wind can also be beneficial to a vineyard by reducing humidity and pest concerns.

SOIL

There are many different types of soil present in vineyards. Some examples include clay, chalk, sand, gravel, silt, slate, marl, loess, and limestone. Grapevines can grow in almost any of them. However, the world's greatest vineyard sites seem to have two things in common:

1. They are not very fertile. In fertile soil, a vine has the tendency to produce an overabundance of shoots and bunches, with sugar and flavor components divided among too many grapes. Theoretically, this can be controlled, but to do so requires considerable labor. Less fertile soils encourage the vine to produce less vegetation and fewer grapes. This is part of the reason why, historically, grapes for wine have been planted in sites that were not amenable to the cultivation of other food crops.
2. Their soils regulate the supply of water to the vine. Ideally, the soil should enable the roots to access water when needed but also ensure that excess water is drained away, so there are no extremes of too much or too little moisture.

These factors help explain why the best vineyard sites maintain consistent quality regardless of vintage year.

Some tasters believe that a soil's composition imparts its unique flavor characteristics to grapes and the wines made from them. For instance, it could be believed that grapes grown in chalky soil will yield a wine with a chalky character. However, there is as yet little scientific evidence to support this concept, and the topic remains a popular source of debate among wine enthusiasts.

A soil type is defined by the sizes of particles it contains and the composition of those particles. The particle sizes are as follows:
- *Clay:* very fine particles that fit together so tightly that water has difficulty passing through
- *Silt:* particles of intermediate size
- *Sand:* coarse particles with relatively little water-retention capability

- *Gravel:* larger pieces of solid inorganic matter; essentially, inert obstacles that roots must pass around, or sometimes through, to reach water and nutrients

Soil normally contains varying proportions of each of these particle sizes. The particles themselves may be composed of one or more minerals, such as quartz, feldspar, or calcium carbonate. Soil also contains organic matter made up of decomposed plant and animal materials. These materials provide most of the nutrients the grapevine needs for continued growth.

PHYSICAL GEOGRAPHY

There will always be innumerable elements related to a vineyard's physical location that cannot be exactly duplicated anywhere else: distance from the ocean, contour of the land, latitude, proximity to mountain ranges and rivers, and so on. These often subtle and sometimes invisible features are what make terroir such an enigmatic influence.

Some geographic factors include the following:
- *Latitude:* In general, a lower latitude (that is, one closer to the equator) translates into hotter climates. Higher latitudes benefit from longer summer days and cooler nights, but they have a shorter growing season and possibly dangerous frosts and freezes.
- *Elevation:* Compared to a valley floor vineyard, a vineyard at a higher elevation will be cooler and windier, and may have less fog. Higher altitudes experience larger diurnal temperature swings, which is a positive factor as long as the nights don't get too cold. Well above sea level, the sunlight is more intense, encouraging photosynthesis.
- *Topography:* The way the vineyard is contoured can have any number of effects. Hillside vineyards have fewer problems with frost, but they can be harder to work if they are steep. Tractors and mechanical harvesters can navigate flat tracts easily, but flat bottomland is often overly fertile. Rolling topography can create a patchwork of low areas that collect too much water and higher areas that are always dry.

- *Aspect:* In the Northern Hemisphere, a vineyard on a slope that faces south gets the most sun, which is highly desirable in cool regions but not so desirable in hotter ones. In the Southern Hemisphere, the north-facing slopes get the most sun exposure.
- *Proximity to bodies of water:* Water tends to change temperature more slowly than soil. The larger the body of water, the more it resists change. For this reason, vineyards located close to water—rivers, lakes, and especially oceans—experience far less temperature variation than those without water's moderating influence. Their diurnal temperature range is less, summers are not as hot, and winters are milder compared to other vineyards at the same latitude but located farther from the water. Bodies of water also provide a source of humidity, which in different areas can mean morning or evening fogs, greater cloud cover, rain, or fungus-encouraging dampness.

These geographic factors combine to produce an incredible diversity of climates around the world, often changing perceptibly in the space of a few miles. Climatologists group these climates into broad categories, but the ones most applicable to wine regions are maritime, Mediterranean, and continental.

- *Maritime climates* are strongly influenced by an ocean and have high rainfall and mild temperatures overall.
- *Continental climates* are the opposite: found in areas far from oceanic effects, they have hotter summers and colder winters—sometimes extreme in both directions—and they may have less precipitation.
- *Mediterranean climates*, typically found within the temperate latitudes, are characterized by warm, dry summers, mild, wet winters, and low humidity. Mediterranean climate zones are associated with high-pressure atmospheric cells found over many of the world's large oceans that pull rain toward the region during the winter while keeping the areas warm and dry during the summer.

Another term that is frequently heard in association with wine is "marginal climate," which refers to an area that has such cool temperatures or such a short summer growing season that grapes are just barely able to achieve enough ripeness for harvesting before autumn frosts arrive.

VINE DISEASES AND PESTS

DISEASES

Grapevine diseases may be caused by viruses, bacteria, or fungi. Different diseases attack different parts of the plant, such as roots, trunk, branches, shoots, flowers, or grapes, and are often most troublesome at a specific time of the year, such as during flowering or right before harvest. Some diseases result in a poor crop, while others threaten the survival of the vine itself.

Viral diseases can be spread by propagating infected vine cuttings, so controlling them is dependent upon avoiding introducing them to new vineyard plantings or grafted vines.

Bacterial diseases are more likely to be spread by insects and animals that carry the microbes. One example is Pierce's disease, a bacteriological contamination of the host vine resulting in premature leaf fall. This disease is spread by several types of sharpshooter insects, most notably the glassy-winged sharpshooter. These insects might feed on an infected vine and then transmit the bacteria to a healthy vine. Typically, these diseases are prevented through the systematic use of insecticides to control the carriers. However, new research has uncovered safe, organic remedies that may cure such diseases from within the plant.

Fungal diseases are generally spread by airborne spores and become a problem mostly in warm, humid conditions, which are ideal for the growth and spread of the fungus. Grape growers usually fight fungus with either sulfur or a commercial fungicide sprayed onto the vines. Two of the most damaging fungal diseases are powdery mildew, also known as *oidium*, and downy mildew, also known as *peronospora*.

Another significant fungus is *Botrytis cinerea*, which, uniquely, can be as beneficial as it can be harmful. When it is present at the wrong time or on grapes that are detrimentally affected by it, it is known as gray mold and wreaks havoc with the ripening grapes. However, when it develops on fully ripe grape varieties that can benefit from it (white grapes, especially Sémillon, Riesling, and Chenin Blanc), botrytis is known as noble rot. Botrytis is known to the French as *pourriture noble* and to the Germans as *Edelfäule*.

Figure 4–4: Grape clusters affected by *Botrytis cinerea*

Botrytis cinerea sends its filaments through the skin of the grape to tap into the juice. By extracting water from inside the berries, it concentrates the grapes' sugars and flavors while adding its own characteristic aroma, which has been described as being similar to honeysuckle. Botrytis develops best under very special climatic conditions: morning fog, which provides a humid environment that nurtures botrytis growth on the berries, followed by afternoon sun, which prevents the fungus from spreading over the entire vine. Under these conditions, botrytis is responsible for some of the finest sweet wines in the world.

PESTS

Grapevine pests come in many shapes and sizes, from microscopic insects to large mammals. Among the insects, the most serious is the tiny louse phylloxera. No other grapevine malady has caused such economic and viticultural damage.

Phylloxera—native to the eastern United States—was accidentally introduced to Europe in the mid-1800s, most likely brought in on the roots of samples or specimens of young vines of native North American origin. Once it became established, phylloxera devastated many of the established vineyards of Europe, spreading from vineyard to vineyard and country to country, killing off the vines on which it fed. The pest eventually made its way to other parts of the world—including Australia, New Zealand, South Africa, the west coast of the United States, and beyond—destroying many of the world's vinifera vines in its path.

Eventually, it was discovered that the native American grapevines had long ago developed a natural resistance to phylloxera. With this in mind, one early attempt at a solution in France was to interbreed native American vines and *Vitis vinifera* in order to develop hybrids that would have the varietal character of the vinifera and the disease resistance of the American species. Many of these hybrids were deemed unsatisfactory, however, so the practice did not gain widespread acceptance. It was ultimately discovered that the prized vinifera varieties could be grafted onto the rootstock of American vines with little, if any, degradation in the flavor profile of the vinifera fruit.

Cultivating grafted vines became standard procedure in most of the world's vineyards, and the destroyed vinifera vineyards in Europe and elsewhere were almost all replanted with grafted plants. This situation remains today, as no method of safely removing phylloxera from an active vineyard has been found. Only a few areas throughout the world can claim to be "phylloxera-free" to the extent that they can sustain ungrafted vines. Such regions are generally isolated from other wine regions, or they are rich in sandy soils that are inhospitable to this pest.

Another soil-based pest is the nematode. This microscopic roundworm also feeds on the vine's roots. In addition to causing direct damage to the vine via the worm's feeding, nematodes also transmit viruses that can kill the plant. This problem has become more prevalent with the increased use of shallow-rooted rootstocks and has been further compounded by the use of drip irrigation, which reduces the vine's tendency to send its roots deep into the soil in search of water. The most common solution to the problem is the use of nematode-resistant rootstocks, but certain cover crops, such as mustard, can act as a natural biofumigant.

By comparison, larger pests in the vineyard are more of a nuisance than a plague. Because the fruit is naturally sweet, many animals, including birds, deer, and wild pigs, like to snack on it. In some areas, this can cause significant economic losses, making it worth the expense to install fencing or netting to keep the animals away from the vines.

THE ROLE OF THE GRAPE GROWER

As is true of any grower regarding any agricultural crop, the grape grower's responsibility is to create the best possible growing conditions for the plants, free of competition from other vegetation, and with sufficient access to water and nutrients. The work of the grape grower often includes the following tasks.

PRUNING

Pruning, typically performed in the winter or early spring, involves removing much of the vegetative growth from the previous year as well as any excess foliage and branches. Pruning is necessary to manage the size, shape, and development of the vine.

Each of the vine's branches has several nodes that may produce a new shoot and, eventually, new fruit in the spring. However, the number of shoots and grape bunches that the plant would generate naturally is typically much higher than is desirable. The vine's roots can gather only a limited amount of nutrients, and uncontrolled leaf and fruit production would spread those nutrients too thinly. To produce quality wine grapes, the grower must remove all but a few of the nodes to allow the grapevine to focus its energies on supplying a small quantity of grape bunches with its entire output of sugar and nutrients.

Pruning is typically approached using one of the following general strategies:

- *Cane pruning:* Using cane pruning, the grower will remove all but one or two canes per vine. The remaining canes are attached to a horizontal trellis and trimmed so that each cane has between six and ten nodes (buds).
- *Spur (cordon) pruning:* Using spur pruning, vines are trained to develop one or more permanent cordons (branches), each of which will support several canes. Annual pruning will cut back the new canes, leaving behind several spurs. Each spur is a portion of a cane— measuring a few inches long—that contains several nodes (buds).

VINE TRAINING AND TRELLISING

Grape plants are climbing vines and will not naturally develop a trunk or central stalk for support, preferring instead to climb up and over nearby trees or other structures. As such, most commercial grapevines are attached to a vine training and trellis system that positions the vine as desired by the grower. The structure can be as simple as a single stake or as elaborate as a multilevel system of posts, crossbars, and wires. The goal in each case is to optimize the quality of the fruit by achieving a balance between the vigor of the vine and the desired yield of grapes per acre.

Trellised vines may utilize a simple vine training system—such as the *Guyot* system—in which one or two canes or cordons from each vine are trained along a wire. Such systems often use a configuration known as vertical shoot positioning (VSP) in which the new year's shoots and leave are trained upward and braced by trellis wires as they grow, with the grape bunches positioned below the leaves in the fruiting area. Benefits of vertical shoot positioning include good air circulation and light exposure as well as ease of use with mechanical harvesters.

In high vigor sites, a divided canopy—with two or more separate fruiting zones, spaced either horizontally or vertically—may be used to provide more space for the vine to spread out. Well-known examples of divided canopies include the Geneva Double Curtain, Lyre, and Scott Henry systems.

Figure 4-5: Bush vine Grenache

Some vines may develop a thick (and often somewhat gnarled) trunk over time. Often referred to as bush vines, head-trained, or *gobelet*-style vines, such vines are typically free-standing (without the need for a stake or other support) and spur pruned.

In the *pergola* system, overhead vines are trained up a tall support and then allowed to spread out horizontally, with the fruit hanging below.

CANOPY MANAGEMENT

Techniques that alter the position or number of shoots and grape clusters are collectively known as canopy management. Canopy management techniques employed during the growing season include shoot thinning, shoot positioning, leaf removal, crop thinning, and other procedures intended to optimize fruit quality through the control of vine yield and vigor.

IRRIGATION

In some regions, vines may require supplemental water as well as fertilizers or chemical nutrients to maintain their rate of growth. In some parts of Europe—particularly in those appellations that are highly regulated in many aspects of production—irrigation is either prohibited or tightly controlled. However, irrigation is used in many parts of the world and in some areas, commercial viticulture would be unsustainable without it.

MANAGING THE HARVEST

In the fall, the grower—often working in tandem with the winemaker—must decide upon the optimal time to harvest the grapes. This decision is based on the ripeness of the grapes and the style of wine to be produced as well as weather, labor availability, and economic considerations.

Figure 4-6: Refractometer in use

There are several different methods used to measure grape sugar concentration; most countries have their preferred scale and many use slightly different forms of analysis. In the United States, the concentration of sugar in the grapes is typically measured in *degrees Brix*. The most common tools used to measure grape sugar include a refractometer, and the more old-fashioned hydrometer. To estimate the potential ethanol level in a finished dry wine, the conversion factor is about 5/9, or 55%, of the Brix value. For example, grapes harvested at 24° Brix will yield a wine with an alcohol level of around 13.3% (24 × 0.55) if fermented dry. For a quick, rough estimate of potential alcohol, simply divide the Brix reading by two.

Other countries use different measurement systems to calculate the anticipated final alcohol level. Baumé, a unit of measurement used primarily in France, reflects the potential alcohol level in milliliters per 100 milliliters of wine. Freshly pressed grape juice with 12° Baumé will produce a wine with a maximum of 12% alcohol.

The system used in Germany and Switzerland, Oechsle, is a bit more complicated. To calculate it, measure the density of the grape must, subtract 1.0, and multiply this figure by 1,000. In other words: Oechsle = (density – 1.0) × 1,000. Must with a density reading of 1.068 will have an Oechsle reading of 68, which is roughly 9% potential alcohol.

Table 4-1: Comparison of Sugar Measurement Systems

COMPARISON OF SUGAR MEASUREMENT SYSTEMS			
	US	FRANCE	GERMANY
Potential Alcohol	Brix (Bx)	Baumé	Oechsle (Oe)
12.0% abv	21.8°	12.0°	89
15.4% abv	28°	15.4°	110.4
16.0% abv	29.1°	16.0°	114.9

SPECIAL VITICULTURAL PRACTICES

ORGANIC VITICULTURE

Organic viticulture is grape growing without the use of manufactured fertilizers or pesticides. Recent focus on protecting the environment has created significant interest in organic agriculture; organic grapes represent one of the fastest-growing segments of viticulture today, and wines made from organic grapes are in great demand among consumers. (Note that there is a difference between organic grapes and organic wines, which will be discussed in chapter 5.)

To be recognized as an organic grower, it is necessary to go through a certification process overseen by an accredited body, such as a state agricultural department or a duly sanctioned private company. In the United States, the US Department of Agriculture's (USDA) National Organic Program (NOP) designates the certifying bodies and provides the criteria that a vineyard must meet to be approved as organic. Other countries have their own certification procedures, but they are not currently recognized for wines imported into the United States.

The NOP maintains a list of banned chemicals, which includes most inorganic and manufactured chemicals. Some chemicals are allowed if there are no acceptable substitutes and if the chemical is generally recognized as safe. A vineyard must be free from all prohibited materials for a minimum of three years before it can become certified as organic.

To produce a quality crop without using synthetic chemicals, the grower must find alternative methods to promote growth and avoid pest and disease damage. For example, chemical fertilizers can be replaced with compost and manure. Rather than using herbicides to keep weeds down, additional mowing can be used to keep them under control. Various sulfur mixes, though inorganic, are allowed as effective fungicides. Natural predators and nonchemical solutions may be used to deal with pests.

INTEGRATED PEST MANAGEMENT (IPM)

Integrated Pest Management is a targeted approach to dealing with pests in a vineyard. Its goal is to eliminate or control only those insects that are actually present and causing damage, rather than applying a more general solution that kills all insects, as some may, in fact, be beneficial.

IPM employs a process in which each pest is considered individually, as directly and uniquely as possible. The life cycle of the pest, its natural predators, and its hosts are examined in order to find a particular vulnerability that can be exploited to kill or ward off the pest with the least amount of intervention and with minimal effect on the vines and the environment.

BIODYNAMIC VITICULTURE

Biodynamic viticulture is essentially organic viticulture with the addition of metaphysical elements and a few mandated procedures. Biodynamic viticulture is gaining in popularity among consumers, many of whom tend to think of it as "more organic than organic," although they may have only a hazy idea of how it differs from organic grape growing. Interpretations of the biodynamic philosophy vary among grape growers as well.

The philosophy of biodynamics, developed in the early twentieth century by Rudolf Steiner, is part of a larger movement that holds that all parts of the universe are interconnected as an ecosystem and that humans have the capacity to tap into the universal energy through meditation and mental practice. Proponents of biodynamic viticulture believe that the alignment of the planets and the phases of the moon should direct the course of work done in the vineyard and in the winery. In the biodynamic calendar, certain days are designated as fruit days, leaf days, flower days, or root days—each of which has its own ideal vineyard activities such as harvest, pruning, watering, or leaving the vines alone! There are nine special preparations that are fundamental to biodynamic viticulture, all compost mixtures that are thought to endow the organic fertilizer with spiritual energy. Certification as a biodynamic vineyard is available through a private organization known as Demeter International.

SUSTAINABLE VITICULTURE

Sustainable viticulture has the same goals as organic and biodynamic viticulture, with one major difference in approach: it abandons the black-and-white criteria of the organic philosophy for a grayscale of relative value in protecting the environment. As with organic farming, the intent is to leave the land for the next generation in better condition than it was when it was inherited by the current farmer. However, sustainability theory does not provide a set of rules about the correct path to follow in pursuit of that ideal. In addition, it includes an analysis of social goals and economic viability.

For example, neither organic nor biodynamic principles really address climate change and greenhouse gases, but sustainability does. A grower might decide that it is more environmentally sound overall and therefore more sustainable to use infrequent applications of a mild herbicide to control weeds rather than use a tractor to mow them under. Another example is water usage: organic practices do not address it, but sustainability recognizes that water is a scarce resource that must be used wisely.

Figure 4-7: Lodi Rules Sustainable Winegrowing Certified Green Seal

By using sustainable practices, a grower demonstrates a commitment to the long-term future of the environment, society, and winegrowing. Certification of sustainable practices is still in its infancy in the United States but is being spearheaded by such programs as the Lodi Winegrape Commission's "Lodi Rules," the Napa Valley Vintners' "Napa Green," and "Vine Balance" in New York State.

FERMENTATION AND STILL WINE PRODUCTION

CHAPTER FIVE

LEARNING OBJECTIVES

After studying this chapter, the candidate should be able to:

- Recall the sequence of events that take place during the winemaking process.
- Recognize key terminology associated with fermentation and wine production.
- Understand the differences between red, white, and rosé winemaking.
- Describe the procedures for making sweet wines.
- Discuss what makes organic, biodynamic, and kosher wines different from other wines.

While much of a wine's character is determined by the qualities of the grapes themselves, winemakers have a great deal of influence as well. In this chapter, we examine the basic art and science of winemaking, or enology, beginning with the basic winemaking process for still (nonsparkling) white wines, followed by a discussion of the production of red wines, rosé wines, dessert wines, and some specialty wines. The production of sparkling and fortified wines will be covered in chapters 6 and 7, respectively.

WHITE WINE PRODUCTION

White wines are produced in a range of styles, from light-bodied and delicately scented to full-bodied, well-oaked, and complex. No matter what the style, the sequence of events in the winery is roughly the same, but with differences in the details. The following idealized description is typical of the production of most white wines in a modern winery. Keep in mind, however, that not all of the following steps will necessarily be carried out for every wine, and that variations are often introduced for the sake of style, tradition, or economy.

PRE-FERMENTATION

In general, it is a priority to begin the winemaking process as soon as possible after harvest. Once grapes are picked, they immediately start to degrade, and oxidation begins to set in. If left alone, unbroken grapes would start to become raisins, while broken grapes and their juice would quickly begin to ferment in unpredictable ways, potentially ending up as vinegar. To minimize these unwanted effects, the winemaker typically keeps the grapes cool and covered and may use sulfur as a preservative while the grapes are en route to the winemaking facility.

Sulfur can be added to the grapes or juice at any of several points during the pre-fermentation period. The sulfur combines with oxygen to form sulfur dioxide (SO_2), which inhibits the growth of both yeast and bacteria, thereby reducing the likelihood of premature fermentation and spoilage. It also prevents the juice from oxidizing and turning brown.

The pre-fermentation portion of the winemaking process is often referred to broadly as the "crush," encompassing not only the actual crushing (if any) of the grapes but also everything that gets the juice ready for the initiation of fermentation.

Sorting

The first stop in grape reception may be some type of *sorting table* where leaves, underripe bunches, damaged fruit, and other debris can be removed before processing begins. This is usually done by hand, but it can be partially mechanized. Rigorous selection results in high production costs and is primarily employed in the production of high-end wines.

Figure 5-1: White grapes in a crusher/destemmer

Crushing and Destemming

From the sorting table, the grapes may be sent through a crusher or crusher-destemmer. This piece of equipment is designed to break open the berries and release their juice. If destemming is intended, the grapes will simultaneously be separated from the stem structure of the bunch. The result of the crush is a quantity of liquid containing the grape skins and the seeds (and, perhaps the stems).

Crushing is differentiated from pressing in that the skins of the grapes are broken and juice is allowed to flow, but no pressure is applied. Crushing is typical but not universal; some wineries eliminate this step for certain wines, preferring instead to crush and press at the same time (which may involve whole-cluster pressing). If done, crushing (and later, pressing) must be done gently, as too much force can cause the release of tannins (and, perhaps, an accompanying bitterness or astringency) from the skins and seeds.

Pressing

When making white wine, contact between the skins and the juice is usually minimized, primarily in order to avoid coloration. However, an exception is often made for some of the more aromatic grape varieties, which may benefit from a short period of time during which they are chilled, and their skins are permitted to macerate with the juice to extract aromas and desirable phenolics. This "cold soak" is generally done for no more than twenty-four hours.

During the pressing stage, fresh grapes, whether crushed first or not, are poured into the press in order to separate the solids from the juice. By this point, the movement of the grapes since harvest has already caused many of the berries to burst open, so a large amount of juice drains out from the press immediately (more if the berries were crushed first). This is known as the "free run" juice and is typically considered to be juice of the highest quality, rich in sugar and low in tannin. Some wineries keep this free-run juice separate from the later "press juice" for use in the winery's best wines.

After most of the free run has been collected, the grapes are subjected to one or more pressings to extract the remaining liquid. Presses were once mechanical devices that smashed the grapes between two hard surfaces to extract the juice, but modern versions are far gentler. Modern presses are usually *bladder presses* that essentially inflate a large balloon with air or water to squeeze the grapes with just as much force as other presses, but with more flexibility, which is less likely to crush seeds or burst open skin cells. As a result, properly operated modern presses can extract more usable liquid from the grapes than ever before while avoiding the negative consequences of too much pressure.

The cake of dry, compressed skins and pips (seeds) that remains after the final pressing is called *pomace* and is often composted or plowed back into the vineyard to improve soil structure. It can also be used to make pomace brandies known as *marc* or *grappa*.

Must Adjustments

Grape juice that is destined for fermentation is referred to as *must*. After pressing, the must may be ready to move into the fermentation phase, or the winemaker may determine that must adjustments are necessary. For instance, as sometimes occurs in warm climates or particularly hot years, the grapes may have a level of acidity that is too low for the accompanying sugar levels. In the case of cool climates or unusually cool-to-cold years, the grapes may have developed insufficient sugar. For these and a variety of other reasons, the levels of sugar or acidity in the must may be out of the range that the winemaker needs for the style of wine he or she wants to create.

The issue of low acidity can be solved by adding acid directly to the must, a process known as *acidification*. This is generally done with tartaric acid, the most common acid naturally found in grapes. Acidification should not affect the flavor significantly apart from sharpening the acidic tang and bringing the wine into balance. If necessary, a degree of de-acidification may be achieved through the use of potassium or calcium bicarbonate.

The problem of insufficient sugar is not uncommon in marginal growing regions where grapes may fail to reach optimal ripeness. In such instances, the winemaker may choose to use some form of *enrichment*, such as blending with grape juice or concentrated grape sugar (known as rectified grape must concentrate/RGCM).

In a related process known as *chaptalization*, sugar is cautiously added to the must before fermentation begins. Chaptalization requires that the winemaker incorporate only enough sugar into the must to achieve an acceptable alcohol level in the finished wine. This is not a method of making wines sweet, as the added sugar—along with the original sugar content of the must—is expected to be converted into alcohol.

There are various other methods available for raising or lowering the concentration of sugar or acid in the must, including adding or removing water. However, such procedures are highly regulated in many parts of the world, and wineries are subject to the stipulations of each country or region.

Juice Settling

After pressing, the winemaker may choose to let the juice settle for a day or two before allowing fermentation to begin. This process is called *débourbage* in French. Juice settling may be done in order to let a must adjustment fully integrate with the juice, to wait for some of the solids to settle out of solution so there will be less sediment after fermentation, or to have time to process more grapes that will go into the same batch.

FERMENTATION

The actual mechanics of fermentation are quite complex in that the biochemical process involves about thirty successive chemical reactions, each *catalyzed* (brought about) by a specific *enzyme* (an organic substance capable of causing a chemical change) in the yeast.

Simply put, yeast cells attack sugar molecules ($C_6H_{12}O_6$) and break them apart to release energy, some of which is given off as heat. The smaller molecules that remain after the yeast cells have split apart the sugar are ethyl alcohol (C_2H_5OH) and carbon dioxide. After the yeast cells have worked their way through a tank of grape must, virtually all of the fermentable sugar has been replaced by alcohol and carbon dioxide, the latter of which mostly dissipates into the air. In other words, the must has become wine.

The basic chemical formula is this:
$$C_6H_{12}O_6 + yeast \rightarrow 2\ (C_2H_5OH) + 2\ (CO_2) + heat$$

Because there are actually many intermediate steps that take place during this process, usually only about 90% of the grape sugars are fully converted into ethanol and CO_2 before fermentation stops. Most of the rest are broken down into various transitional products such as glycerol, succinic acid, acetic acid, lactic acid, acetaldehyde, ethyl acetate, and other alcohols such as methanol.

Figure 5-2: Vintage wine presses

In modern wineries, white wines are often fermented in stainless steel tanks. Stainless steel is considered *inert*, meaning that it does not impact the flavors of the wine. Stainless steel tanks are also airtight and easy to clean, and they provide relatively easy temperature control. Some white wines are barrel-fermented in standard 225-liter (60-gallon) oak barrels to add complexity, introduce some oak flavors, and downplay fruit aromas. Other fermentation vessels, more often seen in older, more traditional wineries, include large wooden casks and concrete vats.

Initiating Fermentation

Yeast cells and spores are commonly found in and around wineries. These include yeasts that were brought into the winery on harvested grapes and others that remain in the winery from previous years' fermentations. Therefore, it is often more difficult to *prevent* fermentation from beginning than it is to make it begin. As soon as the sugar-rich juice is released from the grapes, yeast cells will jump in and begin feasting and multiplying. To stop this from happening too soon or with unwanted strains of yeast, the winemaker will usually add some sulfur. Sulfur is toxic to yeast as well as to other fungi and bacteria. The must may also be refrigerated, which slows or stops most biological activity.

The use of these ambient (native) yeasts—sometimes referred to as natural fermentation—is an important stylistic decision. There are hundreds (if not more) types of yeast, and not all of them are conducive to commercial wine production. In some cases, a certain strain (or strains) of yeast may produce less-than-desirable aromas or flavors, or they may be unable to convert all the fermentable sugar to alcohol (leaving the wine susceptible to spoilage, among other issues). However, native yeast fermentation can be an effective and deliberate wine making technique. In some established wine regions and wineries, generations of natural selection may have fostered a dominant strain of desirable yeast, making native yeast fermentation a possible and positive choice.

The alternative is to add a significant amount of commercially grown yeast. *Inoculation* of the must with cultured yeast gets the fermentation off to a fast start and gives the cultured yeast a substantial advantage over any wild yeast that may be present in the must. The cultivated yeast will rapidly dominate the yeast population.

Most of the yeasts used in winemaking are strains of *Saccharomyces cerevisiae*. Different strains of yeast may be chosen in order to add desirable flavors or aromas to the wine, to speed up or slow down the fermentation process, or to achieve a certain level of alcoholic strength. The specific yeast strain chosen can have a considerable effect on the overall style of the finished wine.

During Fermentation

Once the yeast start to multiply, the must will begin to bubble and foam with escaping carbon dioxide and will grow warm from the heat caused by the fermentation process. The temperature is a critical factor. Cool temperatures between 50°F and 60°F (10–16°C) are best for retaining delicate fruit and floral aromas, which are key features of many white wines.

Figure 5-3: Stainless steel fermentation tanks

As the temperature increases, the yeast cells become increasingly active, converting the sugar into alcohol at a faster pace and further raising the temperature. At elevated temperatures, the fresh fruit and floral essences of white grapes can disappear, giving the wine a more neutral character or even introducing "cooked fruit" aromas more akin to apple sauce than fresh apples. If the fermentation gets out of control and the liquid goes much above 100°F (38°C), the yeast will likely die, and fermentation will stop prematurely. This is the most common cause of a "stuck fermentation," which is very difficult to reverse.

For both stylistic and practical reasons, temperature control is one of the most important things the winemaker is tasked with during fermentation. The job is made much easier with modern technology, which allows for remote monitoring of temperature levels and effective cooling capabilities through the use of refrigerated jackets, coils, or panels. Before such technology existed, winemakers had to rely on chilly fall weather conditions or work in underground wine cellars to keep the fermenting vessels cool, although these nontechnical methods are still in use today.

End of Fermentation

With proper temperature control and a healthy population of yeast, fermentation should continue until the sugar is depleted and there is nothing left for the yeast to consume. This can take anywhere from several days to several weeks. Fermentation may also come to an end if the alcohol content reaches more than 14% or so, at which point the yeast may no longer be able to survive. This may leave a small amount of residual sugar. Another possibility is for the winemaker to intentionally stop the fermentation while there is still a degree of sugar present. This is done for white wines that are intended to be *off-dry* or *medium dry*, as well as for dessert and fortified wines.

The liquid is now officially wine. While some white wines have an alcohol content as low as 7% abv, most white wines have an alcohol content of 12% to 14%. Next, the wine moves into the post-fermentation phase, where it will be prepared for bottling and sale.

POST-FERMENTATION

Malolactic Fermentation

Malolactic fermentation (MLF) is not a true (alcohol-producing) fermentation but rather a conversion process that can take place simultaneously with the primary (alcoholic) fermentation or after the primary fermentation is complete. Malolactic fermentation is often referred to as *secondary fermentation* or *malolactic conversion*. Malolactic fermentation is carried out by a particular strain of lactic acid bacteria that decomposes the sharp malic acid in the wine and converts it to lactic acid. When this happens, the tart, green apple characteristics of malic acid are replaced by the milder and creamier characteristics of lactic acid. An ester known as diacetyl, created as a by-product of malolactic fermentation, often imparts a "buttery" aroma to wines that have undergone this process.

For many white wines—particularly those that rely on fragrant aromas, light body, and crisp acidity—malolactic fermentation is avoided. Certain styles of Chardonnay benefit from the richness added by malolactic fermentation, and these are perhaps best-known examples of white wines that undergo malolactic fermentation. However, some producers are using MLF on Chenin Blanc, Viognier, and other white wines. These wines are often described as having notes of butter, hazelnut, brioche (freshly baked bread), and dried fruit.

Lees Contact

After fermentation is complete, the expired yeast cells and any other solid particles in the wine begin to sink to the bottom of the tank or barrel. This sediment is known as the *lees*. In many cases, the wine is quickly removed from the lees through a method of clarification known as *racking*.

In other cases, the wine is allowed to rest in contact with the lees for an extended period of time. This is known as *sur lie aging*, which is French for "on the lees." As the wine rests on the lees, the dead yeast cells begin to decompose, potentially imparting a yeasty aroma, creamy texture, and increased complexity to the wine. To amplify these effects, the sediment may even be stirred back up into the liquid in a process known as *lees stirring* or *bâtonnage*.

Figure 5-4: White Wine Production Chart

Grape Arrival					
Sorting	Crushing	Destemming			
Pressing					
Must Adjustments	Juice Settling				
Fermentation					
Yeast Inoculation	Temperature Control				
Post-fermentation					
Lees Contact	Malolactic Fermentation	Clarification	Aging	Blending	Cold Stabilization
Bottling					

Sulfur Addition

After fermentation is complete, the sulfur level of the wine is typically checked once again. The addition of more sulfur at this point might be necessary to decrease the chance of microbial spoilage or browning in the finished wine. This is particularly important if there is any residual sugar in the wine, which could potentially lead to unwanted fermentation after bottling.

Clarification

Following fermentation, a new wine has a cloudy, almost murky appearance due to the remaining yeast cells and other solids that remain in suspension. Because modern consumers generally expect their wines to be clear, various methods are used to remove these solids before bottling. Some of these methods are discussed below:

Racking

Racking, the most basic clarification procedure, uses the action of gravity by allowing the suspended matter to settle to the bottom of the fermentation vessel. The wine is then carefully drawn off the sediment and moved into a fresh container. Several rackings may take place over a period of time, each resulting in a brighter, clearer wine.

Although racking removes most of the suspended solids in a wine, some microscopic particles, such as chains of tannins or proteins, will inevitably remain in solution. Although they may be too small to be seen individually, their collective presence may make the wine look dull, or they may eventually coalesce together into larger, visible particles. For these reasons, many winemakers opt for further clarification.

Fining

Fining is a time-honored technique in which an inert material that has an affinity for certain particulates is stirred into the wine. The fining agent falls through the wine, attracting and binding with the unwanted material as it settles to the bottom. Both the fining agent and sediment are then separated from the wine by racking. Fining agents include gelatin and egg white, which bind with and remove excessive tannin, and bentonite clay, which attracts and removes proteins.

Filtering

Filtering involves straining the wine through a barrier with very fine openings in order to trap any particulates over a certain size. With modern technology, filters can eliminate contaminants as small as bacteria. This process, known as *sterile filtering*, removes all microbes (yeast and bacteria) that could cause spoilage later. Filtering must be carefully monitored, as it comes with the risk of reducing some desirable flavor molecules along with the unwanted particles.

Centrifuge

Some wineries may use a *centrifuge* to clarify their wines. A centrifuge is a modern piece of laboratory equipment that uses accelerated gravity to separate the wine from the heavier solids.

After a full course of clarification, a white wine will typically be sparkling clear and have no sediment in the bottle. While this is the norm for white wines, there are winemakers who prefer to bottle some of their white wines unfined and unfiltered, as this can lead to greater depth of flavor, complexity, and texture. Such wines may contain sediment in the bottle or be slightly opaque in appearance.

Barrel Aging

Aging wine in oak barrels allows for a slow oxidation that changes the wine and adds complexity. If the wood is new, it can also add touches of vanilla, oak, wood, coconut, toast, or other aromas to the wine. Such transformations are neither necessary nor beneficial for the majority of light white wines. However, heavier, fuller-bodied styles of white wines, such as those often made with Chardonnay and Sauvignon Blanc, can be produced with some time spent in a barrel.

Blending

Shortly before bottling, many different vats of wine may be blended together to make the finished product. These vats may represent wine from different vineyards, grape varieties, vintages, or even winemakers. Blending is particularly important for branded wines, which need to re-create the desired flavor profile of the brand year after year. Aside from achieving consistency, the practice of blending is also employed to develop complexity or balance, or to create a particular style of finished wine.

Cold Stabilization

White wines, particularly those that are crisp and tart, tend to be quite high in tartaric acid. This acid is a major component of the wine and is not something that can or should be filtered out in the clarification process. However, when the wine gets cold, the acid may precipitate out of solution as tartrate crystals. As previously mentioned, these crystals are known as "wine diamonds." Wine diamonds look like tiny crystals of rock salt and may form in the bottle or on the bottom of the cork.

While tartrates are harmless, many consumers assume they are a defect. In order to prevent wine diamonds from forming in the consumer's or retailer's refrigerator, many white wines are *cold stabilized* before bottling. This is achieved by chilling the wine to around 25°F (–4°C), holding the wine at this temperature for one to three weeks, and racking the wine off of the precipitates.

Figure 5-5: Bottling line

Bottling

If the wine is not to be sold in bulk, the last task is bottling. Most large wineries have their own bottling equipment, while smaller wineries may rent a mobile bottling facility or have their wine bottled at a larger winery. The typical bottling line receives empty bottles at one end, fills them with wine, seals them with a cork, installs a capsule over each bottle's neck, labels them, and packages them in boxes on pallets. Each of these steps is either automated or done manually. From here, the wine is stored until needed for shipment and sale.

RED WINE PRODUCTION

The procedure for the production of red wine is very much the same as that for white. The differences, intended to capture the flavor and color available in the skins of red grapes, are highlighted in the following section.

Figure 5-6: Red grapes in a crusher/destemmer

PRE-FERMENTATION
Crushing and Destemming
Whereas white grapes sometimes skip this step and go straight to the press, crushing is typically required for red grapes because their skins are used during the fermentation process. Red grapes are crushed in order to break the skins, free the juice, and allow the yeast to begin working.

Destemming may be done as well, either by hand before crushing (which is somewhat rare and very labor-intensive) or by using a crusher-destemmer machine. In some cases, the stems may be added back to the must to provide an additional source of tannin, flavor, and complexity.

Must Adjustments
If legally permitted, the winemaker may choose to adjust acidity or sugar levels as necessary to achieve balance and the desired style in the finished wine, just as for white wines. With reds, there is also the option to add tannin if the grapes are deficient in that category. This may be done by leaving stems in the must, as mentioned above, or by adding tannin powder.

Maceration
The most important difference between white and red winemaking is the need to extract phenolics such as color, tannin, and flavor components from the skins of the red grapes. In the majority of red grapes, most of the color components are located in the skins; the juice is just as colorless as that of white grapes. During fermentation, as the skins remain in contact with the juice, the red and blue pigments are extracted out of the skins and move into the darkening juice, along with tannins and flavor constituents. This period of contact between the grape skins and the fermenting grape juice is called *maceration*.

Maceration periods run from a few days to a few weeks or even longer, beginning at or before fermentation and potentially continuing well afterward. The length of maceration is one of the winemaker's most important decisions, and is based on the intended style of the wine and the grape variety. Longer periods of maceration yield highly "extracted" wines that are deeply colored, highly tannic, bursting with flavor, and generally in need of time in the bottle to mature. A shorter period of maceration will yield softer, more accessible wines that are often ready for consumption upon release.

Certain grape varieties, such as Syrah and Cabernet Sauvignon, have an abundance of color and extract that is readily pulled from the grape skins during maceration. Others, most notably Pinot Noir, have relatively little and therefore require more time to extract sufficient color.

If the winemaker chooses to begin maceration before fermentation, the must is chilled to below 55°F (13°C) in order to postpone fermentation. This technique is called a *cold soak*. A cold soak differs from other maceration periods in that the grape solids are macerating in cold grape juice, a large percentage of which is water, as opposed to macerating in fermenting grape juice which contains a percentage of alcohol and is, therefore, a more effective solvent. The cold soak is one of the techniques that allows the winemaker to control the level of phenolics that are extracted from the grape skins during production.

FERMENTATION

The fermentation process for red wines is similar to that of white wines. The main differences are caused by the presence of the grape skins in the must. In order for the appropriate amount of phenolics to be extracted from the skins, contact between skins and the must needs to be maintained throughout the fermentation. The presence of skins also impacts the selection of fermentation vessels, favoring the use of larger tanks—which are easier to clean—over small wooden barrels.

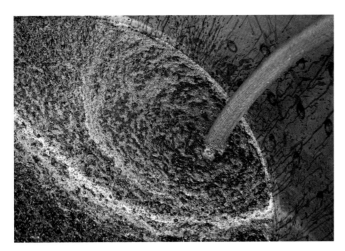

Figure 5-7: Red wine fermentation

Cap Management

Inconveniently, the carbon dioxide that is continuously produced during fermentation forms bubbles that push the grape solids to the top of the fermentation vessel in a fairly dense and compact mass known as *the cap*. Once the cap forms, it becomes the winemaker's job to break up the cap and reintegrate the skins into the liquid, allowing for optimal extraction. This is known as *cap management*.

Cap management is necessary because the proper extraction of phenolics requires the grape skins to be in the liquid, not floating *on top of it*. Potentially, acetobacter may begin to grow on the cap, which may cause the wine to develop excess acetic acid. Trapped carbon dioxide might even cause the cap to burst.

Four of the most common methods of cap management include the following:

- Punching down: physically pushing the cap down into the juice; also known by the French term *pigéage*
- Pumping over: pumping juice from the bottom of the tank and spraying it over the top of the cap; also known by the French term *remontage*
- Rack and return: draining the fermenting juice into a separate holding tank before it is returned to the original tank by spraying it over the now sunken cap, resulting in considerably more aeration than a standard pump-over; also known by the French term *délestage*
- Rotofermentation: agitating the fermenting must in a specialized fermentation vessel that either rotates on its own or contains an inner paddle that mixes the fermenting must; this eliminates the need for punching down or pumping over, as the contents are mixed at regular intervals; usually controlled by a computer.

Fermentation Temperature

Red wine fermentations are typically conducted at higher temperatures than those of white wines, in part because the light floral and fruit aromas emphasized by a cool fermentation are less important in most red wines. Warmer fermentation temperatures allow for increased extraction of phenolics, which creates a good foundation for robust, age-worthy reds. A winemaker might choose a moderate temperature of 60°F to 70°F (16°C to 21°C) for a light, fragrant Pinot Noir, or a warmer fermentation of 85°F to 95°F (30°C to 35°C) when producing a tannic blockbuster Cabernet Sauvignon. At the higher temperatures, the sugar may be completely converted to alcohol within a week.

Figure 5-8: Red Wine Production Chart

Grape Arrival				
Sorting	Crushing	Destemming	Must Adjustments	Cold Soak
Fermentation				
Yeast Inoculation		Temperature Control	Maceration	Cap Management
Post-fermentation				
Extended Maceration		Malolactic Fermentation	Pressing	
	Clarification	Aging	Blending	
Bottling				
Bottle Aging				

POST-FERMENTATION

Extended Maceration

The winemaker decides the precise time to remove the grape skins from the liquid based on the desired amount of extract in the wine. With extremely tannic grapes, some winemakers opt to end the maceration phase *before* the completion of fermentation by pressing the skins away from the still-fermenting juice. More commonly, the skins remain in contact with the wine until it has fermented to dryness and the cap loses its buoyant carbon dioxide support. In some cases, when the fullest extraction of phenolics is desired, the new wine may be allowed to remain in contact with the grape skins for several days to several weeks, or even longer, after fermentation is complete. This is known as *extended maceration*.

Malolactic Fermentation

Malolactic fermentation is more often used in the production of red wines than in the production of white wines. In most reds, high acidity is unnecessary and possibly even undesirable, making the added complexity introduced by malolactic fermentation a plus. MLF can also result in the production of a more microbially stable wine by reducing the amount of malic acid available for bacteria that can cause spoilage to attack. Malolactic fermentation in red wine is often spontaneous, or it may be initiated with an inoculation of lactic acid-producing bacteria. This may be done anytime between the beginning of the alcoholic fermentation and the transfer of the wine into barrels for aging.

Pressing

As the wine rests after fermentation, a considerable amount of solids may build up in the bottom of the fermentation tank. These solids include the former cap, the dead yeast cells, and other precipitated sediment. When it is determined that the wine has absorbed enough phenolics from the solids, the free-run wine is racked off into a different tank or directly into barrels. The remaining solids are then pressed to release any remaining wine. The press wine is very rich in tannin and color and may be added to the free-run wine or used in a separate blend.

Clarification

After pressing, the wine may be moved into a tank for clarification. One or more rackings will likely be performed to remove additional sediment. The wine may be fined or filtered, although this will inevitably take out some of the phenolics as well, so these practices are not done as frequently with red wines as they are with white wines.

Oak Aging

Aging in barrels can be very beneficial for red wines, particularly those high in tannin. The slow infusion of oxygen that seeps through the wood and into the wine helps the tannin molecules combine with each other in a process called *polymerization*. These long, polymerized tannins feel softer and richer in the mouth compared to the shorter, harder type of tannins found in grapes. The use of new or young barrels can also add vanilla, toasty, or woodsy aromas to the wine. When properly balanced with the fruit and other characteristics of the wine, oak aging can add substantial complexity to the finished product.

For these reasons, many mid- and upper-range red wines spend some time in barrels. The most exalted Cabernets and similar wines usually go into new oak barrels for several years or more. Less powerful or less expensive wines may be aged in less costly used barrels or in a mix of new and used barrels.

Variations in Oak Barrels

The choice of barrel affects the results of the aging process in many ways, such as the following:

- New barrels impart significant flavor to the wine. With each year of use, the barrel imparts less oak flavor into, and has less of an influence on, the wine. After about four years of use, most of the flavor components have leached out of the wood.
- Larger barrels have less of an effect than small barrels. The smaller the barrel, the more oak flavor will be imparted to the wine.
- The two principal sources of oak for barrels are France and the United States. French oak is considered more subtle and refined in flavor, due to its tighter grain, while American oak is more assertive and less expensive. Recently, barrels from the Baltic states, Canada, Russia, and other regions have become available internationally, with each region's barrels exhibiting their own qualities and characteristics.
- Barrels are made by hand over an open fire, which softens the wood enough to bend it into shape. The amount of "toast," or charring, on the wood affects the flavors imparted by the barrel.
- Winemakers choose their barrels by shape, size, and type of wood, and by light, medium, or heavy toast.

Figure 5-9: Red wine aging in barrels at Kanonkop Estate in Stellenbosch, South Africa

At a cost of $1,300 per new French oak barrique, the use of barrels is generally reserved for high-end wines. Alternatives to oak barrels—such as oak chips or planks—are available for inexpensive wines that would benefit from oak flavor but cannot support the cost of the barrels. Obviously, the effect is not quite the same without the oxidation that the barrel enables. Some wineries use a procedure called *micro-oxygenation*, which involves bubbling a tiny amount of oxygen into the wine in an attempt to simulate the oxidization effects of barrel aging.

CARBONIC MACERATION

Carbonic maceration is an alternative method of red winemaking involving an enzymatic fermentation that requires neither yeast nor bacteria. It will occur in whole, unbroken grapes in the absence of oxygen. To begin the process, grapes are carefully placed in an enclosed fermentation vessel and blanketed with carbon dioxide. In this environment, enzymes in the grapes themselves will begin to break down the grape sugars and create some alcohol within the berries, along with other compounds that may affect wine flavor.

It is rare for wine to be produced completely using 100% carbonic maceration, as any breakage in the grapes will lead to yeast being introduced to the juice. Instead, carbonic maceration is often used in the initial stages of wine production, after which any remaining sugar is converted by a normal alcoholic fermentation.

Carbonic maceration generally results in red wines that are low in tannin, brightly colored, and showing aromas and flavors of tropical fruit and red berries. Carbonic maceration is used in many parts of the world, but it is primarily known for its use in the Beaujolais region in France–particularly the very popular Beaujolais Nouveau.

ROSÉ WINE PRODUCTION

Rosé is basically defined as a pink wine—although the actual color may range from pale pink to dusty rose, or even an orange-tinged pink sometimes called *salmon* or *onion skin*. Rosé wines are produced—at least in part—from red grapes, and are made in many styles including still (non-sparkling), sparkling, dry, off-dry, and sweet. While many consumers assume that any pink wine is sweet, in reality, the amount of residual sugar in a rosé depends on when the fermentation is halted—a decision that is purely up to the winemaker.

The amount of color in a rosé wine depends on the grape varieties themselves and the amount of time the juice is allowed to remain in contact with the grape skins. Alternative methods of rosé production include fermenting a portion of white grapes together with a batch of red grapes (co-fermentation) or blending a small amount of red wine with a finished white wine (although this practice most often seen in the production of sparkling wine).

The most common method for making a rosé is to limit the contact time between the skins and juice so that only a small degree of color is extracted from the grape skins into the wine. In the process, red grapes are crushed, and fermentation is allowed to take place on the grape skins for anywhere from a few hours to several days. When the juice has extracted the desired amount of color from the skins, it is pressed off the skins, and the fermentation and winemaking process continues using just the juice.

In the *saignée* method of rosé production, red grapes are crushed, perhaps destemmed, and vatted for a length of time, typically from 2 to 20 hours. Next, a certain amount of the juice is run (or bled) off to make rosé. The remaining juice remains vatted with the skins and is made into red wine. The saignée method produces both a rosé and a concentrated red wine from the same batch of grapes.

Very pale rosés, such as those produced in Provence, may be made using the *direct press* method. In this method, the grapes, either destemmed or whole cluster, are crushed immediately after harvest. The juice is then pressed—either straightaway or after a short period of maceration—resulting in pale pink juice, which is then fermented. In France, such wines are often referred to as *vin gris*. (Note: As the term *vin gris* is not regulated in many parts of the world, outside of France it is not unusual to see the term used on the labels of rosé wines produced using other methods as well.)

Rosés should always be fruity and refreshing, with medium to high acidity. Rosés that are slightly sweet are often called *blush* or, if made from a single variety, *white*, as in White Zinfandel. *Rosé* is the French term and is widely used in English-speaking countries as well. Other terms include *rosado* in Spanish, *rosato* in Italian, and *Weissherbst* in German.

THE ROLE OF THE WINEMAKER

There are many schools of thought concerning the role of the winemaker and their appropriate impact on the final style of the wine. One such dichotomy might be informally described as "terroir-focused" versus "process focused." The more traditional, terroir-focused view is that the natural aspects of a vineyard and production facility are paramount; and that grapes and wine should reflect their physical environment as closely as possible. On the other hand, some people believe that while terroir plays a significant role, grapes are simply raw materials to be molded—as far as possible—into a desired form by human artistry, expertise, and technology. Of course, neither of these points of view are absolute, and most winemakers accept the tenets of many different viewpoints.

The winemaker's activities are most intense from just before harvest through the end of the fermentation process. During the remainder of the year, the pace is slower, as the winemaker checks on the progress of the aging wines, decides when to bottle, and plans for the next vintage. Because this schedule is heavily weighted within a three- or four-month time frame, some "flying winemakers" are able to travel between the Northern and Southern Hemispheres to make wine twice a year.

SPECIAL WINEMAKING PRACTICES

SWEET WINES

Sweet wines can be made from many different grape varieties, by using diverse winemaking techniques and, in many cases, by using specific viticultural practices. Some of these include the following:

- *Botrytis:* If the *Botrytis cinerea* (noble rot) fungus affects grapes at the right time, it causes water to evaporate from the berries, thereby raising the concentration of sugar. This most famously occurs in the Sauternes area of Bordeaux in France, but also in the Loire Valley and in other locations that have similar climatic conditions. Sémillon and Chenin Blanc are two grape varieties that have a particular affinity for botrytis due to their thin skins. Noble rot adds distinctive honeysuckle and apricot aromas to the wine.
- *Late harvest:* If growers wait beyond the typical optimal ripeness point to harvest the grapes, the berries will continue to gain sugar as long as there are green leaves on the vine. They will begin to lose some water as well, making them very sweet. However, they also lose acidity during this period, so this technique works best in cool climates and with varieties that have high natural acidity, such as Chenin Blanc and Riesling.

Figure 5–10: Grapes drying for dessert wine

- *Dried grapes:* After harvest, grapes can be allowed to dry out and become partially raisinated. This is an ancient tradition that is still practiced in many places around the Mediterranean. The grapes may be spread out on mats or hung from the rafters of a drying room for as long as several months, retaining sugar but losing water content. The dried grapes may be fermented into a dry, high-alcohol wine, as in Italy's Amarone, or more often, into a sweet wine.
- *Freezing:* In some cold regions, primarily in Germany and Canada, growers may leave the grapes on the vine until the weather turns cold enough to freeze them. This may be as late as January or February in the Northern Hemisphere. By this time, the grapes have developed significant sugar content. Following harvest, the frozen grapes are pressed immediately, resulting in extremely sweet, rich juice. Riesling, Gewürztraminer, Chenin Blanc, and some cold-hardy hybrids are the most common varieties used in these styles of wine, known as ice wine (icewine) or Eiswein. Red versions of ice wine are also produced, typically using Cabernet Franc. A similar style of sweet wine can be achieved using late-harvest grapes and freezing them, post-harvest, in a commercial freezer. This mechanical freezing process is known as cryoextraction. Products produced using cryoextraction are distinguished from true ice wines and may not be labeled as such.

Note that chaptalization is not considered an acceptable way of increasing the sweetness of wine. Chaptalization is allowed only in situations where the grapes are unable to ripen sufficiently, and then only to the degree necessary to bring the alcohol level up to a minimum standard, not to create a sweet wine.

Fermentation begins for a sweet wine the same as for any other wine. However, this can be a difficult fermentation, as the yeast may struggle to stay alive due to the high sugar content.

A winemaker may choose to use one of the following procedures in the making of a sweet wine:
- *Refrigeration:* Chilling the must during fermentation stops yeast activity while there is still sugar left. However, it does not kill the yeast, so additional procedures, such as sterile filtering or sulfur additions, are necessary to make sure that the wine does not begin fermenting again after bottling.
- *Adding sweetness:* The wine can be allowed to ferment dry, and then it is made sweet through the addition of sugar, grape concentrate, or unfermented juice (rectified grape must) after fermentation is complete. This also poses the risk of restarting fermentation unless protective measures are implemented.
- *Fortification:* Adding distilled spirits during fermentation can raise the alcohol level high enough to kill the yeast before all the sugar is gone. This is discussed in greater detail in chapter 7.

Other methods of creating a sweet wine include interrupting the fermentation by killing the yeast via pasteurization or adding large amounts of sulfur.

ORGANIC WINES

The National Organic Program (NOP) of the US Department of Agriculture, which sets labeling rules in the United States, limits the term "Organic Wine" to wines that are made from a minimum of 95% certified organic grapes and that do not use anything in the winemaking process that is defined as "prohibited" according to the NOP's National List of Allowed and Prohibited Substances. Wines that meet these and other specific NOP criteria qualify as "Organic Wine" and are entitled to display the USDA Organic Seal on

the label. Wines that meet these criteria and are made solely using certified organic grapes may use the term "100% Organic." Only a small proportion of the wines produced worldwide are organically made; however, they may be the safest wines for those who have asthma or a sulfur allergy.

Figure 5-11: USDA NOP logo

By far, the most significant restriction in organic winemaking concerns the use of sulfur in the winery. Sulfur is the single most effective substance for controlling the bacteria and fungi that threaten to spoil wine. An effective alternative that does not overtly change the character of the wine is yet to be found. However, sulfur is an inorganic element, not an organic substance, and therefore sulfur additions in the winery are not allowed for wines labeled as "Organic Wine."

A wine may be labeled with the phrase "Made with Organic Grapes" if the wine was sourced from 100% *certified* organic grapes and if any added sulfur dioxide yields less than 100 parts per million in the finished wine. Wines with less than 100% organic grapes or higher sulfite additions cannot use that specific statement, although they can list the percentage of organic content in an ingredient statement on the label. In neither of these cases may the USDA Organic Seal be used.

Because of the careful, hands-on treatment of the grapes, organic wines are often of high quality. Even so, without the protective properties of sulfur, they are unlikely to remain in top form as long as other wines. Accordingly, they must be handled more attentively once they leave the winery, for example, by placing them in refrigerated units when they are sold in retail establishments.

Other countries have their own procedures for certifying wines as organic; however, wines sold in the United States cannot be labeled as organic without being certified by an NOP-accredited body.

As of August 2012, organic wines produced and sold in the European Union may be labeled "Organic Wine" or "Vin Biologique." These wines must contain 30% to 50% less added sulfur than nonorganic wines. No additives are permitted, and the winemaking process must be fully traceable.

For more details on organic viticulture, see chapter 4.

BIODYNAMIC WINES

Starting with 100% biodynamically grown grapes, the production of biodynamic wines is guided by the principles of minimal manipulation and low impact on the environment. Certification is based more on progress toward an extensive list of goals than on a strict set of criteria, although there are a few prohibitions, such as the one against the use of genetically modified materials. Sulfur use is permitted, but it is to be kept to a minimum. Thus, under US regulations, biodynamic wines are subject to less regulation than organic wines. The term *biodynamic* is trademarked and controlled by a private organization known as *Demeter International*, rather than by government regulators.

KOSHER WINES

Kosher wine is certified by Jewish religious authorities to conform to biblical laws as "proper" or "fit" (the literal translation of *kosher*) for consumption by observant Jews. Outside of Israel, kosher wine can generally be made from any grapes. However, from the time the grapes arrive at the winery, the materials may only be handled by observant male Orthodox Jews under the supervision of a rabbi, using equipment that is used for no other purpose. In addition, animal-based products such as gelatin and egg whites for fining may not be used in the production of the wine.

All kosher wines, once bottled, may leave rabbinical control without losing their status until opened. From the point of opening through consumption, the wine must again be untouched by non-Jews or nonobservant Jews.

Mevushal wine, a subcategory of kosher wine, is free from limitations on who may handle it. Mevushal wine is briefly subjected to high heat via flash-pasteurization, either as must or as wine, before leaving the winery.

ORANGE WINES

The tradition of orange wine is thought to have originated in the Republic of Georgia approximately five thousand years ago. In the production of orange wines, juice from white grapes spends a significant amount of time macerating with the grape skins in order to extract tannin and color and to achieve some oxidative resistance. Depending upon the winemaker's preference, contact may last for as short as three days or as long as several weeks or even months. As a result, these wines develop a coppery or orange hue.

SPARKLING WINE PRODUCTION

LEARNING OBJECTIVES

After studying this chapter, the candidate should be able to:

- Describe how sparkling wines are produced.
- Identify which grape varieties are commonly used in sparkling wines.
- Recall the sequence of events that takes place during the traditional sparkling wine production process.
- Recognize the different style categories of sparkling wines.
- Recall the terminology relating to sparkling wines.

Carbon dioxide is a naturally occurring by-product of the fermentation process. During the production of still wines, this gas is encouraged to disperse throughout the winemaking process. However, if fermentation takes place in a sealed container and the gas is not allowed to escape fully, the pressure will build up, and the carbon dioxide will be absorbed into the wine. If the wine is then handled in such a way that the gas remains dissolved in the wine while in the bottle, columns of bubbles streaming continuously toward the surface will appear in the glass upon opening and pouring the wine.

Effervescent wines have been known since antiquity—when they were developed completely by accident—as incompletely fermented wines that had been stored in the chill of winter would begin to spontaneously re-ferment when temperatures rose in the spring. Now known as the *méthode rurale (rural method)* or *méthode ancestral (ancestral method)*, this process remains in use today by a small number of producers.

The most famous and highly regarded process for creating a high-pressure sparkling wine is known as the *traditional*, or *classic, method*. This is the method used in the Champagne region, where it may be referred to as the "Méthode Champenoise." This method involves producing a base wine, adding a measured amount of sugar and yeast, and initiating a second fermentation in the sealed bottle.

Due to the evolution of Champagne's export trade in the late eighteenth and early nineteenth centuries, "champagne" became the default term for sparkling wine worldwide. Even after such wines began to be commercially produced in many other countries, they were still known almost universally as "champagne." Eventually, the Champenois objected to this usage and began a long campaign against the use of the term *champagne* to describe any wine except those sparkling wines made within the boundaries of the Champagne region.

This move by the Champenois was one of the earliest examples of the protection of a place-name, and it has been largely successful. Most countries now outlaw labeling a domestic sparkling wine as champagne. In the United States, certain wines may be labeled as champagne as long as a place-name is appended, such as "California Champagne." Labels submitted for approval after March 10, 2006, however, are not allowed to use the term. Additionally, some producers are voluntarily retiring their grandfathered labels in a show of support for protecting the place of origin.

GRAPE VARIETIES FOR SPARKLING WINE

In principle, it is possible to make sparkling wine out of any grape, and a wide assortment of varieties is used for the production of sparkling wines throughout the world. The main grape varieties that came to be used in the Champagne region for sparkling wine are Chardonnay, Pinot Noir, and Meunier (Pinot Meunier). This combination worked well for the cool climate of the region and for the high-acid, moderate alcohol, yeast-driven style of Champagne.

Other areas in Europe use different indigenous grapes for their sparkling wines, including the following:
• Chenin Blanc in France's Loire Valley
• Riesling in Germany
• Xarel-lo, Macabeo, and Parellada in Spain
• Muscat (Moscato), Brachetto, and Glera (Prosecco) in Italy

Outside of Europe, most wine regions have little or no limitations on the grape varieties that may be used in the production of sparkling wines. Nevertheless, many producers—particularly those able to source grapes from cool climate regions—feature Chardonnay and Pinot Noir in their sparkling wines. However, many regions produce sparkling wines from their most successful locally grown grape varieties. Examples include sparkling Shiraz from Australia, sparkling Sauvignon Blanc from New Zealand, and sparkling Riesling from New York State.

THE TRADITIONAL METHOD OF SPARKLING WINE PRODUCTION

The method of sparkling wine production employed in Champagne—referred to as the traditional or classic method (in various languages)—is used with only minor variations all over the world. Many of Europe's premium sparkling wines—including Cava (produced in Spain), Franciacorta (produced in Italy), and Crémant (produced in certain appellations in France)—use this traditional method (known as the *méthode traditionelle* in French). The highest-quality sparkling wines from California, Oregon, South Africa, Australia, Argentina and beyond do as well.

The traditional method entails making and bottling a dry, still, high-acid, and low-alcohol wine. The winemaker then adds a precise amount of yeast and sugar to the wine, which is immediately capped. The fresh yeast and sugar start a second fermentation in the bottle, which takes about thirty days to complete. After this second fermentation, the wine is aged on the lees while still in the bottle. This allows some of the lees to dissolve and be absorbed into the wine. After aging, an elaborate procedure is used to collect the sediment in the neck of the bottle and dispose of it, leaving the clear, sparkling wine behind in the bottle. The wine is then quickly topped up, presenting the winemaker with options for adding sweetness, and then resealed for eventual sale.

In the United States, sparkling wines made by these procedures are identifiable by the term "Classic Method" or "Traditional Method," or by the phrase "Fermented in This Bottle" on the label.

BASE WINE PRODUCTION

The production of the base wine that will later become sparkling wine typically proceeds like the winemaking for any other light white wine. However, grapes used for traditional method sparkling wines are typically harvested quite early (to maintain a low sugar/high acid character), and there is quite an emphasis placed on gentle handling of the grapes in order to ensure that as few bitter or harsh components as possible are transferred from the skins into the juice. In addition, careful handling minimizes color transfer from red grape varieties, such as Pinot Noir, that are often used for the white base wine.

This emphasis on gentle treatment typically begins with hand harvesting of the grapes (rather than harvesting by machine) and using small bins for storage, so the grapes are not crushed by the weight of other grapes. At the winery, the grapes may be hand sorted to remove damaged bunches. Whole-cluster pressing is the norm, keeping the juice inside the skins until the last moment and then rapidly, and with minimal force, squeezing the juice out and separating it from the skins and seeds.

The traditional Champagne press is a wide, flat basket press still used today, although modern bladder-type presses are more common both in Champagne and elsewhere. The soft and flexible surface of the inflatable bladder is less likely to break the skins' cellular structure and release bitter phenolics than are older mechanical presses.

A series of pressings is conducted, first at a relatively gentle pressure and then at increasingly greater pressures. The first pressing releases most of the juice with minimal force. This juice is of the finest quality, and the winery's best wine will be made from it. Depending on the winemaker's assessment of its quality, juice from later pressings may be combined with the first or may be used for different wines. The last pressings inevitably pick up more bitter components from the seeds and skins and are generally unsuitable for fine sparkling wine. This juice may be used to produce still wine, fortified wines, spirits, vinegar, or other products.

The juice that is destined for sparkling wine is allowed to rest for a short period of time in order to allow any sediment to settle to the bottom of the holding tank. If necessary, must adjustments are carried out to improve the must's balance. A normal fermentation is then initiated; stainless steel tanks, oak casks, and concrete vats are all used in the production of sparkling wine. The winemaker may also elect to complete malolactic fermentation at this stage; however, high acidity is considered a hallmark of these wines.

Table 6-1: Sparkling Wine Vocabulary

SPARKLING WINE VOCABULARY	
Débourbage	Juice settling
Dégorgement	Disgorging, disgorgement
Prise de mousse	"Seizing the foam," the second alcoholic fermentation
Pupitre	Riddling rack
Remuage	Riddling
Réserve	Still wine from earlier vintages, used in blending
Transversage	Transfer between bottles

BLENDING

In a large sparkling wine production facility, the winemaker will have a myriad of separate lots of base wines. These wines may be from different pressings, different grape varieties, and different vineyards, and they may include réserve wines from previous vintages. These wines are sometimes used separately to create a sparkling wine, but far more often they are mixed together in varying combinations and proportions to create one or more blends, or cuvées, that will supply a range of products with different characteristics. The blending stage is referred to by the French term *assemblage*.

Within a single brand's line of sparkling wines, there may be several cuvées. The most often seen are the following:

- *Prestige:* These top-quality wines are also known as *tête de cuvée* and by other superlatives. This is, in theory, the brand's very best wine, made from only the earliest part of the first pressing of the most exceptional fruit and treated with extraordinary care. It is usually also a vintage wine. Prestige wines are often sold in uniquely shaped or decorative bottles and at high prices.
- *Vintage:* These wines are produced from a cuvée of base wines made from grapes all harvested in the same year. The goal is to highlight the quality and unique characteristics brought on by the weather and conditions of that particular year. In Champagne, each production house may determine the years it will produce vintage Champagne.
- *Nonvintage:* These wines are produced from a cuvée that contains wines from more than one year's harvest. The base wines are chosen to construct a consistent flavor profile, or "house style," for which the brand has become known. This is normally the highest-volume category by far, and usually the least expensive.
- *Blanc de Blancs (white [wine] from white [grapes]):* This term refers to a cuvée made from white grapes. In the case of Champagne (or a sparkling wine made to emulate the style of Champagne), blanc de blancs is typically produced using 100% Chardonnay. It may be vintage or nonvintage.

- *Blanc de Noirs (white [wine] from black [grapes]):* This term refers to a cuvée made exclusively from red grapes, in which the grapes are crushed and the juice is pressed off the skins very quickly after harvest. In practice, this usually refers to wines made in the style of Champagne, produced mainly from Pinot Noir. Other red varieties may be added or substituted, such as Meunier (Pinot Meunier) in Champagne. Despite efforts to avoid color transfer from the skins, these wines may take on a pale salmon hue. These wines may be vintage or nonvintage.
- *Rosé:* Rosé sparkling wines may be produced by creating a pinkish base wine or cuvée. Production methods include having both red and white wines in the blend, using a short carbonic maceration of red grapes before pressing, or creating a pink wine via saignée. Pinot Noir is the most common variety used to make the red portion of the cuvée. In some regions, it is permitted to produce rosé sparkling wines by blending in a small amount of red wine along with the dosage; this may help to avoid potential browning during the lees-aging period.

Assemblage is followed by fining, racking, and cold stabilization before the wine is ready for the next stage.

SECOND FERMENTATION AND FINISHING

Up to this point, the traditional method is not markedly different from any other type of winemaking procedure. The differences become apparent during the next phase, when a second fermentation in the bottle traps the newly produced carbon dioxide in the wine.

Initiating Fermentation

When the time comes to begin the second fermentation process, a mixture of yeast and sugar called the *liqueur de tirage* is added to the cuvée. This mixture is immediately placed into heavy glass bottles with indented punts in the base, so designed to help withstand the pressure that will build in the bottle. The bottles are then sealed, usually with a temporary crown cap like that on a typical soda or beer bottle.

With sugar available, the yeast cells begin the second fermentation, breaking down the sugar and creating alcohol and carbon dioxide. The extra alcohol raises the level in the wine by a small amount, usually one to one and a half percentage points by volume. Typically, this causes the alcohol in the wine to increase from 10% or 11% to 11% or 12.5% abv. More importantly, the carbon dioxide gas builds pressure within the sealed bottle, causing the gas to dissolve into the liquid.

This second alcoholic fermentation occurs slowly due to the low temperature in the cellars or caves. The yeast cells also have difficulty multiplying in a wine that already contains 10% to 11% alcohol. The process can easily take a month or even longer.

Lees Aging

By the time the sugar has been used up, the pressure in the bottle is typically 5-6 atmospheres, or 75 to 90 pounds per square inch. At this pressure, the wine can hold a considerable amount of carbon dioxide gas, even though no bubbles can be seen through the glass.

As fermentation runs its course, the yeast cells die and begin to decompose, releasing compounds that create toasty, nutty flavors in the wine in a process known as *autolysis*. This is considered an important aroma and flavor component of traditional method sparkling wines. Also, it is one of the reasons that neutral base wine is used. In this way, the inherent flavor of the grapes themselves will not compete with the yeasty characteristics created through this production method.

The longer the wine remains in contact with the dead yeast before it is removed, the more apparent this flavor may become. Prestige and vintage sparkling wines usually are left for an extended time *sur lie*, that is, on the yeast lees. The longer aging time also allows the carbon dioxide to dissolve more thoroughly into the wine, which will ultimately translate into a finer, smaller bubble size in the glass.

Riddling and Disgorging

When the wine has rested on the lees long enough to achieve the desired style of wine, it is time to remove the sediment from the bottle. The challenge is to avoid letting out too much pressure, which is compounded by the fact that yeast cells tend to stick to the side of the bottle. The solution to this problem is a process called *riddling*, which involves turning the bottle upside down and gently shaking it to get the yeast to collect near the cap. This is followed by a process called *disgorging (dégorgement)* in which the bottle is opened, the yeast extracted, and the bottle resealed as quickly as possible.

Figure 6-1: Riddling racks

The traditional method of riddling, developed in Champagne in the nineteenth century, uses an A-frame rack with holes known as a *pupitre*. Every day for several weeks (or months), the bottles are shaken momentarily, partially rotated, and angled ever more vertically, causing the sediment to move down the side of the bottle and into the neck.

These days, given the amount of wine involved, this traditional practice is mostly done only for show. Instead, the task is often completed by mechanized gyropalettes, which hold 500 bottles per crate and perform the same task in less than one week, compared to two to three months by hand.

When all of the lees are gathered in the necks of the bottles, the bottles may be allowed to rest in an upside-down vertical position—known in French as *sur pointe*—for some time prior to disgorging. When the winemaker determines that the bottles are ready for disgorging, the end of the bottle is typically dipped into an icy brine solution cold enough to freeze the sediment into a slushy "plug." When the bottle is turned upright and opened, the internal pressure shoots the icy plug out of the bottle, leaving nothing but clear sparkling wine behind.

Dosage

Because a small amount of volume is lost during disgorging, the bottle is topped up to the correct level by adding a small wine addition known as the dosage or *liqueur d'expédition*. This step also creates an opportunity for altering the dry wine's style by adding sweetness. This is accomplished by adding some sugar to the dosage, which is often made using the same or a similar cuvée.

Because of the high acidity of the base wine, which is amplified in the mouth by the bubbles, it is standard practice to add at least a little sugar to the wine for balance. With a sugar addition that is barely, if at all, perceptible, the wine style is designated "brut." This is the most common style of Champagne and similar sparkling wines. The next most popular style is called "extra dry," which is a bit of a misnomer since the wine has noticeable sweetness. There are other styles, both sweeter and drier than these, as detailed in table 6-2.

Bottle Aging

After the bottles are topped up with the dosage, they are sealed with a specially manufactured large cork that is able to maintain a seal despite the 6 atmospheres of pressure pushing against it. The cork is super-compressed before insertion. The top part of this cork, extending out of the neck of the bottle, returns to its full width, giving it a mushroom shape when removed. For safety, the cork is held in place with a *muselet* (wire cage). Next, the bottles are generally cellared for at least a few months to give the dosage time to thoroughly integrate with the wine, after which time the wine can be released.

TANK METHOD

Another method of sparkling wine production goes by several names: *tank method*, *Charmat*, *cuve close* (closed tank), and *bulk method*. In Italy, the term *Martinotti method* is often used. This process has a somewhat undeserved bad reputation as a shortcut that is a mere shadow of the traditional method, stemming from the fact that many inexpensive commercial products do use this technique to save time and money. However, numerous quality sparkling wines are made this way as well. Some consider this method the best choice for the production of sparkling wines made using aromatic grape varieties such as Muscat and Riesling, as the yeast aromas characteristic of the traditional method would be distracting and incongruent with these grapes. The tank process yields a wine that emphasizes youthful, floral, and primary fruit aromas. As a bonus, production costs are less than those for bottle fermentations.

In the basic tank method, such as that used in the production of most of Italy's Prosecco and the majority of German Sekt, the second alcoholic fermentation takes place in a pressurized tank rather than in a bottle. The concept is the same as that of the traditional method, but it is performed on a larger scale:

1. Batches of grapes are fermented normally into dry, still base wines, which are then blended as desired into a cuvée.
2. Yeast and sugar are added to the tank of blended base wine.
3. The mixture ferments under pressure, keeping the carbon dioxide dissolved in the liquid.
4. If the intention is to replicate the Champagne style, the wine can be left on the lees for an extended time. However, since the ratio of surface area to wine is reduced, the autolytic character will not be as evident. For aromatic sparkling wines, lees contact is avoided since the emphasis is on fruit character rather than autolytic character.

Table 6–2: Sweetness Levels of Sparkling Wines

SWEETNESS LEVELS OF SPARKLING WINES			
Category/Label Term	Sweetness	Sugar Quantity (g/L)	Percent (%) Sugar
Brut nature, sans dosage, pas dosé, dosage zero, brut sauvage	No sugar added	Less than 3	<0.3
Extra brut	Very dry	Less than 6	<0.6
Brut	Dry	Less than 12	<1.2
Extra dry, extra sec	Off-dry	12–17	1.2–1.7
Sec	Slightly sweet	17–32	1.7–3.2
Demi-sec	Sweet	32–50	3.2–5.0
Doux	Very sweet	More than 50	>5.0

In Champagne, the various categories of sweetness are regulated based on the sugar concentration in the finished wine, which is measured in grams per liter (g/L). These same terms are often used in other countries, but they do not necessarily have legal definitions, or else the regulations may differ, so the actual level of sweetness may vary slightly.

As noted, the most troublesome part of the traditional method for sparkling wine is the removal of the yeast sediment from each individual bottle. The tank method bypasses this stage entirely by keeping the wine in the tank throughout the production process. The sparkling wine is racked to a different tank through a filter to remove the sediment, and the dosage is added to the entire batch all at once. Once bottled, the wine may be bottle aged for a few weeks or months, or it may be considered ready for immediate release.

TRANSFER METHOD

The transfer method is a hybrid procedure that begins like the traditional method and then transitions to the tank method. After following the traditional method through the second fermentation and lees aging, all of the bottles are emptied into a pressurized tank. The wine is then filtered and the dosage is added to the tank. This eliminates the need for riddling and for the individual disgorging and dosage processes. After the bottles are cleaned, the wine can be put back into them for corking and sale.

The transfer method is advantageous in that it saves considerable time and effort by performing three important steps of the process in one pass rather than thousands of times in a row. All else being equal, these wines may achieve similar quality to those produced by the traditional method. However, if economy is the driving motive, the wine is rarely allowed to rest on the lees very long, so the usual flavor characteristics are less prominent. There is also a possibility that the filtration could remove some of the flavor components along with the sediment.

It should be noted that this is essentially the method used in Champagne and elsewhere for very small or very large format bottles that are difficult to work with using the traditional method. While the majority of Champagne's production takes place in standard 750 ml bottles, the wine is also sold in many other sizes of bottles. For piccolos (quarter bottles) and bottles larger than three liters, it is impractical to do the individual riddling, disgorging, and dosage required by the traditional method in each bottle, so something similar to the transfer method is used instead. After the second fermentation, lees aging, and riddling phases, some 750 ml bottles are disgorged and the wine is transferred into tanks, where the dosage is added before filling the differently-sized bottles with wine.

In the United States, sparkling wine made by the transfer method can usually be recognized by the phrase "Fermented in the Bottle" or "Bottle Fermented" on the label. This implies that the wine has not been fermented in that particular bottle.

PARTIAL FERMENTATION METHOD

The partial fermentation method is used for certain low-alcohol, sweet sparkling wines such as Italy's Moscato d'Asti; as such, it is sometimes referred to as the *Asti method*. Rather than conducting a full fermentation of the base wine followed by a later second fermentation, this method involves a single, incomplete fermentation. In many cases, the initial carbon dioxide produced via fermentation is allowed to escape, after which the tank is sealed and pressurized. When the desired levels of alcohol and carbon dioxide pressure are reached, the wine is chilled to the point that fermentation is halted; later, the wine is sterile-filtered and bottled.

The partial fermentation method results in a low-pressure (around 2.5 atm), low-alcohol wine (often containing just 5% to 6% abv). Such wines typically contain significant residual sugar and—with little to no autolytic character—the fruity, often floral scents inherent in the grapes are retained as primary aroma and flavor components. Due to the low pressure, wine produced using this method may be bottled with a standard cork.

Table 6–3: Traditional Champagne Bottle Sizes

TRADITIONAL CHAMPAGNE BOTTLE SIZES		
Size	Equivalent	Volume
Piccolo/split	¼ bottle	187.5 milliliters
Half, or demi-bouteille	½ bottle	375 milliliters
Standard	1 bottle	750 milliliters
Magnum	2 bottles	1.5 liters
Jeroboam	4 bottles	3 liters
Rehoboam*	6 bottles	4.5 liters
Methuselah	8 bottles	6 liters
Salmanazar	12 bottles	9 liters
Balthazar	16 bottles	12 liters
Nebuchadnezzar	20 bottles	15 liters

*Discontinued as an official bottle size in 1989

ANCESTRAL METHOD

The ancestral method, a procedure that predates the traditional method, is still used in a few places for the production of sparkling wine. The best-known example is Limoux Méthode Ancestrale produced in France's Languedoc region. The ancestral method calls for bottling an incompletely fermented and therefore sweet base wine. After the bottle is sealed, the fermentation will continue inside the bottle until the pressure reaches 1–3 atm and 6% to 7% residual sugar remains. In homage to historical practice, the bottle may not be reopened for disgorging, and a small amount of sediment may remain therein. This unique method, also known as the *méthode rurale*, is also used to produce Bugey Cerdon AOC and Gaillac Mousseux Méthode Gaillaçoise AOC.

A variation of the ancestral method, known specifically as the *Méthode Dioise Ancestral*, is used in the production of Clairette de Die Méthode Dioise Ancestral AOC in the Rhône Valley's Pays Diois. During production, the wine is kept chilled to around 50°F (10°C) all throughout the fermentation process, which may last up to six months. This is to mimic the ancient way of fermenting the wines of the region, when they were submerged in the icy waters of the nearby river. For the first few months of fermentation, the wine is kept in bulk tanks. The wine is then bottled and allowed to continue fermenting while still under refrigeration. Fermentation ends while the wine is still slightly sweet, after which the bottles are quickly emptied and the wine is filtered before being rebottled for sale.

Pétillant Naturel: While the term is not officially regulated nor legally defined, sparkling wine produced using the ancestral method (or something similar to it) may be described as *Pétillant Naturel* (a French term that roughly translates as "naturally sparkling"), or *Pét-Nat*. Wine produced in the Pét-Nat style is often lightly sparkling and somewhat rustic. In addition, such wines may be bottled unfiltered, lending a slightly cloudy appearance due to the presence of lees.

CARBONATION

The least expensive method of making a sparkling wine is to inject carbon dioxide directly into a still wine, which is very much like the process for making a carbonated soft drink. Because the carbon dioxide gas is not naturally created molecule-by-molecule through fermentation, it does not integrate as well with the wine. This results in larger, shorter-lived bubbles in the finished product. This method is used only for wines in the lowest price category.

FORTIFIED WINE PRODUCTION

LEARNING OBJECTIVES

After studying this chapter, the candidate should be able to:

- Recall the historical purpose for fortifying wines.
- Discuss how the fortified winemaking process differs from standard table wine production.
- Recognize the differences in the production methods of sweet fortified wines and dry fortified wines.
- Identify the grape varieties commonly used in fortified wines.
- Describe how the solera system works.

Centuries ago, it was discovered that adding brandy to wine helped protect it from spoilage. In fact, it was discovered that wines "fortified" with brandy or other spirits not only lasted longer than unfortified wines but also often evolved in style and improved in quality at the same time. Fortification became standard practice for wines that needed to travel long distances, such as across the oceans to colonial outposts, as well as for wines that could not be kept chilled in a wine cellar. Fortified wines such as Sherry, Port, and Madeira captured a major segment of the world wine trade and were among the most celebrated wines from the sixteenth to the twentieth century.

Although it took a while for scientists to figure out the processes involved, fortification helped preserve wines because it raised the alcohol level of the wine to a point at which spoilage agents, including yeast and bacteria, could not survive. This allowed fortified wines to last much longer than unfortified wines either in the bottle or the barrel, as well as after the container had been opened.

The market for fortified wines declined toward the end of the twentieth century because of changes in consumer tastes away from high levels of alcohol and toward drier wines. While fortified wines no longer command the market share they once did, they are still an important category, and their unique winemaking procedures merit closer examination by wine professionals.

Fortified wines are made in most wine-producing countries. The basic winemaking process is the same as that of unfortified wines, with the added step of fortification. The differences among the numerous fortified wines come from the following:

- The grape varieties used
- The timing of fortification
- The aging regimen applied after fortification

These differences can be considerable.

Quality fortified wines are made in small batches, using traditional procedures that developed over centuries of practice. These wines use specific traditional grape varieties, may be sweet or dry, and often have elaborate procedures for aging in barrels or bottles for extended periods. Port, Sherry, and Madeira are considered the classics, but similar styles of wine are produced in many areas throughout Europe and beyond.

Fortified wines are usually divided into two types, defined by *when* the fortification takes place, which may be either *before* or *after* the wine has finished fermenting on its own. Those that are fortified while fermentation is still going on, such as Port, are sweet. Port, Sherry, and Madeira are considered the classics, but similar styles of wine are produced in many areas throughout Europe and beyond.

This chapter provides a description of the general winemaking procedures for the two basic types of fortified wine. These procedures are replicated by or serve as inspiration to winemakers in many countries. Additional country-specific details about particular fortified wines may be found in the chapters that follow.

Table 7–1: Fortification Sequence and Wine Styles

FORTIFICATION SEQUENCE AND WINE STYLES		
Wine Style	Sweet	Dry
Fortification Sequence	Fortified *during* fermentation	Fortified *after* fermentation
Key Example	Port	Fino Sherry

FORTIFICATION DURING FERMENTATION: THE SWEET STYLE

As described in the section on sweet wine production in chapter 5, one of the primary ways to make a sweet wine is to add alcohol to the wine before or while it is still fermenting and still has a significant amount of sugar in it. This practice is known as *mutage*. If the alcohol level is raised above the point where the yeast can survive, this not only stops the fermentation of the remaining sugar but also ensures that the fermentation will not be able to restart at a later time.

The majority of fortified wines are produced in this manner, as this was found to be an ideal method of making a stable sweet wine. The most renowned of these is Port, made in the Douro Valley of Portugal. This method of fortified wine production is practiced in many parts of the world, resulting in a wide range of products.

Table 7–2: Sweet-Style Fortified Wines

SWEET-STYLE FORTIFIED WINES		
Wine	Country of Production	Grape Varieties
Banyuls	France	Grenache
Commandaria	Cyprus	Xynisteri, Mavro
Madeira (sweeter styles)	Portugal	Malvasia, Boal, Tinta Negra
Madeira (drier styles)	Portugal	Sercial, Verdelho, Tinta Negra
Málaga	Spain	Pedro Ximénez, Muscat
Marsala	Italy	Grillo, Catarratto, Inzolia, and others
Maury	France	Grenache
Mavrodaphne of Patras	Greece	Mavrodaphne
Moscatel de Setúbal	Portugal	Moscatel/Muscat
Muscat de Beaumes-de-Venise	France	Muscat
Muscat de Rivesaltes	France	Muscat
Port	Portugal	Primarily Touriga Nacional, Touriga Franca, Tinta Roriz, Tinta Barroca, and Tinto Cão; however, several other grapes may also be used
Rasteau	France	Grenache
Rutherglen	Australia	Muscat, Topaque (Muscadelle)

BASE WINE PRODUCTION

Many different grape varieties, both red and white, are used for sweet fortified wines. Usually, high sugar levels are desired to make sure the final product is sufficiently sweet. This is not normally a problem in the hot climates where most of these wines are made. Nevertheless, some grapes are late harvested, and others are allowed to dry for a time after picking, before fermentation begins.

The winemaking procedures for the base wines are essentially no different from those for table wines, although some regions follow long-established idiosyncratic practices for the sake of tradition. However, since fermentation is only allowed to proceed for a short period of time, there is less time to extract color and other phenolics from the grape skins; therefore, special methods may be used to extract these components as quickly as possible.

FORTIFICATION

To keep the wine sweet, the base wine's fermentation is stopped by fortification midway through the process. The exact timing of the alcohol addition depends on the regional style and the producer's goals, but it is usually driven by the falling sugar level. The fortification will typically take place when the remaining sugar level reaches the 8%-12% range.

The fermentation is halted through the addition of a high-alcohol spirit. The alcoholic strength and composition of this spirit varies from region to region. It can be nearly pure alcohol or a more dilute mixture, but nearly all jurisdictions require the use of grape-based spirits (brandy). Enough brandy must be added to raise the alcohol level of the entire barrel or tank of wine high enough to quickly kill all the yeast and stop the fermentation, which is normally 18%-20% for these types of fortified wines. The spirit additive may be completely neutral or may introduce its own aromas and flavors; it may also be sweet itself, raising the overall sugar level.

Figure 7-1: Tawny Port aging in a wine cellar

AGING

Aging regimens vary by region and by style of wine. Most newly fortified wines are left in barrels, large wooden vats, or tanks for some time to allow the components to become thoroughly integrated. If wooden vessels are used, slow oxygen seepage through the wood permits a degree of oxidation that helps further stabilize the wines. Some styles, such as tawny Port, may spend years aging in wood.

Unlike unfortified wines, the wine is not necessarily coddled in a cool cellar during this period but is sometimes intentionally left to bake in a hot aboveground warehouse. Madeira and Rutherglen Muscat in particular are given this treatment, which removes any heat-unstable compounds from the wine and makes it nearly indestructible.

BLENDING AND BOTTLING

After a few months to several years of aging in large containers, the wines are blended for style and then bottled. The blends may be formulated in order to re-create a specific, consistent flavor profile for a branded wine, or they may incorporate older vintages for wines that are sold based on average age. They may continue to age in the bottle for several more years before release and, in many cases, may last for several more decades if unopened.

FORTIFICATION AFTER FERMENTATION: THE DRY STYLE

The most well-known fortified wine made in the dry style is Sherry (although not all Sherries are dry). True Sherry is made in the area surrounding the city of Jerez in far southwestern Spain. A similar style of wine is produced in the Montilla-Moriles DO, also in southern Spain. The drier forms of Madeira and Marsala are closer in style to post-fermentation fortified wines than to sweet-style fortified wines in terms of process, although they may be subsequently sweetened.

BASE WINE PRODUCTION

Because the dominant aroma and flavor characteristics of these wines come from the production process rather than the grape varieties themselves, relatively neutral white grapes are most appropriate. For Sherry, this means primarily Palomino and, secondarily, Pedro Ximénez. Madeira's dry fermented wines are made from Sercial or Verdelho. In other regions, any available grapes may be used, but those serious about making a wine in the Sherry style most often use Palomino.

To avoid extracting more phenolics than necessary, the grapes are handled delicately, not unlike those destined for sparkling wines. After careful pressing, the must is fermented at a warm temperature, high enough to evaporate most of the floral and fruit aromas but not so high as to introduce any "cooked" aromas. To keep the wine neutral in flavor, stainless steel tanks are the typical fermentation vessels used.

FORTIFICATION

The dry-style wines go through a complete fermentation to dryness (or nearly so) before being fortified. For the production of Sherry, there are two basic types of wine, *fino* and *oloroso*, with many variations within these two main styles. The degree of fortification depends on the style of wine to be made.

Figure 7–2: Flor yeast in a barrel of fino Sherry

Fino Sherries are pale in color and light-bodied, due to a process known as *biological aging*. Biological aging requires the action of a unique organism known as *flor yeast* during the aging process. Flor yeast floats on the surface of the wine in the barrel, and thrives in a wine that has about 15% alcohol. In this environment, the flor multiplies until it becomes a thick, protective blanket on top of the maturing wine, protecting the wine from oxidation and preventing it from darkening in color. To encourage the development of flor, Sherry winemakers select the best-quality batches of pale, clear, fresh wine to which they add grape spirits mixed with an equal amount of older Sherry in order to bring the overall alcohol level up to 15% to 15.5%, but no higher.

Once fortification has taken place, the flor survives in the presence of oxygen by consuming any remaining sugars and glycerol in the wine, as well as a small amount of alcohol. As a result, these are lighter-bodied wines than those that have not been aged in the presence of flor. The flor also feeds on acetic acid, thereby lowering acid levels in the wine. When all of the sugar is consumed, flor yeast switch to another metabolic phase in which they use oxygen from the atmosphere. In the process, the flor produces chemicals such as acetaldehyde that create a characteristic "flor aroma" often described as "nutty" or "bruised apple."

Under these conditions, the acetaldehyde that is created is not converted to acetic acid, and the protective coating of the flor prohibits direct contact with the air so that no browning occurs. Biological aging, so named because the changes in the wine are largely due to the action of a living organism, results in lower alcohol and acid levels and much higher amounts of acetaldehyde.

Oloroso Sherries are generally produced from base wines that are not considered to have the quality or delicacy to be made into fino. These wines are fortified to 17% to 18% alcohol, which is too high for the development of flor. Without flor, these wines do not build up the high levels of acetaldehyde that characterize finos.

Oloroso Sherries are allowed direct exposure to air in the partially filled barrels of the solera, where they experience *oxidative aging*. During oxidative aging, alcohol and acid levels increase, and the color of the wine deepens. The result is a fuller-bodied, darkened, flavorful wine dominated by oxidative and caramelized aromas. Because water evaporates during oxidative aging, an old oloroso can rise in alcoholic strength to as high as 24%.

MATURATION

Sherry matures in a complex network of barrels known as a *solera system*. While in the solera, young wine is progressively blended together with a series of older, more complex wines. For fino Sherries, new wine is periodically necessary in order to maintain the level of nutrients needed by the flor yeast. The longest that flor may be maintained is six to seven years, although most commercial finos are only aged for two years, the minimum amount of time required by law.

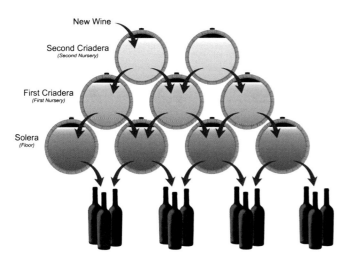

Figure 7–3: Diagram of a solera system

A solera consists of several groups of butts: large (600 L) American oak barrels. One of the groups, containing the oldest wine, is somewhat confusingly also called the solera. The other groups of butts are called *criaderas* (nurseries). The first criadera holds the next-oldest wine, the second criadera holds the next-oldest wine, and so on. There may be a dozen or more "layers," or criaderas, in a large solera system. The final criadera contains the youngest wine.

The criaderas are usually depicted as multiple rows of barrels with the solera (row) on the bottom and the progressively younger criaderas in the upper rows, but the actual positioning varies by *bodega* (winery). A complete solera system may contain hundreds or thousands of butts, and a large facility may have several soleras in operation simultaneously.

At least once a year after each vintage, wine is bottled from the solera row or one of the criaderas, with no more than 40% of the volume removed each year. This is followed by an intricate process known as *running the scales*. Wine from the first criadera (in theory, an equal amount from each butt within the criadera) is used to top up the barrels of the solera row, wine from the second criadera tops up the first criadera, and so on. Finally, the new wine of the vintage goes into the last (youngest) criadera.

This is known as a *fractional blending* system, and, because no barrel is ever completely emptied, it ensures that the average age of the solera continues to grow. Even for the oldest Sherry soleras—many are over one hundred years old—a tiny proportion of the wine from the year the solera was established remains in the mix today.

Soleras are not unique to Sherry or even to Sherry-style wines. Wines from other parts of the world—including Montilla-Moriles (Spain), Madeira (Portugal), Mavrodaphne of Patras (Greece), and Rutherglen (Australia)—may use a form of solera aging.

Figure 7–4: A solera in use

BLENDING, ADJUSTMENTS, AND BOTTLING

Prior to bottling, Sherry-style wines can be sweetened, colored, or both to produce a wide range of different styles. For wines coming out of a solera, blending is not necessary because they have already been well blended from running the scales many times; nevertheless, some bodegas may blend wines from two or more soleras together, or several wines of different styles together into a single wine.

VIN DOUX NATUREL

Vins doux naturels are lightly fortified sweet wines produced throughout the South of France. Vins doux naturels, depending on local regulations, may be made from either white or red grapes and in many styles, including white, red, and rosé. Aged versions known by terms such as *tawny* and *amber* are also produced in certain regions. Specific examples include Muscat de Beaumes-de-Venise (from the Rhône Valley), as well as Muscat de Rivesaltes, Banyuls, and Maury (all from Roussillon).

MISTELLE

Taking the method to the extreme, it is possible to fortify grape must before—or just slightly after—it begins to ferment. A wine made in this style is known in France as a *mistelle*. In Spain, this type of fortified wine goes by the name *mistela* (when the must is unfermented) or *vino licor* (when a small amount of fermentation is allowed). The term *sifone* is used in Italy, where a version is used to sweeten some styles of Marsala.

France produces several well-known examples of mistelle, including Pineau de Charentes AOC and Floc de Gascogne AOC. Pineau de Charentes, produced in the Cognac region, is usually produced from Ugni Blanc, Folle Blanche, and Colombard, and is fortified with Cognac. Other grapes are permitted, including some red varieties used for red and rosé versions. Floc de Gascogne, produced in the Armagnac region, is most often produced in a white version (using mainly the Colombard, Gros Manseng, and Ugni Blanc varieties); a small amount of rosé is produced as well.

Wines such as these may be, and often are, referred to as *vins de liqueurs*. However, the European Union recently changed the definition of "vin de liqueur" to include all fortified wines, so the more specific terms—as discussed above—are considered to be more accurate.

WINE LABELS, LAWS, AND REGIONS

UNIT THREE

INTRODUCTION TO THE WORLD WINE INDUSTRY

CHAPTER EIGHT

79

CHAPTER EIGHT INTRODUCTION TO THE WORLD WINE INDUSTRY

LEARNING OBJECTIVES

After studying this chapter, the candidate should be able to:
- Understand how the history of wine relates to the current state of the wine industry.
- Recognize how geography and climate affect wine production in the various countries of Europe.
- Discuss the European Union system for designating wine quality and the EU labeling laws.

The wine industry is a major segment of world agricultural trade, accounting globally for more than a hundred billion dollars in sales and millions of jobs. The bulk of the wine industry, and approximately 56% of the global vineyard, is located in Europe. However, growth, in terms of both production and consumption, is occurring both inside and outside of Europe.

The industry consists of *producers* (grape growers, winemakers); *distributors* (distributors, brokers, exporters, importers); *retailers* (shop owners, sommeliers, buyers, sales staff, restaurateurs, supermarkets, online retailers); *allied businesses and individuals* (equipment manufacturers, lab technicians, wine writers, auction houses, plant nurseries, advertising agencies, event planners, trade organizations, wine educators); and, of course, *consumers*. While some of these entities are more central to the industry than others, the wine trade would be weakened by the absence of any of these roles.

This chapter provides a broad overview of the world wine community and a more detailed look at the European Union as a multinational confederation. It begins with a very brief synopsis of the history of wine. This is followed by a discussion of where the wine trade is concentrated, both in global terms and with regard to specific wine regions within countries. The chapter concludes with an examination of the wine laws that shape the wine industries of the European Union member countries. The US wine industry is covered separately in chapter 16.

THE GLOBAL WINE INDUSTRY

HISTORICAL DEVELOPMENT

According to Dr. Patrick McGovern, scientific director of the Biomolecular Archaeology Laboratory for Cuisine, Fermented Beverages, and Health at the University of Pennsylvania Museum, evidence uncovered in Jiahu, China indicates that the first alcoholic beverage to incorporate fermented grapes dates to about 7000 BCE. Wine produced from vinifera varieties is believed to have made its first appearance in the Caucasus Mountains in western Asia, spreading from there into eastern Europe and the Middle East.

SOCIETY OF WINE EDUCATORS • CERTIFIED SPECIALIST OF WINE

Figure 8-1: Ancient amphorae found on the island of Delos, Greece

Greece became an early stronghold of wine production, spreading viticulture around the Mediterranean coast and passing the torch on to the ancient Romans once the Roman Empire rose to dominate the Western world. By that time, two millennia ago, grape growing and winemaking were well established around the shores of the Mediterranean Sea. As their empire spread, the Romans carried viticulture throughout their conquered lands, planting the first vineyards in inland areas of Spain, France, Germany, and the Balkans.

When the Roman Empire fell into disarray, much knowledge and many technologies were lost, but winegrowing continued due to the role of the Catholic Church. Needing wine to consecrate the religious ceremony of the Mass, monks and clergymen maintained vineyards and made wine continuously over the centuries, slowly locating prime growing areas, selecting top-performing vines for further propagation, and refining winemaking techniques.

Once science and industry returned to Europe during and after the Renaissance, winemaking grew in importance and expanded well beyond the cloisters and monastery lands to become a major agricultural activity. In the swelling urban areas, where poor sanitation led to problems of insufficient fresh water and widespread disease, wine, free of germs due to its alcohol content, grew increasingly in demand as an everyday beverage. Wine could be transported only relatively short distances across land, both because of its weight and its tendency to spoil if exposed to the elements, so vineyards and wineries were established far and wide to serve the local populations.

When Europeans began exploring the lands across the Atlantic Ocean and established trading colonies and settlements in Africa, Asia, and Oceania, wine traveled with them. It was still one of the most healthful beverages available, as well as a mark of civilized life. Sailors found that fortified wines survived the voyages in much better shape than unfortified wines, leading to a centuries-long love affair with Port, Sherry, Madeira, and similar wines.

Apart from North America, wine grapes did not exist in any of the new colonies, so colonists brought European vines with them to their new homes. Some of the earliest of these new vineyards were in Latin America, where Spanish Catholic missionaries planted grapes to produce wine for religious use. The greatest degree of success was initially achieved in the British and Dutch outposts in South Africa, Australia, and New Zealand.

During the mid-nineteenth century, vinifera grapevines were planted in the Americas by immigrants arriving from Europe, especially Italians, Germans, and eastern Europeans. Commercial wineries started to appear in Argentina, Chile, and California.

A crisis developed in the 1860s when the root louse phylloxera, which is native to the eastern United States, was inadvertently brought to Europe and began killing grapevines—first in France and eventually throughout Europe and much of the rest of the world. For a while, it looked like phylloxera might wipe out the entire global wine industry, but, before that happened, it was discovered that European vines could be grafted onto the rootstock of indigenous North American grapevines, which had a natural resistance to phylloxera. This allowed the wine industry to return more or less to normal after a few decades of disruption. One of the legacies of this crisis was that French and other European winemakers traveled to other parts of the world after their own vineyards were lost, dispersing winemaking expertise and raising the quality of wine the world over.

Figure 8-2: Prohibition in the United States

A second calamity occurred in 1920 when the United States enacted Prohibition, basically outlawing wine production. Several other countries adopted similar legislation, and the (legal) wine trade suffered as demand for wine plummeted in some parts of the world. By 1933, the experiment with Prohibition was over, leaving little lasting damage anywhere except the United States, where the wine industry took decades to recover. The symbolic turning point came in 1976, when California wines were awarded first place over top French wines in a major head-to-head competition now known as the *Judgment of Paris*. This announced to the world that the wines of California—and by extension the wines of the world beyond Europe—had come of age.

Some of the headlines from the past few decades include the following:

- The growth of export-driven wine industries in the Southern Hemisphere
- An increase in wine consumption in the United States, to the point that the United States is now the world's largest wine market, although per-capita consumption remains small
- A revival of the historic wine-producing regions of central and eastern Europe
- An ongoing debate about what defines a "natural" wine

- The rise of Asia as a powerhouse new wine market and potential new producer
- In many parts of the world, an emphasis on environmental stewardship and sustainability
- The ongoing discussion on climate change and its possible impact on viticulture and wine
- The growth of wine tourism—which brings certain advantages as well as potential disruption to specific locations
- The disruption in the industry resulting from the worldwide pandemic of 2020–2021

WORLD WINE PRODUCTION AND TRADE

The global volume of wine produced in 2020 is estimated at 260 million hectoliters (mhl), the equivalent of nearly 2.9 billion cases of wine.

According to the International Organization of Vine and Wine (OIV), 2020 represents just a small (1%) increase in wine production over 2019. These two years combined represent something of a return to typical levels of worldwide wine production after the record high of 2018 (292 mhl) and the record low of 2017 (250 mhl). Aside from these exceptions, the annual global production of wine has remained somewhat stable since 2004, typically amounting to between 260 and 270 million hectoliters per year.

Of the total volume of wine produced throughout the world in 2020, it is approximated that 65% was produced in Europe, 10% in South America, 10% in North America, 6% in Asia, 5% in Oceania, and 4% in Africa.

COMPARISON OF TOP TEN COUNTRIES BY LEADING INDUSTRY INDICES (2020)				
Vineyard Acreage	Wine Production	Wine Consumption	Wine Exports (by volume)	Wine Imports (by volume)
Spain	Italy	United States	Italy	United Kingdom
France	France	France	Spain	Germany
China	Spain	Italy	France	United States
Italy	United States	Germany	Chile	France
Turkey	Argentina	United Kingdom	Australia	The Netherlands
United States	Australia	China	Argentina	Canada
Argentina	South Africa	Russia	United States	China
Chile	Chile	Spain	South Africa	Russia
Portugal	Germany	Argentina	Germany	Belgium
Romania	China	Australia	Portugal	Portugal

Sources: International Organization of Vine and Wine (OIV), Statistical Report on World Vitiviniculture, 2021

The global heavyweights of the wine community have traditionally been Italy, France, and Spain, which, in various orders, are consistently among the world leaders in vineyard acreage, wine production, and wine exports. China has recently joined this rank of world leaders in terms of vineyard acreage; recent statistics show that China is currently in the global top three in terms of total vineyard acreage, following Spain and France.

France and Italy have traditionally led the world in wine consumption, but their per-capita consumption has declined slightly in recent years, and the United States is now the world's largest overall consumer of wine (although per-capita consumption remains low). Another significant aspect of the global wine market is that several large wine-producing countries—including Australia and Chile—produce much more wine than they consume and are therefore net exporters of wine, needing to find markets in other countries.

WINE REGIONS

Wine regions are generally delineated on either political or viticultural foundations. Political regions are administrative districts of various sizes, such as nations, states, provinces, counties, towns, and communes, which are defined for government purposes. These are useful for some purposes, but their boundaries may be relatively weak predictors of wine style. For this reason, the wine community recognizes a parallel system of viticultural regions. In theory, this system is based on the environmental features that define an area (terroir) or—occasionally—on traditional winemaking practices.

Historically, the fame of top wine regions spread by word of mouth, and the names of certain areas such as Champagne, Chianti, and Tokaj became well-known among wine lovers. Soon, it became necessary to issue official decrees defining the boundaries of these places in order to protect their reputation from misuse by impostors. In modern times, almost every country with a significant wine-producing sector has written laws to safeguard its own wine regions and, by reciprocal agreement, the regions of other nations. Officially sanctioned wine regions are known generically in English as *appellations* or *geographic indications* (GIs).

Generally, the more specific an appellation is, the more accurate it will be as a predictor of a wine's characteristics. A small appellation based on terroir should have a relatively uniform climate, topography, and soil structure; as such, its wines should conform to a certain standard. Larger appellations have much more variability in their physical conditions and are therefore less predictive of the character of their wines.

In many cases, wine regions are nested one within another, sometimes several layers deep. For example, in Bordeaux, certain vineyards are located within multiple appellations of varied dimensions. In such cases, the level of specificity can be chosen to suit the situation. This gives winemakers a number of options for sourcing their grapes; for instance, staying local to qualify for a highly regarded small appellation, or combining fruit from several areas and accepting a less prestigious, larger appellation.

The protections of an official appellation run both ways. On the one hand, they restrict the use of a place-name to the actual site, preventing anyone else *in another location* from profiting from or damaging the reputation of the appellation's wines.

For example, no one outside the Rioja region of Spain can legally sell their wine as "Rioja." On the other hand, the laws put certain limitations on what producers *within the designated region* can do, also with the intent of protecting the reputation of the appellation. Thus, the wineries in Rioja must meet a list of requirements, such as yield per acre, alcohol level, and grape varieties used, if they want to use the Rioja name. Outside of Europe, appellations are typically less restrictive and define the boundaries of a geographical place-of-origin with no restrictions on grape varieties or wine style.

Legally defined wine regions have a variety of names in different countries. A few examples include the following:

- *Australia:* Geographical Indication
- *France:* Appellation d'Origine Contrôlée
- *Germany:* Qualitätswein, Prädikatswein
- *Greece:* Onomasía Proeléfseos Anotéras Poiótitos, Topikos Oínos
- *Italy:* Denominazione di Origine Controllata e Garantita, Indicazione Geografica Tipica
- *Portugal:* Denominação de Origem Controlada
- *South Africa:* Wine of Origin
- *Spain:* Denominación de Origen, Vino de Pago
- *United States:* American Viticultural Area

These and other types of wine regions will be described in the respective chapters on particular countries.

THE EUROPEAN UNION

The global wine industry is regulated primarily at the national level. There are no global wine laws, only reciprocal agreements among countries that govern how one nation will treat the wines of the other. However, given its dominant share of the wine industry, the European Union currently represents the closest thing there is to multinational control over the wine trade.

The European Union was created in 1993 out of an earlier, smaller, looser confederation of European countries and has expanded in several stages to its present size. Its goal is to coordinate activities among all of its member states so that Europe can act as a single body with the rest of the world to reduce wasteful and counterproductive duplication of efforts internally.

Producing nearly 60% of the world's wine, the EU is obviously a powerful force in the international wine industry. The EU's rulings have a major effect not only on its own member states but also on producers in other countries who want to sell wine in the EU market. (Note: An agreement between the EU and the United States allows US wines some leeway not granted to most other countries' wine products.)

Figure 8-3: EU flags in front of the Berlaymont building in Brussels, Belgium

Wine Laws

As noted, the European Union was founded as an economic initiative among relatively small nations to help them compete with larger economies in the global marketplace. Its primary goals still include eliminating trade barriers and protectionism within the EU while creating a more unified front for dealing with the rest of the world.

As the EU integrated the economies of its member states, it had to develop trade legislation that would apply equally to products in all countries so that consumers would be able to rely on their quality, safety, and value regardless of their country of origin within the European Union. The EU has brought all member countries' food products, which include wine, in line with its three-tiered structure of quality.

In the case of wine, the EU was faced with a group of traditional wine producing countries—most of which used vastly different systems to classify, protect, and market their wines. In many cases, elements of these systems date back centuries and represent a significant part of the region's heritage, culture, and economy. Accordingly, attempting to replace them would quite possibly have created chaos.

Instead, the EU designed an umbrella framework that defines various terms and sets a general set of standards while allowing each country to retain much of its traditional terminology (and the concepts so represented). The new regulations and their resultant changes took effect beginning on August 1, 2009.

This new EU framework underlies all national systems but is largely transparent. Within the structure, three levels of wines made within the Union are defined, as follows:

- The highest-quality tier of wines is Protected Designation of Origin (PDO). Prior to 2009, these wines were known as Quality Wine Produced in a Specified Region (QWPSR).
- The second quality tier is Protected Geographical Indication (PGI) wine, which includes all of the wines that were previously table wines with a geographic indication.
- The third quality tier is the category designated simply "Wine." This term is intended to describe table wines that do not carry a geographical indication more specific than a single country.

As a result of these changes, some new category terms have been instituted by the member countries. However, the regulations permit the continuing use of preexisting designations of origin, provided that the EU country registered these designations with the European Council by December 31, 2011. Accordingly, current wine labels are not significantly different from those used prior to the implementation of the new system, although there does appear to be broader adoption of the newer terms at the lower levels.

Protected Designation of Origin

Wines that fall into the PDO category must be made entirely from grapes grown in the clearly defined region after which they are named, and must be produced within a given area. The individual countries register these wines along with parameters concerning delimited boundaries of the region, maximum yields, permitted grape varieties, defined viticultural practices, allowed enological practices, and predominant analytical and organoleptic characteristics of the wine.

Protected Geographical Indication

PGI wines are those whose qualities can be attributed to being produced from a registered geographical region or specific place. Compared to a PDO region, a PGI region is typically larger and more heterogeneous. To qualify as a PGI wine, at least 85% of the grapes must come from the defined geographical area after which it is named, and the wine must be produced in this geographical area.

Similarly to PDO wines, these wines must adhere to rules and regulations governing viticultural and enological practices. However, these rules and regulations are generally less restrictive than those for PDO wines and do not necessarily need to be typical of the region (despite the Italian name for this category). For instance, international varieties that are not traditional to the region can often be used.

These wines will carry the PGI designation (or its equivalent in the local language) on their labels unless the producer chooses to use the traditional term, such as *vinho regional* (Portugal) or *indicazione geografica tipica* (Italy).

In addition, these wines may now carry the name of a grape variety and/or a vintage date if the wine is produced from a minimum of 85% of the named variety or vintage. If two or more grape varieties are listed, the wine must be produced entirely from those varieties, shown in descending order of proportions. If 100% of the grapes were harvested exclusively from a named vineyard, it may also be included on the label.

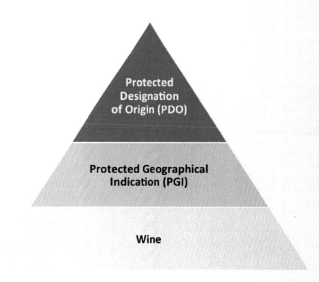

Figure 8-4: EU wine categories

Wine

Products belonging to the EU category "Wine" are table wines without geographical indication more specific than a single country. Grapes for these wines may be sourced from anywhere within a country or the EU. Although these wines previously could not include much information on the label, the new regulations concerning this category permit the grape variety and/or vintage date on their labels as long as they are produced from a minimum of 85% of the named variety or vintage.

European Union Labeling Laws

Within the EU, wine labels are required to state the wine's category and, as permitted, its place of origin. There are a number of other labeling requirements, the most important of which are the following:

- If a protected place-name is stated, the wine must be entirely from that region for PDO wines and at least 85% from that region for PGI wines.
- If a vintage date is stated, at least 85% of the wine must be from that year.
- If a single grape variety is stated, at least 85% of the wine must be from that variety.
- If two or more grape varieties are stated, 100% of the wine must be from those varieties, and they must be listed in descending order of content.

Other labeling changes include a more defined usage of terms for sparkling wines, such as the following:

- Quality Sparkling Wine—for those wines with CO_2 produced wholly by a secondary fermentation in the bottle that are subject to disgorgement, and with a minimum of nine months aging on the lees
- Sparkling Wine—must contain a minimum of 3 atm of pressure, carbon dioxide may come via a first or second fermentation but may not be injected
- Aerated Sparkling Wine—for wines whose "sparkle" is derived from the addition of CO_2

In general, under the new EU regulations, the classic wines of Europe will continue to be produced as they have always been, but in some cases, these changes may affect what is seen on the label.

NON-EU WINES

Wines from outside the EU are legally neither quality nor table wines but are simply "wines," with or without a geographical indication.

FRANCE

LEARNING OBJECTIVES

After studying this chapter, the candidate should be able to:

- Identify the general role and position of France in the global wine industry.
- Recall the geographical location and general climate of France's major wine regions.
- Discuss the hierarchy of wine designations used in France.
- Recall which grape varieties and wine styles are associated with France's important appellations.
- Describe the classification systems of the major wine regions of France.

France almost always leads off any discussion of the world's wines, for several good reasons:

- It has one of the largest national wine industries in the world.
- It has one of the longest histories of exporting fine wine.
- Its wines are emulated the world over and are considered a benchmark for many important grape varieties and styles.
- Its wine laws have been a model for the European Union's and many other nations' wine systems.

This chapter describes France and its wines and, in doing so, establishes a framework for the other countries to come. Like all of the following chapters in this unit of the Study Guide, it begins with a general overview of the country's geography and climate, grape varieties, and wine laws. The discussion then turns to the major French wine regions, all of which are significant on the world stage. The regions covered in detail, starting in Bordeaux and progressing roughly clockwise around the country, are the following:

- Bordeaux
- The Loire Valley
- Champagne
- Alsace
- Burgundy
- Beaujolais
- The Rhône Valley
- Southern France
- Southwest France

FRENCH WINE HISTORY

Wine grapes were probably first brought to France by the Greeks and Romans, who established several colonies along the Mediterranean coast. Later, the Romans spread viticulture farther inland after conquering Gaul and founding cities throughout the area.

Major Wine Regions of France

Figure 9–1: Major Wine Producing Regions of France

A watershed event occurred in the twelfth century when the Bordeaux region came under the English Crown through the marriage of Eleanor of Aquitaine to Henry II. For a variety of reasons, viticulture in the British Isles had declined, so the Bordeaux vineyards were an ideal solution for supplying England with wine, launching what would become the world's most heralded wine region and setting France on the road to leadership in the world wine trade. Warfare in the fourteenth and fifteenth centuries ended English ownership of Aquitaine, but the bond between Britain and Bordeaux wine remained strong.

In the fifth century, when the Roman Empire collapsed and France began to develop as a nation, wine became associated with the Christian monasteries, which produced wine for both sacramental use and profit. Vineyards were often donated to the church by rich patrons seeking divine favor, and monasteries acquired considerable holdings, especially in the Burgundy region (where the Benedictine and Cistercian Orders were based) and in Champagne. Some of the monks took a very scientific approach to their grape growing and winemaking. They experimented with different kinds of grapes and various arrangements in the vineyards, ultimately fine-tuning high-quality vines and matching them to the ideal growing sites. The monks also pioneered many innovations that improved winemaking on a large scale.

Farther north, the Loire Valley was the home of French nobility during the Middle Ages. This concentration of wealth spurred significant wine production in this highly fertile area. Even after the seat of power shifted back to Paris in the fifteenth century, wineries in the Loire Valley continued to prosper.

East of Paris, the Champagne region also had an excellent reputation for wine in the Middle Ages, but it was for still wine, not the well-recognized sparkling wine of today. By the 1600s, the Champagne region was renowned in Paris and London for still Pinot Noir wines. Although the wines of the area would sometimes go through an accidental second fermentation once bottled, producing a bit of "spritz," the deliberate introduction of bubbles to the winemaking process did not commence until the end of the seventeenth century.

The South of France has the country's longest history of viticulture, but for most of the Middle Ages the sunny southern coast produced wine mostly for local consumption or for blending into other regions' wines to give some weight to what otherwise would have been unpleasantly thin wine in most vintages.

The region of Alsace, situated on the border with Germany, has a complicated history of alternating between French and German control and occasional independence. It retains some Germanic traditions, both culturally and in its winemaking, such as an emphasis on Riesling and (to a lesser extent) Gewurztraminer grape varieties, and the use of the tall, thin *Flûte d'Alsace* bottles for many of its wines.

GEOGRAPHY AND CLIMATE

France is shaped more or less like a hexagon. Clockwise from its southwest extremity, the hexagon is formed by the country's Atlantic coastline; the English Channel; low-lying terrain to the north bordering on Belgium and Luxembourg; mountainous terrain on its eastern boundaries with Germany, Switzerland, and Italy; the Mediterranean coast to the south; and the natural boundary with Spain at the Pyrenees. The major topographical features within the country are the Massif Central (the central highlands of the country), a segment of the Alps in the southeast, and several rivers that flow from the mountains to the ocean, especially the Loire, Garonne, Dordogne, and Rhône, plus the Rhine, which forms part of the border with Germany.

The country's climate ranges from sunny Mediterranean to frigid Alpine. The Mediterranean climate, with ample sunshine and little rainfall during the growing season, is found, predictably, along the Mediterranean coast. This is the warmest part of France and is well suited to grape growing. This area, comprising the regions of Roussillon, Languedoc, Rhône, and Provence, plus the island of Corsica, is home to half of all French vineyard land. These areas are largely planted to red grapes and are known for their production of full-flavored, full-bodied red wines as well as a significant amount of rosé.

The western part of France is exposed to the chilly and often stormy Atlantic Ocean and experiences a maritime climate. Compared to the Mediterranean coast, the humidity and rainfall here are higher, there is less sunshine, and summers are cooler. Roughly a third of the vineyard area of France lies in the western maritime-influenced counties, or *départements*. In Bordeaux and surrounding areas in the southwest, temperatures are still high enough to produce full-bodied wines, but with significant acidity. Reds continue to dominate. Farther north, the climate becomes cooler and white grapes preponderate.

The central and northeastern sections of the country have a more continental climate. Because there is little protection from the north, winters are quite cold, and summers are not particularly hot. The northern third of France is, in general, too cold and too wet to grow grapes. South of that, most vineyards are planted in river valleys (in particular those of the Loire, Seine, Saône, and Rhône), which provide some protection from storms and funnel milder weather in from the coasts. White grapes are slightly more prevalent than reds in these cooler regions. The wines here are often highly acidic, light- to medium-bodied, and low in alcohol.

The Alpine climate of the French Alps is far too cold for grapevines, and the higher elevations around the Massif Central are similarly unsuitable. The other topographic feature that has a notable effect on a wine region's climate is the Vosges Mountains, a small north–south range in northeastern France. The Vosges chain provides a barrier to storms coming from the west and shields the vineyards of Alsace, which are therefore warmer and drier than most other vineyards at the same latitude (for example, Champagne and Chablis). As a result, grapes ripen to a much greater degree, and the wines of Alsace can be quite high in alcohol.

Figure 9-2: Merlot vineyards in the Haut-Médoc

FRENCH GRAPE VARIETIES

Many of the world's leading international varieties can be traced back to France. As such, the list of the most widely grown grapes of France will be quite recognizable to wine enthusiasts. However, some of the more traditional areas—such as those found in the far south and southwest of the country—are planted to lesser-known grape varieties (and even some vinous obscurities).

WHITE GRAPE VARIETIES

The major white (*blanc*) grape varieties in France are the following:

- Ugni Blanc (Trebbiano Toscano): At more than 200,000 acres (80,000 ha), this is by far the most widely planted white grape in France (almost double that of Chardonnay). However, it is used almost exclusively for making brandy (Cognac and Armagnac) rather than for wine.
- Chardonnay: Though primarily known as the white grape of Burgundy and Champagne, Chardonnay is grown throughout France, with more acreage under vine in Languedoc-Roussillon than in Champagne.
- Sauvignon Blanc: This widely planted grape is best known as a leading white grape of both Bordeaux and the eastern Loire Valley.
- Melon de Bourgogne: This grape is grown primarily in the western Loire Valley; however, small plantings are found in Beaujolais and elsewhere. Outside of France, this variety is often referred to as *Melon*.

- . Sémillon: This grape is grown primarily in Bordeaux and the southwest; plantings are found in Languedoc-Roussillon and Provence as well.
- Chenin Blanc: Grown primarily in the Loire Valley's Anjou-Saumur and Touraine areas, it produces a wide range of wine styles including dry, sweet, and sparkling.
- Muscat: Muscat is planted mainly in the South of France, where it is primarily used for sweet and fortified wines; the majority of the plantings are the finer-quality subvariety Muscat Blanc à Petits Grains.

RED GRAPE VARIETIES

The major red or black (*noir*) varieties in France are the following:

- Merlot: This is the most widely planted grape variety in France, with close to 250,000 acres (101,000 ha). Merlot can be found in most winegrowing parts of the country, covering over 151,000 acres (61,000 ha) in Bordeaux alone.
- Cabernet Sauvignon: This grape is closely associated with Bordeaux, where more than half of France's Cabernet Sauvignon is grown; however, smaller plantings of Cabernet Sauvignon may be found in many parts of France.
- Cabernet Franc: Tolerating cooler climates, Cabernet Franc is a leading red grape of the Loire Valley and a minor red variety in Bordeaux.
- Grenache: Requiring a warm climate, Grenache is found primarily in the South of France. It is an important ingredient of most southern Rhône blends as well as many wines of Languedoc-Roussillon, Corsica, and Provence.
- Syrah: Another warm-climate variety, Syrah is primarily associated with the Rhône Valley. However, its reputation there (as well as in Australia and elsewhere) has led to much more extensive plantings in other regions as well, including Corsica, Provence, Southwest France, and Languedoc-Roussillon.
- Pinot Noir: A highly respected cool-climate red grape variety, Pinot Noir is the red grape of Burgundy and one of the two red grapes of Champagne. On a smaller scale, it is also the main red variety of Alsace and the eastern Loire.

- Carignan: This is yet another warm-climate variety grown throughout the south of France and Corsica.
- Gamay: Gamay is primarily found in Beaujolais; however, small quantities of Gamay are also located in other cool-climate French regions such as the Loire Valley.
- Cinsault (Cinsaut): A red grape variety found throughout the south of France and Corsica; used as a blending grape and in rosé.
- Meunier (Pinot Meunier): Known primarily as the secondary red grape variety of Champagne.
- Mourvèdre: A warm-climate red variety grown in the Rhône Valley, Languedoc-Roussillon, Corsica, and Provence.

FRENCH WINE LAWS

In the early twentieth century, France was the first country to devise a national system for legally protecting and restricting the use of place-names for wine regions, as well as for other traditional agricultural products such as cheeses and olive oils. This system, administered nationally by the Institut National de l'Origine et de la Qualité (a new name for the organization that still goes by its old acronym of INAO), became a model for the Europe-wide system described in chapter 8.

French wine laws mandate or prohibit a variety of procedures for wineries that plan to use a protected *appellation*, or place-name. The geographic boundaries of the named place are defined, a list of approved grape varieties for that place is given, and viticultural and winemaking practices are specified. Wines that do not meet the standards for the desired appellation must instead be labeled with another, usually larger, appellation (if they qualify for it) or with a lower classification category.

The entry level of French wine is *vin*, formerly referred to as *vin de table*. Wines in this category have few specific regulations apart from those required for health, safety, and commercial trade. As long as all of the grapes come from France, these wines may be labeled as *Vin de France*.

The next tier in the pyramid was formerly known as country wine (vin de pays), and it accounts for more than one-third of French wine. In the new EU system, these are considered table wines with geographical indication (PGI). The wines may be labeled as Indication Géographique Protégée (IGP), with the traditional vin de pays, or by using a combination, as in "IGP–Vin de Pays." There are few restrictions on these wines, except that at least 85% of the grapes must come entirely from within the boundaries of one of the delimited vin de pays regions. In recent years, there has been a great deal of change and consolidation in the IGP regions of France, but as of December 2021, there were a total of 77 IGP/vin de pay designations.

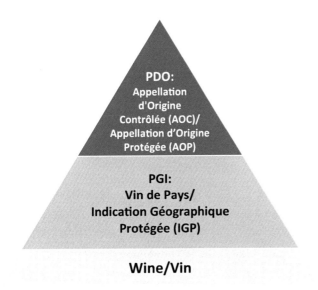

Figure 9–3: French wine categories

The IGP category is subdivided into three levels of geographical specificity. From broadest to most specific, they are regional, departmental, and zone. There are currently eight regional IGP designations, as follows:

- Pays d'Oc IGP: The best-known of the IGPs, covering the western part of the French Mediterranean coast, including Languedoc and Roussillon
- Val de Loire IGP: Covering the Loire Valley and Chablis
- Comtés Rhodaniens IGP: Covering the northern Rhône Valley and Savoie
- Méditerranée IGP: Covering southeast France, including the Rhône Valley, Provence, and Corsica
- Comté Tolosan IGP: Covering southwest France
- L'Atlantique IGP: Covering Bordeaux, Dordogne, and Charentais
- Terres du Midi IGP: Approved in mid-2018 for certain blended wines produced in the Languedoc and Roussillon
- Île-de-France IGP: Approved in 2019; located in the north-central part of the country (including the city of Paris and surrounding areas)

There are 28 departmental IGPs whose boundaries match the political boundaries of a French département (county), some of which are located within the larger regional IGP areas. The remainder of the IGPs—known as vin de pays de zone—are smaller, locally specific areas, often named after a historic or geographical feature of the area.

The top of the French wine classification pyramid—correlating with the EU's PDO tier—is the *appellation d'origine contrôlée* (AOC), "name of controlled origin," category. The name is sometimes shortened to *appellation contrôlée* or AC, and under the new EU system, the term *appellation d'origine protégée* (AOP) may be used. This category includes many of the great wines of France and carries with it the restrictive regulations that have been put into effect to ensure that a French place-name indicates a wine of quality to consumers. There are more than 300 AOCs, producing just under half of all French wine.

FRENCH WINE REGIONS

BORDEAUX

Bordeaux is among the world's most famous wine regions, renowned for long-lived, high-quality, expensive red wines and luscious white dessert wines. For a region with such a reputation, it produces both a greater volume and far more variety than might be expected, including dry whites, rosés, and sparkling wines in a range of price and quality levels. Bordeaux makes about 61 million cases of wine annually, enough to place it twelfth on the list of global producers if it were a separate country. Almost all of this wine qualifies for AOC status, accounting for one-fourth of all French AOC-level production.

Geography and Climate
The wine region of Bordeaux surrounds the city of Bordeaux in southwestern France. Near the city, two rivers, the Garonne and the Dordogne, meet to form the Gironde, a long estuary that flows into the Atlantic. The waterways divide the area into three sections: the *Left Bank*, to the west of the Garonne and Gironde; the *Right Bank*, east and north of the Dordogne and Gironde; and *Entre-Deux-Mers*, between the Garonne and Dordogne Rivers.

The city of Bordeaux lies on the Left Bank. The area of the Left Bank north of Bordeaux city is called the *Médoc*; the area south and west of the city on the Left Bank is known as *Graves*. The main town on the Right Bank of the Dordogne is Libourne. Being so close to the Atlantic, Bordeaux naturally has a maritime climate with a Gulf Stream influence, but the climate is tempered thanks to the protective barrier formed by the Landes Forest along the western coast.

Grape Varieties
The vineyards of Bordeaux are dominated by red grapes, with nearly eighty-five percent of the area planted to red varieties. Merlot takes first place as the most widely planted variety, particularly on the Right Bank and in the Entre-Deux-Mers region. Cabernet Sauvignon—number two on the list—is especially concentrated on the Left Bank. The third most widely planted red grape is Cabernet Franc, although it appears to be declining in importance. Three other red varieties—Malbec, Petit Verdot, and Carmenère—are

planted in much smaller quantities. While blending is not mandated, standard practice is to blend two or more of these varieties together to make red Bordeaux.

The primary white grapes are Sauvignon Blanc and Sémillon, which are blended for use in both the sweet and dry white wines of the region. A minor third grape is Muscadelle, which is sometimes added for its floral notes. Sauvignon Gris (a pink-skinned mutation of Sauvignon Blanc) is sparsely planted; but allowed for use in most white wine appellations. A few other white grapes ("accessory varieties") are permitted (in limited amounts) in some of the white wines of the region; these include Colombard, Ugni Blanc, and Merlot Blanc, among others.

In April of 2021, six new grape varieties—including four red grapes (Arinarnoa, Castets, Marselan, and Touriga Nacional), and two white grapes (Albariño and Lilorila)—were approved for limited use in the wines of the Bordeaux and Bordeaux Supérieur AOCs. The inclusion of these grape varieties represents an effort to lessen the long-term effects of climate change on the wine industry of Bordeaux. The new grapes (combined) cannot exceed 10% of the blend in any given wine.

LEADING GRAPES OF BORDEAUX

Red Grapes	White Grapes
Merlot	Sémillon
Cabernet Sauvignon	Sauvignon Blanc
Cabernet Franc	Muscadelle
Malbec	
Petit Verdot	
Carmenère	

Figure 9-4: Leading Grapes of Bordeaux

Bordeaux Wine Styles
Bordeaux is primarily known for its dry red wines, which typically account for as much as 85% of the region's total production. The region is also quite renowned for its dry white wines and its luscious sweet white wines. Rosé and sparkling wines are produced as well, albeit in limited amounts. Some important styles of Bordeaux wines include the following:

- *Basic red Bordeaux:* Despite the exalted reputation of the top *châteaux* (producers), the majority of Bordeaux production is made for everyday drinking. These wines are usually based on Merlot grown in Entre-Deux-Mers or peripheral areas of the Right Bank. They represent good quality, but they do not have the complexity or age worthiness of their more expensive counterparts.
- *Higher-end Right Bank reds:* The central areas of the Right Bank around St.-Émilion produce some top-quality, long-lived red Bordeaux. Right Bank wines usually feature a substantial contribution from all three major red varieties, with Merlot often leading the blend.
- *Higher-end Left Bank reds:* With a few exceptions, the most celebrated Bordeaux châteaux and wines are found in the Médoc on the Left Bank. Although Merlot is being planted in increasing amounts, these high-end wines are generally made with a majority of Cabernet Sauvignon. Many of these wines are expensive and require careful handling and a long storage time before release. These wines are considered to be some of the world's finest.
- *Dry white wines:* Dry white Bordeaux wines are generally made from Sauvignon Blanc with a minority of Sémillon, although the blend varies by producer and may include small amounts of accessory varieties as well. These wines are typically crisp and high in acidity, with a distinctive Sauvignon Blanc aroma profile. The majority of them come from Entre-Deux-Mers, but some of the best come from Graves, especially Pessac-Léognan.
- *Sweet white wines:* The classic sweet Bordeaux comes from Sauternes on the Left Bank. Other examples are made in several areas along the banks of both rivers, where early morning fogs are common in the autumn and provide perfect growing conditions for botrytis. These sweet wines are normally Sémillon-based, with a small amount of Sauvignon Blanc added. They are harvested late in the season to achieve the highest possible sugar level and, in good years, to give botrytis a chance to develop. The resulting wines are thick and intensely sweet and, if botrytized, have a notable honeyed character.

Bordeaux Appellations

Bordeaux has close to 40 separate appellations, and some of these contain an often-complicated list of subzones within them. Many Bordeaux appellations allow for the production of only one type of wine, while others allow for a range of wines that may include dry reds, dry whites, off-dry whites, sweet whites, rosé, light red wines known as *clairet*, and sparkling wines (crémant).

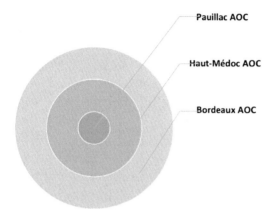

Figure 9–5: Example of Bordeaux appellation hierarchy

The largest appellation, both in physical size and production volume, is the Bordeaux AOC. This appellation covers the geographic area of the entire region and allows for the production of all of the non-sparkling (still) wines approved for production in Bordeaux. The Bordeaux Supérieur AOC, which covers the same geographic area, allows for dry reds and white wines with a minimum of 1.7% residual sugar. The Bordeaux Supérieur AOC has slightly higher standards than the Bordeaux AOC, including lower yields, higher minimum ripeness at harvest, and a half-degree higher minimum alcohol. The sparkling wines of the region, produced in both white and rosé, are classified under the Crémant de Bordeaux AOC. Taken together, these regional appellations account for approximately 55% of Bordeaux's total production.

Wines that fall into one of these general appellations most often come from an area that does not qualify for a higher (smaller) appellation. For instance, the large territory of Entre-Deux-Mers grows a good deal of red grape varieties throughout the region; however, a very small portion of the acreage is located within an AOC that is approved for red wines. Thus, a majority of the red grapes grown within the territory of Entre-Deux-Mers are made into wines

that are labeled as Bordeaux AOC or Bordeaux Supérieur AOC. Similarly, white wines produced in the Médoc have no other appellation but Bordeaux AOC.

The Left Bank

On the Left Bank, north and south of the city of Bordeaux, respectively, are the Médoc and Graves. The Médoc itself consists of the Médoc and Haut-Médoc (Upper Médoc) appellations and six communal AOCs, including four of the most esteemed villages in the wine world: St.-Estèphe, Pauillac, St.-Julien, and Margaux. These are all red wine appellations.

The Graves AOC is approved for dry red and dry white wines; sweet white wines produced in the area may be labeled as Graves Supérieures AOC. In 1987, Pessac-Léognan, the northernmost part of the area and home to many of its most prestigious châteaux, received its own AOC approved for dry red and dry white wines. Farther south, Sauternes and other communal AOCs are the prime sources of Bordeaux's sweet white wines.

Wine Regions of Bordeaux

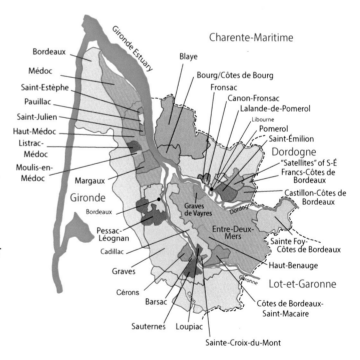

Copyright: The Society of Wine Educators 2022

Figure 9–6: Bordeaux

Entre-Deux-Mers

Entre-Deux-Mers—the large, triangular-shaped area between the Garonne and Dordogne Rivers—is more fertile than other parts of Bordeaux, so its wines tend to lack the concentration of those from either bank. The Entre-Deux-Mers AOC—taking up most (but not all) of this land area—is one of the coolest-climate regions of Bordeaux and approved for dry white wines only. The Entre-Deux-Mers AOC contains a well-known sub-region—Haut-Benauge—tucked along its western edge that is also approved for dry white wines only. (Note: Haut-Benauge is also considered to be a sub-region of the Bordeaux AOC and wines labeled as "Bordeaux-Haut Benauge AOC" may be produced in either the dry white or sweet white styles.)

The Entre-Deux-Mers area also contains several other appellations, each with their own specific regulations. Three appellations—Loupiac AOC, Sainte-Croix-du-Mont AOC, and Cadillac AOC—are clustered along the eastern shore of the Garonne River and approved solely for the production of sweet white wines (which may or may not be affected by botrytis).

Despite the emphasis on white wines, the vineyards of the Entre-Deux-Mers area contain significant planting of red grapes (primarily Merlot and Cabernet Sauvignon). Much of this production is made into dry red wines labeled as Bordeaux AOC or Bordeaux Supérieur AOC. However, a few specific appellations—including Graves de Vayres AOC and Sainte Foy-Côtes de Bordeaux AOC, both located along the banks of the Dordogne—are approved for the production of red wines (in addition to white).

The Right Bank

On the Right Bank, a small area around the town of Libourne has earned a reputation for wines on a par with those of the Médoc communes. The most coveted wines from this area of Bordeaux come from the Pomerol and St.-Émilion AOCs. Several other communes in the area, including Fronsac, Canon-Fronsac, and Lalande-de-Pomerol, also produce highly respected wines, as do the four regions known as the "satellites" of St.-Émilion: Lussac-St.-Émilion, Montagne-St.-Émilion, Puisseguin-St.-Émilion, and St.-

Georges-St.-Émilion. In addition, there is a separate St.-Émilion Grand Cru AOC that comprises the same area as the more basic St.-Émilion AOC but has tighter standards.

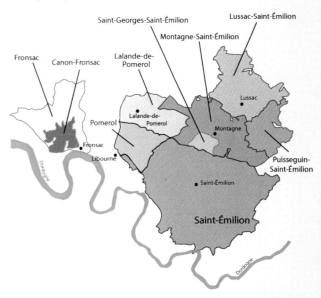

Wine Regions of the Libournais
(Bordeaux's Right Bank)

Copyright: The Society of Wine Educators 2016

Figure 9–7: The Libournais

The Côtes de Bordeaux

In 2009, the Côtes de Bordeaux AOC was created in order to combine some of the more disjointed regions of Bordeaux under a more recognizable and commercially useful banner. Five areas—Francs, Castillon, Blaye, Sainte Foy, and Cadillac—while somewhat dispersed geographically, are now considered to be subzones of the Côtes de Bordeaux AOC. As such, they are allowed to include the term *Côtes de Bordeaux* in the titles of their appellations (and on their wine labels). These five subzones are as follows:

- Blaye-Côtes de Bordeaux
- Cadillac-Côtes de Bordeaux
- Castillon-Côtes de Bordeaux
- Francs-Côtes de Bordeaux
- Sainte Foy-Côtes de Bordeaux

Table 9-1: Bordeaux Appellations

BORDEAUX APPELLATIONS						
	Appellation	Dry White	Rosé	Red	Sweet White	Sparkling
Regional	Bordeaux	•	•	•	•	
	Bordeaux Supérieur			•	•	
	Crémant de Bordeaux					•
Left Bank— Médoc	Haut-Médoc			•		
	Médoc			•		
	Listrac-Médoc			•		
	Margaux			•		
	Moulis-en-Médoc			•		
	Pauillac			•		
	St.-Estèphe			•		
	St.-Julien			•		
Left Bank—Graves	Graves	•		•		
	Graves Supérieures				•	
	Pessac-Léognan	•		•		
	Barsac				•	
	Cérons				•	
	Sauternes				•	
Entre-Deux-Mers	Entre-Deux-Mers	•				
	Cadillac				•	
	Côtes de Bordeaux-St.-Macaire	•			•	
	Graves-de-Vayres	•		•	•	
	Loupiac				•	
	Premières Côtes de Bordeaux				•	
	Ste.-Croix-du-Mont				•	
Right Bank— Libourne Area	Canon-Fronsac			•		
	Fronsac			•		
	Lalande-de-Pomerol			•		
	Lussac-St.-Émilion			•		
	Montagne-St.-Émilion			•		
	Pomerol			•		
	Puisseguin-St.-Émilion			•		
	St.-Émilion			•		
	St.-Émilion Grand Cru			•		
	St.-Georges-St.-Émilion			•		
Blaye, Bourg, & Côtes	Côtes de Bordeaux	•		•	•	
	Blaye			•		
	Côtes de Blaye	•				
	Bourg/Côtes de Bourg	•		•		

Châteaux and the Wine Trade

A *château* in France is a country house, sometimes as grand as a castle. As the wine industry grew in Bordeaux, the most famous wine producers in the area built châteaux on their properties. Over time, *château* came to be used for any Bordeaux wine estate, with or without a mansion, and even for some businesses that made wine but did not own any land at all. This latter group is important in Bordeaux, as it is in many places in France, because a lot of grape growers and winemakers own only small plots of land and do not have the means to age or widely market their wines. Thus, a class of middlemen known as *négociants* developed, buying juice or wine from numerous small farms and blending it under their own label. They would also buy in larger quantities from farmers' cooperatives or large estates, either to add to the blend or to sell directly. Years ago, even the great properties sold almost all their wine to various négociants rather than bottling it themselves. This practice has slowed to some extent, but négociants are still quite important to the Bordeaux trade.

Figure 9–8: Château Pichon Longueville Baron

A particular system has developed in Bordeaux of selling wine *en primeur,* or "in futures." Under this system, most top Bordeaux is sold several years before it is bottled and long before it is drinkable. This provides cash flow for the châteaux, which otherwise would have to wait years to get paid for their work, as well as a potential price break for brokers and retailers who buy the wine early.

Bordeaux Classifications

One of the well-known elements of the Bordeaux wine scene is its system of "classified growths." Several rankings of producers and estates have been drawn up over the years, establishing a somewhat stable hierarchy of prestige and, to a large extent, bottle price.

The most famous of these rankings is the Bordeaux Classification of 1855. This classification was carried out by brokers in Bordeaux city in preparation for the Universal Exhibition in Paris that year. It was essentially a listing of châteaux by the price their wines brought on the market, which, in this case, proved to be an accurate indicator of quality. Because the Right Bank wines did not command the same prestige at the time, they were excluded from the 1855 ranking.

The 61 red wines that were included were subdivided into five levels called *crus,* or "growths." The top level, known as *premier cru,* or "first growth," comprised four châteaux: Haut-Brion, Lafite-Rothschild, Latour, and Margaux. A fifth, Château Mouton-Rothschild, was moved up to the top tier in 1973—one of the few changes ever to be made in the ranking since its initial publication. The estates in the Classification of 1855 were considered at the time to produce most of the very best wines of Bordeaux, and the châteaux owners have tried to maintain their status ever since. Over time, a few châteaux from the second tier—*deuxième cru*—have achieved price levels on a par with higher-ranked wines and have come to be known (quite unofficially) as "super-seconds." Château Cos d'Estournel, Château Montrose, and Château Pichon Longueville Baron are often cited as among the leading super seconds.

Sweet wines, for which Bordeaux was also renowned, were also classified in 1855; the sweet wine classification lists 15 second growths, 11 first growths, and one superior first growth: Château d'Yquem.

Table 9-2: Bordeaux Classification of 1855: First Growths

BORDEAUX CLASSIFICATION OF 1855: FIRST GROWTHS		
Red Wines		
Classification	Château	Commune
Premiers Crus	Château Haut-Brion	Pessac (Graves)
	Château Lafite Rothschild	Pauillac
	Château Latour	Pauillac
	Château Margaux	Margaux-Cantenac
	Château Mouton Rothschild (promoted in 1973)	Pauillac
Sweet Wines		
Supérieur Premier Cru	Château d'Yquem	Sauternes
Premiers Crus	Château Climens	Barsac
	Château Clos Haut-Peyraguey	Bommes (Sauternes)
	Château Coutet	Barsac
	Château de Rayne-Vigneau	Bommes (Sauternes)
	Château Guiraud	Sauternes
	Château Lafaurie-Peyraguey	Bommes (Sauternes)
	Château La Tour Blanche	Bommes (Sauternes)
	Château Rabaud-Promis	Bommes (Sauternes)
	Château Rieussec	Fargues (Sauternes)
	Château Sigalas-Rabaud	Bommes (Sauternes)
	Château Suduiraut	Preignac (Sauternes)

Because of the limited scope of estates considered in the Classification of 1855, other supplementary classifications or special statuses have been developed since.

- *Graves:* Graves châteaux were classified in 1953 and again in 1959. This list contains 16 properties ranked for their white wine, red wine, or both. There is only one level: *cru classé* (classified growth). Château Haut-Brion, the one Graves wine listed in the red wine Classification of 1855, is among this group as well.

- *St.-Émilion Grand Cru Classé:* The only classification system on the Right Bank is the one established in St.-Émilion in 1954. Unlike the Classification of 1855, it requires reclassification every ten years. The classification ranks the châteaux in the St.-Émilion Grand Cru appellation into two categories: *grand cru classé* (great classified growths) and the higher *premier grand cru classé* (first great classified growths). St.-Émilion Grand Cru is an appellation that any grower in the St.-Émilion AOC can theoretically achieve by meeting its higher viticultural standards. As of 2012, 18 producers have premier grand cru classé status. Of these, four—Château Angélus, Château Ausone, Château Cheval Blanc, and Château Pavie—are considered so far superior to the others that they have been given a category A ranking, while the other 14 are listed as category B.

In early 2021, several of the leading châteaux of St.-Émilion announced that they would not be submitting applications for the planned renewal of the *St.-Émilion Grand Cru Classé* classification (scheduled for 2022). As a result, the future of this classification is uncertain.

ST.-ÉMILION PREMIER GRAND CRU CLASSIFICATION (SEPTEMBER 2012)	
Premier Grand Cru Classé A	
Château Angélus	Château Cheval Blanc
Château Ausone	Château Pavie
Premier Grand Cru Classé B	
Château Beauséjour	Château Larcis-Ducasse
Château Beau-Séjour Bécot	Château Pavie-Macquin
Château Bélair-Monange	Château Troplong-Mondot
Château Canon	Château Trotte Vieille
Château Canon-la-Gaffelière	Château Valandraud
Château Figeac	Clos Fourtet
Château la Gaffelière	La Mondotte

LOIRE VALLEY (VAL DE LOIRE)

The Loire Valley is really several different wine regions rolled into one, all joined by their position along the banks of the Loire—the longest river in France. As a whole, the Loire Valley is known primarily for crisp white wines, light red wines, rosés, and some fine sweet and sparkling wines. However, each distinct subregion focuses on different grape varieties. Despite the river's great length, the Loire Valley's vineyards cover only about half as much ground as those of Bordeaux. Three-quarters of the total production of about 45 million cases is at the AOC level.

Geography and Climate

From its origin in the Massif Central in the heartland of France, the Loire River flows north to the twin towns of Sancerre and Pouilly-sur-Loire, which mark the beginning of Loire Valley wine country. The river then makes a broad turn to flow west toward the Atlantic Ocean, south of Brittany. The 300-mile (482-km) stretch of river from Sancerre to Nantes is flanked by vineyards nearly the entire way, especially on its southern side.

The Loire Valley comprises four distinct winegrowing regions, joined together by the river. From west to east, these are as follows:

- *The Pays Nantais* (Nantes Country)
- *Anjou-Saumur*, which is made up of two adjacent but separate areas, Anjou and Saumur
- *Touraine*, situated to the east of Anjou-Saumur
- *The Upper Loire*, the area around Sancerre and Pouilly-Fumé, sometimes referred to as the eastern Loire

In addition, some outlying appellations along tributaries of the Loire River are included in the Loire Valley's wine production.

Given the large span of territory, the various wine regions of the Loire Valley do not have a lot in common apart from the same northerly latitude and, therefore, cool climates. The Pays Nantais, situated on low-lying terrain close to the ocean, has a chilly maritime climate. The maritime influence decreases farther from the shore, and the middle section of the Loire Valley gets more sunshine than the coastal areas. Humidity remains high from the sea air coming up the river, which provides ideal conditions for the botrytis development that is important in the sweet wine appellations. The Upper Loire is far enough inland to have a continental climate, moderated slightly by the continuation of the sea breezes up the valley.

LEADING GRAPES OF THE LOIRE VALLEY

Red Grapes	White Grapes
Cabernet Franc	Melon de Bourgogne
Gamay	Chenin Blanc
Pinot Noir	Sauvignon Blanc
Cabernet Sauvignon	Chardonnay
Grolleau	Folle Blanche
Pineau d'Aunis	Pinot Gris
Négrette	

Figure 9-9: Leading Grapes of the Loire Valley

Figure 9-10: Vineyards in the Loire Valley

Grape Varieties and Wine Styles

The Loire Valley is perhaps the most diverse producer of wine styles in France. These include the following:

- Dry whites
- Sweet whites
- Dry and off-dry rosés
- Sparkling wines
- Dry reds

The key white grape varieties of the Loire Valley include Melon de Bourgogne, Sauvignon Blanc, and Chenin Blanc. Small amounts of Arbois, Chardonnay, Pinot Gris, and Folle Blanche are planted as well.

As the name suggests, Melon de Bourgogne originally hails from Burgundy, although very little of it remains there. Melon is a fairly neutral white grape that produces a light-bodied, very crisp white wine. In the Loire Valley, the Melon de Bourgogne variety is limited to the Pays Nantais area, where it is made into the well-known wines of the Muscadet AOCs.

Chenin Blanc, sometimes called Pineau de la Loire, shows its versatility in this region in dry white wines, sweet white wines, and delightful sparkling wines. Perhaps the most well-known Chenin Blanc–based wines of the Loire are Vouvray and Savennières, two wines that can be markedly different despite their shared heritage. Chenin Blanc's thin skins make it highly susceptible to botrytis, which is instrumental in creating the region's highly acclaimed dessert wines.

Sauvignon Blanc is planted throughout the Anjou-Saumur and Touraine areas, but it is best known for the wines it produces in the Upper Loire. In regions such as Sancerre and Pouilly-Fumé, Sauvignon Blanc produces some of its most classic flavor profiles with vibrant acidity and fine aromatics.

The Loire Valley is also known for its rosés, produced in both dry and off-dry styles. Loire rosés are generally made using a blend of grapes including Cabernet Franc, Cabernet Sauvignon, Pinot Noir, Gamay, Grolleau, and Malbec, among others. The local name for Cabernet Franc is Breton, and Malbec is locally known as Côt.

These same grapes are used in the production of dry red wines. Notable Loire Valley red wines include those made from Cabernet Franc, such as Chinon, and those made from Pinot Noir, such as Sancerre (which is far better known for its white wine). Due to the Loire's cool climate, these wines are nicely acidic, light versions of red wine.

Sparkling wines of the Loire, marketed under the name *Fines Bulles* (fine bubbles), are made in the traditional method. Loire Valley sparkling wines are generally based on Chenin Blanc, with Sauvignon Blanc and Chardonnay sometimes added as a minority component. Red grapes, including Pinot Noir, Cabernet Franc, Cabernet Sauvignon, Grolleau, and Gamay, are also used in the production of sparkling wines. A variety of sparkling wine styles are produced, including both white and rosé with varying levels of sweetness.

The Loire Valley

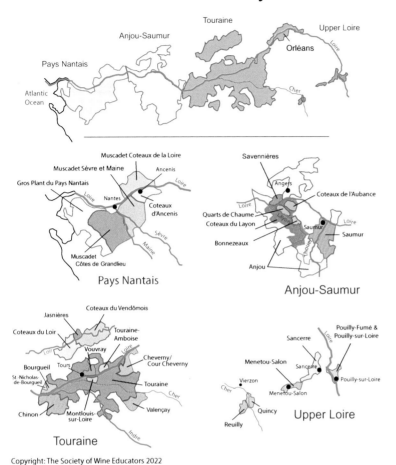

Copyright: The Society of Wine Educators 2022

Figure 9–11: Loire Valley region

Loire Valley Appellations

Given the dissimilarity of terroir and grape varieties, the Loire Valley has no quality wine appellation that covers the entire region comparable to, for example, the Bordeaux AOC. That role is played, at the PGI level, by IGP Val de Loire—one of the seven regional vins de pays in France. IGP Val de Loire replaced the Vin de Pays du Jardin de la France in 2009.

Pays Nantais

While small amounts of wine are made from Chenin Blanc, Gamay, Folle Blanche (Gros Plant), Pinot Gris, and a handful of other varieties, Melon de Bourgogne (Melon) is the leading grape of the Pays Nantais. Melon de Bourgogne represents three-quarters of area's vineyards; and is required to comprise a minimum of 90% of the wines of the Muscadet AOC (the remaining 10% may include Chardonnay).

The rules are a bit stricter for the Muscadet sub-appellations—Muscadet Coteaux de la Loire AOC, Muscadet Côtes de Grandlieu AOC, and Muscadet Sèvre et Maine AOC—which must be 100% Melon de Bourgogne. Due to the neutral character of the grape, many producers of these wines craft a richer, fuller-bodied wine by allowing it to rest on its lees for several months or longer before bottling. These wines may be labeled with the term *sur lie* (provided they originate from one of the three Muscadet sub-appellations and meet the minimum aging requirements). Muscadet Sèvre-et-Maine AOC is by far the leading appellation, accounting for nearly 80% of the total production of Muscadet.

Anjou-Saumur

The Anjou-Saumur is considered part of the Central Loire, along with Touraine, its neighbor to the east.

The Anjou AOC produces a red wine from primarily Cabernet Franc and/or Cabernet Sauvignon, and a white from Chenin Blanc with up to 20% Sauvignon Blanc or Chardonnay. There are also basic Anjou appellations for sparkling (*mousseux*) and lightly sparkling (*pétillant*) wine, and for red wine made from Gamay grapes. On the north bank of the river, Savennières—one of the area's premier white wine appellations—produces unique (typically dry) wines from 100% Chenin Blanc. Savennières, which has been called "the most cerebral wine in the world," is often listed among the world's top Chenin Blancs.

Two regional rosé appellations are Rosé d'Anjou and Cabernet d'Anjou. The off-dry Rosé d'Anjou is most often produced primarily from the Grolleau variety, while the somewhat sweeter Cabernet d'Anjou is made from Cabernet Sauvignon and Cabernet Franc. Dry rosés are more likely to use the Rosé de Loire appellation, which covers Anjou, Saumur, and Touraine.

Sweet dessert wines are a specialty of Anjou, where conditions favor the development of botrytis. The primary sweet wine area of Anjou is the Coteaux du Layon AOC, which has two better-known subregions, Bonnezeaux and Quarts de Chaume. As of 2011, Quarts de Chaume became the Loire Valley's first grand cru, and a new appellation, Coteaux du Layon Premier Cru Chaume, was created. All of these use 100% Chenin Blanc and produce very long-lived dessert wines.

Much of the wine that is produced in the Saumur region is produced under the Saumur AOC; this designation allows for still (non-sparkling) wines in white, red, and rosé as well as sparkling wines (in white or rosé). A small red wine only appellation, Saumur-Champigny, produces unique spicy red wines based on the Cabernet Franc grape. Up to 15% of the blend of Saumur-Champigny may be Cabernet Sauvignon or Pineau d'Aunis (sometimes known as Chenin Noir).

Figure 9–12: Château de Saumur

Saumur, however, is particularly known for sparkling wines. The main sparkling wine appellation is *Saumur Mousseux* (sometimes seen as simply *Saumur*). This traditional method wine may be white or rosé. White versions must contain a minimum of 60% Chenin Blanc, while rosé versions are based on at least 60% Cabernet Franc. Both versions may also include any of the other grapes of the region. In addition, Saumur is the chief source of grapes for Crémant de Loire, a sparkling wine that may be produced anywhere in the Central Loire.

Touraine
Considered part of the Central Loire but located to the east of Anjou and Saumur, Touraine is home to Vouvray, one of the most well-known of the Loire appellations. Vouvray produces white wines based on the Chenin Blanc grape variety. Vouvray is typically a dry, still wine, but the style may range from dry to sweet, and some sparkling wines are produced as well. Across the river from Vouvray, its counterpart, Montlouis-sur-Loire, produces wines very similar in style.

Touraine is also home to Chinon, Bourgueil, and St.-Nicolas-de-Bourgueil. The highly regarded red wines of these appellations must be produced using a majority of Cabernet Franc, but often have a measure of Cabernet Sauvignon added for additional structure and complexity. Of the three, Chinon is considered to be the most elegant. While these three appellations are mainly known for their red wines, Chinon produces a small amount of white wine from 100% Chenin Blanc, and both Bourgueil and St.-Nicolas-de-Bourgueil produce rosé.

The Touraine AOC covers the entire area and allows for the production of red, white, and rosé wines as well as sparkling wines in white and rosé. East of Vouvray, where most of the vineyards that produce grapes for this regional appellation are located, the grapes and wines of Touraine begin to mirror those of the Upper Loire. Thus, Touraine AOC whites are typically made with a majority of Sauvignon Blanc; reds and rosés are produced using a blend based on Cabernet Franc and Malbec.

The Cheverny AOC—well-known for white wines based on Sauvignon Blanc and Sauvignon Gris—is located on the eastern side of Touraine. The red and rosé wines of the Cheverny AOC are based on Pinot Noir blended with Gamay; Malbec is optional.

Upper Loire
East of Touraine, there are fewer appellations, but two of them, Sancerre and Pouilly-Fumé, are among the most famous of the Loire Valley. Known for classic 100% Sauvignon Blanc wines, Sancerre is located on the west bank; Pouilly-Fumé lies across the river on the east bank. It is said that the chalky

limestone of Sancerre gives the wine its crisp acidity, and that the flinty soil of Pouilly-Fumé gives the wine a smoky flavor. Both wines are considered to be among the world's benchmarks for Sauvignon Blanc. Sancerre also produces a small amount of red wine from Pinot Noir. (Note: The Loire Valley's Pouilly-Fumé should not be confused with Pouilly-Fuissé in the Mâconnais area of Burgundy, whose wines are 100% Chardonnay.)

The appellations of Menetou-Salon, just southwest of Sancerre, and Quincy and Reuilly, located some 30 miles to the west on the River Cher, are considered to be part of the district as well. All three of these AOCs make Sauvignon Blanc; Reuilly and Menetou-Salon produce a small amount of Pinot Noir (red and rosé) as well.

CHAMPAGNE

Champagne's development was evolutionary. Its proximity to Paris and the English market accounts for the early demand for its wines, which were at the time light white wines and Pinot Noirs. These wines were basically still, although it was observed that suspended fermentation—caused by the region's cold climate—could lend a few bubbles to the wine. Later on, after discovering that the Champagne merchants' practice of adding sugar to balance the wine's acidity caused an inadvertent second fermentation, the English were the first to deliberately replicate the process and create the second fermentation in the bottle. This discovery was followed by centuries of improvements, led in the early years by Dom Pérignon and his contemporaries, and later by Veuve Clicquot, Louis Roederer, and a host of other leading houses of Champagne.

Champagne production is now a highly prestigious multibillion-dollar industry. Today, the region focuses almost exclusively on this category and makes more than 32 million cases per year, or about 18% of the entire world production of sparkling wine.

Geography and Climate

Champagne is one of the coldest and most northerly winegrowing regions in the world, which is why it is so well suited to the production of sparkling wine. The grapes of Champagne, which barely ripen by most regions' standards, are picked at high levels

of acidity, which is essential in sparkling wine production. Summers are cool, and winters can be quite cold and snowy, with no protection from storms out of the north.

Figure 9-13: Dom Pérignon statue at Moët et Chandon, Épernay

Located in north-central France, the 84,500 acres (34,200 ha) of vineyards in Champagne are divided into five main zones:

- *Montagne de Reims:* a plateau between the Marne River and the city of Reims
- *Vallée de la Marne:* stretching for more than 40 miles along the Marne River west of the town of Épernay
- *Côte des Blancs:* a ridge running south and southwest from Épernay
- *Côte de Sézanne:* a region situated southwest of the Côte des Blancs, stretching in a long thin line beyond the town of Sézanne
- *Côte des Bar:* an isolated area in the Aube department, some 60 miles southeast of Épernay

Although the soils of Champagne are varied, two particular subsoils contribute to the unique terroir for which the region is known: chalk and limestone-rich marl. These soils allow the vine roots to dig freely and deeply and have the ability to retain moisture, while at the same time allowing the excess water to drain away. The high levels of chalk and limestone also keep the soil at a somewhat constant temperature throughout the year. Most of the grand cru villages are situated on these types of soil. The chalk of the area was mined by the Romans, who created miles of subterranean cellars that still exist throughout

Champagne. These cellars are used to store millions of bottles of developing Champagne at the perfect temperature and humidity level.

The Côte des Bar lies on top of a ridge of soil known as Kimmeridgian marl. This is a limestone-rich soil—formed by fossilized marine deposits from an ancient sea that formed the Paris Basin—mixed with clay. This soil extends to England's White Cliffs of Dover and Salisbury Plain. Its characteristics include excellent water retention, heat retention, and heat reflection; when heat is reflected back onto the vine, it helps to optimize the vine's ability to reach phenolic ripeness in an otherwise less than ideal environment. Kimmeridgian marl is also found in the Loire Valley and in Burgundy.

Grape Varieties

Champagne is almost always made from one or more of the three main permitted grape varieties: Chardonnay, Pinot Noir, and Meunier (Pinot Meunier). The region does allow the use of four other grape varieties: Pinot Blanc, Pinot Gris, Petit Meslier, and Arbane. While somewhat obscure, these grapes are appreciated by some producers and are sometimes used in wines that emphasize the uniqueness of the grapes, such as Le Nombre d'Or (Golden Number) Champagne produced by the House of Aubry.

As for the prominent grapes of Champagne, Chardonnay dominates the plantings of the Côte de Sézanne and the aptly-named Côte des Blancs. Pinot Noir is the prominent grape of the Côte des Bar, while the frost-prone Vallée de la Marne is heavily planted to the suitably late-budding and early-ripening Meunier. The Montagne de Reims is largely planted to Pinot Noir, but its diverse terrain supports a good deal of Chardonnay and Meunier as well.

LEADING GRAPES OF CHAMPAGNE

Red Grapes	White Grapes
Pinot Noir	Chardonnay
Meunier	

Figure 9–14: Leading Grapes of Champagne

Champagne Production

The production of Champagne begins with the harvest of high-acid, low-sugar grapes. As most of these wines are intended to be white despite the use of red grapes, producers are very careful in their handling of the fruit. Small boxes are used during harvest to ensure that the grapes don't burst open prior to arrival at the winery, and most press houses are located in or near the vineyards.

Once the grapes are ready to be pressed, regulations define more than twenty criteria that must be followed, including permitted press types and pressing and racking capacity. The traditional measurement for the quantity of grapes allowed in the press is known as a *marc* (from the Old French *marchier*, meaning "to trample"), which is equivalent to 4,000 kilograms (approximately 8,800 pounds).

The juice extracted from the grapes is also carefully controlled, with a maximum of 25.5 hectoliters (roughly 675 gallons) allowed for Champagne production per marc. The total volume of this juice is further defined into two categories:

- The *cuvée* comprises the majority of the juice (20.5 hectoliters) from the free run and the first light pressings. The cuvée is rich in sugars and acids. It comes from the juiciest part of the pulp and is used for premium Champagne production.
- The *taille* is the juice from the next set of pressings. This is juice from the flesh closer to the pips or the skins. It is lower in acid and sugar and is primarily used for demi-sec or extra dry sparkling wine production, as the extra sweetness of the wine will mask its coarser nature. The permitted volume for this fraction of the pressing is 5 hectoliters.

Juice from a third pressing, known as the *rebêche*, may be used to produce still wine (including a local vin de liqueur known as Ratafia de Champagne PGI), spirits, or vinegar.

After a period of juice settling and chaptalization, (if needed), the permitted pressings are fermented and clarified to produce a set of neutral-tasting base wines, known as *vins clairs*. Often, many separate batches are produced from different grape varieties, zones, and vineyards. After several months, the cellar master will assemble these various base wines into a variety of cuvées.

When producing a nonvintage Champagne, which makes up the bulk of production, the cuvée will often include considerable réserve wine as well, with the goal of creating a consistent house style from year to year. The base wine used to craft vintage Champagne does not contain any réserve wine, as it is intended to reflect the product of a sole year's harvest. Regardless of whether réserve wines are used, the cuvée, along with the liqueur de tirage, will be bottled and sealed. In accordance with the region's laws, the wine may not be bottled until January 1, following the harvest.

Once bottled, the wines are stored in underground caves, where the secondary fermentation takes place. After this fermentation is finished and the yeast cells die off, the wine will remain in the sealed bottle for a specified period of time. Specifically, nonvintage Champagne must spend a minimum of 15 months maturing in the producer's cellars, with at least 12 of those months spent aging on the lees. Vintage (*millésime*) Champagne must be aged for a minimum of three years, which also must include at least 12 months on the lees. In practice, most producers exceed these minimums.

The next stage is riddling (remuage), which is now performed most frequently with gyropalettes rather than by hand; hand-riddling is almost exclusively used by small production houses and for the highest-end prestige wines. After riddling is complete, the bottles are disgorged, topped off with additional wine, and adjusted with dosage (liqueur d'expédition), depending on the level of sweetness desired. As previously discussed, wines may be sweetened to any of the following levels, listed from driest to sweetest: brut nature or sans dosage (unsweetened), extra brut, brut, extra sec, sec, demi-sec, and doux. (See chapter 6 for specific residual sugar levels.)

The Champagne Region

Copyright: The Society of Wine Educators 2021

Figure 9–15: Champagne region

In addition to wines with varying sweetness levels, there are several basic styles of Champagne:

- Nonvintage: the standard wine of a Champagne producer ("house"), made to the house style by using a blend of wines from several vintages; this category accounts for three-quarters of Champagne production
- Vintage: Champagne designed to reflect a single year's harvest with no reserve wines used in the base wine/cuvée; the better producers make a vintage Champagne only in exceptional years
- Prestige cuvée, tête de cuvée, or cuvée spéciale: the top-of-the-line product produced by a Champagne house, using the finest grapes and most careful production techniques. Well-known examples include Krug's *Clos du Mesnil* and Bollinger's *Vieilles Vignes Françaises*.
- Blanc de blancs: wine produced from only white grapes, primarily Chardonnay
- Blanc de noirs: wine produced from only red grapes, primarily Pinot Noir, but sometimes with Meunier (Pinot Meunier) included

- Rosé: pink Champagne produced from base wines that have been allowed to macerate on the red grape skins for a short period of time, or by blending up to 20% red wine into the cuvée

Champagne Classification

The wines of Champagne do not have a classification scheme, but the villages do. Known as the *échelle des crus*, this system rates each village in Champagne based on the quality of its grapes. The top-rated villages are those that received the maximum score (or *échelle*, meaning "scale") of 100; these were classified as grands crus. There are 17 grand cru villages. The next tier is comprised of those villages that received scores ranging from 90 to 99%; these are the premier cru villages. There are currently 42 premier cru villages.

The rating of the échelle des crus was originally a true percentage system intended to set the portion of a maximum price that a vineyard could receive for its grapes. The maximum price was set by Le Comité Interprofessionnel du vin de Champagne (CIVC). Under this system, grand cru vineyards received the full price, while others would receive a percentage of the maximum corresponding to their rating. In the early 2000s, the rating system was abolished, but the grand cru and premier cru villages retain their titles. Wines whose grapes come entirely from grand cru or premier cru villages are entitled to use the appropriate term on the label, but because many wines are blends from several small areas, this is not often seen except on the wines of small, independent producers.

The Champagne Trade

The traditional winemaking properties in Champagne are known as "houses." The roughly 300 Champagne houses produce more than two-thirds of the region's wine but own only a tenth of the vineyards, so they must buy most of the grapes they use from the thousands of independent growers.

Some growers also make and sell their own Champagne, accounting for a quarter of the market. Well-known producers of these *grower Champagnes*—which can be recognized by the initials RM (*Récoltant-Manipulant*) on the label—include Cédric Bouchard and Jacques Selosse. The remainder of the production of Champagne is done by cooperatives that do not own any vineyards but produce and sell *vins clairs* (still wines) to the bigger houses, produce Champagne for their grower-members, or produce Champagne to sell directly.

Champagne Appellations

There is only one sparkling wine appellation for this entire region: Champagne AOC. All of the many variations of Champagne are simply styles, not separate appellations. The region does have two other AOCs used for nonsparkling wines, which are made in very small quantities. The Rosé des Riceys AOC covers still rosé wines made from the Pinot Noir grape variety in the commune of Riceys, at the far south end of the Champagne region. The Coteaux Champenois AOC, which covers most of the area in Champagne, is used for still wines. Coteaux Champenois may be white, red, or rosé.

ALSACE

Alsace has strong cultural roots in the history of Germany as well as France, and accordingly, its wines show elements of both German and French tradition. The average vineyard holding in Alsace is small, and the number of producers is large. The 38,300 acres (15,500 ha) of vineyard land is divided among more than 4,930 growers. Annual sales amount to about 12.3 million cases.

Geography and Climate

Alsace is located at the northeast corner of France, stretched out in a north–south band 75 miles long, sandwiched between the Vosges Mountains on the west and the Rhine River on the east. It lies across the river from the German wine region of Baden and south of the Pfalz. The Alsace area is comprised of the Bas-Rhin department (consisting of the area to the north, but at a lower elevation), and the Haut-Rhin department (comprising the area to the south, but at a higher elevation).

Alsace has a cold continental climate due to its northerly location and distance from the ocean. It is also one of the driest areas of France as a result of the rain shadow created by the Vosges. The mountains block rain and humidity coming off the Atlantic and give the region an abundance of sunshine. The sunny, dry summers allow grapes in Alsace to ripen much more fully than those in Champagne and Chablis to the west.

The Alsace Region

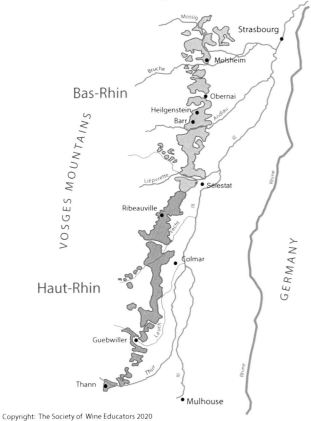

Copyright: The Society of Wine Educators 2020

Figure 9–16: Alsace region

Grape Varieties

Alsace is overwhelmingly white grape territory, with Pinot Noir being the only red grape variety permitted in the AOC wines of the region. The primary white grapes are Riesling, Gewurztraminer, Pinot Gris, and Muscat. Pinot Blanc is also grown in significant quantity. (Unlike Germany, Alsace does not use the umlaut over the *u* [ü] when spelling *Gewurztraminer.*)

Alsace Appellations

There are three types of appellations in Alsace: Alsace AOC, Alsace Grand Cru AOC, and Crémant d'Alsace AOC. Most wines fall under the general Alsace AOC, which covers the entire district. Under appellation rules, if a winery labels wine with the name of a grape variety, it must be produced 100% from that grape. Varietal wines in the Alsace AOC may be produced from the following ten grape varieties: Riesling, Gewurztraminer, Pinot Gris, Pinot Noir, Pinot Blanc, Sylvaner, Muscat, Chasselas, Auxerrois, and Klevener de Heiligenstein (Savagnin Rose). Klevener de Heiligenstein wines

are restricted to the village of Heiligenstein and a few other specific communes. An eleventh grape, Chardonnay, may only be used in Crémant d'Alsace.

Alsace has a hierarchy system for its vineyards, with the top ones accorded grand cru status. There are presently 51 grand cru vineyards. As of 2011, each of these vineyards was recognized as an appellation in its own right. With few exceptions, such as those where blended wines and Sylvaner are allowed, Alsace Grand Cru vineyards are permitted to grow only the "noble varieties" of Gewurztraminer, Muscat, Pinot Gris, or Riesling. Alsace Grand Cru wines have slightly higher standards for yields and minimum ripeness levels, and chaptalization is not allowed. The majority of grand cru vineyards are located in Haut-Rhin.

The Crémant d'Alsace AOC is approved for traditional method sparkling wines made from Pinot Blanc, Pinot Gris, Riesling, Chardonnay, Pinot Noir, and/or Auxerrois. Crémant d'Alsace accounts for approximately 23% of the wine produced in Alsace.

Wines that do not adhere to the appellation rules, such as still wines made from Chardonnay, are declassified as Wine, since no IGP exists for the region.

Alsace Wine Styles

Placing the emphasis on the grape variety, typical Alsace white wines are single variety, with aromatic, fresh-fruit-driven profiles and moderate acidity. There is little to no use of oak, even for red wines.

Blends of the permitted white varieties, though not common, are allowed and are labeled as "Edelzwicker." Those blends produced with a minimum of 50% of the noble varieties may include the designation "Gentil" on the label. In addition, a wine labeled simply as "Pinot" or "Pinot d'Alsace" may contain any quantity of Pinot Blanc, Pinot Gris, Pinot Noir, or Auxerrois, vinified as a white wine.

Most Alsatian whites are fermented dry, a style for which Alsace has long been noted. However, in recent years, warmer summers have produced a series of vintages with grapes so concentrated in sugar that they often do not ferment completely dry. Thus, although the wines are not intentionally made sweet, many

LEADING GRAPES OF ALSACE

Red Grapes	White Grapes
Pinot Noir	Riesling
	Pinot Blanc
	Gewurztraminer
	Pinot Gris
	Sylvaner
	Muscat*
	Chasselas
	Auxerrois
	Klevener de Heiligenstein
	Chardonnay

*Includes Muscat Blanc à Petits Grains, Muscat Rosé à Petits Grains, and Muscat Ottonel

Figure 9–17: Leading Grapes of Alsace

Alsace whites in the last few years have had noticeable residual sugar as well as high alcohol levels.

Alsace is also highly regarded for its excellent dessert wines. Among these, there are two distinct styles of wine:

- *Vendange tardive* is produced from late-harvested grapes, which may or may not be affected by botrytis (these wines can be made into a dry style, as well).
- *Sélection de grains nobles* indicates a sweet wine made from botrytis-affected grapes.

BURGUNDY (BOURGOGNE)

Burgundy is another French wine region that is among the world's greatest. Burgundy is renowned for elegant, silky, complex Pinot Noirs and well-structured dry white wines produced from Chardonnay.

Compared to Bordeaux, Burgundy has only about one-fourth the acreage and produces about one-quarter of the volume of wine (71,500 acres [29,000 ha] and nearly 17 million cases). The ownership of the vineyard land is notoriously splintered, due to both the French Revolution (during which the Church's and aristocracy's vineyards were expropriated and redistributed to peasant supporters) and the Napoleonic Code of inheritance, which dictated that land was to be inherited equally by all heirs, forcing the repeated division of privately held land among numerous people.

As a result, many growers are not able to make enough of their own wine to be profitable, so they sell their grapes to négociants. Even named vineyards often have multiple owners, leading to a situation where many different producers may make competing wines from the same vineyard.

Geography and Climate

Burgundy is located in eastern central France, east of the Loire Valley wine regions, south of Champagne, and southwest of Alsace. Burgundy, *Bourgogne* in French, was once a powerful duchy with a long and dramatic history both before and after it came under the French Crown in the fifteenth century. Today, Burgundy is part of the Bourgogne-French Comté region of France. The wine-producing areas of Burgundy are divided into the four distinct vineyard areas of Chablis, the Côte d'Or, the Côte Chalonnaise, and the Mâconnais.

Chablis is about 80 miles (129 km) from the Côte d'Or and is actually closer to the Aube district of Champagne than it is to the vineyards of Burgundy. The weather in Chablis is essentially the same as that in Champagne: cold winters and cool summers, which makes it difficult to fully ripen grapes. However, Chablis's vineyards are slightly farther south and are located on and around the south-facing slopes of a celebrated outcropping of Kimmeridgian marl, which provides better sun, some protection from northerly winds, and an excellent base of mineral nutrients.

The Côte d'Or lies southwest of the city of Dijon along a narrow limestone ridge that parallels the west bank of the Saône River. The Côte d'Or is divided into two segments: the Côte de Nuits to the north and the Côte de Beaune to the south. The Côte de Nuits takes its name from the town of Nuits-St.-Georges, and the Côte de Beaune is named for the town of Beaune, the commercial heart of Burgundy's wine trade. A wide belt of hills to the north and west of the Côte d'Or provides shelter from the chilly influence of the Atlantic, resulting in a more fully continental climate of hot summers and cold winters. Summer hailstorms are a bigger concern than winter gales.

Farther south, the Côte Chalonnaise and the much larger Mâconnais share the general geographical characteristics of the Côte d'Or, but their slightly more southerly site closer to the Mediterranean helps to moderate the winter temperatures. The limestone that is so important to Burgundy's terroir is less prevalent here.

Grape Varieties

The legendary wines of Burgundy are made primarily from Chardonnay and Pinot Noir, two local grape varieties that have become favorites worldwide. Chardonnay, which accounts for 60% of production, is grown throughout the region. Pinot Noir, likewise, is grown throughout the region, with the exception of Chablis. Pinot Noir dominates in the Côte de Nuits but becomes much less prevalent as one moves south. Gamay is grown in small amounts in the region, primarily in the Mâconnais. Aligoté is a minor second white variety of Burgundy. A handful of other grape varieties—including César, Pinot Gris, Pinot Blanc, and even Sauvignon Blanc and Sauvignon Gris—are grown in small amounts, and are approved for use in a few appellations.

LEADING GRAPES OF BURGUNDY

Red Grapes	White Grapes
Pinot Noir	Chardonnay
Gamay	Aligoté

Figure 9-19: Leading Grapes of Burgundy

Burgundy Wine Styles

Over 90% of the wines exported from Burgundy to other markets are dry and still; the remainder is crémant. Hallmarks of the Burgundy style include moderate alcohol, acidity, and tannin; complexity in aromas and flavors; and a characteristic earthiness. While minor grape varieties are allowed, most white wines are 100% Chardonnay, and most reds are 100% Pinot Noir.

Main Wine Regions of Burgundy

Figure 9-18: Burgundy region

The distinctive terroir of Chablis produces Chardonnay wines with a pronounced minerality or "flinty" character that is not common elsewhere in Burgundy. Chablis also has considerable acidity. South of Chablis, the Chardonnays are richer and less sharply acidic.

In the Côte d'Or, both the whites and reds have multilayered aroma profiles suggestive of wet earth, the outdoors, forest undergrowth, or farmland. Additional elements from oak aging and the typical varietal characteristics of Chardonnay and Pinot Noir are also present. Both whites and reds from the best vineyards can continue to improve and increase in complexity for decades. The wines of the Côte Chalonnaise and the Mâconnais also exhibit some of this same complexity, but in a lighter style.

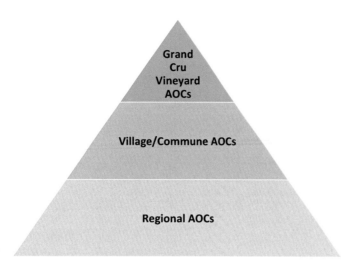

Figure 9-20: Burgundy appellations

Burgundy Classification

Burgundy is made up of many different plots of land, referred to as *climats*, with very precise boundaries based on terroir. These distinct vineyards are classified according to their quality. The highest-ranking sites are designated *grand cru* (great growth), with the second tier designated as *premier cru* (first growth). This classification differs significantly from that of Bordeaux in that the vineyard land is classified in Burgundy, whereas the classifications of Bordeaux are attributed to the châteaux themselves.

The grands crus, of which there are 33, are each granted an AOC of their own, named after the vineyard. The more than 600 premiers crus, on the other hand, do not qualify as separate AOCs; they fall under the appellation of their commune. However, a wine from a premier cru climat is allowed to include the vineyard name and "Premier Cru" or "1er Cru" on the label alongside the commune name. Vineyards that are neither grand nor premier cru may also be named on a wine label with the commune name if the grapes in the wine came from the named vineyard.

Despite the large number of premiers crus, they are relatively easy to spot because the label will usually state "Premier Cru" or "1er Cru" along with the vineyard name and the commune name. On a premier cru label, the name of the commune will come first and will typically be in larger type.

The appellation names of the 33 grands crus and the various communes, however, tend to look quite similar on many wine labels. It is thus helpful that many times the phrase *Grand Cru* will appear on the label of a wine designated as such. However, to really know the status of a Burgundy wine, sometimes there is no alternative to consulting a list, mental or otherwise. Adding to the difficulty, several communes decided years ago to take advantage of free self-promotion by appending the name of one of their grand cru vineyards to their own name. Only experience or an inventory will reveal that Griotte-Chambertin is a grand cru vineyard, while Gevrey-Chambertin is a commune- or village-level wine.

Burgundy Appellations

As of December 2021, the Burgundy region contains over 80 separate appellations for quality wines, testimony to the numerous variations in soil and climate along with its history of designating specific vineyards by terroir. These appellations are often overlapping and/or nested, and it is quite common for small, vineyard-specific AOCs to lie within one or more of the larger communal or regional appellations.

There are half a dozen appellations that cover the entire Burgundy wine region, of which the most important by far is AOC Bourgogne, a generic appellation for white, red, or rosé wines from anywhere in the area. The AOC Bourgogne includes 14 sub-appellations for specific parts of the region, including the Bourgogne Côte d'Or, Bourgogne La Chapelle Notre-Dame, and Bourgogne Tonnerre AOCs. Other regional appellations of Burgundy include Crémant de Bourgogne—for traditional method sparkling wines (white and rosé)—and Bourgogne Aligoté.

Chablis

The Chablis region produces white wine exclusively, and Chardonnay is the only permitted grape. Its prime land comprises the Chablis Grand Cru AOC. The majority of the vineyard area surrounding both the Chablis Grand Cru and the town of Chablis qualifies for Chablis AOC status.

The renowned 254-acre (103-ha) Chablis Grand Cru vineyard is located on a hill northeast of the town. This single vineyard is divided into seven parcels whose names normally appear on the wine's label. They are, from largest to smallest: Les Clos, Vaudésir, Bougros, Blanchot, Les Preuses, Valmur, and Grenouilles.

The 40 premier cru vineyards (created from 79 eligible climats) within the Chablis AOC region are generally grouped in 17 "principal" premiers crus. The best known of these include Fourchaume, Montée de Tonnerre, Vaillons, Mont de Milieu, and Vosgros. The vineyards of the Petit Chablis appellation are tucked between and around some of the more prestigious vineyards, and occupy primarily those areas where the soils and sun exposure are significantly less desirable.

The Côte d'Or

The top vineyards of the Côte d'Or and the wines they produce are some of the most famous in the world. The district includes 32 of Burgundy's 33 grand cru vineyards (the other being Chablis Grand Cru). The two parts of the Côte d'Or are differentiated by subtle variations in soil, topography, and climate that make the northern subregion of the Côte de Nuits ideal for Pinot Noir, and the southern subregion of the Côte de Beaune better for Chardonnay.

The Côte de Nuits is the spiritual home of Pinot Noir, which makes up almost 90% of its production. It has 24 grand cru vineyards, all of which are for red wine, with the exception of Musigny, which also produces a tiny amount of Chardonnay. Its commune appellations are Marsannay, Fixin, Gevrey-Chambertin, Morey-St.-Denis, Chambolle-Musigny, Vougeot, Vosne-Romanée, and Nuits-St.-Georges. Some of the best-known grands crus of this part of the Côte d'Or are Chambertin, Musigny, Clos de Vougeot, and Romanée-Conti.

Chablis

Note: The premier cru vineyards indicated on the map represent the groupings of the 17 "major" premiers crus of Chablis.

Copyright: The Society of Wine Educators 2016

Figure 9-21: Chablis

Grand Cru
Premier Cru
Chablis
Petit Chablis

The Côte de Beaune is known as a white wine region, although just over half of its production is actually red. However, seven of its eight grands crus produce only white wine, and it is the superb quality of these Chardonnays that has earned the Côte de Beaune its reputation. (The eighth grand cru, Corton, is mostly red, producing only a small amount of white wine.) The primary communes of the Côte de Beaune are Aloxe-Corton, Pernand-Vergelesses, Beaune, Pommard, Volnay, Meursault, Puligny-Montrachet, Chassagne-Montrachet, and Ladoix-Serrigny.

The Côte Chalonnaise

The Côte Chalonnaise is located just south of the Côte d'Or, west of the town of Chalon-sur-Saône, from which it derives its name. It produces a good amount of commune-level wine every year and is a large source for regional-level wines, especially Aligoté and sparkling wine. There are five communal AOCs, of which the largest is Mercurey; there are no

The Côte de Nuits

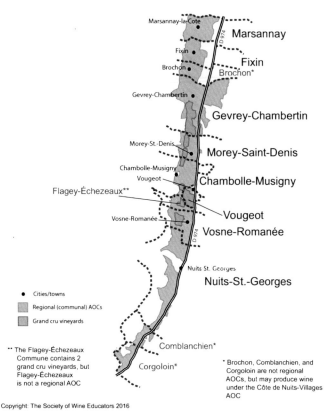

Marsannay-la-Cote
Marsannay
Fixin
Fixin
Brochon
Brochon*
Gevrey-Chambertin
Gevrey-Chambertin
Morey-St.-Denis
Morey-Saint-Denis
Chambolle-Musigny
Chambolle-Musigny
Vougeot
Vougeot
Flagey-Échezeaux**
Vosne-Romanée
Vosne-Romanée
Nuits St. Georges
Nuits-St.-Georges

● Cities/towns
▨ Regional (communal) AOCs
▨ Grand cru vineyards

Comblanchien*
Corgoloin*

** The Flagey-Échezeaux Commune contains 2 grand cru vineyards, but Flagey-Échezeaux is not a regional AOC

* Brochon, Comblanchien, and Corgoloin are not regional AOCs, but may produce wine under the Côte de Nuits-Villages AOC

Copyright: The Society of Wine Educators 2016

Figure 9–22: Côte de Nuits

only. The Mâconnais area is also home to five specific white wine-only AOCs—Pouilly-Fuissé, St.-Véran, Pouilly-Loché, Pouilly-Vinzelles, and Viré-Clessé. These five appellations are also approved for white wines produced from 100% Chardonnay only.

The Yonne Département

Just to the south (and slightly west) of Chablis, there are several small—and in some cases, quite unique—appellations located within the Yonne Département of Burgundy. The newest of these is Vézelay AOC, approved in 2017 for dry white wines produced using 100% Chardonnay. Irancy AOC is approved for dry red wines using primarily Pinot Noir, with up to 10% (combined) César or Pinot Gris allowed. The Saint-Bris AOC—long considered a Burgundian outlier—is approved for dry white wines made from Sauvignon Blanc and/or Sauvignon Gris.

The Burgundy Wine Trade

The fragmentation of vineyard ownership here has resulted in over 4,000 domaines. The quintessential example is the grand cru vineyard Clos de Vougeot. Prior to the French Revolution, this 125-acre (51-ha) vineyard belonged to the Catholic Church; today, it has some 80 owners. In any given vintage, more than a hundred different Clos de Vougeot wines are produced, varying in quality from good to exceptional.

The average grower's holding in Burgundy is about 15 acres (6 ha), usually scattered among several appellations. This creates an important opportunity for négociants-éleveurs, who buy grapes from these small domaines and make a blended wine sold under the négociant's own label. The négociant trade represents about three-quarters of Burgundy's annual wine output, but a growing number of small domaines, especially in the Côte d'Or, have begun bottling and marketing at least a portion of their own wines. In addition, there are several growers' cooperatives, mostly in the Mâconnais.

grands crus, but there is an array of premiers crus. In addition, a unique white wine using 100% Aligoté is produced in the Bouzeron AOC.

The Mâconnais

The southernmost part of Burgundy proper is the Mâconnais, which lies directly north of Beaujolais. This relatively large district is well-known for its Chardonnay-based white wine, however, the area does produce a small amount of red and rosé as well. More than 90% of the vineyards here are planted to Chardonnay, with the remainder planted largely to Gamay and Pinot Noir.

The district-wide appellation, the Mâcon AOC, is approved for the production of red, white, and rosé. The Mâcon AOC includes twenty-seven specific villages (geographical designations) that have earned the right to append their name to the region's name on the label, such as Mâcon-Lugny or Mâcon-Verzé. However, most of the wine produced in the Mâconnais falls into the higher-level Mâcon-Villages designation, which is approved for 100% Chardonnay-based white wines

The Côte de Beaune

Figure 9-23: Côte de Beaune

BEAUJOLAIS

Beaujolais is technically a part of Burgundy, and the two areas are often grouped together on account of their proximity. However, apart from some blurring of boundaries with the Mâconnais, the two areas do not have a lot in common. Beaujolais is devoted to the Gamay grape, has a different terroir, and produces its own unique style of wine. Beaujolais, whose harvests have been declining, now produces about 9.4 million cases of wine annually.

Geography and Climate

Beaujolais is situated directly south of the Mâconnais along the Saône River. By virtue of its more southerly position, Beaujolais is somewhat warmer than Burgundy and begins to see some moderation in the continental climate due to the closer proximity of the Mediterranean Sea. The most significant difference in terroir between Beaujolais and Burgundy, however, is in the soils; Beaujolais has granitic soils that are ideal for Gamay, rather than the limestone that defines Burgundy.

Grape Varieties

Gamay comprises about 95% of the approximately 50,000 acres (20,200 ha) of grapevines planted in Beaujolais. The remainder of the vineyards are planted mainly to Chardonnay, Aligoté, and Pinot Noir; small amounts of Melon de Bourgogne and Pinot Gris are found as well.

Beaujolais Wine Styles

Wines of Beaujolais are generally intended for early consumption rather than for extended aging. They typically exhibit bright red fruit aromas and flavors with tropical notes that are characteristic of the carbonic maceration technique commonly employed for at least a portion of the fermentation. This process produces exceptionally fruity, low-tannin wines with a vivid purple-ruby color that can be ready to drink almost as soon as the fermentation is complete. In fact, a considerable volume is bottled within weeks of the fermentation and sold worldwide as "nouveau" or "primeur" beginning on the third Thursday in November. The release of Beaujolais Nouveau is celebrated each year as one of the first French wines of the vintage.

However, despite the reputation for these light wines, in the northernmost part of the district, where the granite soil is most prevalent, Gamay can have a more substantial character. Made by using more typical production techniques, the wines from this area are often richer, more structured, and capable of improving with a couple of years of bottle aging. These wines represent the best expression of Gamay and can be remarkably similar to Pinot Noir in nature.

Beaujolais Appellations

There are 11 appellations in the Beaujolais district: Beaujolais (which now includes those wines that, prior to 2011, were bottled under the Beaujolais-Villages AOC), and a group of ten villages designated as the Beaujolais Crus. While the great majority of the wine produced in the area is red, white and rosé wines are authorized under the Beaujolais AOC as well. Much of the wine considered to be "standard" Beaujolais AOC is produced from Gamay grapes grown in the

Table 9-4: Burgundy Appellations

BURGUNDY APPELLATIONS			White	Red	Rosé	Sparkling
Appellation						
Regional	**Bourgogne**		•	•	•	
	Bourgogne Aligoté		•			
	Bourgogne Mousseux					•
	Crémant de Bourgogne					•
	Bourgogne Passe-Tout-Grains			•	•	
	Coteaux Bourguignons		•	•	•	
Chablis	**Chablis**		•			
	Chablis Grand Cru	GC	•			
	Petit Chablis		•			
Côte de Nuits	**Marsannay**		•	•	•	
	Fixin		•	•		
	Gevrey-Chambertin			•		
	• Chambertin	Grands Crus		•		
	• Chambertin-Clos-de-Bèze			•		
	• Chapelle-Chambertin			•		
	• Charmes-Chambertin			•		
	• Griotte-Chambertin			•		
	• Latricières-Chambertin			•		
	• Mazis-Chambertin			•		
	• Mazoyères-Chambertin			•		
	• Ruchottes-Chambertin			•		
	Morey-St.-Denis		•	•		
	• Clos St.-Denis	Grands Crus		•		
	• Clos de la Roche			•		
	• Clos des Lambrays			•		
	• Clos de Tart			•		
	• Bonnes Mares, small part			•		
	Chambolle-Musigny			•		
	• Bonnes Mares	GC		•		
	• Musigny		•	•		
	Vougeot	GC	•	•		
	• Clos de Vougeot			•		
	Vosne-Romanée			•		
	• Échezeaux*	Grands Crus		•		
	• Grands-Échezeaux*			•		
	• La Grande Rue			•		
	• Richebourg			•		
	• La Romanée			•		
	• Romanée-Conti			•		
	• Romanée-St.-Vivant			•		
	• La Tâche			•		

Note: The grand cru vineyards of Échezeaux and Grands-Échezeaux are actually located in the commune of Flagey-Échezeaux; however, there is no communal appellation for Flagey-Échezeaux, so they are typically categorized under the heading of their neighbor, Vosne-Romanée.

Table 9-4: Burgundy Appellations, *continued*

BURGUNDY APPELLATIONS			White	Red	Rosé	Sparkling
Côte de Nuits	Nuits-St.-Georges		•	•		
	Côte-de-Nuits-Villages		•	•		
Côte de Beaune	Ladoix-Serrigny		•	•		
	GC	• Corton, part	•	•		
		• Corton-Charlemagne, part	•			
	Aloxe-Corton		•	•		
		• Charlemagne, part	•			
	GC	• Corton, part	•	•		
		• Corton-Charlemagne, part	•			
	Pernand-Vergelesses		•	•		
		• Charlemagne, part	•			
	GC	• Corton, part	•	•		
		• Corton-Charlemagne, part	•			
	Chorey-lès-Beaune		•	•		
	Savigny-lès-Beaune		•	•		
	Beaune		•	•		
	Pommard			•		
	Volnay			•		
	Monthélie		•	•		
	Auxey-Duresses		•	•		
	St.-Romain		•	•		
	Meursault		•	•		
	Blagny			•		
	Puligny-Montrachet		•	•		
	Grands Crus	• Montrachet, part	•			
		• Bâtard-Montrachet, part	•			
		• Chevalier-Montrachet	•			
		• Bienvenue-Bâtard-Montrachet	•			
	Chassagne-Montrachet		•	•		
		• Montrachet, part	•			
	GC	• Bâtard-Montrachet, part	•			
		• Criots-Bâtard-Montrachet	•			
	St.-Aubin		•	•		
	Santenay		•	•		
	Maranges		•	•		
	Côte de Beaune		•	•		
	Côte-de-Beaune-Villages			•		

BURGUNDY APPELLATIONS		White	Red	Rosé	Sparkling
Appellation					
Côte Chalonnaise	Rully	•	•		
	Bouzeron	•			
	Mercurey	•	•		
	Givry	•	•		
	Montagny	•			
Mâconnais	Mâcon	•	•	•	
	Mâcon + village name	•	•	•	
	Mâcon-Villages	•			
	Pouilly-Fuissé	•			
	Pouilly-Loché	•			
	Pouilly-Vinzelles	•			
	St.-Véran	•			
	Viré-Clessé	•			
Yonne Département	Irancy		•		
	Saint-Bris	•			
	Vézelay	•			

southern part of the region; of this, approximately one-half is sold, beginning on the third Thursday of November, as Beaujolais Nouveau.

Within the Beaujolais AOC, there are 38 designated villages that are allowed to use the term "Beaujolais-Villages" on a Beaujolais AOC wine label. Wines labeled as such must meet the somewhat higher standards detailed for a Beaujolais-Villages wine, including higher minimums for alcohol by volume, riper grapes at harvest, and lower allowed yields. These villages are primarily located in the midsection of the region, generally north of the area that grows grapes for use in the "basic" Beaujolais AOC. Ten of the most northern villages, the Beaujolais crus, are considered to produce superior red wines and have each earned AOC status for themselves. These wines are marketed with only the name of the village on the label. Among the best known are Moulin-à-Vent, Fleurie, and Morgon. As a group, the crus produce a third of the wine of Beaujolais.

Table 9–5: Beaujolais Cru Styles

BEAUJOLAIS CRU STYLES		
Lighter Styles	Fuller-Bodied Styles	Age-Worthy Styles
Chiroubles	Brouilly	Chénas
Fleurie	Côte de Brouilly	Moulin-à-Vent
St.-Amour	Juliénas	Morgon
	Régnié	

Wine Regions of Beaujolais

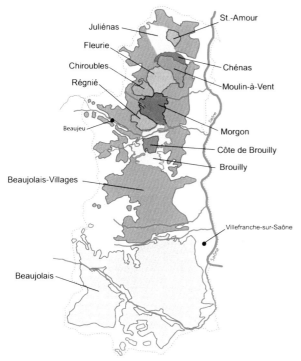

Copyright: The Society of Wine Educators 2022

Figure 9-24: Beaujolais

THE RHÔNE VALLEY

The Rhône Valley, like the Loire Valley, makes more sense as a geographical unit rather than as a viticultural area. The region is made up of two rather distinct districts—referred to as the Northern Rhône Valley and Southern Rhône Valley—both located along the banks of the Rhône River, but with significant differences in terms of both terroir and wine styles. Nevertheless, this is clearly big red wine country. It is also one of the oldest winegrowing areas of what is now France, with a collection of indigenous grape varieties grown alongside the more recognizable varieties of Syrah and Grenache. The Rhône Valley produces over 37 million cases of wine annually, making it the second largest producer of AOC-level wine after Bordeaux.

Geography and Climate

The prime viticultural areas of the Rhône Valley lie on either side of the Rhône River beginning roughly 20 miles (32 km) south of the city of Lyon and ending approximately 120 miles (193 km) south at the city of Avignon. The area is clearly divided into two subregions, north and south, separated by a 30-mile (48-km) gap.

The northern Rhône vineyards lie in a narrow strip about 45 miles (72 km) in length along both banks of the river. The valley is steep-sided through much of this stretch of river as it passes through the divide between the Massif Central and the French Alps; it had to be terraced to allow vines to be planted. The climate is still more continental than Mediterranean, with hot summers and cold winters. The northernmost appellation in the Northern Rhône Valley, Côte-Rôtie, has some of the steepest vineyards in France—with gradients as high as 55° or more in spots.

The vineyards of the southern Rhône are situated below the point at which the Rhône breaks out of the mountains and opens into a broad area of lowlands that run all the way to the Mediterranean. This area enjoys the Mediterranean climate of the South of France, with abundant sunshine, warm temperatures, and minimal precipitation during the growing season, although there can be sudden, violent rainstorms. One well-known feature of the southern Rhône's terroir is a profusion of large rounded stones called *galets* that have been washed down from the mountains and cover the ground in several places, especially around Châteauneuf-du-Pape.

In both sections of the Rhône Valley, but more intensely in the south, the strong, cold wind from the north known as the *mistral* can impact the local climate and damage the grapevines.

Figure 9-25: Vineyards in Châteauneuf-du-Pape

Grape Varieties

The roster of grape varieties grown in the northern and southern Rhône is one of the main differences between the two sections. The north is fairly straightforward: Syrah is the only red variety; the whites are Viognier, Marsanne, and Roussanne.

In the south, over two dozen grape varieties are allowed, and wines are normally based on a blend of at least three or four. The most important of the southern Rhône varieties by far is Grenache, accounting for two-thirds of the red grapes. Among the other permitted red grapes are Syrah, Carignan, Mourvèdre, and Cinsault. The dominant white grape is also Grenache—Grenache Blanc, a white mutation of Grenache Noir. Clairette, an aromatic white variety, is also widespread, along with smaller amounts of Viognier, Ugni Blanc, Roussanne, Marsanne, Muscat, and others. All of these grapes are considered "Rhône varieties" among the international grapes adopted in other countries.

Wine Regions of the Rhône Valley

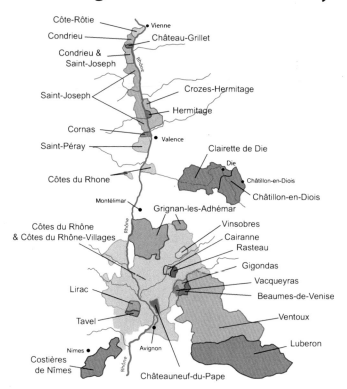

Copyright: The Society of Wine Educators 2016

Figure 9-27: Rhône Valley region

LEADING GRAPES OF THE RHÔNE VALLEY	
Red Grapes	**White Grapes**
Grenache Noir	Viognier
Syrah	Grenache Blanc
Carignan	Clairette
Cinsault	Marsanne
Mourvèdre	Roussanne

Figure 9-26: Leading Grapes of the Rhône Valley

Rhône Valley Wine Styles

Red wine is the standard fare for the Rhône Valley, north and south. The Syrahs of the north are typically deeply colored, tannic, powerful, and long-lived. The wines of the south, based on Grenache, have less tannin and pigment but are still high in alcohol. They are lower in acidity and potentially quite concentrated.

While accounting for a relatively small 9% of production, rosé is a particular area of expertise. Due to its low tannin levels and attractive color, Grenache is often a key component of Rhône rosé. Rhône rosés are relatively hearty, deeply colored, and full flavored.

White wines account for only 5% of the region's output. A few appellations are well regarded for dry, sweet fortified, or sparkling wines. The Viognier of the northern Rhône, for example, has set a benchmark for the proliferation of Viognier around the world. These wines are full-bodied, viscous, and very aromatic.

Rhône Valley Appellations

The northern Rhône is relatively compact, but its varying terroirs have been divided into eight appellations. Among the reds, Côte-Rôtie, Hermitage, and Cornas are small, commune-size AOCs that are highly regarded for their excellent, long-aging wines. St.-Joseph and Crozes-Hermitage are larger AOCs that have a little more variability in terms of wine quality. Of these, only Cornas requires 100% Syrah. The other red wine appellations of the northern Rhône allow a small proportion of white grapes to be mixed with the Syrah (Viognier for Côte Rôtie; Marsanne and Roussanne for the others).

While the northern Rhône is indisputably red wine country, three appellations are approved for white wine only. Two of these, Condrieu AOC and the tiny

Château-Grillet AOC, produce highly regarded wines from 100% Viognier. Saint-Péray AOC produces still and sparkling white wines from a blend of Marsanne and Roussanne.

The southern Rhône covers much more ground than the northern vineyards and is the source for 95% of the Rhône's total production. The regional Côtes du Rhône appellation covers most of the area (including the northern Rhône, although wine from the north rarely sacrifices a more famous appellation for the Côtes du Rhône label) and by itself accounts for more than half of the Rhône Valley's output. The Côtes du Rhône AOC is approved for red, white, and rosé wines produced from a range of permitted Rhône grape varieties. Most of the wine is produced at cooperatives.

More than 90 villages within the Côtes du Rhône AOC (all in the southern Rhône) are allowed to use the Côtes du Rhône-Villages appellation. Of these, 22 are permitted to append their names as official subzone designations to the name "Côtes du Rhône-Villages." The Côtes du Rhône-Villages appellation has somewhat stricter production standards than the basic Côtes du Rhône in terms of yield, vine density, minimum alcohol levels, and other such factors.

Table 9–6: Grapes Authorized for Use in Châteauneuf-du-Pape

GRAPES AUTHORIZED FOR USE IN CHÂTEAUNEUF-DU-PAPE
Grenache–Noir, Gris, and Blanc
Mourvèdre
Syrah
Cinsault
Counoise
Bourboulenc
Roussanne
Brun Argenté (Vaccarèse)
Clairette, Clairette Rosé
Muscardin
Picardan
Piquepoul–Noir, Gris, and Blanc
Terret Noir

Note: All grapes are authorized for use in the red wines of the region, but white must is required to be blended together with red must before fermentation.

A few other communes have distinguished themselves sufficiently enough to warrant their own AOCs. Foremost among them is Châteauneuf-du-Pape, known for its hearty red blend of 13 (or 18, depending on how they are counted) grapes, as well as a small amount of white wine. (See table 9–6 for a list of the grapes authorized for use in the wines of Châteauneuf-du-Pape.) The nearby AOCs of Gigondas, Lirac, Rasteau, Cairanne, and Vacqueyras are also known for hearty red blends (although small amounts of white and rosé are produced in some areas as well).

The southern Rhône is also home to several producers of sweet wine. Muscat de Beaumes-de-Venise is a vin doux naturel made from the Muscat grape variety; it has an alcohol level of 15% or more and a minimum of 10% residual sugar. While usually produced as a white wine, rosé and red versions of Muscat de Beaumes-de-Venise are made as well, using red Muscat grapes in addition to white. Another vin doux naturel, this one based on Grenache (including its noir, blanc, and gris versions), is produced in the Rasteau appellation. Rasteau vin doux naturel is generally red, although white, tawny, and rosé versions are also produced.

The southern Rhône appellation of Tavel produces rosé exclusively. Tavel rosé, made primarily from Grenache and Cinsault, is considered to be one of the finest dry rosés of France.

Four small appellations are located about 25 miles (40 km) southeast of Cornas on the Drôme River (a Rhône tributary). These include the Clairette de Die AOC, which produces traditional method sparkling wines as well as a historically significant, sweet sparkling white wine made using the Méthode Ancestrale Dioise.

The nearby Crémant de Die AOC produces dry, traditional method sparkling wines. Grapes used in the sparkling wines include Clairette, Muscat, and Aligoté. Still wines are also produced in the area: the Coteaux de Die AOC produces dry, still white from 100% Clairette, and the Châtillon-en-Diois AOC produces dry white wines from Chardonnay and Aligoté, as well as rosés and reds from Gamay, Pinot Noir, and Syrah.

Table 9–7: Rhône Valley Appellations

RHÔNE VALLEY APPELLATIONS					
Appellation	White	Rosé	Red	Fortified	Sparkling
Regional					
Côtes du Rhône	•	•	•		
Côtes du Rhône-Villages	•	•	•		
Northern Rhône					
Château-Grillet	•				
Condrieu	•				
Cornas			•		
Côte-Rôtie			•		
Crozes-Hermitage	•		•		
Hermitage	•		•		
St.-Joseph	•		•		
St.-Péray	•				•
Diois					
Châtillon-en-Diois	•	•	•		
Clairette de Die					•
Coteaux de Die	•				
Crémant de Die					•
Southern Rhône					
Beaumes-de-Venise			•		
Châteauneuf-du-Pape	•		•		
Gigondas		•	•		
Grignan-les-Adhémar	•	•	•		
Lirac	•	•	•		
Muscat de Beaumes-de-Venise				•	
Cairanne	•	•	•		
Rasteau			•	•	
Tavel		•			
Vacqueyras	•	•	•		
Vinsobres			•		
Outlying Regions					
Clairette de Bellegarde	•				
Costières de Nîmes	•	•	•		
Côtes du Vivarais	•	•	•		
Duché d'Uzès	•	•	•		
Luberon	•	•	•		
Ventoux	•	•	•		

The Southern Rhône Valley wine region includes six appellations located outside the boundaries of the Côtes du Rhône AOC in the hills to the east and west of the Rhône River. Five of these—Ventoux AOC, Costières de Nîmes AOC, Luberon AOC, Duché d'Uzès AOC, and Côtes de Vivarais AOC—produce white, red, and rosé wines from an assortment of typical Rhône varieties. The sixth—the tiny Clairette de Bellegarde AOC—produces a small amount of white wine from 100% Clairette.

SOUTHWEST FRANCE

The large, rather spread-out area referred to as Southwest France (*Sud-Ouest*) comprises those vineyards and appellations located south and southeast of Bordeaux. This area is not covered under a general AOC; rather, it can be defined so as to include those appellations located within the Comté Tolosan IGP. Winemaking in this area has been traced as far back as 125 BCE. Bordeaux's key grapes, Cabernet Sauvignon, Cabernet Franc, and Merlot, are planted here, as are the Rhône Valley's Syrah and Beaujolais's Gamay. Even more remarkable, these same grapes come together in a single glass.

Other, less familiar varieties found in the region include the white grapes Petit Manseng, Gros Manseng, Mauzac, and Arrufiac. Red grapes include Fer Servadou, Prunelard, and Négrette, among many others. The vast diversity is impressive; the styles of wines produced include tannic reds, easy-drinking reds, dry whites, sweet whites, and even sparkling wines produced by ancient methods that predate Champagne's rise to prominence.

The Malbec-based "black wine" of Cahors and the powerful reds produced from the Tannat grape variety in the Madiran AOC are among the best-known wines of Southwest France. Others include Gaillac, which produces a wide range of wine styles, and Jurançon (not to be confused with the Jura, located in northeast France), which produces both dry and sweet whites.

SOUTHERN FRANCE

The wine growing areas of the South of France include the island of Corsica (which will be discussed later in this chapter) and the regions of Roussillon, Languedoc, and Provence, which stretch along the Mediterranean coast between Spain and Italy. In general, this picturesque area consists of low, rolling hills occasionally punctuated by rugged ridges. The climate is Mediterranean with ample sun, low humidity, little rainfall, and moderate temperatures during the growing season. Winters range from chilly to cold but are never severe.

LEADING GRAPES OF THE LANGUEDOC-ROUSSILLON

Red Grapes	White Grapes
Syrah	Chardonnay
Grenache Noir	Sauvignon Blanc
Carignan	Muscat Blanc à Petits Grains
Merlot	Grenache Blanc
Cabernet Sauvignon	Viognier
Cinsault	Muscat of Alexandria
Mourvèdre	
Cabernet Franc	
Alicante Bouschet	

Figure 9–28: Leading Grapes of the Languedoc-Roussillon

Red grapes thrive in the warm climate of the south of France with many vineyards planted to Syrah, Grenache, Mourvèdre, Merlot, and Cabernet Sauvignon. Accessory red varieties include Cinsault, Carignan, and Terret Noir (among others). The primary white varieties of this area include Chardonnay, Sauvignon Blanc, Viognier, Clairette, and Muscat.

Wine styles in this geographically diverse and huge-volume area are naturally quite varied. While most of the region's output is red, dry, and still; the region also produces white and rosé wines, several sweet dessert wines, and even some sparkling wines.

Wine Regions of the Languedoc-Roussillon

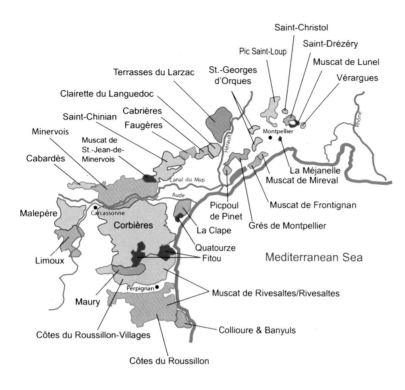

Figure 9-29: Languedoc-Roussillon region

Languedoc-Roussillon

A large amount of the IGP wine produced in France comes from the southern portion of the country. This includes a good deal of wine produced in Languedoc-Roussillon, under the Pays d'Oc IGP, which covers the entire area. More than 50 million cases of Pays d'Oc IGP wine are produced annually, much of it from classic international grape varieties.

The Languedoc AOC (formerly known as the *Coteaux du Languedoc AOC*) covers much of the entire Languedoc-Roussillon area from the Spanish border to the French city of Nîmes. This large appellation allows many growers in the region the opportunity to move up from Pays d'Oc IGP to AOC status for wines based on the grapes traditional to the region. The long list of red grape varieties approved for use in the Languedoc AOC includes Grenache, Syrah, Mourvèdre, Cinsault, and Carignan. White wines are based around the Piquepoul Blanc variety and may include Bourboulenc, Clairette, Grenache Blanc, Marsanne, Roussanne, and Vermentino (among others).

In addition to the over-arching Languedoc AOC, the region is home to over 20 more specific appellations. Perhaps the best-known examples (and the largest areas in terms of production) are Corbières AOC and Minervois AOC. Red wines based on G-S-M (Grenache, Syrah, and Mourvèdre) are the focus in these appellations, but both regions allow for whites and rosés as well. A smaller appellation, Fitou—located in two separate areas, both within the boundaries of the larger Corbières AOC—is one of the oldest AOCs in the area, dating to 1948. Fitou produces red wine only, based on Grenache and Carignan.

In July of 2014, Terrasses du Larzac was approved as an AOC, producing red wine only. Prior to this promotion, the area had been a subzone of the former AOC Coteaux de Languedoc. La Clape, another former subzone, was approved as an AOC in 2015. La Clape AOC produces both red and white wines.

The Languedoc and Roussillon regions are also noted for vins doux naturels and sweet fortified wines. Banyuls AOC and Maury AOC are perhaps best-known for their red vin doux naturel based on the Grenache grape variety, but both also produce white and amber versions based on Grenache Blanc. Muscat de Rivesaltes AOC is a white vin doux natural produced using the Muscat grape (both Muscat Blanc à Petits Grains and Muscat of Alexandria). Muscat de Rivesaltes is also produced in a unique "Christmas version" known as *Muscat de Noël* that must be bottled no later than December 1 of the harvest year.

Sparkling wines are also produced in the area, particularly around the town of Limoux. These include Crémant de Limoux AOC—a traditional method sparkling wine based on Chardonnay—as well as Blanquette de Limoux and Limoux Méthode Ancestrale (both produced under the Limoux AOC and based on the Mauzac grape variety). Limoux Méthode Ancestrale is said to be the oldest purposefully-produced sparkling wine in France.

Table 9–8: Languedoc-Roussillon Appellations

LANGUEDOC-ROUSSILLON APPELLATIONS					
Appellation	White	Rosé	Red	Fortified	Sparkling
Languedoc					
Cabardès		•	•		
Clairette du Languedoc	•			•	
Corbières	•	•	•		
Corbières-Boutenac			•		
Crémant de Limoux					•
Faugères	•		•		
Fitou			•		
La Clape	•		•		
Languedoc	•	•	•		
Limoux	•		•		•
Malepère		•	•		
Minervois	•	•	•		
Minervois-La Livinière			•		
Muscat de Frontignan				•	
Muscat de Lunel				•	
Muscat de Mireval				•	
Muscat de Saint-Jean-de-Minervois				•	
Pic Saint-Loup		•	•		
Picpoul de Pinet	•				
Saint-Chinian	•	•	•		
Terrasses du Larzac			•		
Roussillon					
Banyuls				•	
Banyuls Grand Cru				•	
Collioure	•	•	•		
Côtes du Roussillon	•	•	•		
Côtes du Roussillon Villages	•	•	•		
Grand Roussillon				•	
Maury			•	•	
Muscat de Rivesaltes				•	
Rivesaltes				•	

Provence

Blessed with nearly perfect Mediterranean climatic conditions, Provence prides itself on being the birthplace of all French wine. In fact, winemaking in the region dates to 600 BCE, representing a total of 26 centuries of wine production in France. The regional IGP area is the Méditerranée IGP, but Provence produces much more AOC-level wine than IGP-level. Its largest AOC is Côtes de Provence, which produces (along with its five subzones) a great deal of the region's well-known rosés.

Provence produces only a small amount of red wine (9%), supplemented by an even smaller production of white wine (3.5%). Rosé accounts for nearly 88% of the wine produced in Provence. Provence rosé is generally made from a blend of grapes; the leading grapes include Grenache, Cinsault, Syrah, Mourvèdre, and Tibouren. Provence accounts for 40% of all AOC rosé production in France, making it at least partially responsible for France's position as the number one producer of rosé wine worldwide.

The 65,000 acres (26,300 ha) dedicated to rosé production are centered in three appellations:
- Côtes de Provence, which has five sub-appellations and is the largest, at 75% of overall production
- Coteaux d'Aix-en-Provence, which comprises an additional 15%
- Coteaux Varois en Provence, which accounts for the remaining 10%

Table 9-9: Provence Appellations

PROVENCE APPELLATIONS			
Appellation	White	Rosé	Red
Bandol	•	•	•
Bellet	•	•	•
Cassis	•	•	•
Coteaux d'Aix-en-Provence	•	•	•
Coteaux Varois en Provence	•	•	•
Côtes de Provence	•	•	•
Subzones: Sainte-Victoire		•	•
Fréjus		•	•
La Londe	•	•	•
Pierrefeu		•	•
Notre-Dame des Anges		•	•
Les Baux-de-Provence	•	•	•
Palette	•	•	•
Pierrevert	•	•	•

Bandol, Provence's best-known communal AOC, is known for its rich, aromatic reds and fine, dry rosés that focus on Mourvèdre. Grenache and Cinsault complement the blend, with Carignan and Syrah also planted in the area. The Bandol AOC is also approved for white wines based on the Clairette grape variety.

Corsica

The island of Corsica—located in the Mediterranean Sea about 110 miles (170 km) from the coastline of southeast Provence—has been part of France since 1769. However, geographically speaking, it is closer to Tuscany than France, and the Italian influence is evident in the wines of Corsica. Red wines here are just as likely to be produced from Nielluccio (a grape that is either identical to or closely related to Sangiovese) as they are from grapes more typical to southern France such as Grenache, Mourvèdre, and Syrah. The leading white grape varieties include Muscat à Petits Grains Blanc and Vermentino (also known as Rolle or Malvoisie de Corse).

Corsica has a long history of wine production and, like many other similar regions, has been experiencing a renewed focus on quality. At present, approximately 25% of the island's production is AOC-level wine, with another 50% bottled under the elegantly titled departmental L'Île de Beauté (Isle of Beauty) IGP.

The main AOC of Corsica is the Vin de Corse AOC, which allows for white, red, and rosé wines vinified in dry, off-dry, or semi-sweet styles. White Vin de Corse AOC requires a minimum of 75% Rolle (Vermentino), while red and rosé versions are made with at least 50% (combined) Grenache, Sangiovese, and Sciaccarello (an aromatic, historically significant Tuscan variety also known as Mammolo).

Cap Corse—the mountainous peninsula extending from the northern part of the island—is home to some of Corsica's highest-quality wines, including dry white, red, and rosé wines bottled under the title Coteaux du Cap Corse (a subregion of the Vin de Corse AOC). Muscat du Cap Corse AOC—a vin doux naturel traditionally produced at least partially from sun-dried grapes—is produced using 100% Muscat Blanc à Petits Grains grapes.

Figure 9-30: The port city of Ajaccio, on the west coast of Corsica

ITALY

LEARNING OBJECTIVES

After studying this chapter, the candidate should be able to:

- Identify the general role and position of Italy in the global wine industry.
- Recall the physical location and general climate of Italy's major wine regions.
- Discuss the hierarchy of wine designations from vino to DOCG.
- Recall the grape varieties, wine styles, and important appellations in the Veneto, Piedmont, and Tuscany.
- Identify the major appellations and grapes of other regions in Italy.

Italy's winemaking tradition has been well established for three millennia. In modern times, Italy is recognized as one of the world's leading producers of wine, often vying with France from year to year for the top spot. It has also long been the top wine exporter and is among the biggest wine-consuming nations.

Italian wines cover the full spectrum of wine styles and include excellent examples of whites, reds, rosés, sweet wines, dry wines, still wines, sparkling wines, and fortified wines. Some of Italy's unique wines perpetuate traditional winemaking techniques rarely seen outside the country. There are some Italian wines that are in intense demand, fetch steep prices, and represent classic wine styles that have no direct imitators, as the distinctive Italian grape varieties from which they are made have yet to be widely planted outside of Italy. There is also a large volume of well-made, extremely food-friendly, reasonably priced wine for everyday consumption, much of which finds its way to the United States.

GEOGRAPHY AND CLIMATE

The climate is one of the main reasons that Italy is such a fruitful place for grape growing. Its position in southern Europe is well within the temperate zone where summer days are long and hot, there are clearly recognizable springs and falls, and winters are cold.

Italy's most notable topographic feature is its long Mediterranean coastline. Shaped like a boot, Italy is suspended from the middle of Europe into the Mediterranean Sea. The sea surrounds Italy everywhere except in the north, and few places in the country are more than 75 miles (121 km) from it. The Mediterranean acts as a moderating influence on the weather, reducing the summer heat by a few degrees and warding off the worst winter cold. Nevertheless, there is a considerable difference in climate between the cool northern and hot southern parts of the country.

Regions of Italy

Copyright: The Society of Wine Educators 2016

Figure 10–1: Regions of Italy

The Italian Peninsula is extremely mountainous, with very little flatland except in the Po River Valley in the north, and in Puglia—the heel of the boot.

The rugged terrain, along with continual political discord, served to restrict travel in centuries past, which led to the remarkable profusion of different types of vines and winemaking techniques. The Apennines mountain chain runs the length of the peninsula, and has peaks that reach nearly 10,000 feet (3,048 m). The entire northern border of Italy is formed by the Alps, which rise above 15,000 feet (4,572 m) and form a solid wall to hold back most of the Arctic air masses that strike northern Europe in the winter. The mountains also provide high-altitude vineyard sites with wide diurnal temperature ranges.

Politically, the country is subdivided into 20 administrative regions: 18 on the mainland, plus the two large islands of Sicily and Sardinia located in the Mediterranean to the west of the peninsula. The northern tier is the most prosperous part of

the country, containing the majority of Italy's industrial infrastructure; the cities of Milan, Turin, and Venice; and the rich agricultural lands of the Po River Basin. This area has a relatively cool climate, particularly in the Alpine foothills, and it features some of the most highly respected Italian wine regions, including Piedmont and Veneto.

Tuscany is another internationally renowned Italian wine region, famous not only for its wines but also for its cultural sites and beautiful scenery. Tuscany is situated on the more populated and touristic western coast along the Tyrrhenian Sea. Farther south, the cities of Rome and Naples are also located along the length of the Tyrrhenian coast. The eastern coast, on the Adriatic Sea, is more rural and agricultural and is a major source of wines made from indigenous Italian grapes. The islands, especially Sicily, are widely planted with vineyards.

ITALIAN GRAPE VARIETIES

The wines of Italy are largely reliant upon the country's assortment of indigenous grape varieties, despite the fact that some international grapes have been well established in certain areas of the country for more than a century. Some of Italy's native grapes—such as Sangiovese and Barbera—can now be found throughout the world, while many others—such as Nebbiolo and Cortese—remain planted *almost* exclusively at home.

Sangiovese is the leading red grape of Italy, and while it is grown in many regions, it is known primarily for its use in the most famous wines of Tuscany. Other leading red grapes of Italy include Montepulciano, Barbera, Nero d'Avola, and Primitivo; Merlot and Cabernet Sauvignon are well-represented as well.

Trebbiano Toscano (known elsewhere as Ugni Blanc) and Pinot Grigio (Pinot Gris) are the leading white grapes of the country. Both of these grapes are grown in several regions across the country. Other important white grapes include Glera, Catarratto, Garganega, Moscato (Muscat), and Chardonnay.

Many Italian varieties have been growing in isolated areas for so long that they have diverged into an array of clones or subvarieties with distinct characteristics. Thus, Italian wines made from a given grape variety may vary widely in quality and flavor profile due not only to the differences in terroir, but also to the variations among clones. Some varieties have mutated into red, white, and pink versions. Often, the major subvarieties have names based on locations—such as Trebbiano Toscano—or based on other notable characteristics—such as Sangiovese Grosso (large). There are more than 400 grape varieties allowed for use in the quality wines of Italy; including the subvarieties, the number comes closer to 2,000.

LEADING GRAPES OF ITALY

Red Grapes	White Grapes
Sangiovese	Trebbiano Toscano
Montepulciano	Pinot Grigio
Merlot	Catarratto
Barbera	Chardonnay
Nero d'Avola	Glera
Cabernet Sauvignon	Garganega
Primitivo	Moscato Bianco
Negroamaro	

Figure 10-2: Leading Grapes of Italy

ITALIAN WINE LAWS

Italian efforts to protect the names and origins of wine date back to the early 1700s when the Grand Duchy of Tuscany delineated areas of production for Chianti. Modern Italian wine laws regulate many aspects of wine production, such as which grape varieties can be planted, crop yield, viticultural practices, and winemaking techniques. Although the modern Italian system was modeled after the French appellation contrôlée structure, it developed somewhat differently, resulting in four quality designations instead of three. They are as follows, in order of increasing quality:
- Vino (basic table wine)
- Indicazione geografica tipica (IGT)
- Denominazione di origine controllata (DOC)
- Denominazione di origine controllata e garantita (DOCG)

In principle, the lowest level is basic wine, previously called *vino da tavola*. As in the rest of Europe, the table wine designation was intended for simple wines that were subject to few rules and regulations or whose grapes were grown outside of recognized quality production areas. Initially, no vintage date, grape variety, or zone of production was allowed on the label, but, as elsewhere in the EU, that has now changed (see chapter 8). Wines in this category presently are referred to as either wine (*vino*) or varietal wines (*vini varietali*) and account for approximately 40% of Italy's production.

The *indicazione geografica tipica* (IGT) category was created in 1992, largely in response to winemakers who felt that the DOC/DOCG designations involved excessive restrictions. For example, many wanted to use a grape variety not approved in their area or to modify the percentages of the sanctioned grape varieties in a blend. They felt that by doing so they would produce a higher-quality wine than if they chose to follow the DOC restrictions, yet these often excellent wines would therefore not qualify for any classification level other than basic table wine. Some of these wines met with great commercial success and commanded high prices. Because the first wines of this type were from

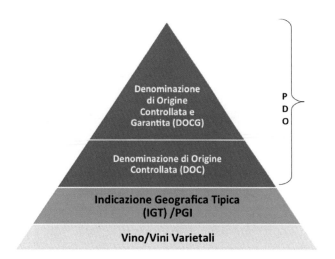

Figure 10-3: Italian wine categories

Tuscany, the term *Super Tuscan* was coined to refer to these outstanding, limited production wines.

In the EU scheme, IGT represents the category of table wine with geographical indication (PGI). These wines must rise to a higher standard of production than basic wines, but the winemakers have considerably more leeway in their choice of grapes and methods than do those producing wines in a higher classification category. IGT wines are allowed to carry a vintage date, the name of a grape variety (provided the wine has at least 85% of the named variety), and the name of the IGT region on the label. There are now close to 120 IGT zones, producing almost 30% of all Italian wine.

PDO wines are divided into two categories in Italy. The primary designation is *denominazione di origine controllata* (DOC). As with other PDO wines, DOC wines are subject to a lengthy set of specifications that are meant to protect the reputation of a place-name by maintaining high standards and by ensuring that the wine fits the typical style of the area.

The *denominazione di origine controllata e garantita* (DOCG) designates a higher level classification among quality (PDO) wines that are not only controlled but also guaranteed. DOCG wines that have been successfully evaluated bear a special, numbered government seal over the cork. Although the category was originally created in 1963, the first DOCGs were not awarded until 1980. Brunello di Montalcino, Barolo, and Vino Nobile di Montepulciano were among the first wines to be awarded DOCG status.

As of December 2021, Italy had 76 DOCGs and just over 330 DOCs, and these numbers are sure to remain in flux for the foreseeable future.

TERMINOLOGY

Within the PDO category of Italian wines, the following terms may be seen on a wine label:

- *Classico* – This term indicates a central or historic subzone within a larger geographic region. Such a territory is often the original center of wine production in the area and is often considered to be superior to the surrounding areas.
- *Superiore* – This term indicates a wine that has a specific higher level of alcohol by volume than required of the corresponding *normale* wine. These wines are usually produced using a lower yield of grapes per acre or riper grapes.
- *Riserva* – This term is applied to wines that have been aged for a longer minimum period of time than regular wines. The total aging time varies according to the type and style of wine.

These terms are often themselves part of the name of the wine region, such as Chianti Classico DOCG and Soave Superiore DOCG.

Table 10–1: List of Italian DOCGs by Region

Region	DOCG
Abruzzo (2)	Colline Teramane Montepulciano d'Abruzzo
	Tullum/Terre Tollesi
Basilicata (1)	Aglianico del Vulture Superiore
Campania (4)	Aglianico del Taburno
	Fiano di Avellino
	Greco di Tufo
	Taurasi
Emilia-Romagna (2)	Colli Bolognesi Pignoletto
	Romagna Albana
Friuli–Venezia Giulia (4)	Colli Orientali del Friuli Picolit
	Lison (shared with Veneto)
	Ramandolo
	Rosazzo
Lazio (3)	Cannellino di Frascati
	Cesanese del Piglio (Piglio)
	Frascati Superiore
Lombardy (5)	Franciacorta
	Moscato di Scanzo (Scanzo)
	Oltrepò Pavese Metodo Classico
	Sforzato di Valtellina
	Valtellina Superiore
Marche (5)	Castelli di Jesi Verdicchio Riserva
	Cònero
	Offida
	Verdicchio di Matelica Riserva
	Vernaccia di Serrapetrona
Piedmont (18)	Alta Langa
	Asti – Moscato d'Asti
	Barbera d'Asti
	Barbera del Monferrato Superiore
	Barbaresco
	Barolo
	Brachetto d'Acqui (Acqui)
	Diano d'Alba (Dolcetto di Diano d'Alba)
	Dogliani
	Erbaluce di Caluso
	Gattinara
	Gavi (Cortese di Gavi)
	Ghemme
	Nizza
	Ovada (Dolcetto di Ovada Superiore)
	Roero
	Ruchè di Castagnole Monferrato
	Terre Alfieri

Region	DOCG
Puglia (4)	Castel del Monte Bombino Nero
	Castel del Monte Nero di Troia Riserva
	Castel del Monte Rosso Riserva
	Primitivo di Manduria Dolce Naturale
Sardinia (1)	Vermentino di Gallura
Sicilia (1)	Cerasuolo di Vittoria
Tuscany (11)	Brunello di Montalcino
	Carmignano
	Chianti
	Chianti Classico
	Elba Aleatico Passito (Aleatico Passito dell'Elba)
	Montecucco Sangiovese
	Morellino di Scansano
	Suvereto
	Val di Cornia Rosso (Rosso della Val di Cornia)
	Vernaccia di San Gimignano
	Vino Nobile di Montepulciano
Umbria (2)	Montefalco Sagrantino
	Torgiano Rosso Riserva
Veneto (14)	Amarone della Valpolicella
	Asolo Prosecco (Colli Asolani)
	Bagnoli Friularo (Friularo di Bagnoli)
	Bardolino Superiore
	Colli di Conegliano
	Colli Euganei Fior d'Arancio
	Conegliano Valdobbiadene Prosecco
	Lison (shared with Friuli-Venezia Giulia)
	Montello Rosso (Montello)
	Piave Malanotte (Malanotte del Piave)
	Recioto della Valpolicella
	Recioto di Gambellara
	Recioto di Soave
	Soave Superiore

*As of December 2021

WINE REGIONS

VENETO

Veneto is among the foremost wine-producing regions of Italy, in terms of both quality and quantity. Veneto produces a large percentage of the country's total wine, as well as the largest quantity (by volume) of DOC/DOCG wines from among the 20 wine-producing regions.

Geography and Climate

Located in northeastern Italy, Veneto is bordered to the north by Austria and Trentino–Alto Adige, to the west by Lombardy, to the south by Emilia-Romagna, and to the east by the Adriatic Sea and Friuli–Venezia Giulia. It divides topographically into two distinct sections. The south and east are flat, formed by deposits of sediment from rivers that empty into the Adriatic. The Po, Italy's longest river, forms part of the region's southern border. Other important rivers include the Adige and the Piave.

The region's northern and western sections become abruptly mountainous, and it is here, in the band of Alpine foothills and valleys between the plains and the rugged mountains, that most of Veneto's renowned grapes are grown.

The climate in this region, so close to both the Alps and the Mediterranean, is quite varied. The broad river delta and flatlands can get quite hot and humid in the summer, while the mountain slopes remain cooler and breezier. In the winter, this is one of the colder parts of Italy, but the Alps keep the coldest continental air at bay. Lake Garda, on the western side of Veneto, moderates the temperatures in its vicinity.

Grape Varieties

The red varieties most closely associated with Veneto are Corvina, Corvinone, and Rondinella, which have traditionally been blended together in several of the region's best-known red wines. Corvina is generally considered to be the quality grape of the three and typically makes up the largest part of the blend. For a long time, it was believed that Corvinone was a clone of Corvina, but new evidence has revealed it to be a distinct (although closely related) variety. As such, regulations regarding its use have been in flux.

The primary white grape of Veneto is Garganega—well known for its use in Soave. Glera, another indigenous white variety, provides the basis for the region's highly successful sparkling wines. International varieties—including Merlot, Cabernet Sauvignon, Cabernet Franc, Pinot Grigio (Pinot Gris), Pinot Bianco (Pinot Blanc), and Chardonnay—are also well represented in Veneto.

Veneto Wine Styles

Veneto produces a wide range of wine types and styles. In most years, as much as 75% is white wine, including Pinot Grigio, Soave, and Prosecco—the region's incredibly popular sparkling wine. Valpolicella and Bardolino are among the best-known red wines of Veneto.

The region is also noted for its dried-grape wines, both white and red, produced by the *appassimento* process. Ripe bunches of grapes are handpicked at harvest time, but instead of going to the press, they are set out to dry. Different wineries use different methods, but the grapes are traditionally placed carefully in special slatted boxes, laid on open shelves, or hung from ceiling rafters by hooks. The challenge is to keep the area well aerated to avoid humidity, which may promote mold growth. The grapes are left to dry until mid-January or longer, by which time they have lost as much as 60% of their water content through evaporation.

LEADING GRAPE VARIETIES OF VENETO	
Red Grapes	**White Grapes**
Corvina	Pinot Grigio
Corvinone	Glera
Rondinella	Garganega
Molinara	Trebbiano Toscano
Oseleta	Trebbiano di Soave
Negrara	Pinot Bianco
Cabernet Sauvignon	Vespaiola
Merlot	Chardonnay

Figure 10–4: Leading Grape Varieties of Veneto

Wine Regions of Veneto

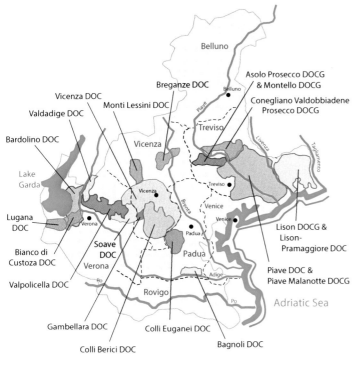

Figure 10-5: Veneto wine regions

and Recioto della Valpolicella DOCG—produced within the boundaries of the Valpolicella DOC (located in the hills north of Verona). Due to its appassimento production method, Amarone requires a minimum of 2 years of aging and a minimum of 14% alcohol by volume, although most producers achieve alcohol levels of at least 15% abv.

The four styles of Valpolicella are all based on Corvina or Corvinone grapes, along with a small amount of Rondinella. Traditionally, Molinara was included in the blend but is now optional. Small percentages of other grapes varieties are allowed as well. Producers in the heart of the historic Valpolicella growing district have the right to the classico designation. The Bardolino area—home to Bardolino DOC and Bardolino Superiore DOCG—is located alongside Lake Garda, just to the west of Valpolicella. Bardolino produces red wines and rosé—known here as *chiaretto*—based on Corvina and Rondinella.

The dried grapes are then brought into the winery, and a long, cool fermentation is begun that extends into March, April, or even May. For most appassimento wines, the fermentation is arrested by chilling the wine after the alcohol level reaches approximately 12%, which still leaves considerable residual sugar and produces a sweet wine called *recioto*. If the carbon dioxide produced via fermentation is retained in a pressure tank, the wine can also be made into a sparkling version. Another variation is to allow the wine to ferment completely dry, which results in a wine of 15% to16% alcohol. Amarone della Valpolicella is the model for this technique. Another traditional production technique called *ripasso* reuses the sediment, or lees, of Amarone or recioto. Young wine is combined with the lees and goes through a short second fermentation, becoming a ripasso wine with more flavor, tannin, and alcohol.

Veneto Appellations

Veneto has 14 DOCGs, with Amarone della Valpolicella DOCG among its most distinguished. Amarone is one of the four styles of wine—along with Valpolicella DOC, Valpolicella Ripasso DOC,

Among the still white wines of Veneto, Soave DOC is preeminent. Along with the Soave Superiore and Recioto di Soave DOCGs, Soave represents a large production volume in Italy. Its main ingredient is Garganega, which must comprise at least 70% of the wine and may be blended with Trebbiano di Soave (Verdicchio), Chardonnay, or both. Soave also has a central classico zone.

The region's other archetypal wine is Prosecco DOC, based on the Glera grape variety (minimum 85%) and typically produced as a white sparkling wine. Updates in the wine laws now allow for the production of Prosecco Rosé DOC, which includes 10% to 15% Pinot Nero (Pinot Noir) fermented on the skins. The Prosecco DOC appellation covers a large area, including the northern and eastern portions of the province of Veneto as well as all of Friuli-Venezia Giulia. In addition, there are two relatively tiny DOCGs that produce Prosecco: Conegliano-Valdobbiadene Prosecco DOCG and Asolo Prosecco (Colli Asolani) DOCG, both located in the historical center of Prosecco production.

Wine Regions of the Tre Venezie

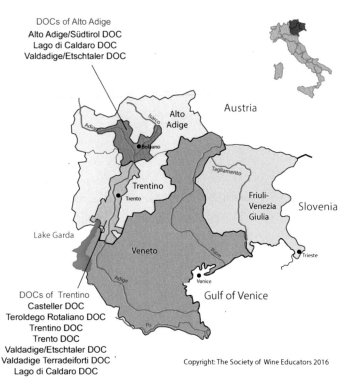

DOCs of Alto Adige
Alto Adige/Südtirol DOC
Lago di Caldaro DOC
Valdadige/Etschtaler DOC

DOCs of Trentino
Casteller DOC
Teroldego Rotaliano DOC
Trentino DOC
Trento DOC
Valdadige/Etschtaler DOC
Valdadige Terradeiforti DOC
Lago di Caldaro DOC

Copyright: The Society of Wine Educators 2016

Figure 10-6: Tre Venezie (Trentino-Alto Adige, Friuli-Venezia Giulia, Veneto)

The Lugana DOC—shared between Veneto and Lombardy—is becoming quite well known as well. This appellation produces light, pleasant white wines based on the Turbiana grape variety (also known as Trebbiano di Lugana and closely related to, but not quite identical to Verdicchio).

A few areas of Veneto produce several styles of wine under separate appellations (which often occupy the same geographic location). For instance, Piave DOC produces both dry and appassimento wines from a range of grapes. However, Piave Malanotte DOCG—which occupies the same location as the Piave DOC—is only approved for red wines based on the indigenous Raboso grape variety. Likewise, the Lison-Pramaggiore DOC (which extends into the Friuli-Venezia Giulia area) produces a range of red and white wines from both traditional and international varieties, while the Lison DOCG— located in the same geographic area—is approved only for white wines made using the Friulano grape variety.

International varieties are also important in Veneto and are used in both IGT and DOC wines. A new three-region DOC, the delle Venezie DOC, was created in 2017. The delle Venezie DOC encompasses the total area of the Veneto, Friuli-Venezia Giulia, and Trentino regions, and thus allows a good deal of multi-regional varietal wine—such as the area's popular Pinot Grigio—to be labeled as a DOC wine. In addition, ten IGTs are available in Veneto, including the general Veneto IGT and the even larger Trevenezie IGT.

TRENTINO–ALTO ADIGE

Trentino-Alto Adige is the northernmost region in Italy. Most of its northern border abuts Austria, to which the upper part of this region, Alto Adige, used to belong. In Alto Adige, also known as Südtirol, German is the predominant language, and wine styles and labels reflect that cultural heritage. The southern half of the region, Trentino, has as its center the town of Trento and is primarily Italian-speaking. It is quite cold in the more mountainous regions and progressively milder closer to Lake Garda in the south. The rugged mountain terrain does not leave much land for agriculture, but vineyards are found throughout the main valley, often planted on terraces.

More than 80% of the region's wine output is of DOC status, and almost all of the rest qualifies as IGT. The primary DOCs—Alto Adige, Trentino, and the overarching Valdadige—allow a wide selection of grape varieties and styles. Most of the wine is varietally labeled. The principal white varieties cultivated in the region include Chardonnay, Pinot Grigio, Pinot Bianco, Müller-Thurgau, and Traminer (Gewürztraminer). The main reds include Cabernet Franc, Cabernet Sauvignon, Lagrein, Merlot, Marzemino, Schiava, and Teroldego. Trento DOC (locally known as "Trentodoc") is the appellation for the region's highly respected traditional method sparkling wine.

Wine Regions of Friuli-Venezia Giulia

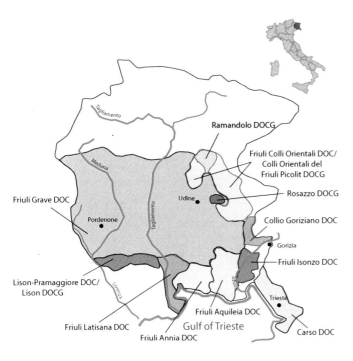

Copyright: The Society of Wine Educators 2016

Figure 10-7: Friuli-Venezia Giulia regions

FRIULI-VENEZIA GIULIA

In recent years, Friuli (the name is usually shortened) has made great strides in white wine production with both international and indigenous varieties, but red grapes also do well here. International varieties such as Cabernet Sauvignon, Chardonnay, Pinot Nero (Pinot Noir), Pinot Grigio, Riesling, and Sauvignon Blanc are commercially important, but some ancient varieties such as the red Refosco and the whites Verduzzo, Friulano (a Sauvignon Blanc relative, until recently called Tocai Friulano), and Picolit are enjoying renewed popularity.

The appellations considered to be among the best for quality wines in Friuli are Friuli Colli Orientali DOC (and its associated DOCG for sweet white wines made from the Picolit grape, Colli Orientali del Friuli Picolit) and Collio Goriziano DOC (often called simply Collio). Both are in the eastern part of Friuli near the Slovenian border, and both have a long list of allowed grape varieties that are often bottled as single-variety wines. Collio also produces white blends labeled as Collio Bianco, as well as skin-fermented "orange" wines from the indigenous Ribolla Gialla grape, which are often made in an oxidized style.

Two other outstanding wines of the area are Ramandolo DOCG and Rosazzo DOCG. The Ramandolo DOCG produces sweet white wines from the Verduzzo variety, a unique white grape rarely seen outside of northeast Italy. The Rosazzo DOCG makes dry white wines with a minimum of 50% Friulano; other allowed grapes include Sauvignon Blanc, Chardonnay, Pinot Bianco, and Ribolla Gialla.

PIEDMONT (PIEMONTE)

Piedmont is known among wine connoisseurs as the home of the great red wines Barolo and Barbaresco, and also, among a wider audience, for its sparkling wines. It is the second largest producer of DOC and DOCG wines in Italy behind Veneto. Though Piedmont's total production volume is well behind that of Veneto, it has the highest proportion of PDO wine of any of Italy's regions.

Geography and Climate
Piedmont forms the northwest of Italy, bordered by France on the west, Valle d'Aosta and Switzerland on the north, Lombardy on the east, and Liguria on the south. The region is sort of a half bowl with a relatively flat basin—the upper (western) part of the Po Valley—surrounded on three sides by the Alps and the Apennines. The flat alluvial expanses are too fertile for quality wine grapes, but the areas of low hills and ridges within the central basin are ideal, especially the Langhe and Monferrato hills south of the town of Asti.

The topography and soils of Piedmont are quite diverse. Partially cut off from the moderating influence of the Mediterranean by the mountains of Liguria, Piedmont's winters are cold with abundant snowfall. The summers are warm and dry, with frequent fog in autumn.

Grape Varieties
Piedmont's most famous grape is the tannic, high-acid Nebbiolo, which produces the region's blockbuster wines. However, the lighter but still high-acid, low-tannin Barbera is the most widely planted variety of the region. Other red varieties include Dolcetto, Freisa, Grignolino, and Brachetto. The leading white varieties are Moscato, Arneis, and Cortese. Piedmont has not rushed to plant international varieties, but

because it has physical and historical connections to France, some French varieties—particularly Chardonnay and Pinot Noir—have been present here for over a century.

LEADING GRAPE VARIETIES OF PIEDMONT

Red Grapes	White Grapes
Barbera	Moscato Bianco
Nebbiolo	Arneis
Dolcetto	Cortese
Brachetto	Erbaluce
Grignolino	
Bonarda	
Vespolina	
Freisa	
Ruchè	

Figure 10–8: Leading Grape Varieties of Piedmont

Piedmont Wine Styles

About two-thirds of Piedmont's wine output is red. Piedmontese red wines come in a full range of intensity from powerful, concentrated, and full-bodied to light and easy-drinking reds. One common feature of the red wines is a notable acidity that helps to give the big wines their longevity and makes the lighter styles particularly refreshing. Given the relatively cool climate of Piedmont, it is not surprising that sparkling wines are well established. These include wines produced via the traditional method, tank method, and partial fermentation techniques that range from dry to sweet and from white to red. The still whites are typically medium bodied with delicate aromatics.

Piedmont Appellations

Piedmont has more high-level wine appellations than any other Italian region: 18 DOCGs and more than 40 DOCs. With no IGTs in the region, the most general appellation is Piedmont DOC, which covers the entire region and allows still and sparkling wines from more than a dozen grape varieties. A large area is also covered by the Langhe DOC, which surrounds and includes the vineyards of Barolo, Barbaresco, and Roero, as well as the areas surrounding the towns of Alba and Ovada.

Many of the main appellations of Piedmont are tied to single grape varieties, and the standout variety is Nebbiolo. It is the sole or primary ingredient in seven DOCGs and several DOCs. Chief among these are the Barolo and Barbaresco DOCGs, based around two historic hill towns of the same names, which produce the two highest-regarded wines of Piedmont from 100% Nebbiolo. Barolo is an intense, dry, robust, but velvety red wine, usually quite tannic and high in alcohol. It requires a minimum aging period of 38 months; riserva wines must be aged for 62 months. Barbaresco resembles Barolo but is considered slightly more elegant and less powerful—though critics and enthusiasts continually debate this. Its aging requirements are less strict than Barolo's, with a minimum of only 26 months, and 50 months for the riserva.

Piedmont is also the home of Asti—the wildly popular, intensely fruity and aromatic sparkling wine made from Moscato Bianco (Muscat Blanc à Petits Grains) grapes. Asti is produced in a range of styles. The best-known, Asti DOCG, is a spumante (fully sparkling) version typically produced using the Charmat/Martinotti method. Asti DOCG is traditionally a semi-sweet to sweet wine, however, dry versions—known as Asti Secco—are permitted as well. Asti may also be produced via the *metodo classico*; such versions must undergo second fermentation in the bottle and age on the lees for a minimum of 9 months.

The calmer Moscato d'Asti DOCG is a *frizzante* (lightly sparkling) version made using the partial fermentation method of sparkling wine production—often referred to as the Asti Method—in which a single fermentation in a pressurized tank is halted by refrigeration, leaving a substantial amount of residual sugar in the wine (see chapter 6).

Other Piedmont appellations include the following:
- Barbera d'Asti DOCG: A large region covering over 9,700 acres (3,900 ha) in the area surrounding the town of Asti, the Barbera d'Asti zone was approved in 2008 as a DOCG for red wines containing at least 90% Barbera.
- Nizza: As of December 2014, Nizza, a former subregion of the Barbera d'Asti DOCG, became a separate DOCG. The regulations for Nizza DOCG require 100% Barbera grapes and a minimum of 18 months of aging (30 months for riserva).

- Roero DOCG: Both a red and a white wine are entitled to use the Roero DOCG. The red version is a less concentrated, earlier-drinking Nebbiolo from the hills across the Tanaro River from Barbaresco. The white version, Roero Arneis, is a highly regarded wine from the fragrant Arneis grape variety.
- Gattinara and Ghemme DOCGs: These regions produce Nebbiolo-based blends in the northern part of Piedmont, where Nebbiolo goes by the name Spanna. Five neighboring DOCs also feature blends built around Spanna.
- Gavi DOCG: This DOCG, located in the southeast corner of Piedmont, produces crisp, floral white wine made from the Cortese grape. The DOCG is also known as Cortese di Gavi or Gavi del Comune di Gavi.
- Brachetto d'Acqui: Also known as Acqui, this DOCG produces a range of wines based on the (red) Brachetto grape. The most widely-distributed style is slightly sweet, sparkling, and redolent with red berry and floral aromas.
- Various grape-named appellations such as Barbera d'Alba DOC, Dolcetto d'Acqui DOC, and Grignolino d'Asti DOC, whose wines are typically made from 100% of the named variety.

One more important economic product of Piedmont is vermouth, an aromatized and fortified wine flavored with herbs, spices, aromatic woods, and other natural ingredients. Italian vermouth is normally red and sweet.

LOMBARDY (LOMBARDIA)

Lombardy is situated at the center of the semicircle of the Alps that forms Italy's northern border. It is particularly known for the sparkling wines of the Franciacorta DOCG. These *metodo classico* sparkling wines are primarily produced with Chardonnay, Pinot Bianco, and Pinot Nero grape varieties. As of the 2017 vintage, limited amounts of Erbamat (a white variety) may be used as well.

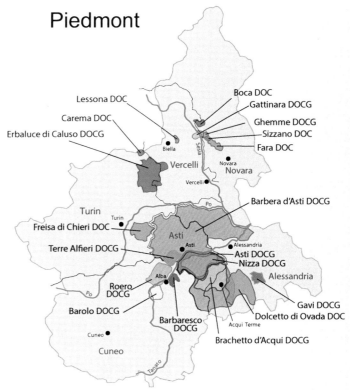

Piedmont

Figure 10-9: Piedmont Regions

Nonvintage Franciacorta must be aged for a minimum of 18 months on the lees. Vintage-dated versions require 30 months of lees aging, while those labeled "Riserva" require 60 months. Satèn, a brut blanc de blancs with only 5 atmospheres of pressure, and rosé styles require 24 months on the lees. For all versions of Franciacorta, the required time spent aging on the lees may not begin until February 1 of the year following the harvest.

Another important wine of Lombardy comes from the Valtellina, a long, narrow, east–west valley in the foothills of the Alps. This is one of the very few successful wines made outside Piedmont using the Nebbiolo grape, which is known locally as Chiavennasca. Valtellina Rosso DOC and Valtellina Superiore DOCG both require a minimum of 90% Chiavennasca. The same area also produces Sforzato di Valtellina DOCG, a dry, high-alcohol wine made with a minimum of 90% Chiavennasca grapes that are partially dried before fermentation. The resulting passito-style wine is rich, dry in character, and has a minimum alcohol content of 14%.

Subzones of the Valtellina Superiore DOCG include:

- Grumello
- Inferno
- Maroggia
- Sassella
- Valgella

TUSCANY (TOSCANA)

Tuscany is Italy's most famous wine region, due partly to its familiarity to tourists and partly to Chianti, one of Italy's largest-volume quality wines. Chianti and most of the other famed wines of Tuscany are based on Sangiovese, the region's signature grape variety.

Geography and Climate

Tuscany is situated on the west coast of the Italian Peninsula, north of Rome. Its primary cities are Florence, Pisa, and Siena, and its neighbors are Emilia-Romagna to the northeast and Umbria and Lazio to the southeast. The climate is typically Mediterranean, with greater extremes of temperature in the inland valleys, where the summers can get quite hot.

LEADING GRAPE VARIETIES OF TUSCANY

Red Grapes	White Grapes
Sangiovese	Trebbiano Toscano
Canaiolo Nero	Malvasia Bianca Lunga
Colorino	Vernaccia
Cabernet Sauvignon	Chardonnay
Merlot	Sauvignon Blanc
Cabernet Franc	

Figure 10–10: Leading Grape Varieties of Tuscany

Grape Varieties

Sangiovese is the grape variety most identified with Tuscany. There are hundreds of different clones or subvarieties of Sangiovese. Some give more color; others, more aromatics; still others, more tannin. Most producers, therefore, grow an assortment of clones to give their wine optimal complexity. There has been a good deal of research into the subvarieties and clones of Sangiovese, and the Chianti Classico Consortium has recently identified seven key clones as being the best for use in the region.

In addition to Sangiovese, there are several indigenous red varieties that are used in small quantities as blending grapes. Canaiolo Nero—prized for its velvety texture—is the most significant, along with Colorino—appreciated for its deep pigment and tannins, which add color and structure to a blend. International red varieties—including Cabernet Sauvignon, Cabernet Franc, Merlot, Syrah, and Pinot Noir (among others)—appear in blends or as varietal wines.

The leading white grapes of Tuscany include Trebbiano Toscano, Malvasia Bianca Lunga, Vermentino, and Vernaccia. International varieties—including Chardonnay, Sauvignon Blanc, and Viognier—are being grown in increasing amounts as well.

Tuscany Wine Styles

Only one other Italian region (Calabria) is more intently focused on red wines than Tuscany. Almost 90% of the region's output is red (including a small proportion of rosato). The traditional reds, all containing a majority of Sangiovese, are generally light-colored, high in acid, moderate in tannin, and full of bright cherry and red berry aromas and flavors. The upper-end versions that are 100% Sangiovese are similar, but they have greater depth of flavor and complexity. Sangiovese blended with Cabernet Sauvignon or other international varieties demonstrates higher levels of tannin, deeper color, and black fruit character, usually without losing much acidity.

A traditional winemaking technique known as *governo* is allowed to be used in the wines of Chianti. This practice involves the use of grapes that have become overripe on the vine or dried after harvest that are added to a batch of fermenting wine just as it is finishing fermentation. This extends the fermentation and often initiates malolactic fermentation, resulting in a richer, rounder wine with softer acids and less volatility. The practice is somewhat rare and if used, must be indicated on the wine's label via the term *Governo all'uso Toscano*.

Of the relatively few white wines produced in Tuscany, most are simple wines made for local consumption. One exception is Vernaccia, a white wine with delicate pear and almond aromas produced in and around the hilltop town of San Gimignano.

Another specialty of Tuscany, though it is made all over Italy, is *vin santo,* a dessert wine made by a unique process. Grapes are harvested and hung in attic rafters to dry, as is done for the Veneto's recioto, concentrating their sugars and flavor. The grapes are then crushed and put into small barrels that contain a bit of the vin santo lees from a previous vintage, which initiates a new fermentation. The barrels are sealed tight, and the vin santo is kept in an attic for a minimum of three years, where it is exposed to the natural temperature extremes over the course of the year. The better producers generally exceed the minimum aging period by two or three years.

Vin santo is typically a white wine, made primarily from Trebbiano Toscano and Malvasia Bianca Lunga grapes. However, a light red or amber-hued version known as *occhio di pernice* ("eye of the partridge") may be produced based on Sangiovese. Vin santo is typically sweet, although dry versions are produced as well. Vin santo is considered to be the ideal accompaniment to Italian cookies such as *cantucci* or *biscotti.*

The Super Tuscans

While not an "official" category of wines, the Super Tuscans are a well-known and highly regarded style of Tuscan wine. The term *Super Tuscan* originated in the 1970s as a result of the Chianti DOC regulations in place at the time, which required that Chianti be made from Sangiovese blended with several other indigenous grape varieties, including a small percentage of white grapes. Winemakers began to question the formula, believing that the required blend of grapes was limiting the quality potential of their wine. Some producers wanted to stop using white grapes in the blend; others felt that the wine should be 100% Sangiovese; and still others wanted to use international varieties such as Cabernet Sauvignon and Merlot.

In the late 1960s, some of these winemakers began releasing wines produced outside the guidelines set for the Chianti DOC, using the (then in use)

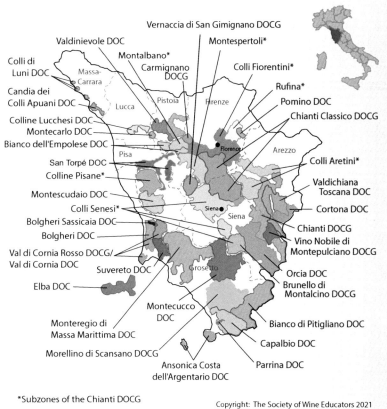

Major Wine Regions of Tuscany

*Subzones of the Chianti DOCG

Copyright: The Society of Wine Educators 2021

Figure 10–11: Tuscany regions

vino da tavola designation as opposed to a DOC. These wines eventually came to be known as Super Tuscans. The original Super Tuscan is generally agreed to be *Sassicaia,* Tenuta San Guido's Cabernet Sauvignon–Cabernet Franc blend commercially released for the first time in 1968 after several decades of being made for family use only. Soon thereafter, Marchese Piero Antinori released a Sangiovese–Cabernet Sauvignon blend known as *Tignanello,* and another wine, *Solaia,* made with Cabernet Sauvignon and Cabernet Franc. (The base grapes and blends of these wines have evolved, and will continue to evolve, over time.) Other producers quickly followed suit, and soon the repute and prices for these Super Tuscans were sky-high.

The rules of Chianti have since been modified to allow 100% Sangiovese wines, and Chianti Classico now allows up to 20% "other local red varieties," which include Cabernet Sauvignon, Merlot, and Syrah. Other Chianti DOCG regions have changed their rules as well. In addition, several small DOCs have been established specifically for this style of wine, while other Super Tuscans use the IGT Toscana designation.

Tuscany Appellations

Although there are certainly other prominent appellations in the region today, Chianti is the one that put Tuscany on the viticultural map, and it remains Italy's biggest wine in terms of name recognition. The original zone of Chianti wine, known today as the Chianti Classico region, lies in the hills and valleys between Florence and Siena. The Chianti appellation, initially demarcated in 1716, has been expanded over time to encompass a much larger area surrounding the classico zone and has also been subdivided into smaller zones.

Basic Chianti DOCG can be made anywhere in the Chianti zone, with the exception of the Chianti Classico zone. It must contain a minimum of 70% Sangiovese and can be 100% Sangiovese. Other permitted varieties are Canaiolo Nero, the white grapes Trebbiano Toscano and Malvasia, and "other suitable red varieties" (an intentionally vague provision in the law that opens the door for winemakers to use international varieties).

Within the Chianti DOCG region are seven defined subzones, not counting Chianti Classico, which, as of 1996, is a separate, independent appellation. The subzones of the Chianti DOCG are:

- Colli Aretini
- Colli Fiorentini
- Colli Senesi
- Colline Pisane
- Montalbano
- Montespertoli
- Rufina

Each of these subzones has its own set of standards, which may be stricter than those pertaining to the Chianti DOCG in parameters such as vineyard density, yield, minimum alcohol level, and aging. For instance, Colli Senesi requires a minimum of 75% Sangiovese, while the Chianti DOCG and the other six sub zones require a minimum of 70%.

Chianti Production Zones

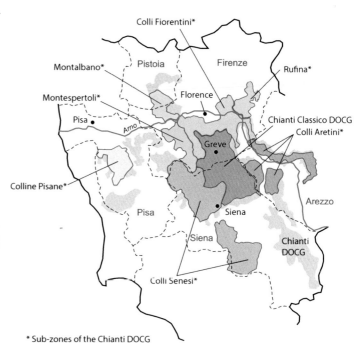

* Sub-zones of the Chianti DOCG

Figure 10-12: Chianti production zones

The Chianti Classico DOCG was the historic heart of Chianti dating back to the Middle Ages, but in recent times it separated itself from the Chianti DOCG to become a separate appellation with somewhat higher standards. The formula was modified such that Chianti Classico must contain at least 80%, but can be up to 100%, Sangiovese; and as of 2006, white grapes were excluded from the blend. Chianti Classico must have a minimum of 12% alcohol and cannot be released for sale until a year after harvest; a Riserva requires two years of aging and an additional half degree of alcohol.

In 2014, the Chianti Classico Consortium added a new category to its wine pyramid—Chianti Classico Gran Selezione (Chianti Classico Grand Selection). This category is meant to be the top wine of the region, with wines produced exclusively from estate-grown grapes, and with longer aging requirements (30 months minimum) and stricter technical and sensory parameters.

Besides Chianti and Chianti Classico, Sangiovese and its subvarieties comprise the sole or predominant portion of several other wines, including the following:

- Brunello di Montalcino DOCG: Made with 100% Brunello, the local name of Sangiovese, in the idyllic hill town of Montalcino. Brunello is typically one of the most powerful expressions of Sangiovese. Brunello di Montalcino must be aged for a minimum of just over four years before release. More specifically, it must be aged for at least two years in wood and at least four months in the bottle (the remainder of the time is not specific as to the vessel) and it may not be sold before January 1 of the 5th year following the harvest. Montalcino growers also have the Rosso di Montalcino DOC available to them for lighter, shorter-aged wines made from the same grape variety.
- Vino Nobile di Montepulciano DOCG: A highly respected Sangiovese-based wine from Montepulciano, another hill village in the Tuscan area. Vino Nobile uses a blend similar to Chianti's, based on a minimum of 70% Prugnolo Gentile, another local synonym for Sangiovese. (Note that Vino Nobile di Montepulciano should not be confused with Montepulciano d'Abruzzo. Vino Nobile is a blend based on Sangiovese grown near the Tuscan town of Montepulciano, whereas Montepulciano d'Abruzzo is made from the Montepulciano *grape* in the Abruzzo region.) Similarly to Brunello, a Rosso di Montepulciano version requiring a shorter aging period also exists.
- Carmignano DOCG: Carmignano, a red wine based on a minimum of 50% Sangiovese, is unique in that it introduced the use of small amounts of Cabernet Sauvignon and Cabernet Franc over a century ago, long before the Super Tuscans. It currently requires 10% to 20% of either Cabernet—or both combined—in the blend.
- Morellino di Scansano DOCG: A blend based on 85% or more Sangiovese, known as Morellino in this southernmost part of Tuscany.

The coastal area of Tuscany, known as the Maremma, is fast establishing itself as Tuscany's most exciting wine district. Unimpeded access to Mediterranean breezes keeps this area from getting as hot as the interior valleys, and the terroir is proving ideal for world-class vineyards. The Super Tuscan movement was born here near the town of Bolgheri with the introduction of the Cabernet-based Sassicaia, first commercially released

in the late 1960s. The excellence of this and other wines from the area led to the creation of new official appellations for them, including the Bolgheri DOC (for red and white blends), the Bolgheri Sassicaia DOC (created in 2013 for red wines made from a minimum of 80% Cabernet Sauvignon), and the Maremma Toscana DOC, elevated from IGT status in 2011.

Figure 10–13: San Gimignano

Tuscany's best-known white wine, Vernaccia di San Gimignano DOCG, is produced from the Vernaccia grape grown around the town of San Gimignano on the fringes of the Chianti area. The indigenous Vernaccia grape is quite ancient, with historical evidence of its existence dating to the thirteenth century, and with literary mentions of it found in Dante's *Divine Comedy*.

Despite its illustrious past, the Vernaccia grape fell out of favor until after World War II. However, the grape and its wine were soon resurrected, with the Vernaccia di San Gimignano appellation earning denominazione di origine controllata (DOC) status in 1966 and a promotion to DOCG in 1993. Vernaccia di San Gimignano characteristically offers up notes of almond, mineral, and earth, which can evolve with bottle age.

There are four DOCs specifically for vin santo in Tuscany. They are:
- Vin Santo del Chianti DOC
- Vin Santo del Chianti Classico DOC
- Vin Santo di Montepulciano DOC
- Vin Santo di Carmignano DOC

Vin santo can also be produced under the DOCs of several other Tuscan areas, including Pomino and Elba.

EMILIA-ROMAGNA

Emilia-Romagna is a triangular-shaped region that stretches diagonally across the top of the Italian Peninsula almost from one side to the other. Much of it lies in the fertile Po Valley. It is among Italy's largest wine-producing areas. Emilia-Romagna is home to the Romagna Albana DOCG (known as Albana di Romagna prior to 2011), the first white Italian wine to earn the DOCG designation.

Lambrusco, one of the most famous wines of the region, is produced in three Lambrusco DOCs (Lambrusco Salamino di Santa Croce DOC, Lambrusco Grasparossa di Castelvetro DOC, and Lambrusco di Sorbara DOC), as well as in both the Reggiano and Modena DOCs. While often thought of as a slightly sweet, simple red wine, Lambrusco is a slightly frizzante wine produced in both dry and sweet, as well as red and rosé, versions. (Note: The Lambrusco Mantovano DOC produces Lambrusco outside of Emilia-Romagna, in the Lombardy region.)

With ample sunshine and moderate temperatures, the hills and mountains of Emilia-Romagna are well suited for the production of quality wines. While the region may seem obscure to students of wine, culinary enthusiasts know it well as the home of Parmigiano Reggiano cheese, Prosciutto di Parma, and traditional balsamic vinegar from Modena.

LE MARCHE (MARCHES)

On the Adriatic coast, the Marches region (Le Marche) features five DOCGs and 15 DOCs. The area has become well-known for its white wines produced from the Verdicchio grape. Other white varieties grown in the region include Pecorino and Passerina. Montepulciano and Sangiovese are the leading red varieties. Marche's best-known wines include the following:
- Castelli di Jesi Verdicchio Riserva DOCG and Verdicchio di Matelica Riserva DOCG: crisp but neutral white wines made with the Verdicchio grape.

- Cònero DOCG and Rosso Cònero DOC: red wines from the same small area, blending the Montepulciano grape with Sangiovese. Both wines must be made with a minimum of 85% Montepulciano, with a permitted addition of 15% Sangiovese. The DOCG wine has higher standards for aging and alcohol levels than the DOC wine.
- Rosso Piceno DOC: a red blend that includes 35% to 85% Montepulciano and 15% to 50% Sangiovese.

ABRUZZO

The Abruzzo region (just to the south of Marches) is also identified with the Montepulciano grape. One of the area's most popular wines—Montepulciano d'Abruzzo DOC—is made from a minimum of 85% Montepulciano, with Sangiovese permitted in the blend. A separate Cerasuolo d'Abruzzo DOC was created in 2010 for the cherry-colored, lighter style of this wine, which undergoes a much shorter maceration period, resulting in lower-tannin wine with bright fruit flavors. Abruzzo's two DOCGs— Colline Teramane Montepulciano d'Abruzzo DOCG and Tullum (Terre Tollesi) DOCG also specialize in red wines based on the Montepulciano grape variety. The region's leading white wine—Trebbiano d'Abruzzo DOC—is based on the *Trebbiano Abruzzese* grape variety.

UMBRIA

Umbria, a land-locked region located in the rugged Apennines between Marches and Tuscany, is perhaps best known for Orvieto DOC. Orvieto is a white wine based on Trebbiano Toscano (known locally as Procanico) and Grechetto grapes. Orvieto is typically dry (*secco*); however, it is also available in off-dry (*abboccato*), semi-sweet (*amabile*), and sweet (*dolce*) styles. Umbria is also home to two DOCG wines, both red: Montefalco Sagrantino (100% Sagrantino), and Torgiano Rosso Riserva (minimum 70% Sangiovese).

Figure 10–14: Cathedral of Santa Margherita, Montefiascone

LAZIO

Situated on the west coast of the Italian Peninsula surrounding the city of Rome, Lazio (sometimes referred to as Latium) enjoyed a good reputation for its wines in ancient Roman times. Lazio produces a range of types and styles of wine; however, the most recognized examples are Frascati DOC, Frascati Superiore DOCG, and Est! Est!! Est!!! di Montefiascone DOC. (These are all white wines, and mostly [but not exclusively] dry). An obscure sweet wine of the region, Cannellino di Frascati DOCG, is a fascinating wine that traditionally tied its very late harvest dates to the festival of San Crispino. The white wines of Lazio are typically based on the Trebbiano Toscano, Trebbiano Giallo, Malvasia Bianca di Candia, and Malvasia del Lazio grape varieties (among others).

CAMPANIA

Campania—the region surrounding the city of Naples and Mount Vesuvius—is the most populated region of the southern peninsula. This area is familiar to tourists, and therefore its wines are relatively well-known abroad. One of the best-known wines of Campania is Taurasi DOCG, a red wine with fine aging potential made from the bold, red Aglianico grape. Aglianico is found in many places around the southern peninsula, including the neighboring Basilicata region. The volcanic soil of Campania also produces several white wines of great character, notably Fiano di Avellino DOCG—an elegant white wine based on the Fiano grape—and Greco di Tufo DOCG (made predominantly from the Greco di Tufo variety, believed to be a clone of Greco Bianco).

CALABRIA

The most prominent appellation of Calabria, located on the boot's toe, is Cirò DOC. Its rosso uses the Gaglioppo grape, and its white, produced in very small quantities, is based on Greco Bianco. Riserva versions of Cirò Rosso have long aging potential. A copper-colored dessert wine made from partially dried grapes, Greco di Bianco DOC is produced here in the region surrounding the town of Bianco. Somewhat confusingly, the name of the town is Bianco, the name of the grape is Greco Bianco, and the name of the wine is Greco di Bianco.

PUGLIA

Puglia (also known as Apulia)—the heel of the boot—produces mainly red wines and is well-known for Salice Salentino DOC, a red wine based on Negroamaro. Negroamaro is a robust, dark-colored grape grown mainly in Puglia. Other important grapes in Puglia include Montepulciano, Sangiovese, Barbera, Aleatico, and Primitivo. A sweet, late-harvest wine, Primitivo di Manduria Dolce Naturale, became the region's first DOCG in 2011. Later that same year, three more DOCGs were awarded: Castel del Monte Nero di Troia Riserva DOCG, Castel del Monte Rosso Riserva DOCG, and Castel del Monte Bombino Nero DOCG.

SICILY (SICILIA)

Located off the southwest tip of the Italian Peninsula, Sicily is the largest island in the Mediterranean Sea. Mount Etna—an active stratovolcano with a current height of 10,900 feet/3,325 meters—dominates the island's skyline. With its reliable sunshine, warm temperatures, and mineral-rich volcanic soils, Sicily has been viticultural powerhouse for over 2,000 years. The island-wide Sicilia DOC and Terre Siciliane IGT allow for the production of a broad range of wine styles and accordingly, in most years, Sicily is one of the largest producers of Italian wine (by total volume).

The region's only DOCG, Cerasuolo di Vittoria, produces a vividly colored red wine from a blend of Nero d'Avola (one of the island's most important red grapes) and Frappato (a low tannin red variety known for its cherry-berry aromas and flavors). The Etna DOC—located on (and up) the eastern side of the mountain—produces crisp white wines from grapes such as Carricante and Catarratto as well as reds and rosatos based on Nerello Mascalese. Nerello Mascalese is a highly regarded red grape named after the Mascali plain—a region near Mount Etna where it is believed to have originated. Historically, Sicily was known as a producer of sweet wines and while in decline, this tradition continues in the wines of the Malvasia delle Lipari DOC, Moscato de Noto DOC, and Moscato di Pantelleria DOC (produced on the satellite island of Pantelleria).

Perhaps most famously, Sicily is home to the Marsala DOC, one of the world's greatest fortified wines. Marsala is made in a range of styles according to levels of sweetness, color, and aging regimes. Grillo and Inzolia (both white varieties) are traditionally used in the production of Marsala; several other varieties – including Catarratto and Nerello Mascalese—are allowed as well.

Styles of Marsala

There are three types of Marsala: oro (golden), ambra (amber), and rubino (ruby/red). Each style can be made secco (dry, maximum 4% residual sugar), semisecco (semi-dry, 4% to 10% residual sugar), or dolce (sweet, more than 10% residual sugar). There are also variations based on the minimum length of aging: Marsala Fine (one year), Marsala Superiore (two years), and Marsala Superiore Riserva (four years). Marsala Vergine and Marsala Solera are aged for a minimum of five years in a solera system like that used for the production of Sherry. The most highly esteemed version of Marsala, Vergine Stravecchio Riserva, is dry and requires a minimum of ten years' aging in cask.

Figure 10–15: Olive trees and vineyards in Sicily

SARDINIA (SARDEGNA)

Located to the west of the Italian peninsula and south of Corsica, the island of Sardinia has been home to various kingdoms and empires over the years. This is reflected in the wine industry of the island, which includes grapes of Spanish and French heritage alongside some unique Italian varieties such as Monica (red) and Nuragus (white).

One of the most famous wines of the region is produced in the island-wide Cannonau di Sardegna DOC. This is a red wine made from a minimum of 85% Cannonau (a minimum of 90% Cannonau is required for the riserva). *Cannonau* is the Sardinian name for Grenache or Garnacha; experts have long debated whether Spain introduced the variety to Sardinia or if it was the other way around.

The island's only DOCG—Vermentino di Gallura DOCG, produced in the island's northeastern corner—is an aromatic white wine produced using the Vermentino grape variety. While typically seen as a dry, still (non-sparkling) wine, Vermentino di Gallura may be produced in a variety of styles (dry, sweet, still, sparkling, and late harvest/passito).

SPAIN

LEARNING OBJECTIVES

After studying this chapter, the candidate should be able to:

- Identify the general role and position of Spain in the global wine industry.
- Recall the physical location and general climate of Spain's major wine regions.
- Recognize the hierarchy of Spanish wine designations.
- Describe the grape varieties and wine styles of Rioja, Sherry, and Cava.
- Recall the wine regions and major grapes of Galicia, the Duero Valley, Navarra, and Catalonia.
- Discuss the differences between the fino and oloroso production methods and styles for Sherry.

Spain is another of the world's major wine countries. After enjoying a brief reign as the world's largest wine producer (by volume) in 2013, Spain has returned to its usual spot as the third largest wine producer in the world, after France and Italy.

Although its domestic wine consumption is substantial, it produces enough excess to be among the world's top three wine exporters. With over 2.5 million acres (1.01 million ha) under vine, Spain continues to have–by far–the largest grape acreage in the world.

Some of Spain's most famous wines include Rioja, Sherry, and Cava. The country is closely associated with the Tempranillo grape variety, which is the main grape of the Rioja region and the foundation of many other standout red wines from Spain.

Major Wine Regions of Spain

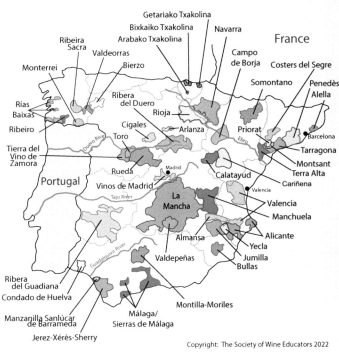

Copyright: The Society of Wine Educators 2022

Figure 11–1: Spain's wine regions

GEOGRAPHY AND CLIMATE

Spain is a moderately large country in southwestern Europe where, along with Portugal, it makes up the Iberian Peninsula. The country is very mountainous, with most of the interior raised on a large plateau known as the Meseta. Almost 60% of Spain lies above 2,000 feet (610 m) in elevation.

To the north of Spain lie the Bay of Biscay off the Atlantic Ocean and, across the Pyrenees Mountain range, France. Its western boundary includes Portugal and a small section of Atlantic coastline. Spain's southern and eastern borders are situated along the Mediterranean Sea coastline. Spain's climate is mostly continental (hot summers, cold winters, rainfall fairly evenly spread throughout the year) despite the fact that the country is nearly surrounded by water. This is a result of the network of mountains that block much of the maritime influence. The Pyrenees Mountains and the *Cordillera Cantábrica* (Cantabrian Mountains) along the north coast are particularly important in that they shield the peninsula from many of the winter storms and colder influences coming from the north.

Only the relatively exposed northwest corner of the country is truly maritime in climate (mild summers, mild winters, considerable rainfall year-round), while the southwest and Mediterranean coastal areas have a classic Mediterranean climate (hot, dry, sunny summers and mild, wetter winters). The months of June, July, and August are quite dry everywhere in Spain.

There are 17 autonomous communities in Spain. Of these, fifteen are located on the Spanish mainland and two are island groups—the Balearic Islands in the Mediterranean and the Canary Islands in the North Atlantic. The autonomous cities of Ceuta and Melilla—exclaves located on the northern coast of Africa—are also part of the country of Spain.

Languages other than Spanish predominate in several of the northern regions of Spain, which introduces variations in terminology and pronunciation for wines from these areas. Galician (*Galego*) is spoken in Galicia, including Rías Baixas; Basque (*Euskara*) in the Basque Country (*Euskadi*) and Navarra; and Catalan (*Català*) in Catalonia (*Catalunya*), Valencia, and the surrounding areas.

SPANISH GRAPE VARIETIES

Spain's vast vineyard acreage is heavily oriented toward the country's indigenous grape varieties, including Airén, which accounts for almost 25% of plantings. An undistinguished white variety used primarily for making brandy and commercial bulk wine, Airén is widely grown in the central regions of Spain.

LEADING GRAPE VARIETIES OF SPAIN

Red Grapes	White Grapes
Tempranillo	Airén
Bobal	Cayetana Blanca
Garnacha Tinta	Albariño
Monastrell (Mourvèdre)	Macabeo (Viura)
	Palomino
Mazuelo (Carignan)	Verdejo
Mencía	Parellada
Cabernet Sauvignon	Xarel-lo
Syrah	Moscatel
Alicante Bouschet	Pedro Ximénez
Merlot	Garnacha Blanca

Figure 11–2: Leading Grape Varieties of Spain

The next most prevalent grape, at just over 20% of plantings, is Spain's illustrious Tempranillo, which is widely grown around the country, especially in the northern part of the Meseta. Tempranillo is known by many different names, depending on the region in which it is planted. Tempranillo is prized for its long-lived wines with moderate acidity and aromas of spice, chalk, strawberries, and tobacco, often accompanied by a hefty input from oak aging.

TEMPRANILLO SYNONYMS

Name	*Region/Town*
Tempranillo	Rioja
Tinta de Toro	Toro
Tinta del País	Ribera del Duero, Cigales
Tinto Fino	Ribera del Duero
Ull de Llebre	Catalonia
Cencibel	La Mancha, Valdepeñas
Aragonêz	Portugal
Tinta Roriz	Douro (Portugal)

Other well-respected varieties found in many parts of Spain include the red grapes Garnacha and Monastrell (known in France as Grenache and Mourvèdre, respectively) and the white Macabeo (also known as Viura).

Most other grape varieties tend to be regionally based, including the following:
• Palomino and Pedro Ximénez in Jerez
• Parellada and Xarel-lo in Penedés
• Albariño in Rías Baixas

SPANISH WINE LAWS

Like all EU member countries, Spain has a classification system for its wine divided along several tiers.

- Basic Spanish wine that does not warrant a geographical indication is designated as *vino de mesa* (literally, table wine).
- Spain currently has 42 areas with protected geographical indication (PGI) status; these are identified on wine labels as "*Vino de la Tierra de*" followed by the name of the region.

Wines with a protected designation of origin (PDO) are divided into several subcategories:

- *Vino de calidad con indicación geográfica* (VCIG): Established in 2005, this status is intended for up-and-coming regions that are expected to prove themselves worthy of DO status before too long. These wines are indicated on the label by the phrase "Vino de Calidad de," followed by the region name. As of December 2021, there were seven regions that held this classification: Cangas, Valles de Benavente, Valtiendas, Sierra Salamanca, Las Islas Canarias, Cebreros, and Legrija.
- *Denominación de origen* (DO): These highly regarded wines are sourced from a demarcated zone whose production is prescribed with regard to grape varieties, crop yields, winemaking methods, and aging regimens. As of December 2021, Spain has 68 DOs; this number has remained relatively stable for several years, but it could change in the future. Each DO is supported by a *consejo regulador* (regulating council) that controls local production areas and practices.
- *Vino de pago:* Established in 2003, the vino de pago category is intended to recognize specific, single vineyard wines of distinction. The vino de pago title is a government-granted protected designation of origin that is—in some respects—equivalent to a DO, although some argue that they should be considered superior to the DOs based on their regional specificity and mandate for estate bottling. As of December 2021, there were 21 vinos de pago, but this number is likely to increase. Currently, Spain's two DOCa regions do not contain any vinos de pago; however, if one were be established, it would be designated a *vino de pago calificado*.

Figure 11-3: Spanish wine categories

- *Denominación de origen calificada* (DOCa): This status is reserved for wines that have demonstrated superior quality as a DO for at least ten years. So far, this classification has been awarded to only two wines: Rioja and Priorato (often written in Catalan as *Priorat DOQ*).

Figure 11-4: Barrel aging at Bodegas Bilbainas in Rioja

AGING REQUIREMENTS AND TERMINOLOGY

Aging wine in oak barrels (*barricas*) is a common practice in Spain. Labeling terminology to indicate a wine's age is strictly regulated by Spanish wine law. There are two sets of terminology: one set that both PGI and PDO wines can use, and another whose use is restricted to PDO wines.

PGI and PDO terms include the following:

- *Vino noble* (noble wine): wine that has spent a minimum of 18 months aging in barricas or in the bottle

- *Vino añejo* (aged wine): wine that has spent a minimum of 24 months aging in barricas or in the bottle
- *Vino viejo* (old wine): wine that has spent a minimum of 36 months aging in a strongly oxidative environment exposed to any combination of light, oxygen, and heat

PDO-Only Terms

Quality wines may use the terms *Crianza, Reserva,* or *Gran Reserva* on their labels to indicate a level of aging prior to release. The general minimum requirements for the use of these terms are shown in the table below. Several DOs and DOCa's have higher minimum aging times for their wines; however, many producers elect to age their wines even longer (sometimes much longer) than the stated minimums.

Joven (young) may be used for PDO wine released the year after it was made and, if oak-aged at all, aged for a shorter period than the legal minimum requirement for Crianza. As of 2018, some regions use the term *genérico* (generic) in place of the term *joven*.

Table 11-1: Spanish Wine Aging Designations

SPANISH WINE AGING DESIGNATIONS				
	RED WINES		WHITE WINES AND ROSÉS	
	Aging in Barrel (Months)	Total Aging (Months)	Aging in Barrel (Months)	Total Aging (Months)
Crianza	6	24	6	18
Reserva	12	36	6	24
Gran Reserva	18	60	6	48

* Note: Specific regions (notably the Rioja DOCa) may have additional aging requirements to accompany these terms.

WINE REGIONS

GALICIA

Galicia is located in the northwest corner of Spain, part of the area often referred to as Green Spain. The area—being exposed to the Atlantic Ocean—is decidedly cooler and wetter than the rest of the country, and its wines are notable for their crisp flavors and high acidity.

Galicia contains five DO wine regions. The best-known of these include the following:
- Rías Baixas: Rías Baixas—a single DO, broken up into five noncontiguous subregions—produces dry, crisp white wines known for their fruity, floral aromas. Rías Baixas is made primarily from the Albariño grape variety, along with Loureira and Treixadura.
- Ribeiro: Located along the Miño (Minho) River just to the east of Rías Baixas, the Ribeiro DO is one of the oldest recognized wine regions in Spain. The area is best known for its crisp white wines based on Treixadura and other (mainly local) grapes, including Loureiro, Torrontés, Albariño, and Godello.
- Valdeorras: Valdeorras is located on the eastern (inland) edge of Galicia. It is known for white wines based on the Godello grape variety, as well as rich, fruity red produced from Mencía.

Figure 11–5: Vineyards in Ribeiro

CASTILLA Y LEÓN

On its way to northern Portugal, where it is called the Douro, the Duero River flows through the heart of Castilla y León and past the regions of Toro, Rueda, Cigales, and Ribera del Duero. This area lies on the high plains of the northern Meseta, where winters are very cold and summers can be quite hot. Because of the protection of the mountains to the north, these vineyard areas get much less rain than Green Spain, yet more than most of southern Spain. The leading wine regions of Castilla y León include the following:

- Toro: Named for the town of Toro, the Toro DO is primarily known for powerful red wines based on Tempranillo, locally known as *Tinta de Toro*. The area is also planted to small amounts of Garnacha (used in some red wines, but primarily vinified into rosé), and an even smaller percentage of white grapes, most notably Malvasia Blanca, Verdejo, and Albillo Real. The Toro DO is located on a high plateau between two mountain ranges, with most vineyards planted at altitudes of 2,000 to 2,800 feet (600–800 m) above sea level.

- Rueda: With its significant diurnal variation, it is not surprising that Rueda has long been prized for its white wines. The region's dry, aromatic white wines (Rueda Blanco) are typically based on the Verdejo grape, which takes up as much as 88% of the total vineyard area. Rueda Blanco may also be made with a majority of Sauvignon Blanc; limited amounts of Viura, Palomino Fino, Viognier, and/ or Chardonnay are permitted as well. Red wines and rosados—based on Tempranillo, Cabernet Sauvignon, Garnacha, and/or Merlot—comprise about 5% of Rueda's production.

- Bierzo: The Bierzo DO lies just to the east of the border between Castilla y León and Galicia. Accordingly, its climate can be described as somewhat transitional—between the cooler influences of Green Spain and the warmer, drier areas inland. Bierzo is best known for its flavorful red wines (and some rosado) produced from the Mencía grape variety.

- Cigales: Cigales produces mostly reds and rosados based on Tempranillo, here known as Tinta del País. The rosés are often blended with Garnacha.

- Ribera del Duero: Ribera del Duero is one of the stars of the Spanish wine industry, considered by many to be on par with Rioja for the quality of its wines. The area's climate can be a challenge, with extremes of both hot and cold. However, at around 2,500 feet (760 m), the region's vineyards are among the highest elevated in Spain, resulting in good diurnal shifts from day to night. Rich, flavorful red wines based on Tempranillo (locally known as *Tinta del País* or *Tinto Fino*) are the focus in Ribera del Duero; rosado and clarete (light reds) are also allowed. In 2020, the regulations were revised to allow the production of white wines—Ribera Blanco—using a minimum of 75% Albillo Mayor grapes.

NAVARRA

The autonomous region of Navarra lies between La Rioja and the French border to the northeast. Castles dotting the region recall Navarra's heritage as a separate kingdom, which maintained its independence until it was subsumed by the Castilian Empire in 1512. While a small portion of the Rioja DOCa crosses over into southwestern Navarra, the rest of southern Navarra, which has a climate similar to Rioja's, falls mostly within the Navarra DO. This traditional region, historically famous for its rosé, has reinvented itself with international grape varieties. The area's principal grapes are Tempranillo and Garnacha, with Cabernet Sauvignon, Merlot, and Chardonnay growing in importance.

RIOJA

Rioja is the most famous red wine of Spain and unquestionably one of its best. Wines of Rioja are widely exported and are respected around the world. Given its long history of quality production, it is no surprise that Rioja was the first region designated as a DO (in 1925) as well as the first region to be elevated to DOCa status (in 1991). The region produces about one-sixth of Spain's DO-level wine.

Geography and Climate

The Rioja DOCa is located in north-central Spain, inland from the Cantabrian Mountains. These mountains help to moderate the area's climate by blocking much of the cold influence that would otherwise flow inland from the Bay of Biscay/Atlantic Ocean. The region—located primarily in the *autonomía* of La Rioja, with some vineyards situated in Basque Country and Navarra—lies in the valley of the Ebro River. The combined influences of the Cantabrian Mountains, the Ebro River, and the Mediterranean Sea—located at the eastern edge of the Ebro Valley—help to provide warm summers and milder winters than those experienced in the open, exposed Meseta. The Rioja DOCa has three sub-appellations, referred to as zones:

- *Rioja Alta:* the high-altitude, hilly area covering most of the western half of the region
- *Rioja Alavesa:* essentially, the part of Rioja Alta north of the Ebro
- *Rioja Oriental:* the lower, flatter eastern portion of the Rioja DOCa (formerly known as the *Rioja Baja*)

The Rioja Oriental is the hottest and driest of the zones. In comparison, the Rioja Alta and Rioja Alavesa zones enjoy a relatively mild climate and produce much of the area's finest grapes. Rioja DOCa

Copyright: The Society of Wine Educators 2019

Figure 11–7: Zones of the Rioja DOCa

wines may be produced from the wines of a single zone and labeled as such; however, many wines contain a blend from two or all three of the zones.

Grape Varieties

Red varieties cover well over 90% of the vineyard area in Rioja, and Tempranillo comprises most of that. The other permitted red grapes include Garnacha, Mazuelo (also known as Cariñena or, outside of Spain, Carignan), and Graciano. Viura is by far the leading white grape. Other allowed white varieties include Chardonnay, Sauvignon Blanc, Malvasia, Garnacha Blanca, Maturana Blanca, and Verdejo.

Rioja Wine Styles

Although Rioja also produces white and rosé, it is most famous for its red wine. Rioja's prominence is largely due to the jump-start provided by the Bordeaux winemakers who settled here for a brief time in the late nineteenth century after phylloxera had destroyed their own vineyards in France. They brought extensive winemaking experience with them and set about making a Bordeaux-style wine from the indigenous grape varieties they had available. After phylloxera spread to the Spanish vineyards, many of the French departed, but they left behind radically improved vinification techniques, including the use of 225-liter oak barrels for aging.

Figure 11–6: Marqués de Riscal Hotel and Winery in Rioja

Tempranillo is the backbone of the region's finest red wines. Traditional red Riojas are Tempranillo-based blends, aged for extended periods in oak barrels. American oak has been used almost exclusively, although some producers are beginning to introduce French oak. Rioja tends to be tannic and can improve in the bottle for decades. Traditionally, there has been less of a focus on fruit flavors and more of a focus on earthiness, minerality, and the distinctive "leathery" bouquet that can develop as the wine ages. However, as in many places, there is a new emphasis on making single-vineyard and single-variety wines, as well as wines that are more approachable at a younger age.

The Rioja DOCa has stricter aging requirements than many of the other wines of Spain. These include the following standards for red wines:

- Crianza: A minimum of 24 months total aging, to include at least 12 months in the barrel
- Reserva: A minimum of 36 months total aging, to include at least 12 months in the barrel and at least 6 months in the bottle
- Gran Reserva: A minimum of 60 months total aging, to include at least 24 months in the barrel and at least 24 months in the bottle

Viura is the principal grape used in the production of white Rioja. It is usually cold-fermented and released young, but some wineries still produce white Rioja in the traditional barrel-fermented, oak-aged style. Rosé Rioja is often produced using a majority of Garnacha blended with the other red grapes of the region. As of 2018, traditional method sparkling wines—known as Vino Espumoso de Calidad de Rioja DOCa—are also allowed to be produced under the Rioja designation.

ARAGÓN

The former kingdom of Aragón, east of both Navarra and La Rioja, is now an autonomous region of the same name. The region can be very hot in summer and very cold in winter. To date, the Somontano DO in the foothills of the Pyrenees has developed the province's best reputation for modern wines, with a mix of indigenous and international varieties planted. Eight red varieties are grown, including Cabernet Sauvignon, Merlot, Syrah, and Garnacha. Among the area's specialties are the bright, intensely hued rosados produced primarily from Garnacha. Seven different white grape varieties are grown, with Chardonnay and Macabeo being the most widely planted.

CATALONIA (CATALUNYA)

The province of Catalonia, known as Cataluña in Spanish and as Catalunya in Catalan, makes up the northeastern corner of Spain. The Mediterranean climate provides good growing conditions and presents fewer challenges to producing quality grapes than many other parts of Spain.

Within Catalonia, there are several DOs of distinction, including the following:

- Priorat DOQ (known as "Priorato DOCa" in Spanish): Promoted in 2009, Priorat is only the second of Spain's wine regions to be granted DOCa status. The DO was initially established in 1950, but it was the pioneers of the late 1980s who revolutionized the local wines and brought a renewed focus on quality to the region. Located in a mountainous region just inland from Barcelona, the area is only 18 miles (29 km) from the Mediterranean Sea, but mountains shield most of the region from the damp sea air and Ebro Valley winds. Priorat is known for its llicorella soils of flat, easily breakable stones made of decomposed slate flecked with mica and other minerals. These famous soils impart a distinct herbal and mineral character to the powerful, deep red wines of the area. Garnacha is the primary grape of Priorat, but Cariñena is almost as prominent. Several other red grapes—including Tempranillo, Cabernet Sauvignon, Cabernet Franc, Merlot, and Syrah— are also among the allowed varieties. Some rosé (*rosat* in the Catalan language) is also produced

Figure 11–8: Garnacha vine in Priorat

in Priorat, as well as some white wine produced from Garnacha Blanca, Macabeo, Pedro Ximénez, and other approved white grapes of the region.

- Tarragona: One of the largest of Catalonia's DOs, Tarragona has a diverse mix of soils and climates, which permits it to produce a range of wines from young reds, rosés, and whites to Port-style fortified wines. However, nearly 75% of production is devoted to full-bodied, aromatic whites, although the younger red wines are starting to find their way to the market.
- Montsant: A relatively new DO (2001) created from Falset, a former subzone of the Tarragona DO adjacent to Priorat, Montsant features many mature vineyards of Garnacha and Cariñena, along with smaller but significant plantings of Ull de Llebre (Tempranillo), Cabernet Sauvignon, and Syrah.
- Costers del Segre: Consisting of several noncontiguous subzones where more than a dozen indigenous and international varieties are planted, Costers del Segre is another region that has seen sudden and dramatic improvements in quality with the introduction of capital, state-of-the-art equipment, and young, well-educated enologists with nontraditional outlooks on winemaking. Wines are typically blends of traditional grapes and international varieties.
- Penedès: The region that started the modern wine revolution in the 1970s, Penedès became the first area in Spain to use stainless steel equipment and temperature-controlled fermentation techniques. The Penedès DO focuses primarily on white wines. Although it encompasses the main production areas for Cava, most of the Penedès DO wines are still whites made from the Xarel-lo, Macabeo, and Parellada grape varieties. The leading white grape is Xarel-lo. International varieties have a strong presence here as well, with Chardonnay being the next most common white grape. Red wines feature both indigenous and international varieties.
- DO Catalonia: The Catalonia (Cataluña) DO encompasses the land (and approved grape varieties) included in all of the other DOs of the autonomía; this allows for a wide range of wine types and styles to be labeled as Catalonia DO.

CASTILLA-LA MANCHA

Castilla–La Mancha, in the central Meseta, is a flat, hot, and dry area dotted by windmills reminiscent of the story of Don Quixote. This area is home to Spain's vast acreage of Airén grapes, most of which make their way into Spanish brandy. The region's La Mancha DO is, physically, Spain's largest, although its output is comparatively low for such a large area, as vineyards tend to be very widely spaced with small vines. In addition to Airén and Cencibel (Tempranillo), international varieties are widely grown in the La Mancha DO. Valdepeñas (Valley of the Rocks) is a well-known DO nearly surrounded by the La Mancha DO. The Valdepeñas DO carries a somewhat better reputation due to variations in the soil that allow for better water retention—an important advantage in this arid environment. As of December 2021, Castilla-La Mancha is home to 12 vinos de pago; this is more than any other region of Spain.

MURCIA

Murcia is located in the southern portion of the Levant (eastern coast) of Spain. The vineyards of Murcia are located somewhat inland, and are thus influenced by the hot, arid climate of Spain's interior—just slightly moderated by the Mediterranean coast. Murcia contains three DOs: Jumilla, Yecla, and Bullas. All three of these regions produce a variety of wines, including red, white, rosé, and—in some cases— sparkling wines and vinos de licor (fortified wines). However, the majority of the output for all three of these regions consists of deep, concentrated reds and flavorful rosés based on the thick-skinned Monastrell (Mourvèdre) grape variety.

Figure 11-9: Cathedral of Jerez de la Frontera

JEREZ

Jerez, also known as Xérès, is the region of production for Sherry. Along with Port, Sherry (produced under the Jerez-Xérès-Sherry DO) is one of the two best-known fortified wines in the world. Though not as popular in modern times as it once was, Sherry is still exported widely, particularly to Britain and the Netherlands.

Geography and Climate

The Sherry region lies in the southwest of Spain, in Andalusia, between Cádiz and Seville. The center of the industry is the so-called Sherry Triangle formed by the towns of Jerez de la Frontera, Sanlúcar de Barrameda, and El Puerto de Santa María.

Although Andalusia's climate is hot and dry, the climate of Jerez is somewhat cooler due to its proximity to the Atlantic Ocean. Sanlúcar de Barrameda and El Puerto de Santa María are both seaports, and the vineyards closest to the water are markedly cooler than those slightly more inland. The summer months feature continually cloudless days with no rain at all.

Grape Varieties

Three grapes are grown throughout Jerez for use in the production of Sherry. The primary grape is the indigenous Palomino, which is the sole or majority grape variety in most Sherries. Pedro Ximénez, often shortened to "PX," is the principal sweetening agent in the sweeter styles of Sherry and is also used to produce an intensely sweet and rich dessert Sherry. Moscatel (Muscat of Alexandria) is grown in small quantities, but it may be added as a sweetener or used to impart a fruity characteristic to younger Sherries.

Soil Types

Each of the three grape varieties of Sherry has an affinity for one of the three soil types found in the Jerez region: Palomino prefers the brilliantly white *albariza* soil, composed of about 30% limestone-rich chalk along with some clay and sand; PX grows well on *barro*, a clay soil with iron oxide and a little chalk and sand; and Moscatel thrives on *arena*, a predominantly sandy soil.

Sherry Wine Styles

Sherry is produced in a wide range of styles from light and dry to rich and sweet, and is found in a wide range of colors from pale yellow, tan, and brown to nearly black. The majority of Sherry is based on the Palomino grape variety and is produced using a base wine that is fermented dry before it enters the aging and blending process. This process is used to create the two basic styles of Sherry– *fino* and *oloroso*–with a wide range of styles available within each of these two main categories. In addition, a small amount of Sherry is produced using partially-dried Pedro Ximénez or Moscatel grapes; these wines are typically sweet.

- Fino-Style Sherry: As discussed in chapter 7, the base wines that will be made into Sherry are classified based on their style and quality. Those that are chosen for the production of fino Sherries are fortified to a low level of alcohol in order to permit the flor to flourish.
- Hybrid-Style Sherry: These styles of Sherry begin as a fino Sherry, aging under flor. However, during the aging process, the flor dies out, allowing the wines to age both biologically and oxidatively while in the solera.
- Oloroso-Style Sherry: Oloroso Sherries are those that are initially fortified to a higher alcoholic strength in order to prevent the development of flor at a later point. Without the protection of the film yeasts, the wine ages in the presence of oxygen, resulting in a rancio (oxidized) character and light-to-deep brown color.
- Dried Grape Sherry: Sweet Sherry, produced primarily from Pedro Ximénez or Moscatel grapes, is produced using grapes harvested at a high level of ripeness with the sugars further concentrated by drying the grapes, post-harvest, on straw mats in the hot sun. This process is known as *soleo*. After

being dried, the grapes are pressed and partially fermented before being fortified and aged.

Descriptions of some of the better-known types of Sherry are found in table 11-2. Commercial Sherry is often marketed under a variety of names that are meant to evoke a unique style or character, including "East India," "brown," "golden," "milk," and "amoroso." These styles are generally a variant or blend of the major styles described in table 11-2.

Age Classifications

In the early 2000s, the Sherry Consejo Regulador introduced two new Sherry designations to recognize exceptionally old and rare wines. These designations, which are given to individual soleras and reviewed periodically, may only be applied to amontillado, palo cortado, oloroso, and Pedro Ximénez wines—finos are excluded.

Two general classifications are specified. The lower classification is known as *vinos con indicación de edad* (Sherries with an age indication) and may be earned by Sherries that have been aged for 12 to 15 years. The higher classification is *vinos de vejez calificada* (Sherries of certified old age), which consists of two levels:
- *Vinum optimum signatum* (VOS/very old Sherry): minimum of 20 years of solera aging
- *Vinum optimum rare signatum* (VORS/very old rare Sherry): minimum of 30 years of solera aging

En Rama Sherry

These days, most dry Sherries are fined and filtered before bottling so that the wine has a high degree of clarity. However, historically, some of the best Sherry was unfiltered and unfined or, perhaps, just minimally filtered. This natural style of Sherry, while still somewhat rare these days, is enjoying a renaissance of sorts and is referred to as *en rama*.

Figure 11-10: Sherry tasting

Vintage Sherry

The solera system of fractional blending seems to rule out any single-vintage bottlings. However, throughout history, single-vintage (*añada*) Sherry bottlings were a regional tradition, carried out alongside solera aging. The tradition all but died out by the late 1800s; however, these days, single-vintage Sherry bottlings are becoming fashionable, and therefore more available, once again. These single-vintage, aged Sherries are typically quite expensive due to their rarity as well as the enhanced oxidation and evaporation experienced by these wines.

MONTILLA-MORILES

The Montilla-Moriles DO, located to the east of Jerez, is known for rich dessert wines that are often compared to the wines of Jerez. However, its position further inland provides a more continental climate, and Montilla-Moriles is, overall, warmer and drier than parts of the Sherry region. For this reason, the Pedro Ximénez grape variety, which accounts for over 70% of the overall plantings, thrives here. The intense summer heat often means that the grapes ripen to very high sugar levels, so much so that even the unfortified wines of Montilla-Moriles may reach alcoholic strengths of 14% to 16% (or even higher). Montilla-Moriles also produces a small amount of dry, still wines and dessert wines from very ripe Moscatel grapes.

Table 11–2: Styles of Sherry

Style	Type	Notes
Fino-Style Sherries	Fino	A pale, delicate, dry wine produced primarily from the Palomino grape under the influence of flor yeast and, thus, showing the unmistakable characteristics of the flor to both the nose and palate. At 15% abv or so, it is among the least alcoholic of the fortified wines. Unless deliberately sweetened, fino Sherries are dry on the palate.
	Puerto Fino	A fino Sherry from the coastal town of El Puerto de Santa María. The cool climate of the coast encourages a thick covering of flor, resulting in a light, crisp wine with a hint of saltiness.
	Manzanilla	A fino Sherry that is matured in the seaside town of Sanlúcar de Barrameda, produced according to the Manzanilla Sanlúcar de Barrameda DO. It has a slightly different flavor than other finos, often described as *briny* due to the maritime humidity, which encourages a more vigorous flor yeast population.
	Pale Cream	A sweetened style of fino Sherry that originated in Bristol. Aside from the addition of a sweetening agent, no other color, aroma, or flavor is added.
Hybrid-Style Sherries	Amontillado	A Sherry that starts as a fino and is aged under a layer of flor but that loses its protective flor after a few years (naturally or through additional fortification). It is thereafter aged like an oloroso, in the presence of oxygen. Amontillado Sherries tend to have intense, nutty aromas.
	Palo Cortado	This unique Sherry is made from fino-quality base wine, but it never quite develops flor as initially expected. It then continues aging oxidatively, but it never quite develops into an oloroso. It has the nutty characteristics of an amontillado but without the flor aroma. Palo Cortado has the color and full body of an oloroso Sherry.
Oloroso-Style Sherry	Oloroso	A Palomino-based Sherry aged in partially filled barrels without flor and with considerable oxidation. Oloroso Sherry changes in color from its original shade of gold to light brown to deep brown as it ages, increasing in alcohol, body, and aroma.
	Cream Sherry	A sweetened Oloroso Sherry, typically produced using a blend of Sherries and often showing a distinctly darkened amber or brown color. Harvey's Bristol Cream Sherry—so named for its creamy texture—is one of the original commercial brands of cream Sherry.
Dried-Grape Sherry	Pedro Ximénez	A very dark, very sweet, almost syrupy Sherry produced using thin-skinned Pedro Ximénez grapes. Plantings of Pedro Ximénez grapes are quite limited in Jerez, so grapes from the nearby Montilla-Moriles DO are permitted for use in these wines.
	Moscatel	While many of the Moscatel grapes grown in the Jerez region are used as a sweetener for other styles of Sherry, a small amount of Moscatel-based Sherry is produced as well. These wines are made from grapes that are left to dry for a short time after harvest and are typically made into a sweet, golden wine with fruity and floral aromas.

CAVA

Cava is one of Spain's leading, high-quality sparkling wines. The term *Cava* refers to the process by which the wines are made, since these *método tradicional* sparkling wines are aged in a cellar or a cave. Cava may be produced as a white (blanco) or rosé (rosado) sparkling wine.

GEOGRAPHY OF THE CAVA DO

The geography of the Cava designation is unique in that it is scattered across the country. The majority of the vineyards (representing as much as 95% of the total Cava production) are located in Catalonia, within the Comtats de Barcelona Zone. This zone—considered to be the "spiritual heart" of the Cava designation—is centered around the municipality of San Sadurní de Noya (Sant Sadurní d'Anoia), where the first bottles of Cava were produced in 1872.

Other areas that are approved for the production of Cava DO include the Ebro Valley, the Levante (located in the province of Valencia), and the Viñedos de Almendralejo (Almendralejo vineyards), located further south in Extremadura.

GRAPE VARIETIES

The three classic grape varieties for Cava are Macabeo, Xarel-lo, and Parellada, all of which are white. Other varieties have been added to the list of approved grapes, including Chardonnay, Malvasia (Subirat Parent), Pinot Noir, Garnacha, Monastrell, and Trepat (a red grape believed to be native to Catalonia).

CAVA DE GUARDA

In 2021, *Cava de Guarda*—a new tier of high-quality wines tied to specific qualitative standards—was introduced. To qualify as a Cava de Guarda, a wine must be traceable from the vineyard to the bottle. To further qualify as a Cava de Guarda Superior, the wine must meet guidelines for maximum yield as well as the following standards: the vines must be at least 10 years of age, the grapes must be grown organically (granted with a five-year period allowed for transition), and the wine must be vintage-dated.

CORPINNAT

Beginning in 2015, a group of mostly small-scale Cava producers decided to forgo the use of the Cava DO in favor of a new designation to be known as *Corpinnat*. Corpinnat is not a protected geographical indication; but is rather an EU-recognized brand name with its own set of standards—including a delimited area within the central Penedès region and the use of organic farming. Other requirements include hand-harvested grapes, minimum lees aging, and the use of at least 90% "historic" varieties (Xarel-lo, Macabeu, Parellada, and Malvasia for whites; Garnacha, Monastrell, Sumoll, and Xarel-lo Vermell for reds). Corpinnat producers can opt to include the Penedès DO designation on the label, provided the wine meets the standards of the appellation.

Table 11–3: Cava Production Requirements

CAVA PRODUCTION REQUIREMENTS	
CAVA DESIGNATION	PRODUCTION REQUIREMENTS
Cava	Minimum 9 months of lees aging
Cava de Guarda	Minimum 9 months of lees aging Additional production standards (see above)
Cava Reserva	Minimum 18 months of lees aging
Cava de Guarda Superior	Minimum 18 months of lees aging Additional production standards (see above)
Cava Gran Reserva	Minimum 30 months of lees aging Must be brut-level sweetness or drier
Cava de Paraje Calificado	Minimum 36 months of lees aging Must be sourced from a single, qualified location/vineyard Must be brut-level sweetness or drier

Table 11-4: PDO Wines of Spain

Autonomous Community	PDO Wines
Andalusia (Andalucía)	Condado de Huelva DO Granada DO Jerez-Xérès-Sherry DO Lebrija VCIG Málaga DO Manzanilla Sanlúcar de Barrameda DO Montilla-Moriles DO Sierras de Málaga DO
Aragón	Calatayud DO Campo de Borja DO Cariñena DO Somontano DO Vino de Pago Aylés
Asturias	Cangas VCIG
Balearic Islands (Islas Baleares/Illes Balears)	Binissalem DO Pla i Llevant DO
Basque Country (País Vasco/Euskadi)	Arabako Txakolina / Chacolí de Álava DO Bizkaiko Txakolina/ Chacolí de Bizcaia DO Getariako Txakolina / Chacolí de Guetaria DO
Canary Islands (Islas Canarias)	Abona DO El Hierro DO Gran Canaria DO La Gomera DO La Palma DO Lanzarote DO Las Islas Canarias VGIC Tacoronte-Acentejo DO Valle de Güímar DO Valle de la Orotava DO Ycoden-Daute-Isora DO
Castilla y León	Arlanza DO Arribes DO Bierzo DO Cebreros VCIG Cigales DO León DO (formerly Tierra de León) Ribera del Duero DO Rueda DO Sierra de Salamanca VCIG Tierra del Vino de Zamora DO Toro DO Valles de Benavente VCIG Valtiendas VCIG Vino de Pago Urueña
Castilla-La Mancha	Almansa DO La Mancha DO Manchuela DO Méntrida DO Mondéjar DO Ribera del Júcar DO Uclés DO Valdepeñas DO Vino de Pago Calzadilla Vino de Pago Campo de la Guardia Vino de Pago Casa del Blanco

Table 11-4: PDO Wines of Spain, *continued*

Autonomous Community	PDO Wines
Castilla-La Mancha, *continued*	Vino de Pago Los Cerrillos Vino de Pago Dehesa del Carrizal Vino de Pago Dominion de Valdepusa Vino de Pago Finca Élez Vino de Pago Florentino Vino de Pago Guijoso Vino de Pago La Jaraba Vino de Pago Vallegarcía Vino de Pago El Vicario
Catalonia (Catalunya/Cataluña)	Alella DO Cataluña DO Conca de Barberà DO Costers del Segre DO Empordà DO Montsant DO Penedès DO Priorato DOCa (Priorat DOQ) Pla de Bages DO Tarragona DO Terra Alta DO
Extremadura	Ribera del Guadiana DO
Galicia	Monterrei DO Rías Baixas DO Ribeira Sacra DO Ribeiro DO Valdeorras DO
La Rioja	Rioja DOCa*
Madrid	Vinos de Madrid DO
Murcia	Bullas DO Jumilla DO** Yecla DO
Navarra	Navarra DO Vino de Pago Bodegas Otazu Vino de Pago Prado de Irache Vino de Pago Arínzano
Valencia	Alicante DO Utiel-Requena DO Valencia DO Vino de Pago Chozas Carrascal Vino de Pago El Terrerazo Vino de Pago Los Balagueses Vino de Pago Vera de Estenas
Multi-Regional	Cava DO

*Portions of the Rioja DOCa are located in Basque Country and Navarra
**A small portion of the Jumilla DO is located in Castilla-La Mancha
Source: Government of Spain—Ministry of Agriculture, Fisheries, and Food (2021)

PORTUGAL

CHAPTER TWELVE

LEARNING OBJECTIVES

After studying this chapter, the candidate should be able to:

- Identify the physical location and general climate of Portugal's major wine regions.
- Recognize the hierarchy of wine designations from Vinho de Portugal to DOC.
- Describe the major grape varieties and wine styles of Port and Madeira.
- Recall significant DOCs for unfortified wine and their primary grape varieties.

Portugal has been well-known in international wine circles for centuries because of Port and Madeira, its famous fortified wines. Portugal has also enjoyed considerable success with white Vinho Verde, which remains very popular among consumers, particularly in the United States. Its other wines are making headway in the export market as well, despite language issues and high domestic demand. A new generation of adventurous consumers is finding much to like about the wines of Portugal and its colorful history, fascinating stories, and diverse pool of indigenous grape varieties.

GEOGRAPHY AND CLIMATE

Portugal occupies the southwestern section of the Iberian Peninsula, bordered by the Atlantic Ocean to the west and south, and by Spain to the north and east. It is a small nation, with nearly all of the country covered by rugged ridges and valleys. If it weren't for the rugged terrain, vineyards could thrive almost anywhere in Portugal. Some, especially in the Douro, cling to the sides of steep valley walls despite the difficulty.

Despite its small size, Portugal is made up of three distinct climates. The coastal part of northern Portugal is lush and green with abundant rainfall, much like Green Spain to its north. Influenced by the Atlantic, temperatures are moderate and humidity is high. Continuing south along the coast, the climate becomes more Mediterranean, with warmer summers, mild winters, and very little precipitation during the growing season. Because of the patchwork of mountain ranges in Portugal's interior, the humidity quickly dissipates and the ocean no longer provides a temperature-moderating influence, so the climate turns decidedly continental and arid. The inland valleys, especially those close to the Spanish border to the east, feature blisteringly hot summers and very cold winters, with minimal precipitation.

PORTUGUESE GRAPE VARIETIES

The inventory of Portugal's major grape varieties is daunting in its length and unfamiliarity. The Instituto da Vinha e do Vinho lists almost 350 varieties. Apart from a small amount of crossover with the Spanish stock, most of these grapes are virtually unknown in other countries. International varieties have not been widely planted in Portugal, although that is slowly changing.

Several of the leading red varieties in Portugal are considered to be among the most important varieties used in the production of Port; however, these grapes are also used to make excellent unfortified wines. These include:

- Touriga Nacional: capable of producing complex wines with firm structure and black fruit flavors
- Touriga Franca: typically used in blends, offering floral, blackberry, and plum notes

- Tinta Roriz: known elsewhere in Portugal as Aragonêz and to the rest of the world as Tempranillo, this variety has red fruit, olive, and herbal characteristics

Castelão, another important red variety, is often referred to as Periquita. Castelão is predominantly planted in the south, where it is often used to produce age-worthy wines with a complex, herbaceous character. Castelão is, however, quite adaptable to many growing conditions and as such may also be used to make fruit-forward, easy-drinking reds and rosés.

Significant red varieties also include Baga and Trincadeira (also known as Tinta Amarela). Baga can be extremely tannic. Consequently, it is often aged in older barrels so as not to impart additional tannins. Baga often yields age-worthy, robust wines with plum and tobacco notes.

While difficult to grow, Trincadeira does best in hot, dry areas such as the Alentejo and Tejo. Trincadeira produces wines with vibrant acidity and aromas of blackberry, herbs, and pepper.

As less than one-third of Portuguese wine is white, white grape varieties are less significant overall. However, white varieties are regionally prominent in the cooler areas in the north and on the islands. In Vinho Verde, Loureiro and Alvarinho (known across the border in Spain's Rías Baixas as Loureira and Albariño) are the stars. Alvarinho is distinctly tart and mineral in character, with peach and citrus aromas and flavors.

Portugal's most-planted white grape variety is Fernão Pires, also called Maria Gomes. It is found mainly in the south (Palmela, Tejo, and Setúbal) and on the central coast (Bairrada). The variety is very aromatic and is produced in a range of styles, including both still and sparkling wines.

Madeira's reputation is based primarily on white grapes:
- Sercial
- Verdelho
- Boal (or Bual)
- Malvasia, also referred to as Malmsey

LEADING GRAPE VARIETIES OF PORTUGAL

Red Grapes	White Grapes
Castelão	Fernão Pires (Maria Gomes)
Touriga Nacional	Encruzado
Touriga Franca	Arinto
Tinta Barroca	Alvarinho (Albariño)
Tinto Cão	Sercial
Tinta Roriz (Aragonêz)	Verdelho
Jaen (Mencía)	Boal (Bual)
Alfrocheiro	Malvasia (Malmsey)*
Trincadeira (Tinta Amarela)	
Baga	

*Originally known as Malvasia Candida, now also known as Malvasia Branca de São Jorge

Figure 12–1: Leading Grape Varieties of Portugal

PORTUGUESE WINE LAWS

The Portuguese classification pyramid, simplified in recent years, is in conformity with EU regulations. There are currently three levels:

- *Vinho (Vinho de Portugal):* basic wine, formerly known as *vinho de mesa;* this category represents about one-fourth of Portugal's production.
- *Vinho regional* (VR): country wine from one of the VR regions, making up another quarter of production. Portugal has 14 VR designations, covering 12 regions in Portugal proper, plus the islands of the Azores and Madeira. The Vinho Regional category represents the PGI wines of Portugal (referred to in Portuguese as *Indicação Geográfica Protegida*, or IGP).
- *Denominação de origem controlada* (DOC): the primary category for quality wine; there are 31 DOCs at present, including Porto and Madeira. The DOC category represents the PDO wines of Portugal (referred to in Portuguese as *Denominação de Origem Protegida*).

WINE REGIONS

MINHO

The Minho is located in the northwestern corner of Portugal, just south of the Spanish region of Rías Baixas. This is the coolest and wettest part of Portugal, so it is not surprising that this area produces more white wine than red. While there is a Minho VR available, the majority of the area's production is quality wine for the Vinho Verde DOC. This appellation is Portugal's largest in vineyard area after the Porto DOC.

Despite its name, which literally means "Green Wine," Vinho Verde can be red, white, or pink; the word *green* implies youth, meaning that the wine is meant to be consumed young. This is sometimes evidenced by a slight effervescence in these light, high-acid wines. There are fully sparkling (*espumante*) versions as well.

White Vinho Verde is produced mainly from Loureiro and Alvarinho grapes, sometimes blended with Arinto, Trajadura, and other grapes. Loureiro provides richness on the palate, while Alvarinho is leaner and higher in acidity. Vinho Verde can be produced as a single-variety wine or a blend. Compared to Rías Baixas wines, Alvarinho-led Vinho Verde is more pétillant, mineral, and tart. Regardless of the varieties used, white Vinho Verde is generally low in alcohol and high in acidity, with a fresh citrus character. In fact, the minimum alcohol level for white Vinho Verde is just 8.5%.

Red Vinho Verde is made mostly from Vinhão. This grape variety produces deeply colored, full-bodied wines. Unlike with the production of the white wines, malolactic fermentation is encouraged in the production of red Vinho Verde, although it is still known as a wine with high acidity. Most red and rosé Vinho Verde remains within Portugal for domestic consumption.

Officially recommended grapes for use in Vinho Verde include the following:

White	Red
Alvarinho	Amaral (Azal Tinto)
Arinto (Pedernã)	Alvarelhão (Brancelho)
Avesso	Borraçal
Azal	Espadeiro
Batoca	Padeiro
Loureiro	Pedral
Trajadura	Rabo de Anho
	Vinhão

Figure 12–2: Portuguese wine categories

DOURO

The Douro was among the first demarcated wine regions in the world, with its boundaries defined in 1756. Although primarily known for its production of Port, the Douro is also a well-regarded producer of unfortified wines. Long just a footnote to Port, these wines are now considered some of the best the country has to offer. About two-thirds of the Douro's production is released under the Porto DOC, but most of the rest is high-quality unfortified wine (along with a small amount of fortified Moscatel do Douro), labeled as Douro DOC. Wines produced under the Douro DOC are made from the same grape varieties used for Port production. Wines made from international varieties such as Cabernet Sauvignon

Wine Regions of Mainland Portugal

Figure 12–3: Wine regions of Portugal

do not qualify for the Douro DOC and are released under the regional appellation, VR Duriense.

Geography and Climate

The vineyards of the Douro begin approximately 40 miles (64 km) east of the city of Oporto and extend 60 miles (96 km) eastward to the Spanish border (where the river's name changes from Douro to Duero). For the most part, the Douro is rugged, wild, and remote. The area is divided into three subregions:

- *Baixo Corgo:* The westernmost section, Baixo Corgo is a relatively fertile area with ample rainfall and makes mostly lighter styles of Port.
- *Cima Corgo:* The central core of the Port region, this subzone has steep rocky slopes of schist and granite that have been terraced. The Cima Corgo has hotter summers, colder winters, and less rain than the Baixo Corgo, and it is considered to produce the finest Ports. The majority of the vineyards used in the production of Port are located here.
- *Douro Superior:* The upriver, eastern part of the valley, this subregion has even more extreme temperatures than the Cima Corgo and very little rainfall. This is the largest subzone in terms of physical size, but less than one-quarter of its area is under vine for Port. This subzone is the source of much unfortified wine.

Grape Varieties

There are dozens of grape varieties that are theoretically authorized for Port production, but the number of grape varieties actually used in significant quantity is shrinking. Years ago, most vineyards were field blends with many different varieties growing side by side. New plantings, however, are usually single-variety vineyards using one of the preferred varieties, which include:

- Touriga Nacional
- Touriga Franca
- Tinta Roriz (Tempranillo)
- Tinta Barroca
- Tinto Cão

Subregions of the Douro DOC

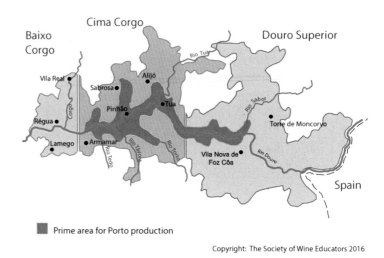

Prime area for Porto production

Copyright: The Society of Wine Educators 2016

Figure 12-4: Subregions of the Douro DOC

For white Port, the predominant grape varieties include Gouveio and Malvasia Fina.

The same red and white grape varieties used in Port production, particularly Touriga Franca, Touriga Nacional, and Tinta Roriz, are used for the unfortified wines of the Douro DOC.

Port Wine Production

Within the Douro Valley, the DOC for Port has a unique and complex vineyard ranking system called the *cadastro* that assesses 12 factors, including altitude, yield, and locality, awarding or subtracting points to arrive at a final total score. Based on this mark, vineyards are classified from A (high) to F (the lowest grade allowed for use in Port). Each year, the ranking, along with harvest conditions, determines each grower's *beneficio* authorization—the maximum amount of wine that is allowed to be fortified and used to produce Port in that year.

Once harvested, the grapes are brought to the winery, where the grapes may be fully or partially destemmed. Traditionally, the grapes were then foot-crushed in low, open granite or concrete troughs known as *lagares*. This practice continues to a certain extent, but many modern Port producers now use mechanical means. After a short, rather fast fermentation, the wine is fortified to 19% to 22% alcohol by volume via the addition of neutral grape spirits (causing fermentation to end). The wine is then moved into containers (of various styles) and left to rest through the winter.

Traditionally, sometime after the winter season, the young Port was placed into barrels (referred to as *pipes*) and sent downriver to the city of Oporto via ornate flat-bottomed boats known as *barcos rabelos*. Here, the wines would be aged and prepared for eventual transport to market. Beginning in the late 1800s, the center of the Port trade shifted across the river to the town of Vila Nova de Gaia, where dozens of lodges used for the storing and aging of Port are now located. The high humidity and cooler temperatures of these towns on the coast proved to be much better for aging the Port with minimal evaporation or maderization.

Figure 12–5: Barcos rabelos on the Douro River

The dangerous boat trip has today been replaced by truck transport, and the structure of the trade is changing slowly. Vila Nova de Gaia is still home to most of the big Port lodges, but more and more quintas now do their own blending and aging in temperature-controlled facilities in the Douro.

Port Wine Styles

Generally, Ports are sweet, high in alcohol, and rich in complex flavors and aromas. However, there are a number of styles, differentiated to a large degree by how long and in what type of container they are aged. Of course, the styles that get the most care and longest aging usually start with the finest grapes from the outstanding vineyards, which multiplies the aging regimen's effect on quality.

The major styles of Port include the following:

- *Ruby:* This is the simplest of Ports, comprising a large share of all Port produced. Rubies have a vibrant red color and youthful aromas but lack the longevity and complexity of flavors found in other styles of Port. Ruby Port is aged in large oak casks for about two years before being bottled and ready to drink.
- *Reserve:* A blend of premium ruby Ports bottled after four to six years' aging in oak vats, reserve Ports are more like tawny Ports in style.
- *Late-Bottled Vintage (LBV):* Wine from a single year, matured in large oak vats for four to six years after harvest; most LBVs are filtered before bottling and are intended to be consumed upon release.
- *Tawny:* Essentially, tawny Port is a version of ruby Port that is aged long enough in oak for the color to oxidize from ruby red to a golden brown shade, developing richer, more oxidized flavors along the way. Basic tawny Port is sometimes aged for just a few years, but those labeled "Reserve Tawny Port" reflect the true style and are required to be aged in oak for at least seven years before bottling. Those with a specific indication of age, such as 10-, 20-, or 30-year-old tawny, have spent considerable time in cask. The age stated on the label is an average, so some of the wine in the bottle is likely to be quite a bit older. These are highly complex and rich wines that represent the pinnacle of quality for wood-aged Ports.
- *Vintage:* Vintage Port is the rarest and most expensive style of Port produced. Whereas most Ports are blends of wine from several harvests, vintage Port is from a single year's harvest and is only produced in the best years. A vintage year is declared at the discretion of the producer, sometimes in as few as three years out of ten. Vintage declarations must be approved by the Instituto dos Vinhos do Douro e Porto (IVDP). Vintage Port is aged in cask, but must be bottled by July 30 of the third year after harvest. After bottling, the wine is usually cellared for many more years before release. Consequently, the wine may spend decades aging in the bottle. Each vintage Port is unique and reflective of the growing conditions of a single year.
- *Single Quinta Vintage:* Single quinta vintage Port—a variation on the vintage Port style—is produced from the grapes of a specific estate or vineyard. Some controversy exists, as single

quinta vintage Port is sometimes produced in years that were not considered good enough for a producer to declare a vintage year for their entire estate. In these cases, specific vineyards that did have excellent-quality harvests may be bottled under this designation, which requires the same handling as other vintage Ports. Examples of single quinta vintage Port produced in recent years include Dow's Quinta do Bomfim and Taylor's Quinta de Terra Feita.

- *Colheita:* A single-vintage tawny Port. The wine must remain in cask for at least seven years, but in practice it usually spends a much longer time in wood before being bottled. Very few vintners produce this style.
- *White:* Although much less common than red styles, a small quantity of white Port is produced using Malvasia Fina, Gouveio, Rabigato, and other white grapes of the region. White port is made in both off-dry and sweet styles and is often served as an aperitif.
- *Rosé:* In a turnabout to the traditional character of Port, Croft introduced a rosé Port called Croft Pink. Originally released in 2008, pink Port was intended to appeal to a new generation of wine drinkers. The style proved quite popular, and several other shippers quickly followed suit.

MADEIRA

Madeira, an island located in the Atlantic some 400 miles (644 km) off the coast of Morocco, is home to the second of Portugal's classic fortified wines. Back in the days of sailing ships, the fortuitous position of the island of Madeira made it an important resupply point for ships en route to the Far East or the Americas. Ships typically took aboard local wines, which were fortified so they wouldn't spoil during the long voyage. It turned out that all that time spent in the stiflingly hot cargo hold of the ship as it sailed through the tropics did something to the wine that dramatically improved its character, resulting in an amber-colored wine with nutty, caramelized flavors. The term *maderization* was coined to describe this "cooking" process.

Fortified wines classified under the Madeira DOC are produced on the island of Madeira as well as the island of Porto Santo, located 27 miles (43 km) to the northeast of Madeira. Unfortified table wines are also made on both islands—in red, white, and rosé—and may be labeled as Madeirense DOC or Terras Madeirenses VR.

Figure 12-6: Vineyards on the island of Madeira

Geography and Climate

Madeira is a small volcanic island, with its highest point more than 6,000 feet (1,830 m) above sea level. The vines are planted on the steep, terraced slopes of the central mountain spine. Situated in the Atlantic Ocean at 33° north latitude, the island has a mild subtropical climate with little annual temperature variation. Rainfall in the grape-growing regions is moderate, although rare in summer, with 75% of the annual precipitation received in the autumn and winter months. Vineyards are irrigated through a system of canals called *levadas,* a practice that dates to the mid-fifteenth century.

Grape Varieties

The varieties that are considered the "noble" grapes of Madeira are Sercial, Verdelho, Boal, and Malvasia (also referred to as Malmsey). They are typically planted at different elevations on the island, with Sercial halfway up the mountain, Verdelho a little lower, and Malvasia and Boal closer to sea level. The most widely planted variety on the island, however, is Tinta Negra (formerly known as Tinta Negra Mole), which takes on some of the characteristics of the noble grapes grown at the same elevations.

Madeira Wine Production

Madeira comes in both dry and sweet styles, and, depending upon which style is being produced, the wine is fortified either during fermentation or after. The dry styles, made with Sercial, Verdelho, or Tinta Negra, are fortified after the wine has fermented to dryness. Sweet styles of Madeira, made from Boal, Malvasia, or Tinta Negra, are fortified during fermentation, which halts the process while the wine is still sweet. All of these types then go through a maderization period to give them the true Madeira character.

There are two main ways to re-create the sunbaked conditions of those long-ago ocean voyages under sail:

- *The canteiro method:* The wine is placed in casks and stored in the rafters of an uncooled warehouse. Here, it will be subjected to high temperatures under the subtropical sun for a minimum of two years. With time, some evaporation occurs and the remaining wine becomes more concentrated, developing more complex flavors and aromas. Wines produced using the canteiro method are considered to be of the highest quality. Vinho de Canteiro may be bottled at a minimum of three years of age; however, the finest examples may remain in cask for 20 years or more.

- *The estufagem method:* Most wine aged using the estufagem method undergoes a process known as *cuba de calor*. In this method, the wine is left in a concrete or stainless steel vat known as an *estufa*. Hot water is circulated through a submerged coil within the vessel for a minimum of three months, heating the wine to 113°F to 122°F (45°C to 50°C). After this process, the wine rests in the estufa for a minimum of 90 days. Following this period of rest, the wine is transferred to a cask for aging. This is the least expensive aging method in terms of not only cost but also of the time required.

A second estufagem method, known as *armazem de calor*, involves leaving the wine in vats in a large room that is heated by steam to over 120°F (49°C) for six months to one year. The wine itself reaches temperatures of 86°F to 100°F (30°to 38°C). This process, used mainly by the Madeira Wine Company, utilizes lower temperatures and a longer period of time than the cuba de calor method. This method is gentler on the wine and is considered an intermediate method in terms of both the time required and the cost. Wines produced using either of the estufagem methods may be released a minimum of two years after harvest.

Madeira Wine Styles

The classic styles of Madeira take the names of the noble grapes traditionally used for that style. From driest to sweetest, these styles are as follows:

- *Sercial:* extra dry or dry, highly acidic; excellent as an aperitif
- *Verdelho:* off-dry or medium dry; honeyed, somewhat smoky character
- *Boal:* sweet, raisiny, medium rich, highly aromatic
- *Malmsey:* very sweet, somewhat soft, very rich

Figure 12-7: Barrels of Madeira aging at Blandy's

As EU law requires any wine using the name of a grape variety in its name to contain at least 85% of that variety, a good deal of Madeira is sold either under a proprietary name or simply as Madeira—perhaps with one of the following stylistic terms on the label:

- *Rainwater:* a traditional name for an off-dry blend with a golden or semi-golden color; intended to be a lighter style of Madeira
- *Age indication:* including 5, 10, 15, 20, 30, 40, and 50 years old as well as over 50; must be assessed and approved by a tasting panel
- *Colheita:* produced from a single vintage (85% minimum) and aged for at least 5 years before bottling
- *Frasqueira:* vintage Madeira, cask aged for a minimum of 20 years

BAIRRADA

Located within Beira Atlântico VR, the Bairrada DOC lies just inland from the coast and has a cool maritime climate. A diversified appellation, Bairrada produces white, red, rosé, and sparkling wines, with the majority of the output being red wine. The Baga grape, known for being high in acid and highly tannic, forms the basis of Bairrada DOC red wines. Other regional red grapes and, increasingly, international varieties are grown as well. Bairrada sparkling wines are made using the traditional method of sparkling wine production and are aged for at least nine months before being sold. The Maria Gomes grape (also known as Fernão Pires) is the main white grape used in the sparkling and white wines of the region.

DÃO

The Dão DOC is located between the sea and the mountains, just south of the Minho region. Compared to Bairrada, the Dão DOC is farther inland, is surrounded by mountains, and has a more continental climate. Although this area produces white, red, rosé, and sparkling wines, the Dão DOC focuses on complex, full-bodied red blends. Key red grape varieties include Alfrocheiro, Tinta Roriz, Jaen (Mencía), and Touriga Nacional. Encruzado and Bical are the leading white varieties of the region.

LISBOA

West and north of the city of Lisbon, the Lisboa VR produces a great deal of Portugal's regional wine. White wines—based on the Arinto grape—are fresh and crisp, while reds are fruit-forward with a good value-to-quality ratio. Key red grapes include Bastardo, Trincadeira, and Ramisco, but international varieties (both red and white) are now permitted. The area is also known for its brandy—including those made in the Lourinhã DOC, an appellation for aguardente (brandy) rather than wine.

The small DOC of Colares—located alongside the Atlantic coastline and dangerously in the path of suburban sprawl—is known for its unique vineyards planted among the sand. Due to the strong ocean breezes, many of the vineyards are surrounded by protective windbreaks created out of sand dunes and wooden fences. Wines produced in Colares include high-acid, high-tannin reds based on the Ramisco grape variety and aromatic whites based on Malvasia.

TEJO

To the east of Lisboa, the region of Tejo (formerly known as Ribatejano) is a significant producer of regional (VR Tejo) wine and an even more significant producer of vinho de Portugal. Covering the same area as the Ribatejo Province, this flat, fertile wine region spans both sides of the Tejo River. A small portion of the region's 55,000 acres (22,300 ha) of vineyards are included in Do Tejo DOC, which produces red, white, rosé, sparkling, and *licoroso* (fortified) wines from a wide range of approved grape varieties. Castelão and Trincadeira are the leading red varieties; Fernão Pires is the leading white grape variety.

PENÍNSULA DE SETÚBAL

Situated just south of Tejo, the Península de Setúbal is protected from the sea by the Arrábida Mountain range and comprises the DOCs of Setúbal and Palmela. The former is regarded for its vins doux naturels, produced from the Muscat of Alexandria grape and, when produced from a minimum of 85% Muscat, labeled as Moscatel de Setúbal. The Palmela DOC is mainly red and based on the Castelão grape, which thrives in the area's sandy soils.

ALENTEJANO

Moving farther east, we find the Alentejano region in southeastern Portugal, which is a significant source of quality wine from DOC Alentejo or the huge Alentejano VR. Given the continental climate in which they are grown, the wines are rich, fruit-forward, and full-bodied, while still retaining good acidity. The leading grapes in the DOC are Aragonêz (Tempranillo) and Trincadeira (Tinta Amarela), along with Alicante Bouschet, but the VR is seeing new plantings of international varieties such as Cabernet Sauvignon and Syrah.

ALGARVE

As the southernmost region on the mainland, the Algarve region has a range of climates depending on proximity to the Atlantic coast. A chain of mountains running along the northern border of the region from Spain to the ocean blocks much of the heat that plagues the Alentejo just to the north. Although the region is limited in its production, it contains four separate DOCs: Lagos, Portimão, Lagoa, and Tavira. Grape varieties are similar to those planted in Alentejo.

THE AZORES

The Azores region is located on a chain of nine islands approximately 1,000 miles (1,610 km) off the west coast of Portugal. Collectively, the islands are covered by the Azores VR, but three islands have their own DOCs: Biscoitos, Graciosa, and Pico. The island of Madeira is about 700 miles southeast of Pico. The majority of the wine produced in the Azores is white (either dry or fortified), much of it based on the Verdelho, Arinto (Pedernã), or Terrantez grape varieties.

Figure 12–8: Vineyards on Pico Island in the Azores

Table 12-1: Wine Designations of Portugal

WINE DESIGNATIONS OF PORTUGAL	
Vinho Regional (PGI) Designation	**PDO Designations**
The Açores (Azores) VR	Biscoitos DOC Graciosa DOC Pico DOC
Alentejano VR	Alentejo DOC
Algarve VR	Lagoa DOC Lagos DOC Portimão DOC Tavira DOC
Beira Atlântico VR	Bairrada DOC
Duriense VR	Douro DOC Porto DOC
Lisboa VR	Alenquer DOC Arruda DOC Bucelas DOC Carcavelos DOC Colares DOC Encostas d'Aire DOC Lourinhã DOC Óbidos DOC Torres Vedras DOC
Minho VR	Vinho Verde DOC
Península de Setúbal VR	Palmela DOC Setúbal DOC
Tejo VR	Do Tejo DOC
Terras da Beira VR	Beira Interior DOC
Terras de Cister VR	Távora-Varosa DOC
Terras do Dão VR	Dão DOC Lafões DOC
Terras Madeirenses VR	Madeira DOC Madeirense DOC
Transmontano VR	Trás-os-Montes DOC

Source: Wines of Portugal, 2021

UNIT THREE WINE LABELS, LAWS, AND REGIONS

GERMANY

LEARNING OBJECTIVES

After studying this chapter, the candidate should be able to:

• Discuss the general role and position of Germany in the global wine industry.
• Recall the physical location and general climate of Germany's major wine regions.
• Recognize the importance of Riesling to the German wine industry.
• Understand the hierarchy of wine designations from Wein to Prädikatswein, along with the progression of Prädikat levels from Kabinett to Trockenbeerenauslese.
• Discuss the differences among Anbaugebiete, Bereiche, Grosslagen, and Einzellagen.
• Identify the grape varieties and wine styles of the key wine regions of Germany.

Germany is home to some of the world's coldest-climate vineyards. The northernmost winegrowing regions of Germany are well above the 50th parallel of latitude and are far from the moderating influence of a large body of water. Yet through determination, centuries of experience, and carefully chosen vineyard sites, Germans have found ways of producing world-class wines.

Germany's wine reputation is built upon its world-class Rieslings. Riesling is one of the most cold-hardy grape varieties, and German Rieslings have a worldwide reputation for quality, complexity, and, in many cases, the ability to age for a long time. However, German wine is about more than just Riesling, as still white wines of many varieties, sparkling wines, and even some cold-hardy reds are produced here.

Beyond being a wine-producing country, Germany is also a major wine-consuming country. It makes the styles of wine it can and imports those styles it cannot. As a result, Germany is consistently among the world's largest importers of wine. Despite the domestic demand, Germany is also among the top ten nations in exporting wine.

GEOGRAPHY AND CLIMATE

Germany is located in north-central Europe, reaching as far north as Denmark and the Baltic Sea. However, with the exception of a few small districts in eastern Germany, all of the winegrowing areas are in the southwest quadrant of the country. The majority are found near a river or on the shores of Lake Constance (*Bodensee* in German).

The lifeblood of the German wine industry is the Rhine River and its tributaries. The Rhine forms most of Germany's border with Switzerland and France as it flows westward from Lake Constance to Switzerland, then along the French–German border north past Alsace, continuing on through western Germany until it flows out of the winegrowing region altogether and into the Netherlands.

The second most important wine river in Germany is the Mosel. It winds its way out of France's Vosges Mountains (where it is the Moselle), past Luxembourg, and then northeast through prime wine territory, until it empties into the Rhine. Other significant tributaries of the Rhine include the Ahr, Nahe, Main, and Neckar Rivers.

Figure 13-1: The Old Town Hall in Bamberg, Germany

Germany's climate is northern continental with mild summers, cold winters, and moderate precipitation year-round. In such a cool climate, wine grapes struggle to ripen before winter arrives, which is why the vineyards are concentrated near waterways. The flowing water moderates local climates and reflects sunlight back onto the vineyards, helping to warm the vines in this marginal climate. At this northerly latitude, south-facing hillside vineyards have a distinct advantage, maximizing both sun exposure and warmth. In Germany, as well as the rest of the Northern Hemisphere, vineyards on the north side of a river also benefit from extra sunlight reflecting off the water. Many of the top vineyard sites, notably in the Mosel and Rheingau, have dark blue and red slate-based soils that are ideal for absorbing solar heat during the daytime and radiating it back at night.

Germany is divided into 16 states (*Länder*). The winegrowing regions are primarily in the states of Baden-Württemberg, Hesse, and Rhineland-Palatinate.

GERMAN GRAPE VARIETIES

As might be expected in this climate, white grape varieties predominate in Germany, accounting for two-thirds of the total. More than 100 varieties are permitted, but in practice about 20 or so comprise almost all of the vineyard acreage.

Riesling is the most widely planted grape in the country, taking up more than one-fifth of the vineyard acreage. It is especially dominant in the Rheingau and Mosel areas. Müller-Thurgau, a Riesling X Madeline Royale cross developed for hardiness but somewhat lacking in resemblance to Riesling with regard to taste and longevity, is the second most common grape. Other leading white grape varieties include Silvaner, Grauburgunder (Pinot Gris, also known as Ruländer), and Weissburgunder (Pinot Blanc). German Gewürztraminer is well-known, but it is not widely grown. Chardonnay, Sauvignon Blanc, and Kerner (a Riesling X Schiava Grossa cross) are present as well.

Spätburgunder (Pinot Noir)—the leading red grape variety—is surprisingly widespread; in recent years its acreage has increased such that it is now the country's second most widely planted grape overall (after Riesling). Other important red grape varieties include Dornfelder, a deeply-hued red grape renowned for its floral aromas, and Blauer Portugieser, much of which is used in light red wines or rosé.

LEADING GRAPE VARIETIES OF GERMANY

Red Grapes	White Grapes
Spätburgunder	Riesling
Dornfelder	Müller-Thurgau
Blauer Portugieser	Silvaner
Trollinger	Grauburgunder
Blaufränkisch	Weissburgunder
St. Laurent	Kerner
	Gewürztraminer

Figure 13-2: Leading Grape Varieties of Germany

GERMAN WINE LAWS

Quality Levels
In keeping with the EU wine blueprint, German wine law, reformed in 2009, divides wines into three broad categories. These categories are further defined both by geographic location and the degree of ripeness achieved by the grapes at harvest.

The various levels of the classification hierarchy, in ascending order of quality, are as follows:

- *Wein:* This category, previously referred to as *Tafelwein,* or table wine, is used for basic wine. There are very few guarantees of quality at this level. Most wein is made for the domestic market. These wines may be enriched or chaptalized to increase the final alcohol level. Some of the wine available at this level is imported bulk wine, mostly from Italy. In order to use the term *Deutscher Wein,* the wine must be 100% German in origin.
- PGI — *geschützte geographische Angabe (ggA):* This category contains what used to be referred to as *Landwein* (country wine). At this level, the grapes are required to be slightly riper than those for allowed for use in *wein;* however, chaptalization is permitted. A minimum of 85% of the grapes must be grown in one of Germany's 26 designated Landwein regions, with the region specified on the label. These wines are typically produced in either a dry (*trocken*) or off dry (*halbtrocken*) style.
- PDO — *geschützte Ursprungsbezeichnung (gU):* This category contains the highest tiers of quality wine, as defined by the German government. These wines must be produced using grapes from one of the thirteen Anbaugebiete (specified winegrowing regions) and denote a place-name on the label (with 100% of the grapes sourced from the named place).

The subcategories of German PDO (gU) wines are as follows:

- *Qualitätswein* is the lower level of the two PDO subcategories. These wines represent the largest proportion of German wine output. Grapes used for Qualitätswein must reach sufficient ripeness for recognition as a quality wine. However, chaptalization is permitted for this category.
- *Prädikatswein* is the highest quality level designation. (The term *Prädikat* means "distinction.") These wines must be produced using grapes of sufficient ripeness, and chaptalization is not permitted. One of the six levels of the *Prädikat* must be stated on the label.

Figure 13–3: German wine categories

The subcategories for Prädikatswein, in ascending order of grape ripeness, are as follows:

- *Kabinett:* light- to medium-bodied wines made from grapes with the lowest ripeness level of the Prädikat. These wines average 7% to 10% alcohol.
- *Spätlese* (late harvest): wines of additional ripeness made from grapes harvested after a designated picking date. With the extra ripening time, the grapes develop more intense flavors and aromas than Kabinett.
- *Auslese* (selected harvest): wines made from grapes that have stayed on the vine long enough to have a required level of sugar. These wines can be intense in bouquet and taste, and have a potential alcohol level in excess of 14%.
- *Beerenauslese* (BA; selected berries): rich, sweet dessert wines made from individually harvested berries that are sweeter than Auslese and that may also be affected by the honeyed influence of botrytis, known in German as *Edelfäule.*
- *Eiswein* (ice wine): wines made from frozen grapes harvested at a BA level of ripeness or higher. Having already become overripe from staying on the vine until as late as January, these grapes are harvested after they freeze in the vineyard. They are crushed immediately, and much of the water in the berries is discarded as ice, leaving grape must with a very high sugar level (see chapter 5).

- *Trockenbeerenauslese* (TBA; selected dried berries): wines from individually picked berries that are overripe to the point of being raisins and often further shriveled by botrytis. TBAs are considered to be among the world's greatest dessert wines.

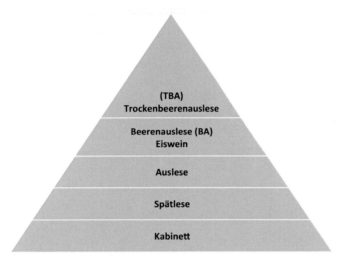

Figure 13–4: German Prädikat levels

The six Prädikat levels are not necessarily a hierarchy of quality. Kabinett wines are certainly the most basic of the Prädikat wines, but after that the differences are more stylistic and a matter of taste than indicative of an absolute scale of quality. The three dessert wines, Beerenauslese, Eiswein, and Trockenbeerenauslese, make up a very small fraction of production.

The Prädikat levels ensure that the grapes used in a specific wine have achieved a minimum level of ripeness. The riper levels are considered desirable, as the use of underripe grapes may result in wines that are highly acidic, light in alcohol, and with flavors that are not fully developed. The ripeness of the grapes is assessed by measuring the amount of sugar present in degrees *Oechsle*, a system based on the density or must weight of the juice (the more solids, primarily sugar, in the juice, the denser the liquid will be).

Despite the emphasis on sugar content in the grapes, the Oechsle value does not necessarily translate to sweetness in the finished wine. High sugar content can lead to either high alcohol content in a dry wine or high sweetness levels in a low-alcohol wine, or anything in between, depending on the winemaker's preference. Approximately two-thirds of all German wine production is dry.

OECHSLE

The Oechsle scale is based on the density of the grape must:

- Oechsle = (density − 1.0) × 1,000

Must with a density reading of 1.074 is said to measure 74° Oechsle. Oechsle values can range from the 40s (seriously underripe) to well over 150 in dried grapes. Kabinett grapes may range from 70° to 85° Oechsle.

Figure 13–5: Hierarchy of place-names for German PDO wines

GEOGRAPHICAL INDICATIONS

- *Anbaugebiete*: Germany has 13 recognized wine regions, known as Anbaugebiete, for PDO wines. Both Qualitätswein and Prädikatswein require a single Anbaugebiet as a place of origin. These Anbaugebiete are further divided into the following progressively more exclusive geographical areas: Bereiche, Grosslagen, and Einzellagen.
- *Bereiche:* There are approximately 40 Bereiche. A Bereich can be thought of as a regional or district appellation, along the lines of AOC Côtes du Rhône, DO Catalunya, or a county in the United States. Each Anbaugebiet contains at least one Bereich. A Bereich is often indicated by the word *Bereich* on the label, as in *Bereich Bernkastel*.

- *Grosslagen:* There are approximately 160 Grosslagen. A Grosslage is a grouping of numerous vineyards into a convenient administrative package. There was little, if any, effort to take terroir into account when these areas were established, so they are largely meaningless from a terroir standpoint. Each Bereich includes multiple Grosslagen.

- *Einzellagen:* There are more than 2,700 Einzellagen. Each Grosslage contains numerous Einzellagen. An Einzellage is, in theory, a single vineyard, but this ignores the fact that these areas were created by cobbling together tiny vineyards (there were once 30,000 Einzellagen) into new vineyards with a minimum of 5 hectares (12.4 acres). Again, the logic appears more administrative than viticultural. Nevertheless, these are still relatively small vineyard areas with reasonably homogeneous conditions. The vineyards are often divided among many different owners.

If a Grosslage or Einzellage appears on a wine label, the name is typically preceded by a village name. The addition of the village name is helpful, as many of the Grosslagen and Einzellagen stretch across several towns—such as the famous Sonnenuhr vineyard that encompasses *Wehlener Sonnenuhr* (in the village of Wehlen) and *Zeltinger Sonnenuhr* (in the adjacent village of Zeltingen). In addition, some names occur more than once, at separate locations—such as *Rauenthaler Rothenberg* (in the village of Rauenthal) and *Geisenheimer Rothenberg* (in the village of Geisenheim).

The Future of Geographical Indications in Germany

Beginning in 2020, a few new PDO regions were registered in Germany. These regions—which include the *Monzinger Niederberg* PDO in the Nahe and the *Uhlen Blaufüsser Lay* PDO in the Mosel—are small, very specific areas within the larger Anbaugebiete. In addition, their rules dictate the use of approved grape varieties, limits on yield, and certain required methods of production—similar to an *appellation d'origine contrôlée* (AOC) as used in France. These new PDOs represent a departure from the typical label designations previously used in Germany.

Furthermore, in April of 2021, new guidelines were announced regarding the future of geographical indications in Germany. The new regulations—which include an expanded emphasis on village-, commune- and vineyard-specific appellations—are expected to be implemented as of the 2025 vintage.

GERMAN WINE LABELS

In addition to the information provided on a German wine label described in figure 13-6, wines made by the grape growers are designated *Erzeugerabfüllung* or *Gutsabfüllung*. Gutsabfüllung is the equivalent of "estate bottled." Erzeugerabfüllung also includes cooperatives of growers and means "producer bottled." The term *Abfüller* indicates a wine produced at a commercial winery that buys grapes from other sources. All German PDO wines will also show an *Amtliche Prüfungsnummer* (AP Number) on the label. The AP number is issued after government approval and identifies the wine and the specific testing center where it was approved, as well as the village of origin, winery of origin, and other information.

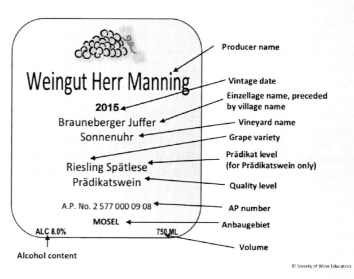

Figure 13-6: German wine label and explanation of its content

VDP CLASSIFICATION

The Association of German Prädikat Wine Estates (Verband Deutscher Prädikatsweingüter, or VDP) is an organization of Germany's leading wine estates committed to terroir-driven viticulture. In 2002, it announced Germany's first classification system for individual vineyards, using the system of vineyard classification in Burgundy as its model. The VDP system was further refined in 2012.

There are four levels of classification in the VDP system, listed from highest to lowest:

- *VDP Grosse Lage:* The highest-level vineyards of the estate, translated as "great site." A dry wine from a VDP Grosse Lage vineyard may be designated by the initialism "GG" (Grosses Gewächs) and is labeled with the term "Qualitätswein Trocken." A VDP Grosse Lage wine with natural, ripe sweetness is labeled with one of the traditional Prädikat levels: Kabinett, Spätlese, Auslese, Beerenauslese, Eiswein, or Trockenbeerenauslese.
- *VDP Erste Lage:* The second-highest-level vineyards of the estate, translated as "first site." Dry wines at this level are also labeled as "Qualitätswein Trocken," while each region can define the taste profile of off-dry (halbtrocken or feinherb) wines. Naturally sweet wines at the Erste Lage level will be labeled with one of the traditional Prädikat levels.
- *VDP Ortswein:* Translates as "classified site wine." These wines are sourced from vineyards at the equivalent of a village appellation. These wines may also be labeled as "Qualitätswein Trocken" if dry and, if naturally sweet, with the terms *halbtrocken* or *feinherb*, or one of the levels of the Prädikat.
- *VDP Gutswein:* Represents good entry-level wines, equivalent to an estate wine or regional wine. The wines originate from an estate's holdings within a region, and they meet the stringent standards prescribed by the VDP.

One interesting item of note concerning the label terms used in the VDP classification is that for the top three tiers—Grosse Lage, Erste Lage, and Ortswein—the Prädikat levels are reserved for use with wines that retain some natural sweetness. Under the VDP system, dry wines produced under these three tiers are labeled with the term *trocken* (in addition to the *GG* used by the Grosse Lage properties) as opposed to a Prädikat level. According to the VDP, this enables the levels of the Prädikat to reflect their original meaning, indicating natural sweetness, as opposed to the modern usage of the Prädikat terminology, which—it may be argued—does not reflect a correlation between Prädikat level and actual taste profile.

Figure 13-7: VDP logo

GERMAN WINE STYLES

In Germany's northern climate, grapes are typically left on the vine as long as possible to get as ripe as they can, and are often brought into the winery just before winter sets in. Historically, the cold temperatures after harvest had a tendency to cause the new wine to stop fermenting before all of the sugar had been converted to alcohol. Given the high acidity of Riesling and some of the other grape varieties grown in Germany, especially when they are underripe, the residual sugar was beneficial. Thus, the typical style of German wine became white wine somewhere between off-dry and fully sweet. This style was very popular both at home and on the export market, and the country's sweet wines were prized internationally for centuries.

When tastes changed in the late twentieth century, consumers began drinking drier wines, and Germany's exports plummeted. These days, the German wine industry is trying to promote both the production of dry wines at home and consumer awareness of these wines abroad. In addition, red varieties are increasingly grown throughout the country. Today, more than one-third of German wine production is red, and a large proportion of whites are dry.

WINEMAKING CONSIDERATIONS

In principle, grapes at any ripeness level can be made into sweet or dry wine. In the lowest categories, the natural sugar in the grapes is often so low that the potential alcohol level is barely enough for the wine to be stable and to meet the legal definition of wine. In these cases, for wines up to and including Qualitätswein, the winemaker's choices are as follows:

- Make a low-alcohol dry wine (probably thin and extremely acidic).
- Chaptalize—that is, add sugar to the must before fermentation to increase the potential alcohol level.
- Make a low-alcohol sweet wine by adding *süssreserve* (unfermented grape juice) to the wine after fermenting it dry.

Grapes at the Prädikatswein level have sufficient potential alcohol to produce stable wine even if the fermentation is stopped early. For these wines, chaptalization is not allowed. The winemaker's choices for Prädikatswein, therefore, especially at the Spätlese or Auslese level, are a little different:

- Make a medium- to high-alcohol dry wine.
- Make a medium-alcohol, moderately sweet wine by stopping the fermentation prior to completion.
- Make a low-alcohol, very sweet wine by stopping the fermentation even earlier.

INDICATIONS OF SWEETNESS

With so many choices of styles, it can be difficult for consumers to know what to expect from a bottle of German wine. There is as yet no mandatory industry-wide system in place that makes it clear to consumers how sweet a particular German wine is or how its sweetness was achieved. Nevertheless, there are clues available on every label, and various groups of German winemakers and individual producers have come up with ways to make the style apparent.

The simplest way to advise the consumer of the wine's sweetness level is to state it plainly. Many labels carry the exact residual sugar level in grams per liter. Others use qualitative terms that give a general idea of the sweetness. English-language words may be used on some wineries' exports to English-speaking countries, but the traditional German terms are seen more often:

trocken	dry	up to 9 g/L*
halbtrocken	off-dry	9–18 g/L**
feinherb	off-dry	legally undefined, but in the same range as halbtrocken
lieblich, halbsüß	half-sweet	18–45 g/L
süss or *süß*	sweet	more than 45 g/L

* No more than 2 g/L above acidity level
** No more than 10 g/L above acidity level

Figure 13-8: Riesling taste profile

In 2008, in an attempt to clarify matters for the consumer, the International Riesling Foundation created the Riesling Taste Profile, which permits Riesling producers to use a scale on their back labels to indicate the wine's sweetness level to consumers. While participation is voluntary, its use has caught on among some producers. The individual winery determines the placement of the arrow based on a set of technical guidelines in concert with its tasting assessment.

DESSERT WINES

The three highest Prädikat levels, BA, TBA, and Eiswein, represent some of the world's exemplary dessert wines. These wines are normally low in alcohol, high in acid, and very sweet. Botrytis aromas and flavors may be present in the BA and TBA wines, but grapes for Eiswein have not necessarily been affected by noble rot.

Required minimum ripeness levels for BA, Eiswein, and TBA grapes vary somewhat by Anbaugebiet. However, they are within the range of 110° to 125° Oechsle for BA and Eiswein and between 150° and

154° Oechsle for TBA. Grapes for German Eiswein must be harvested while frozen on the vine at an ideal temperature of at least –8°C/18°F. For this reason, most grapes for Eiswein are harvested in the early hours of the morning, often before dawn. While the harvest for Eiswein often begins in November or December, it is quite possible for it to occur in January or February of the year following the harvest for the more typical styles of wine. If this is the case, the vintage date of the finished wine will reflect the calendar year of the growing season.

RED WINES

Red wines are an increasingly important part of German wine production. In the past two decades, red grape varieties have more than doubled in vineyard area and now account for some 36% of Germany's acreage. These vineyards are mostly found in the warmer south of the country, particularly in Württemberg and Baden. This is still a fairly cool area, so German red wines are often on the light side, all the more so because the most prominent red variety is Spätburgunder (Pinot Noir), which is typically light in color and tannin. Germany also produces a substantial amount of rosé. A rosé made from a single variety of at least Qualitätswein quality may be labeled with the term *Weissherbst*.

SPARKLING WINES

High-acid, slightly underripe grapes are the perfect ingredient for sparkling wine, and Germany makes a lot of it. Germans reportedly have the world's highest per-capita consumption of sparkling wine. A good deal of German sparkling wine is known as *Sekt*, which is typically produced via by the tank method (although use of the traditional method is allowed). Off-dry and semisweet versions of Sekt are widely produced and very popular. Simple, fruity aerated sparkling wines known as *Schaumwein* ("foam wine") are produced by carbonation. Spätburgunder and wide range of white grape varieties are used for making German sparkling wine.

Figure 13–9: Vineyards in the Mosel

WINE REGIONS

MOSEL

The Mosel is one of the best-known wine regions of Germany, famous for its high-acid Rieslings. It is one of the larger areas in terms of production, responsible for almost one-sixth of the country's wine.

Geography and Climate

The Mosel River snakes its way past some of Germany's most famous vineyard sites as it flows from Trier northeast to Koblenz, where it joins the Rhine. The river is tortuously winding, and its banks are often very steep. This is the most northerly great wine region in the world, and its cool climate makes it difficult to fully ripen even the most cold-hardy grapes.

The best-performing vineyards are those facing south on steep slopes, providing the ideal aspect for maximizing sun exposure. In many spots, the thin, sandy topsoil is scattered with bits of broken slate that help with heat retention and prevent erosion of the soil. Despite the overall cold climate, Germany's continental setting allows some hot summer days during the peak growing season that help to raise sugar levels without sacrificing acidity.

The Mosel has several side tributaries, the most important in wine terms being the Saar and Ruwer Rivers (until 2007, the Anbaugebiet was known as Mosel-Saar-Ruwer). The central area, known as the Mittelmosel, is home to many of the most famous sites.

Figure 13-10: Vineyards in Zell-Merl in the fall

Grape Varieties and Styles

Riesling dominates the Mosel with about 62% of the vineyard land. Other leading white grapes include Müller-Thurgau, Elbling, and Grauburgunder. Red grapes, led by Spätburgunder, account for just slightly over 10% of the total plantings.

Acidity is the hallmark of Riesling, and the Mosel produces Rieslings that exemplify this trait; yet these wines are balanced by rich flavors of stone fruits and honey and, sometimes, a moderate sweetness. Wines of the Mosel usually contain no more than 10% alcohol, and they are traditionally bottled in tall, slender green bottles.

Mosel Appellations

The Mosel Anbaugebiet has six Bereiche, including Bernkastel, Burg Cochem, Saar, and Ruwertal. The region's quality is attested to by the fact that it has over 500 Einzellagen, more than any other region.

RHEINGAU

The most famous stretch of vineyards along the Rhine is the Rheingau. This small area produces just 2% of Germany's total wines, but its reputation is at least equal to the Mosel's.

Geography and Climate

The Rheingau's vineyards have the most favored position on the Rhine. For about 15 miles (24 km) after passing the cities of Mainz and Wiesbaden, the Rhine flows westward, giving the entire right bank an ideal southern exposure, with additional sunlight reflecting up from the wide river. This macroclimate affords maximum sun and warmth, along with protection from cold north winds. Red slate soils hold heat during the day and radiate it onto the vines overnight.

Grape Varieties and Styles

The vineyards of the Rheingau with the best reputations are heavily invested in the country's classic grape, Riesling, which takes up more than three-quarters of the region. The excellent southern exposure of the vineyards produces elegant, full-bodied Rieslings. It also provides enough warmth to ripen Spätburgunder well; this variety takes up more than half of the remaining vineyard space.

Rheingau Appellations

This Anbaugebiet has just one Bereich, Johannisberg, with more than 120 Einzellagen.

NAHE

The Anbaugebiet of Nahe lies southwest of the Rheingau, where the river of the same name flows into the Rhine. The Nahe Valley, west of Rheinhessen, produces Rieslings that are well respected, if not especially well-known. However, while white wine does dominate, Riesling represents only about one-quarter of the production here. The region has many fine vineyard sites on the south-facing slopes of the mainly east–west valleys of the Nahe and its tributaries.

RHEINHESSEN

Rheinhessen is located on the south and west bank of the Rhine across from the Rheingau and north of the Pfalz. It leads Germany's winegrowing regions both in area under vine and overall wine production. The Rheinhessen forms a low, flat plateau and has a generally warm, dry climate. Most of its vineyards are currently planted to Riesling and Müller-Thurgau, but Dornfelder is not far behind.

PFALZ

The Pfalz lies to the west of the Rhine, and its southern edge is not far from the northern tip of French Alsace. It is the second largest Anbaugebiet in terms of acreage. With the region's name coming from the Latin word *palatium,* meaning "palace," it is often referred to by the English equivalent, Palatinate. Quite sunny and warm during the growing season, this fertile region is known mainly for simple, inexpensive wines produced in large quantities, but that is changing as some vintners begin to focus on low yields and premium bottlings. Riesling accounts for nearly 25% of the total plantings in the Pflaz. Other leading grape varieties include Müller-Thurgau and Grauburgunder, along with the red varieties Dornfelder and Spätburgunder.

FRANKEN

The easternmost Anbaugebiet of the former West Germany, Franken covers a large area of the Main River Valley, but with fairly sparse plantings of vines. Due to the region's cold climate and short growing season, the earlier-ripening varieties of Müller-Thurgau and Silvaner play a significant role, and the area is primarily known for everyday white wines. Franconian wines are easily recognizable by the region's use of a traditional squat green or brown flask called a *Bocksbeutel.*

HESSISCHE BERGSTRASSE

A tiny region with only 1,150 acres (465 ha) planted to vines, Hessische Bergstrasse is a spur off the northern part of the Baden region. The area is known for white wines, with almost half of the acreage currently planted to Riesling. The name of the region means "Hessian Mountain Road."

WÜRTTEMBERG

Württemberg is a large region that focuses on red wine, with almost 75% of the vineyard area dedicated to red grape varieties such as Trollinger, Schwarzriesling (Pinot Meunier), and Lemberger. Most of the vines are planted on the slopes of the Neckar River Valley and on the banks of the

Wine Regions of Germany

Copyright: The Society of Wine Educators 2021

Figure 13–11: German wine regions

Neckar's tributaries, but a few are isolated well south on the shore of Lake Constance. Rainfall and humidity are higher in Württemberg than in other German wine regions.

BADEN

Geographically, Baden covers the most ground of the 13 winegrowing areas, stretching 150 miles (240 km) along the eastern bank of the Rhine between Mannheim and Switzerland. However, only a fraction of the area is planted to grapes, making it the third largest Anbaugebiet in vineyard acreage, after Rheinhessen and Pfalz. Baden consists of two large unconnected segments along the east side of the Rhine, plus three small subareas along western Lake Constance. Baden's Kaiserstuhl Bereich is considered the warmest of Germany's growing areas. Spätburgunder is by far the most widely planted grape variety in Baden, followed by Müller-Thurgau and Grauburgunder. Weissherbst—a single-variety, high-quality rosé—based on Spätburgunder is a specialty of the region.

AHR

One of the northernmost regions, Ahr is among Germany's smallest, with just over 1,300 acres (526 ha) planted to vines. Ahr is (somewhat surprisingly) known for red wines, which account for over 80% of total production. Spätburgunder is the leading grape variety, although Portugieser and Dornfelder are widely planted as well. The region follows the short path of the Ahr River from its source in the village of Blankenheim to its confluence with the Rhine. The land surrounding the Ahr River consists of a series of sheltered valleys lined with steep, south-facing slopes. This topography, combined with the heat-retaining properties of the dark slate and greywacke (sandstone) soils, allows the red grapes of the area to reach a consistent level of ripeness. The red wines of the Ahr tend to show relatively high tannins and oak-derived notes of spice—despite the northerly latitude (50°N).

MITTELRHEIN

Another small region, the Mittelrhein is located along a stretch of the Rhine Valley downriver (north) from the Rheingau. The Mittelrhein features steep banks dotted with castles and small vineyards. Most of the terraced vineyards are planted to Riesling.

SACHSEN AND SAALE-UNSTRUT

These two areas, part of the former East Germany, are the northernmost and easternmost of the German Anbaugebiete. Together, they comprise 2,600 acres (1,050 ha) and produce very little wine. Müller-Thurgau, Riesling, and Weissburgunder are the most widely planted grape varieties.

Figure 13–12: German vineyards in winter

Table 13-1: German PDO Wine Regions

GERMAN PDO WINE REGIONS				
Anbaugebiete		**Bereiche**	**Grosslagen**	**Einzellagen**
Ahr	1	Walporzheim/Ahrtal	1	43
Baden	9	Badische-Bergstrasse, Bodensee, Breisgau, Kraichgau, Kaiserstuhl, Markgräflerland, Ortenau, Tuniberg, Tauberfranken	17	315
Franken	3	Mainviereck, Maindreieck, Steigerwald	23	216
Hessische Bergstrasse	2	Starkenburg, Umstadt	3	23
Mittelrhein	2	Loreley, Siebengebirge	11	111
Mosel	6	Bernkastel, Burg Cochem, Moseltor, Obermosel, Saar, Ruwertal	19	524
Nahe	1	Nahetal	6	328
Pfalz	2	Mittelhaardt-Deutsche Weinstrasse, Südliche Weinstrasse	23	325
Rheingau	1	Johannisberg	10	123
Rheinhessen	3	Bingen, Nierstein, Wonnegau	24	434
Saale-Unstrut	3	Mansfelder Seen, Schloss Neuenburg, Thüringen	4	18
Sachsen	2	Elstertal, Meissen	3	17
Württemberg	6	Bayerischer Bodensee, Kocher-Jagst-Tauber, Oberer Neckar, Remstal-Stuttgart, Württembergisch Unterland, Württembergisch Bodensee	15	207

Source: German Wine Institute, 2021

CENTRAL AND EASTERN EUROPE

CHAPTER FOURTEEN

LEARNING OBJECTIVES

After studying this chapter, the candidate should be able to:

- Discuss the physical location and general climate of Austria's major wine regions.
- Recognize Austria's signature grape variety and other important grapes.
- Describe Austrian wine law and the hierarchy of Austrian wine designations.
- Discuss the other main wines and wine regions of central and eastern Europe.

Eastern Europe has as old and rich a tradition of winegrowing as the western parts of Europe, but its wine industry was halted and much of its infrastructure destroyed by World War II and the subsequent Soviet domination of most of the area. Of the countries discussed in this chapter, only Austria and Switzerland in central Europe remained outside of communist rule, which seemingly focused on high output, resulting in a decrease in quality.

Austria maintained a wine industry that competed on the world wine market during this time, although it ran into its own quality issues in the 1980s, which seriously damaged its reputation for more than a decade. Meanwhile, Switzerland kept its wine production levels constant, but its wines are largely unseen outside of the country, partly because they are domestically consumed and partly because the Swiss franc is higher in value than other currencies, which makes Swiss wines prohibitively expensive.

Since the fall of the Soviet Union, some progress has been made in reviving eastern Europe's wine production. At the same time, the European Union has spread eastward in a series of expansions, drawing much of eastern Europe into its sphere, and greatly influencing the wine of many eastern European countries.

AUSTRIA

Austria's wine industry has become a source of fine wines after many years of acting as a supplier of bulk wines for the German wine market. The change was brought on by a public relations crisis in the mid-1980s when a few brokers chemically adulterated some wines to artificially give them added richness. After several subsequent years of disastrous export sales, the Austrians tightened controls and began focusing on quality. As a result, Austria's reputation has rebounded, along with its exports. It is still a relatively small player on the international market, but its wines are well regarded.

GEOGRAPHY AND CLIMATE

Austria is centrally located in Europe, southeast of Germany and northeast of Italy. The Alps cover much of the country, especially toward the west, so only the lower hills and plains in the eastern part of the country are really suitable for winegrowing. The majority of Austria's vineyard land lies in the three eastern states of Niederösterreich (Lower Austria), Burgenland, and Steiermark (Styria), which border the Czech Republic, Slovakia, Hungary, and Slovenia.

Wine Regions of Austria

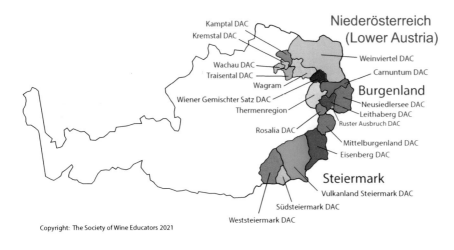

Copyright: The Society of Wine Educators 2021

Figure 14-1: Austrian wine regions

As in most of central Europe, the climate in eastern Austria is cool continental. Summers are mild and winters are very cold. The climate is similar to that of Baden in southern Germany, which lies at the same latitude just to the west. Its viticultural conditions are similar, as well.

GRAPE VARIETIES

There are 40 grape varieties authorized for use in Austrian wine bottled at the PGI or PDO level. These include 26 white and 14 red varieties.

White wine production dominates in Austria, accounting for over 66% of the total. The country's signature grape variety is the indigenous Grüner Veltliner, a spicy white grape that is popular internationally and is known for citrus, white pepper, and mineral characteristics. Young examples provide fresh fruit and vibrant acidity, while wines produced from older vines and better vineyards are capable of aging for three to ten years. Outside Austria, Grüner Veltliner is found only in a few places, mostly in eastern Europe. Approximately one-third of Austria's total acreage under vine—nearly 35,530 acres (14, 380 ha)—is planted with Grüner Veltliner.

- Welschriesling: not true Riesling, but a variety that makes fragrant, perfumed, high-acid wines
- Müller-Thurgau: a cross of Riesling and Madeleine Royal, this grape is a reliable producer, but it makes wines that are low in acid and relatively unremarkable

- Weissburgunder: Pinot Blanc
- Riesling: most commonly produced in a dry style, but also in the full range of sweetness levels up to Trockenbeerenauslese
- Chardonnay: also known here as Morillon

The second most widely planted grape, and the most prominent red, is Zweigelt. This cross between Blaufränkisch and St. Laurent, when well made, displays a medium body and cherry flavors with a peppery finish.

Other significant red varieties include the following:
- Blaufränkisch: Also known as Lemberger or Kékfrankos, this is one of the few Austrian grape varieties with commercial importance in the United States. It produces a full-bodied wine with high acidity, solid tannins, and dark-berry fruit flavors.
- St. Laurent: Although this variety makes up only a small percentage of planted acreage in Austria, it is increasingly exported. This member of the Pinot family produces medium-bodied wines with medium tannins and cherry-berry flavors.

LEADING GRAPE VARIETIES OF AUSTRIA

Red Grapes	White Grapes
Zweigelt	Grüner Veltliner
Blaufränkisch	Welschriesling
Spätburgunder	Riesling
Blauburger	Weissburgunder
St. Laurent	Müller-Thurgau
Portugieser	Chardonnay (Morillon)
Merlot	Sauvignon Blanc
	Muskateller/Muscat

Figure 14-2: Leading Grape Varieties of Austria

KMW CONVERSION

The Austrian measure for must weight is called *Klosterneuburger Mostwaage (KMW)*. KMW can be converted to other systems through these approximations:

- 1° KMW = about 1.2 Brix
- 1° KMW = about 5 Oechsle

AUSTRIAN WINE LAWS

The place-of-origin and classification categories used for Austrian wines are similar, but not identical, to the system currently used in Germany. The classification hierarchy, based on minimum levels of ripeness, as well as other attributes, is as follows:

- *Wein:* The basic category, Wein was recently renamed from the more old-fashioned term *tafelwein.* Wein may be labeled with a vintage date and/or a grape variety, but may not carry a place-of-origin more specific than "Österreich" (Austria).
- *Landwein:* The Landwein category represents wine with a geographical indication and is considered PGI-level wine. Wines produced under this category are labeled with one of three *Weinbauregionen* (Landwein regions): Weinland Österreich, Steierland, or Bergland.
- *PDO wines:* Austria uses three distinct terms to refer to its PDO-level wines: Qualitätswein, Prädikatswein, and *Districtus Austriae Controllatus* (DAC). These wines must be sourced from a single quality wine region (Weinbaugebiet), subregion, or a specifically-defined Districtus Austriae Controllatus (DAC). These wines account for approximately two-thirds of Austria's total production. While a great majority of the PDO-level wine in Austria is produced in its easternmost states, all nine of Austria's Federal States are designated as PDO wine-producing appellations.

Austrian Qualitätswein must be produced from grapes harvested at a minimum of 15° KMW; those that are harvested at a minimum of 19° KMW may qualify for Prädikatswein status.)

Austria's Prädikatswein are divided into subcategories based on ripeness levels very much like the categories used for German Prädikatswein. However, there are a few distinct differences in the two systems:

- In Austria, Kabinett wines are considered a subset of Qualitätswein rather than the beginning rung on the ripeness ladder of the Prädikat.
- The Austrian Prädikat includes guidelines for a dried-grape wine, known as *Strohwein* or *Schilfwein*.

With Kabinett wines moved down to the lower quality wine category, the Prädikatswein levels for Austrian wine, from least to most ripe, are as follows:

- Spätlese: minimum 19° KMW
- Auslese: minimum 21° KMW; unripe grapes must be removed from the bunches
- Beerenauslese (BA), Eiswein, and Strohwein/Schilfwein: minimum 25° KMW
- Trockenbeerenauslese (TBA): minimum 30° KMW; the majority of the grapes must be affected by botrytis

Although Austria's wines have historically used must weight (sugar content) as a designation of quality, there was concern among Austrian producers that their wines would be broad-brushed as being universally sweet. Accordingly, Austria sought to further define quality for its dry wines. For instance, in the Wachau, an industry organization known as *Vinea Wachau* (*Vinea Wachau Nobilis Districtus*) instituted the terms *Steinfeder* (the lightest style), *Federspiel* (classic, or middleweight wines), and *Smaragd* (the fullest-bodied wines) to indicate increasing levels of ripeness for wines that are dry on the palate. However, many in the industry felt that a more appellation-based system was needed.

Consequently, in 2003, Austria introduced an appellation system that follows the terroir-based concept developed in France and promoted by the European Union. The Austrian system designates classified grape-growing regions as *Districtus Austriae Controllatus* (DAC), which may be considered the highest level of quality in Austria.

The DAC designation can only be used for the specified grape varieties considered the most outstanding and most typical of the delineated region. Each DAC also specifies alcohol levels, aging regimens, and other specific details. Wines that are produced within these DAC areas but that don't meet the DAC requirements must be labeled with a more generic area.

In addition to the more general *Klassik* (classic) level, some DACs also have a Reserve level with slightly higher standards for alcohol level and specifics in terms of flavor profile. As of July 2016, the wines of the Kamptal, Kremstal, and Traisental DACs will be further classified according to a three-tier quality ladder, beginning with regional, and moving up to village and single vineyard wines.

For the majority of Austrian wines that do not qualify for the DAC designation, classifications are still based primarily on the ripeness of the harvested grapes rather than on the terroir of the winegrowing zone, as noted on the previous page.

AUSTRIAN WINE STYLES

A key difference between Austrian and German wine styles is that Austrian wines (excluding dessert wines) are typically dry. Austria also produces some wine styles unique to the area. These include the following:

- *Strohwein (Schilfwein)* is a dried-grape wine that uses grapes of at least BA ripeness that have been air-dried on mats made of *Stroh* (straw) or *Schilf* (reeds) or hung on strings, much like the recioto wines of Veneto (Italy). Grapes for Strohwein/Schilfwein must be dried for a minimum of three months if picked at 25° KMW. Otherwise, they may be picked at 30° KMW and stored for two months. The raisinated grapes are then pressed, and the juice is fermented into a sweet wine.
- *Bergwein* (mountain wine) is produced using grapes that are grown on extraordinarily steep mountain slopes with at least a 26% gradient.

Figure 14–3: Vineyards in Austria, during the Südsteiermark-Classic auto rally

AUSTRIAN APPELLATIONS

Niederösterreich (Lower Austria)

Niederösterreich is the largest winegrowing region in Austria in both geographical area and vineyard acreage. This landlocked area has a continental climate with warm, dry summers and severe winters. The Danube River flows southeast through the region, and many of the more renowned vineyards are planted along its path. Subregions of the Niederösterreich include:

- Weinviertel DAC: Weinviertel is the largest subregion of Niederösterreich, stretching from the Danube Valley to the borders of the Czech Republic and Slovakia. DAC wines must be 100% Grüner Veltliner, and tend to be quite pungent, spicy, and peppery. Reserve DAC wines may have a subtle botrytis character.

Table 14-1: Austrian Wine Regions

AUSTRIAN WINE REGIONS		
Weinbauregionen (Landwein Regions)	Weinbaugebiete (Quality Wine Regions/ Federal States)	Subregions
Weinland Österreich		Eisenberg DAC
		Leithaberg DAC
	Burgenland	Mittelburgenland DAC
		Neusiedlersee DAC
		Rosalia DAC
		Ruster Ausbruch DAC
		Carnuntum DAC
		Kamptal DAC
		Kremstal DAC
		Thermenregion
	Niederösterreich (Lower Austria)	Traisental DAC
		Wachau DAC
		Wagram
		Weinviertel DAC
	Wien (Vienna)	Wiener Gemischter Satz DAC
Steierland		Südsteiermark DAC
	Steiermark (Styria)	Vulkanland Steiermark DAC
		Weststeiermark DAC
Bergland	(None)	(None)

Source: Austrianwine.com, 2021

Note: All nine of Austria's Federal States are registered with the EU as PDO wine-producing regions (Weinbaugebiete); this would include Carinthia (Kärnten), Tyrol (Tirol), Salzburg, Vorarlberg, and Oberösterreich (Upper Austria) in addition to the four major Weinbaugebiete/ Federal States listed above.

- Traisental DAC, Kamptal DAC, and Kremstal DAC: These three areas have similar climates, and all produce DAC wines from either Grüner Veltliner or Riesling. The Grüner Veltliner produced in these regions tends to be lighter and more delicate in style as compared to those of the Weinviertel.
- Wachau DAC: Located in a valley following the path of the Danube River, the Wachau DAC produces a variety of grapes and wine styles. However, the top-tier wines of the DAC—produced from designated, single-vineyard sites known as *Rieden*—are made exclusively from Riesling and Grüner Veltliner.
- Wagram: The Wagram area—located along the Danube River to the east of Wachau, Kremstal, and Kamptal—was known as Donauland prior to 2007. Grüner Veltliner is the most widely-

planted grape in the region, and is typically made into rich, flavorful, and characteristically spicy white wines. Other leading grapes include Roter Veltliner (a pink-skinned grape that—despite its name—has no direct genetic link to Grüner Veltliner), Riesling, Pinot Noir, and Zweigelt.
- Thermenregion: Thermenregion is located quite far from the moderating influence of the Danube, and produces a good deal of red wine, focusing on Zweigelt. Some unique grapes, such as Rotgipfler and Zierfandler (Spätrot), are grown here as well.
- Carnuntum DAC: The Carnuntum DAC, located to the south and east of Vienna, is approved for the production of dry wines (single-variety as well as blends). White wines may be produced using Chardonnay, Weissburgunder (Pinot Blanc), or Grüner Veltliner; red wines may be based on Zweigelt or Blaufränkisch. All varietally-labeled

wines produced under the Carnuntum DAC must contain 100% of the named variety. Blended wines must contain at least 67% (two-thirds) of the aforementioned grape varieties.

Burgenland

Burgenland is located to the south of Niederösterreich and shares a border with Hungary. The presence of Lake Neusiedl, the largest closed-basin lake in Europe, creates ideal conditions for the growth of *Botrytis cinerea* in parts of the area.

Burgenland contains six DAC regions, as discussed below.

- Mittelburgenland DAC: This area produces red wines based on the Blaufränkisch grape variety. These wines are known for full body, deep color, and spicy aromas as well as red and black fruit flavors. Classic wines must be matured in stainless steel or used oak and should not show any oak influence. Reserve wines, which require an additional year of aging, are often aged in new oak.
- Eisenberg DAC: Surrounding Eisenberg Hill in the southern portion of Burgenland, the Eisenberg DAC produces red wines from the Blaufränkisch grape variety under regulations similar to those of the Mittelburgenland DAC.
- Neusiedlersee DAC: Located to the east of Lake Neusiedl and stretching to the Hungarian border, the Neusiedlersee DAC produces red wines based on the Zweigelt grape variety. In 2020, sweet white wines were approved for production in the Neusiedlersee DAC as well.
- Leithaberg DAC: The vineyards of Leithaberg stretch between Lake Neusiedl to the east, and the Leitha Mountains (Leithagebirge) to the west. The warm winds around the lake encourage ripeness, while the mountains provide for a significant diurnal swing and cool temperatures at night. White wines of the Leithaberg DAC may be single-varietal or blended wines produced using Grüner Veltliner, Pinot Blanc, Chardonnay and/or Neuburger (an indigenous cross of Roter Veltliner and Sylvaner). The red wines of the Leithaberg DAC are based on Blaufränkisch, with an allowed (combined) maximum of 15% Zweigelt, St. Laurent, and/or Pinot Noir.
- Rosalia DAC: The Rosalia DAC is named for the *Rosaliengebirge*—Rosalia Mountain Range—that comprises a portion of the Alpine Foothills on the border between Burgenland and Niederösterreich. The DAC is approved for dry wines only, in red or rosé. Red wines are produced from the Blaufränkisch or Zweigelt grape varieties; rosé may be made from any red grape varieties approved for PDO wines in Austria.
- Ruster Ausbruch DAC: Ruster Ausbruch, one of the most famous wines of Austria, is produced on the western shore of Lake Neusiedl in the town of Rust. This sweet, botrytis-affected white wine was awarded DAC certification in 2020. The grapes used in Ruster Ausbruch—including Chardonnay (Morillon), Muskateller (Muscat), Pinot Gris, and Pinot Blanc, among others—must be harvested at a minimum of 30° KMW, equivalent to TBA (Trockenbeerenauslese) levels of ripeness. The tiny Ruster Ausbruch DAC is located within the larger Leithaberg DAC.

Steiermark (Styria)

Steiermark, the southernmost wine-producing region in Austria, is home to less than 10% of the nation's vineyards. This is a hilly, almost mountainous region with deep valleys and many vineyards planted on south-facing slopes in order to intercept the vivid sunlight. The climate here is slightly warmer than most other viticultural areas in Austria (although the winters can be just as cold). As such, viticulture here is quite different than the rest of the country, with Sauvignon Blanc and Chardonnay among the leading varieties.

As of the 2018 vintage, each of Steiermark's three subregions has been promoted to a DAC, and new *Verordnungen* (regulations) are now officially in force. These three DACs are discussed below:

- Südsteiermark DAC: Sauvignon Blanc, the leading grape of the Südsteiermark, is planted in nearly 20% of the region's vineyards. However, this is a large growing area—currently there are 6,234 acres (2,563 ha) planted to vine—and Riesling, Pinot Gris, and Chardonnay are well-represented as well. The area makes for a stunning landscape, with rolling hills punctuated by staggering slopes—some with an incline as steep as 45°. The soils in the flatter regions are primarily marine sediment, while the hills and slopes contain marl and conglomerate soils. The climate during the vegetative cycle typically consists of warm and humid days combined with cool nights, allowing for a long growing season and complex, concentrated grapes.

- Vulkanland Steiermark DAC: As its name implies, Vulkanland Steiermark is rich in volcanic soils that set this region apart from much of the rest of Austria. The area has 3,765 acres/1,524 ha planted to vines, many of them planted on the slopes of the area's long-dormant volcanoes, some reaching elevations as high as 1,968 feet/600 meters. A wide range of vines are cultivated in the region, including Welschriesling, Chardonnay (Morillon), Weissburgunder (Pinot Blanc), Grauburgunder (Pinot Gris), Sauvignon Blanc, and Zweigelt.

- Weststeiermark DAC: Weststeirmark, characterized by steep hills and deep valleys, is one of the smallest wine-growing regions of Austria (by acreage) with just over 1,200 acres (500 ha) planted to vines. The area is primarily known for its Schilcher Rosé, now labeled as "Schilcher Klassik Westeiermark DAC." Schilcher Rosé is produced from the red Blauer Wildbacher (Schilcher) grape variety—which accounts for nearly 85% of all vine plantings in the area. Other styles of wine produced in Weststeiermark include Weissburgunder (Pinot Blanc), Welschriesling, and Müller-Thurgau; red wine (albeit a small amount) is produced from Blauer Wildbacher as well.

Wien (Vienna)

The city of Vienna (Wien) lies on the Danube River and is the only European capital city to have a PDO within its city limits. The vineyard area is tiny—just over 1,500 acres (610 ha)—but quite significant in terms of culture and history. In the past, much of the economy of the area was based on viticulture and wine production. *Heurigen* (seasonal wine taverns) were a popular annual tradition, where the local winemakers served their newly-produced wine in and around the vineyards at harvest time.

Another tradition of the area (shared in other parts of Austria as well) was *Gemischter Satz*—wines made from several different grape varieties fermented together. The Wiener (Viennese) Gemischter Satz DAC was approved in 2013 for white wines

produced using at least three grape varieties. The grapes must be harvested, pressed, and fermented together, with no more than 50% from any single grape variety, and a minimum of 10% each of at least three varieties. The wines are meant to be fruit-forward and are not allowed to show significant influence of oak. An unusual factor of this DAC is that the grapes must not only be processed together but also must be grown together in a field blend (side by side in the vineyard).

While the regulations require a minimum of three different varieties, 15 varieties are approved for use and may be present in a single wine. Approved varieties include traditional Austrian varieties such as Grüner Veltliner, Sylvaner, Traminer, Rotgipfler, Neuburger, Weissburgunder, and Grauburgunder, as well as international varieties such as Chardonnay.

Figure 14-4: Hungarian vineyards at Badacsony

HUNGARY

Over 70% of Hungary's wine production is white. The Furmint grape variety is often used to produce dry white wines and is used as part of the blend in Hungary's famous dessert wine, Tokaji Aszú. One of the best-known red wines of Hungary, Egri Bikavér (*Bull's Blood of Eger*) is a full-bodied wine traditionally made from Kadarka grapes blended with other red varieties such as Kékfrankos (Blaufränkisch), Kékoportó (Portugieser), Cabernet Sauvignon, Cabernet Franc, Merlot, Menoire, Pinot Noir, Syrah, Blauburger, and Zweigelt. A newer

Figure 14-5: The Old Town of Dubrovnik, Croatia

version of this traditional wine, Egri Bikavér Superior, was introduced in 2004 when Hungary became a member of the EU. Egri Bikavér Superior requires that at least five of the recommended varieties be used.

Tokaji Aszú

The most famous wine from Hungary is the dessert wine Tokaji Aszú. The luscious, sweet Tokaji Aszú has a centuries-old history and managed to survive Soviet control in the twentieth century. Tokaji Aszú is produced in the Tokaj PDO located in Northern Hungary (a small part of the region extends into eastern Slovakia as well).

The authorized grape varieties of the Tokaj region include Furmint, Hárslevelű, Kabar, Kövérszőlő, Sárgamuskotály (Muscat), and Zéta. The climate in certain portions of the vineyard region in Tokaj is ideal for encouraging the development of botrytis in the vineyards. In addition to its famous dessert wines, the area produces dry white wines and sparkling wines.

The primary grape varieties used for Tokaji Aszú are Furmint and Hárslevelű, which provide enough acidity and aromatic character to keep the wine from being cloying. The production of Tokaji Aszú starts with late-harvested, botrytis-affected grapes; in this condition, the grapes are called aszú. The aszú grapes are gently mashed into a thick paste and then mixed with a normally fermented base wine for a day or two, allowing the wine to absorb the sugar and flavors of the aszú. The wine is then racked and aged in small casks for a few years in underground tunnels where film-forming yeast similar to the flor of the Sherry region grows.

Eszencia

Also produced in the Tokaj region, Eszencia is often referred to by its English name, Essencia. Eszencia is made from the free-run juice of the sweetest, most-botrytized, hand-selected berries. This type of wine requires a minimum of 45% residual sugar and often takes years to ferment to a content of 5% to 6% alcohol by volume.

CROATIA

Croatia has a winemaking tradition stretching back more than 2,000 years. However, like the other member states of the former Yugoslavia, it was somewhat wracked by warfare or controlled by a communist dictatorship for most of the last century. Despite this, Croatia has been an independent democratic republic since 1991 and is working to revitalize its wine industry, which has the benefit of the fine winegrowing conditions along the Adriatic Sea. Croatia became a member of the European Union in 2013.

Croatia is well-known as the native home of the Crljenak Kaštelanski grape variety—also known as Tribidrag—that was taken to the United States and eventually renamed Zinfandel. Crljenak Kaštelanski also made its way to Italy, where it is known as Primitivo.

The most widely grown white grape in Croatia is Graševina, known elsewhere as Welschriesling. White wine accounts for nearly two-thirds of the wine produced, with Malvasia, the high-yielding Bogdanuša, and international varieties such as Sauvignon Blanc, Pinot Gris, and Chardonnay among the other leading white grapes. Widely grown red grapes include Frankovka (the local name for Blaufränkisch), Teran, and Plavac Mali (a close relative of Crljenak Kaštelanski), as well as international varieties such as Cabernet Sauvignon and Merlot.

Croatia's wine country is divided into two broad regions—a coastal region and an inland region—separated by the Dinaric Alps. The two regions are very different in terms of climate, terroir, and wines produced. The inland region, *Kontinentalna Hrvatska* (Inland Croatia), stretches eastward over 150 miles (240 km), covering much of the eastern half of the country to the border with Hungary. A majority of wine produced in Inland Croatia is white, and most is consumed locally.

The western half, *Primorska Hrvatska* (Coastal Croatia), extends along the Adriatic coastline for 330 miles (530 km), with vineyard areas interspersed among islands and inlets formed by the Kvarner Gulf. The climate is overall Mediterranean, with maritime influences in the south and warmer areas in the north, particularly around the Istrian Peninsula. The majority of the wines and an even greater majority of the high-quality wines of Croatia are produced in these coastal areas.

SWITZERLAND

Switzerland—a relatively small producer of wine—exports little of its output, as the country's domestic demand is three times its production volume. Swiss wines are also very expensive outside of Switzerland, given the high value of the Swiss franc.

Switzerland, not a member of the European Union, has its own governing body in charge of wine law. This organization, typically referred to as the OIC, has three different official titles—one for each of the country's three official languages: *Organisme Intercantonal de Certification* (French), *Interkantonale Zertifizierungsstelle* (German), and *Organismo Intercantonale di Certificazione* (Italian). Official wine regions and controlled appellations similar to the French AOC system began to be implemented in the 1990s. These appellations, many of which specify grape varieties and some of which specify winemaking and wine styles, are largely overseen by the individual cantons (states).

Despite being set amid the rugged Alps, Switzerland has many protected valleys with fine weather for winegrowing. The primary areas of production are in the French-speaking part of the country along the northern shore of Lake Geneva and in the Valais, the valley of the Rhône River, to its east. Switzerland now produces slightly more red wine than white, with Pinot Noir the leading red grape, followed by Gamay and Merlot. Chasselas, an indigenous white grape also known as Fendant, is the leading white variety.

ROMANIA

The former Soviet satellite Republic of Romania spent most of the twentieth century making large amounts of bulk wine to send east to the Soviet Union. However, in recent years, Romania has begun to restore its quality wine industry, and Romania's 2007 entry into the EU has led to an influx of investment and expertise, as well as easier access to markets in the West.

Romania is, in general, home to a continental climate—moderated in places by the Black Sea, Danube River, and Carpathian Mountains. Romania is home to over 40 appellations, and wine is produced in many areas throughout the country. The country's oldest appellation—the Târnave DOC—is located in the center of the country surrounding the Carpathian Mountains; while the well-known sweet wines of the Cotnari DOC are produced in the Moldovan Hills (near the eastern border).

As victims of the original phylloxera epidemic, many of Romania's vineyards were replanted to French varieties at that time. Today, a dual focus on both indigenous and international grapes has led to varietally labeled wines as well as unusual blends of both French and Romanian varieties. The two most widely planted white grapes are Fetească Albă and Fetească Regală, both of which produce light, aromatic wines with varying levels of sweetness. Widely planted international white varieties include Muscat, Aligoté, and Sauvignon Blanc. Pinot Noir is often thought to be the leading red grape for the export market, while the native Fetească Neagră is considered to be the flagship red variety of the country.

BULGARIA

Bulgaria (officially, the Republic of Bulgaria) has a long history of wine production and was for a time—as recently as the 1970s and early 1980s—a leading producer and exporter of wine in terms of volume. Tumultuous political forces in the years that followed served to halt the growth and progress of the industry for a time. However, Bulgaria began its transformation to democracy in 1990 and became a member of the European Union in 2007. During this same time, the country began to slowly modernize and improve its wine industry. For now, the majority of the country's wine is made from international grape varieties and positioned for export. Boutique projects, traditional practices, and native grape varieties remain a small but thriving part of the industry.

Located in the eastern portion of the Balkan Peninsula, Bulgaria has a diverse topography and a temperate continental climate with hot summers, long, cold winters and four distinct seasons. The Danube River defines a portion of the northern border of the country and separates Bulgaria from Romania, its neighbor to the north. The northern portion of the country consists mainly of the vast lowlands of the Danube Plain, while the southern portion is dominated by highlands and elevated plains. The Black Sea borders the country to the east.

Vine plantings are more or less split evenly between red and white varieties. Cabernet Sauvignon and Merlot are the most widely planted international red varieties, followed by Syrah, Pinot Noir, and Zinfandel (among others). Mavrud, Rubin (a Nebbiolo X Syrah cross), and Gamza (known elsewhere as Kadarka) are considered to be native to Bulgaria and are grown throughout the country. Other red varieties include Melnik, a highly tannic variety mostly planted in the Struma River Valley, and Pamid, a thin-skinned, early-ripening variety.

Rkatsiteli and Dimiat, common throughout Eastern Europe, are the two most widely planted white grapes. The native Misket Cherven (which translates literally as "Red Misket") is a highly aromatic, pink-skinned variety grown throughout the hillier areas of the country. In addition, many international white grape varieties, including Chardonnay, Sauvignon Blanc, Riesling, and Viognier, are grown throughout Bulgaria.

SLOVENIA

Slovenia (officially the Republic of Slovenia) is a small European country with a long history of wine production. Its location on the Mediterranean coast and sharing a border with four established wine-producing countries (Italy to the west, Austria to the north, Croatia to the south and southeast, and Hungary to the northeast), places it at the crossroads of Europe's wine culture.

Slovenia has been an independent nation since 1991 and a member of the European Union since 2004. PDO wines are categorized as *zaščiteno označbo porekla* (ZOP). There are currently 14 defined ZOP designations, as well as several variations within the ZOPs, such as those for traditional method sparkling wines, botrytis-affected wines, and wines with a certain degree of aging. The 14 ZOPs are contained within the country's three designated PGI wine regions, known in the Slovenian language as *zaščiteno geografsko označbo* (ZGO). These three regions are:

- Podravje: The Podravje ZGO is located in the inland east of the country, surrounding the valleys of the Pesnica, Drava, and Mura Rivers. This is the largest of the three regions, producing roughly half of the country's wine.
- Primorska: The Primorska ZGO is located on the coast, across the Adriatic Sea from Venice and sharing a border with Italy's Friuli region. Several of the wine areas located within Primorska straddle the Italian-Slovenian border, divided only by politics; Slovenia's Goriška Brda ZOP becomes Italy's Collio Goriziano DOC across the Italian border, and Slovenia's Kras ZOP becomes Italy's Carso DOC.
- Posavje: The Posavje ZGO is located in the southeast of Slovenia, along the border with Croatia. The name Posavje (Lower Sava) refers to its proximity to the end of the Sava River valley. This is the country's smallest–and perhaps most old-fashioned–wine-producing region.

Figure 14-6: Political map of Central and Eastern Europe

Grape varieties grown in Slovenia reflect the influence of Italy, Germany, and Austria, and include French (international) varieties as well. White wines are the leading product here; widely planted white grapes include Riesling, Gewürztraminer (Traminec), Müller-Thurgau (Rizvanec), Pinot Gris (Sivi Pinot), Sauvignon Blanc, and Chardonnay. White grapes popular in Friuli such as Tai (Friuliano) and Ribolla Gialla are grown primarily in Primorska, near the Italian border. Leading red grape varieties include Cabernet Sauvignon, Merlot, St. Laurent, Pinot Noir (known as Modri Pinot), and Refosco.

GEORGIA

Many archeologists believe that a portion of present-day Georgia is the site of the world's first cultivated vineyards. While we may never know the exact location of the world's first vineyards, it is certain that Georgia has one of the oldest and most unique wine-producing cultures in the world, such that the Georgian tradition of aging wine in large, egg-shaped earthenware vessels known as *kvevris* (often spelled "qvevri") has recently been added to UNESCO's list of the Intangible Cultural Heritage of Humanity.

The Republic of Georgia has been an independent state since 1991 and, as such, has its own regulations and standards for wine. The constitution of Georgia currently contains the "Law of Georgia on Wine and Vine," first passed in 1998. These laws specify winemaking zones (controlled appellations recognized by the EU), as well as specifications for grape varieties, definitions of approved wine styles, and a list of approved winemaking and viticultural practices. Georgia and the European Union have maintained trade relations since 1996; however, at present, Georgia does not have official status as a candidate for EU membership.

Today, Georgia has just over 110,000 acres (44,500 ha) under vine, widely distributed throughout the country. In some parts of the country, wild vines of the *Vitis vinifera silvestris* subspecies are still found. The country's long involvement with grape growing—both wild and industrial—has led to over 500 identifiable indigenous varieties. Close to 90% of Georgia's wine is made from these indigenous grapes, however, only about 35 are used for commercial winemaking. The most widely grown grape is the white variety Rkatsiteli, which is also the predominant white grape of eastern Europe. Rkatsiteli makes light, floral, crisp white wines. Saperavi, the leading red grape, makes high-alcohol wines with good potential for aging.

CRIMEA

Crimea, shaped basically like a peninsula that extends into the Black Sea, has the best viticultural conditions of the former Soviet Union. The area has a long history of sparkling wine production, beginning with the 1878 founding of Novy Svet Winery. Novy Svet Winery is famous for producing a sparkling wine known as "Brut Paradiso," which won the "Grand Prix de Champagne," beating out many famous Champagne producers at the 1900 World's Fair in Paris.

During Soviet times, the Crimean Peninsula was the largest wine supplier in the USSR, some of which used to be known by the colorful name *Sovetskoye Shampanskoye* (Soviet Champagne). These sparkling wines have retained their popularity and are increasing in production. Still wines made primarily using international varieties, and a fortified wine known as *Etalita*, are produced in Crimea as well.

Figure 14-7: Monument to the founder of the Novy Svet Winery in Crimea

EASTERN MEDITERRANEAN

CHAPTER FIFTEEN

LEARNING OBJECTIVES

After studying this chapter, the candidate should be able to:

- Identify the physical location and general climate of Greece's major wine regions.
- Understand the hierarchy of wine designations used in Greece.
- Recognize significant appellations in Greece and their primary grape varieties.
- Describe the style and source of Commandaria.
- Understand the general status of the Israeli wine industry.

The eastern Mediterranean region is the historic cradle of wine trade. Wine and wine grapes reached the shores of the Mediterranean from the East before recorded history, and the great civilizations that developed there did much to advance viticulture and wine production. From Phoenicia and Greece, the culture of wine spread first to the Romans and then to other western Europeans. War and, in some cases, religious influences that restrain the use of alcohol ended much of the winegrowing in the region, although Greece remains a preeminent producer in the eastern Mediterranean. Today, wine production is a rising phenomenon in Israel, Lebanon, Cyprus, and Turkey.

GREECE

Greece has a long vinous history dating back at least 4,000 years. Greek wines were exported all over the Western world in ancient times. However, during the Middle Ages, Ottoman rulers placed heavy taxes on wines that were sold to outsiders. This crippled the potentially thriving industry, and for a time Greek wines disappeared from the international market.

It wasn't until quite recently that Greece once again became recognized as a world-class producer of wine. Even into the late twentieth century, the only Greek wine known to most consumers was retsina, a unique wine flavored with pine resin. Pine resin had been used as a preservative and a means of preventing oxidation in Greek wine in ancient times, and modern retsina is seen as a traditional product. However, for the majority of wine consumers, retsina only reinforces the impression of Greek wines as outdated and poorly made.

Conversely, today's Greek wines are clean, fresh, balanced, and food-friendly. A new generation of modern winemakers, aided by Greece's entry into the European Union, has initiated a remarkable renaissance. Increasing numbers of well-crafted Greek wines have appeared, made from interesting but unfamiliar indigenous grape varieties. These products are eclipsing the memory of Greece's resinated and oxidized wines and are giving consumers new alternatives to wines made from international grape varieties.

Figure 15–1: Vineyards in Santorini

GEOGRAPHY AND CLIMATE

Greece is located in southeastern Europe, south of Albania, Macedonia, and Bulgaria. It consists primarily of a mountainous peninsula surrounded on three sides by the Mediterranean Sea. Geographically, it resembles an outstretched hand reaching into the water. To the west, across the Ionian Sea, is the tip of the Italian Peninsula; to the south, Libya and Egypt; and to the east, across the Aegean Sea, Turkey. Greece also includes the major island of Crete and several archipelagoes with 3,000 smaller islands. Some of these islands are in the Ionian Sea, but most are in the Aegean.

The upper part of the Greek peninsula comprises the political and historical areas of Thrace, Macedonia, Epirus, and Thessalia. Farther south is the region of Attica and the capital city, Athens. Not far from Athens, the almost insular Peloponnese Peninsula clings onto the rest of Greece at the narrow Isthmus of Corinth. The Peloponnese has the highest concentration of vineyards in all of Greece.

With the sea never far away, the climate throughout Greece is classic Mediterranean, with slight temperature variations from north to south and substantial differences due to elevation. High mountains run the length of the country, especially along the western side, blocking much of the rainfall and causing the rain-shadowed eastern side of the peninsula to be significantly drier than the Ionian side.

The warm, sunny Mediterranean climate makes Greece a natural country for viticulture. Vines are planted throughout the mainland and on almost every habitable island. The trend in new plantings has been toward hillside vineyards at higher elevations, some above 2,500 feet (760 m), in order to take advantage of cooler temperatures.

Figure 15–2: View of the Acropolis and Likavitos, Athens, Greece

Grape Varieties

With over 300 cataloged indigenous grapes, Greece provides great diversity and originality in its wines.

Its standouts include three reds:

- *Agiorgitiko:* One of the most widely planted red varieties of Greece, Agiorgitiko ("Saint George's grape") is named for the Chapel of Saint George, located in the town of Nemea. Grown mainly in the Peloponnese region, Agiorgitiko is often used to produce tannic, spicy, flavorful red wines (both dry and sweet). It may also be used to produce lighter red wines (often made by carbonic maceration) as well as rosé.
- *Xinomavro* (alternately, Xynómavro): Another of the most widely planted red grapes of Greece, Xinomavro—meaning *acid black*— is a specialty of the northern areas, including Macedonia and Thessalia. Xinomavro, best-known as the sole variety allowed in the wines of the Naoussa PDO, is used to produce a range of wines from dry, spicy red wines with aromas of red fruit to sparkling wines and rosé in a range of sweetness levels.
- *Mavrodaphne*: Mavrodaphne (meaning *black laurel*) is primarily used to produce sweet fortified wines—such as Mavrodaphne of Patras and Mavrodaphne of Cephalonia. These wines—silky, sweet, and complex—are often compared to ruby or tawny Port.

The most respected white varieties include the following:

- *Moschofilero:* A pink grape akin to Pinot Gris that comes from the Mantinia region of the Peloponnese. It has high acidity with floral and spicy aromas.
- *Assyrtiko* (alternately, Asyrtiko or Assyrtico): A high-acid white variety originally from Santorini but now found throughout the country. Assyrtiko is used for dry and sweet white wines.
- *Muscat* (Moschato): The well-known ancient variety found throughout the Mediterranean; almost always used for sweet wines such as Muscat of Samos, as well as those from Rio Patras and Patras. Muscat often produces wines with notes of apricot, honey, orange peel, and spice.
- *Athiri:* Grown in Rhodes and Santorini, this grape provides wines with low acidity, good weight, and high aromatics.
- *Roditis:* One of the most widely planted white grapes in the nation, Roditis produces easy-drinking white wines with crisp, fruity flavors.

Among the international varietals, Chardonnay, Sauvignon Blanc, Cabernet Sauvignon, Merlot, and Syrah are well-known in Greek vineyards. Syrah, in particular, has made significant inroads, especially on the mainland. International grape varieties such as these are generally considered to be nontraditional and are rarely found in wines at the PDO level.

Greek Wine Laws

Greece has a quality system in accordance with EU standards and overseen by the Greek Wine Institute.

- Basic Greek table wine—categorized as *epitrapézios oínos* (EO)—accounts for approximately one-half of the country's total wine production.
- Greece has over 100 areas with protected geographical indication (PGI) status; the traditional term for this category is *topikos oínos* (TO). Many of these appellations correspond to the major political regions of Greece such as Crete, Thessalia, and Peloponnese; others may be as small as a district or a single estate.
- Greek PDO wines fall into two categories—OPE (*onomasía proeléfseos eleghoméni*), typically

reserved for sweet wines, and OPAP (*onomasía proeléfseos anotéras poiótitos*), used for dry, unfortified wines. However, these terms are rarely seen on wine labels; most of the top-quality wine destined for export will be labeled with the phrase "PDO Wines of Greece" and one of the country's numerous appellations.

The country's best-known wines include Retsina (traditionally flavored with resin) and Verdea, an oxidative white wine. A special category—*onomasía katá parádosi* (OKP/appellation by tradition)—protects these traditional wines of Greece without tying them to a specific area.

Greek Appellations

Few of Greece's appellations are particularly well-known outside the country. Many of Greece's modern winemakers are currently dissatisfied with the limitations of the appellation system and want to experiment with non-traditional varieties, blends of indigenous and international varieties, or unconventional blends of native varieties. Therefore, some of the most exciting Greek wines do not conform to the quality wine definition and must be labeled as TO or even EO. In such cases, grape variety and producer, not appellation, are the determinants of quality.

Among the existing appellations, the following regions and wines are well-known and generally well respected internationally:

Macedonia
- Amyndeon (Amyndaio): dry to off-dry red and rosé, made from Xinomavro
- Côtes de Meliton: red and white wines, produced using Greek and French varieties
- Goumenissa: dry red, from Xinomavro and Negóska
- Naoussa: dry to off-dry red, from Xinomavro

Peloponnese
- Mantinia: dry white, from Moschofilero
- Mavrodaphne of Patras: sweet fortified red, from Mavrodaphne
- Nemea: the largest red wine appellation in Greece; highly regarded reds (both dry and sweet) from Agiorgitiko

- Patras: elegant, dry whites from Roditis, known for citrus aromas and flavors

Aegean Islands

The volcanic island of Santorini has an extremely dry and windy climate that requires vines to be trained low to the ground to avoid being damaged. The vines are often trained in a basket or wreath shape known as a *stefani*. In spite of this inhospitable climate, Assyrtiko thrives here, producing wines that have vibrant acidity and minerality and that develop a beautiful richness over time. The dry white wines of the Santorini PDO must be produced using a minimum of 75% Assyrtiko.

- Vinsanto: Dried-grape wines known as Vinsanto are also produced in the Santorini PDO. These wines are typically unfortified and naturally sweet, although the production of fortified Vinsanto is also allowed. Vinsanto must be barrel-aged for a minimum of two years, although many versions are aged for much longer.

Main Wine Regions of Greece

Copyright: The Society of Wine Educators 2016

Figure 15-3: Greek wine regions

CYPRUS

Cyprus is a large island in the far-eastern Mediterranean that is currently divided politically between Greek and Turkish factions. It has a long history of wine production, but today it is known primarily for Commandaria, a sweet amber-colored dessert wine with an ancestry dating back four millennia. Commandaria is made using sun-dried Mavro (red) and Xynisteri (white) varieties, vinified separately or as a blend. Due to the high sugar content of the dried grapes, Commandaria generally reaches high levels of alcohol via natural fermentation (although it is also allowed to be fortified with grape spirits). The wine is required to be aged for at least two years in wood, although the aging regimen typically goes on for much longer. Traditionally, producers of Commandaria used a complex aging system known as the *mana system* (somewhat similar to the solera system used in Jerez).

TURKEY

Turkey, a relatively liberal Islamic state with one foot in Europe and the other in Asia, is one of the largest grape-growing countries in the world by volume, but the vast majority of the grapes are eaten fresh or as raisins. While most of Turkey's wines are rarely seen outside the country, its largest producer, Kavaklidere, does export its wines internationally. Production includes wines from both native and international varieties.

Turkey began accession negotiations to join the European Union in 2005 and is currently an official candidate to become a member of the EU. As such, the country's wine law is likely to change radically in the future. Currently, however, most of the laws and regulations regarding wine are administered by the Tobacco and Alcohol Market Regulatory Council, which focuses mainly on the sales and distribution side of the industry. Other current wine law includes a basic set of viticultural standards, written into the country's overall "Law of Agricultural Insurance" in 2005.

Table 15-1: PDO Wines of Greece

Region	PDO Wines
Aegean Islands	Lemnos OPAP
	Malvasia Paros OPAP
	Muscat of Rhodes OPE
	Muscat of Lemnos OPE
	Paros OPAP
	Rhodes OPAP
	Samos OPE
	Santorini OPAP
Crete	Archanes OPAP
	Candia OPAP
	Dafnes OPAP
	Malvasia Candia OPAP
	Malvasia Sitia OPAP
	Peza OPAP
	Sitia OPAP
Epirus	Zitsa OPAP
Ionian Islands	Mavrodaphne of Cephalonia OPE
	Muscat of Cephalonia OPE
	Robola of Cephalonia OPAP
Macedonia	Amynteo OPAP
	Goumenissa OPAP
	Naoussa OPAP
	Slopes of Meliton OPAP
Peloponnese	Mantinia OPAP
	Mavrodaphne of Patras OPE
	Monemvassia-Malvasia OPAP
	Muscat of Patras OPE
	Muscat of Rio Patras OPE
	Nemea OPAP
	Patras OPAP
Thessalia	Anchialos OPAP
	Messenikola OPAP
	Rapsani OPAP

Source: New Wines of Greece, winesofgreece.org, regional websites, 2021

Many of the efforts concerning the modernization and regulation of the wine industry are being spearheaded by the Wines of Turkey organization, founded in 2008. These projects include the definition of specific wine regions (separate from the country's current agricultural regions), standards for vineyard yield, and a database of authorized grape varieties.

LEBANON

Lebanon is a multicultural country with a sizable Christian minority and a long connection with the French, and thus it is not too surprising that there is a small wine community here. Most of the vineyards are located at fairly high elevations in the western Bekaa Valley to take advantage of nighttime cooling. Some producers are experimenting with areas in the eastern Bekaa Valley as well as in Batroun and Jezzine. The country's wine industry is based largely on the reputation of one producer, Chateau Musar, although a handful of others are gaining recognition as well. International grapes (mainly French) are grown in most regions, as well as a handful of ancient, indigenous varieties such as Obeideh and Merwah (both white).

Founded in 1997, the *Union Vinicole du Liban* (Viticultural Union of Lebanon) is leading the efforts to formulate a comprehensive modern wine law for Lebanon, and a significant set of such laws was passed in 2000. These new regulations replaced the previous set of laws that had been in place since 1938. Based loosely on the French AOC system, Lebanon's new wine laws outline many of the significant elements of wine production, including regions of origin, labeling terminology, and viticultural practices.

Figure 15-4: Vineyards in Lebanon's Bekaa Valley

ISRAEL

Israel is a small country located on the eastern edge of the Mediterranean Sea. The region's ancient history of grape growing, wine production, and exportation of wine before the common era (BCE) is well-known and widely documented. Throughout the centuries—and despite the obstacles of desert heat, intermittent drought, and periodic warfare—the area has persisted in the production of high-quality grapes and wine.

The present-day wine industry in the region dates to the late 1800s. In 1855, the Cremisan Wine Estate—along with the Cremisan Monastery of the Salesian Order—was established in the area between Jerusalem and the West Bank. Around this same time, Baron Edmond de Rothschild (1845-1934), one of the owners of Bordeaux's Château Lafite, began to invest in the region. He purchased property in the area around Mount Carmel, imported modern production equipment, and provided vine cuttings from Château Lafite. The enterprise thus founded—Carmel Winery—is now the largest-producing winery in the area.

Despite the country's small size—it measures about 263 miles/424 km from north to south and about 84 miles/135 km across its widest point—there are significant differences in the climate and terroir across the area. The wine map of the region and the official designation of appellations are still evolving. However, much of the quality wine is produced in Galilee (a high-elevation region located in the north of the country), the Central Mountains (covering the center of the country, including the Judean Hills and Mount Carmel, and the Judean Foothills (nestled between the Mediterranean Coast and the mountains west of Jerusalem). Viticulture in the semi-arid Negev region, located in the southern part of the country, is made possible by drip irrigation, invented by Israeli water engineer Simcha Blass in in the mid-20th century.

Classic international grape varieties—including Cabernet Sauvignon, Merlot, Syrah, Carignan, Chardonnay, Sauvignon Blanc, and Viognier—make up a large proportion of Israel's vineyards. Indigenous varieties, including Argaman (a red Carignan X Sousão cross created in 1972), Marawi (a white grape traced back to the 17th century), and Dabouki (a red variety) are being planted as well.

UNITED STATES AND NORTH AMERICA

CHAPTER SIXTEEN

LEARNING OBJECTIVES

After studying this chapter, the candidate should be able to:

- Identify the general role and position of the United States in the global wine industry.
- Understand the structure of the US wine industry, especially the three-tier system.
- Describe the differences between native American grapes, French-American hybrids, and vinifera.
- Discuss the differences between American viticultural areas and European appellations.
- Recall the major required and optional elements of a wine label in the United States.
- Recall the minimum content requirements for the use of place-of-origin terms, vintage dates, and grape variety names on a US wine label.
- Discuss the factors that make California of such great importance to the US wine industry.
- Identify the primary appellations, climatic zones, and major grapes of California, Washington, Oregon, and New York.
- Discuss the major wine-producing regions of Canada and Mexico.

UNITED STATES

Wine production in the United States now totals over 350 million cases, placing it just behind France, Italy, and Spain in terms of volume output. For the past several years, the US has been among the leading countries in terms of both exports and imports of wine. More recently, it has earned the title of the largest consumer of wine in the world. Furthermore, American wine drinkers overall tend to drink better quality and more expensive wines than their counterparts in most other countries. Thus, the United States by many measures now drives the global wine industry.

Within the United States, the center of the wine industry is firmly situated in California. Of the American total, California produces just over 81%. Washington State, New York State, and Oregon are the next largest producers, typically followed by Virginia, Texas, Pennsylvania, Michigan, Missouri, Ohio, and Florida—although not necessarily in that order (which changes often). The other states contribute only a small fraction to the total, although many have thriving local wine scenes. According to the American Association of Wine Economists (AAWE), there are now more than 16,000 bonded wineries in the US, with at least one in all fifty states.

Canada and Mexico also have wine industries, albeit on a much smaller scale, producing wine near the US borders. Canada's wineries are found mainly in inland British Columbia and the Great Lakes area of Ontario, while Mexico's are primarily in Baja California. These countries will be discussed in more detail at the end of this chapter.

HISTORY OF AMERICAN WINE

The United States has a long history of winemaking. However, the development of a strong wine tradition was brought to an abrupt halt in the early twentieth century by a national alcohol ban known as Prohibition. It took many years after the repeal of Prohibition for the industry to reemerge as a significant sector of the domestic economy, and even longer to establish an international standing.

It is believed that many Native American tribes produced fermented beverages — including beer, fruit wine, grape wine, and other products — well before contact with European colonists. For instance, the Pueblo peoples produced a type of corn-based beer, as witnessed by pottery fragments dating back to 828 BCE discovered at an archeological dig at Pueblo Bonito (in Chaco Canyon, New Mexico). Likewise, the Apache and Maricopa people produced wine from the fruit of the saguaro cactus, and it is believed that the Zuni people made a range of fermented beverages using aloe, corn, prickly pear, agave, and/ or grapes. Other examples — including raspberry wine produced by Native Alaskans and a fermented beverage produced from the roots of Hawaiian ti plant — abound.

European colonists arrived in North American with a taste for — and knowledge of the production of — vinifera-based wine. Upon their arrival on the American East Coast, the colonists discovered native North American grapes growing in the wild. These grapes were used to produce wine as early as the 1560s in Florida and in the Jamestown colony by the 1600s. However, these early attempts at winemaking in the eastern colonies proved difficult, as the native grapes had an unexpected flavor that was considered somewhat unpalatable. Sometime later, when European vines were brought to the colonies, they failed to thrive and eventually died off. It is now known that the imported grapevines had little resistance to the local plant diseases and especially to the root louse phylloxera. However, elsewhere in North America, vinifera grapes were successfully planted — and vinifera-based wine was produced — in Texas and New Mexico by the 1620s, and in California beginning in the 1770s.

In the West, which was Spanish and then Mexican territory until the mid-1800s, there were no native grapevines, nor was there initially much demand for wine among the sparse inhabitants. The first vineyards were established by Catholic missionaries for the small-scale production of sacramental wine. The sole grape variety grown at that time was what has come to be called the Mission grape, a hardy but unexciting wine grape propagated for centuries after being brought to the Americas from Europe.

Figure 16–1: Napa Valley landmark locally referred to as "the Grape Crusher Statue"

All of that changed in the 1800s when the West Coast became part of the United States following the Mexican War and, above all, when gold was discovered in California in 1849. The population of California and the other western territories skyrocketed, as did the demand for alcohol. Commercial wineries, which had already begun to appear in Southern California, sprang up in Northern California as well. New vineyards, planted primarily by immigrants from Italy, Switzerland, and Germany, were stocked with vines imported from various places in Europe. By the turn of the century, the California wine industry was thriving and gaining a respectable reputation.

Problems started to develop in the late nineteenth and early twentieth centuries. First, the spread of phylloxera, which was being unknowingly carried around the world with grapevine cuttings, reached California. The bigger problem, however, was a political and cultural one. Moral crusaders on the East Coast promoted the idea that alcohol was responsible for many of society's ills and pushed for the prohibition of all forms of alcohol. The 18th Amendment to the US Constitution eventually won passage in 1919, which ushered in Prohibition as of January 1920.[1]

---

[1] The National Archives indicates that the 18th Amendment was passed by Congress on December 18, 1917, was ratified on January 16, 1919, and took effect one year after its ratification.

During the 13-year period of Prohibition, alcohol was illegal for general consumption, although there were liberal exceptions granted for wine used for religious and medicinal purposes. Individuals were even allowed to make up to 200 gallons of wine at home for family consumption. These exemptions made it possible for a few of the existing wineries to stay in business producing sacramental wine or grape juice for home winemaking, but most commercial wineries went out of business.

Surprisingly, grape production in California increased during this period as winegrowers switched from noble varieties to less distinguished, high-yielding varieties such as Thompson Seedless. The long-term impact on the US wine industry after Prohibition was that wines were made from blends that were less distinctive in flavor and intensity than before Prohibition, and therefore they had to be marketed using familiar, if misleading, names—such as Burgundy or Chablis—to identify the styles being sold.

As is well-known, the "noble experiment" of Prohibition proved to be a failure, as the laws were widely ignored by many Americans and little demonstrable good came out of it. Finally, with the Great Depression making alcohol tax revenue seem preferable to forced abstinence, the 21st Amendment was passed in 1933, repealing Prohibition on a national level and returning decisions about alcohol control to state and local governments.

With the onset of the Depression and World War II, it took several decades for the wine industry to rebuild itself and its consumer base. Beginning in the 1960s, wine became fashionable again, and increased demand helped the US wine industry (led by California) to grow in size and quality. Much of this success can be attributed to Robert Mondavi, Mike Grgich, Warren Winiarski, and several other winemakers who focused on producing quality wines able to compete with their French counterparts.

Figure 16-2: Clos Pegase Winery in Napa, California

The Paris Tasting of 1976, which placed Californian Chardonnay and Cabernet Sauvignon side by side with the finest white Burgundy and Bordeaux-classified growths, is now known to be "the vinous shot heard round the world." This seminal event changed the course of American winemaking, as the top wines chosen in both the red and white categories were California wines. The first place winner among the red wines was Stag's Leap Wine Cellars 1973 S.L.V. Cabernet Sauvignon (Napa), made by Warren Winiarski from three-year-old Cabernet vines. The first place in the white category was awarded to Chateau Montelena 1973 Chardonnay (Calistoga), made under the leadership of Jim Barrett. In an instant, Californian wine producers learned that they could compete with the well-established French, and winemakers all over the world realized their potential to compete as well.

By this time, US wine consumers had reached a new level of sophistication and began to pay attention to wine quality. Varietally labeled wines rather than semi-generic labels became standard, and place of origin became significant to buyers. The American wine industry has been on an upward path ever since.

IMPORTANT NAMES IN AMERICAN WINE HISTORY

- Ernest and Julio Gallo: brothers who were almost singlehandedly responsible for ensuring that there was consistent and reasonably priced wine on the American table after Prohibition
- Agoston Haraszthy: Hungarian immigrant who helped found the California wine industry and brought many European vines to Sonoma in 1861
- Charles Krug: founder of the first Napa Valley winery in 1861
- Nicholas Longworth: founder of the first successful US commercial winery in the 1830s and who—using grapes grown in the Ohio River Valley—produced the first sparkling wine in America
- Robert Mondavi: California winemaker who was most instrumental in establishing the reputation of Californian (and, by extension, US) wine quality among consumers
- Frank Schoonmaker: wine journalist credited with introducing and promoting the concept of varietal labeling to help California better define its wines
- André Tchelistcheff: California winemaker who introduced many modern techniques to the US and mentored many other winemakers
- Bob Trinchero: son of Sutter Home Winery's co-founder, Mario Trinchero, Bob Trinchero developed the idea to create a white wine from the red Zinfandel grape, which, given its commercial success, saved many of California's Zinfandel vines from being uprooted or abandoned

STRUCTURE OF THE US WINE INDUSTRY

THE THREE-TIER SYSTEM

The way the wine industry is organized within individual countries varies considerably around the world. In the United States, it is structured as a *three-tier system*. What this means is that the wine trade in the US is divided into three distinct groups that, in theory, are entirely separate with regard to ownership. This system is intended to allow the government to oversee the industry's activities at the points between tiers where wine and other alcoholic beverages change hands and to collect tax revenues on sales and corporate profits.

The three tiers are as follows:
- *Producers* or *suppliers:* essentially synonymous with wineries, but also including importers as the US-based representatives of foreign wineries that are otherwise beyond the reach of US law
- *Distributors* or *wholesalers*
- *Retailers:* including both "on-premise" licensees (those that sell for consumption on the spot, such as restaurants, bars, hotels, and clubs) and "off-premise" vendors (retailers that sell wines to take away, such as wine shops, liquor stores, and, where permitted, supermarkets)

Under a strict interpretation of the three-tier system, each of the following is true:
- Wineries can sell only to distributors, not directly to retailers or consumers.
- Foreign wineries must sell their wine through a US-based import company.
- Distributors cannot have direct ownership of wineries or retail establishments and cannot sell directly to the public.
- Retailers must remain independent of the other tiers.

The wine industry has been able to secure a variety of exceptions to these rules—for example, allowing sales directly to consumers at winery tasting rooms—but the overall philosophy is still implemented.

At the federal level, the Alcohol and Tobacco Tax and Trade Bureau (TTB) of the Department of the Treasury is responsible for enforcing laws relevant to businesses engaged in alcohol production, importation, and wholesale operations, and for ensuring that alcohol labeling and advertising meet federal regulations. This bureau is also responsible for alcohol excise tax collection. The Bureau of Alcohol, Tobacco, Firearms, and Explosives (ATF), part of the Department of Justice, is responsible for enforcement of laws aimed at illegal alcohol production and smuggling. In addition, every state and most counties, cities, towns, and other local jurisdictions have alcoholic beverage control departments that oversee and enforce further state and local laws relating to wine and other alcoholic beverages.

Producers

The first tier consists of the production segments of the wine industry: wineries and, by extension, importers. Producers may also be known as suppliers.

The producers' wine may be sold in the following ways:

- to a distributor
- to an importer, if crossing international borders
- in bulk to another winery
- direct to consumers at the winery, if allowed by state and local laws
- direct to consumers by shipping courier, if allowed by state and local laws

Distributors

The middle tier is collectively known as the distribution tier, although there may be any number of other brokers and intermediaries involved besides the actual distributor. Distribution companies are licensed state by state, and while many of them operate in several states, none yet operates in every state. In theory, distributors are supposed to operate completely independently of both producers and retailers, but some wineries or importers skirt this principle by establishing technically separate companies that cooperate closely.

Wineries' distribution arrangements vary state to state, as each state's laws may be different. In some states, it may be possible or even necessary to have more than one distributor. In other states, known as control states, the state government itself has taken over the role of the distributor and is the only legal distribution agent. Another variation is the franchise state, wherein state laws grant distributors exclusive relationships with suppliers' brands, often giving them considerable leverage over suppliers in their relationship, such that it can be nearly impossible for a winery to change distributors. The supplier–distributor relationship is more equal in nonfranchise states.

Figure 16–3: US Capitol Building

Distributors typically have salespeople who visit on- and off-premise retail accounts to try to get their suppliers' wines onto the store's shelves or the restaurant's wine list. They also warehouse a stock of wines to deliver to accounts as sales are made. To help sales, some distributors may host trade tastings, do product promotions, conduct training, and so on.

Retailers

Retailers are the usual interface between the wine industry and the consuming public. They buy wine from distributors, mark it up to cover their overhead and other costs, and make it available to consumers. Retail is divided into the on- and off-premise trade, but there are many different types of retailers, including the following:

- Restaurants
- Bars, wine bars, and nightclubs
- Hotels
- Fine wine shops
- Liquor stores
- Supermarkets and grocery stores

- "Big-box" retailers (e.g., Target, Walmart) and membership club stores (e.g., Costco, Sam's Club)
- Online retailers
- Wine-of-the-month clubs
- Airlines and cruise lines

US WINE LAWS

AMERICAN VITICULTURAL AREAS

The place-of-origin, or appellation, system used in the United States is quite different from the appellation system of Europe. Unlike European appellations, there are no rules regarding approved grape varieties, minimum or maximum crop yields, planting densities, or vinification techniques that must be followed in order to be permitted to use the place-name. This is not to say that place-names are unimportant in the United States, but simply that they do not dictate a specific style of winemaking.

The TTB maintains the list of defined areas that may be used to describe the place of origin of a wine. At a general level, a place of origin may be defined along political boundaries such as the entire country, a single US state, multistate (three maximum), a single US county, or multicounty (three maximum).

However, while such areas are acceptable, these political units are usually too large and too arbitrarily drawn to adequately identify a unique winegrowing region of distinction. For that reason, US wine law has a procedure for delineating areas that have unifying viticultural characteristics regardless of where they fall relative to political boundaries. These areas are called *American Viticultural Areas,* or AVAs.

There is no maximum or minimum size for an AVA; they vary from as small as one-quarter of a square mile to as large as several thousand square miles—the latter creating an AVA of dubious usefulness. It is not uncommon for AVAs to nest one within another or to partially overlap. In such cases, the smaller AVAs would be expected to produce wines of greater distinction than the larger ones. As of December

2021, 260 distinct AVAs had been approved in over 30 different states; of these, 142 are in California (and these numbers are sure to increase in the future).

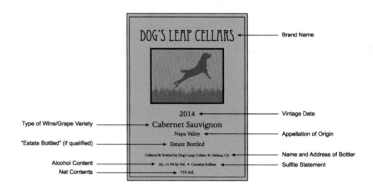

Figure 16-4: American wine label

US WINE LABELING LAWS

Beyond regulating the distribution of wine and approving AVAs, the TTB is also responsible for ensuring that wine labels meet federal labeling laws. Specifically, all wine labels in the United States, whether for wine made in America or imported from another country, require these elements:

1. A brand name
2. The class or type of wine (although this may be implicit rather than explicit)
3. The alcohol content
4. The name and address of the bottler or importer
5. The place of origin (country or more specific) for all imports or if a vintage date is included on the label
6. The net contents (volume) of the bottle
7. A sulfite statement (in almost all cases)
8. A health warning

Additional items that may appear on a wine label include the following:
- Vintage date
- Grape variety (or varieties)
- Appellation of origin
- The term "estate bottled"
- Optional information about the wine, the winery, or related subject matter
- Label art

The brand name, class/type of wine, and alcoholic content must appear on the brand label. The other items may also appear on the brand label or may be printed on one or more separate labels. For example, a small vintage label may be affixed to the bottle neck, avoiding the requirement to reprint new labels every year if nothing changes apart from the vintage date. The brand label and a second, informational label are sometimes called the front and back labels, respectively, but this can be confusing because many wineries put all of the mandatory information on a minimalist "front label" and then make the back label more visually appealing; these wines are inevitably shelved with the "back label" facing forward.

Brand Name
Usually the most prominent word(s) on a label, the brand name may be the name of the producing winery, a certain product line from a large producer, or a proprietary name that identifies the wine.

Wine Class or Type
The label must include some indication of the *kind* of wine contained within. For most wines, this requirement is satisfied by citing a grape variety or an appellation on the label. In other instances, the label must specify one of the TTB-designated classes or types of wines, such as "table wine," "sparkling red wine," or "fruit wine."

Semi-Generic Names
In (and before) the 1900s, European placenames were often used to describe American-made wines produced in a comparable style. This practice was commonplace throughout the wine-producing world over a century ago. However, in recent times, the US government has agreed to ban the use of many such placenames on American-made wines. For example, US wines cannot be labeled "Rioja" or "Bordeaux," regardless of the style of wine or grape varieties used.

However, a number of other European place-names, including Chablis, Burgundy, Chianti, Port (but not Porto), and Madeira, are considered by the US to be *semi-generic* names, meaning that although they clearly refer to European wine regions, they have been used outside of those regions for so long that they have lost their explicit reference to the original wine zone. These names may be used on US wine labels provided a US geographic term is also used, for example, "American Chablis" or "California Port Wine," and only if the labels were approved prior to March 2006. The European Union will not allow such wines to be imported, but there remains a large market for these wines in the United States. Since the signing of the US–European Community Trade in Wine Agreement, new applications for the use of these terms will not be accepted nor approved by the TTB for use on wine labels.

Similarly, for years *Champagne* was one of the TTB's semi-generic names, and sparkling wines that had been using the term on their labels (such as *California Champagne*) prior to 2006 may still use that designation. However, no labels submitted to the TTB after that point have been or will be approved for use of the term.

Alcohol Content
The alcohol level of a wine is provided in percentage by volume and usually falls in the range of 11% to 15%. Some styles of wine have lower alcohol levels; fortified wines have higher levels. For wines of 14% alcohol or less, the designation "table wine" may be used in place of giving an exact percentage.

If a percentage *is* stated, the TTB allows a variance of plus or minus 1.5% between the declared and the actual alcohol content; the allowed variance for wines with more than 14% abv is plus or minus 1%. This is a convenience for large wineries that produce millions of gallons of wine each year. As alcohol content may vary from batch to batch, this variance allows them to avoid printing new labels for each batch. The winery may also choose to disclose the exact level of alcohol on the label, as is often done with vintage-dated wines.

Name and Address of Bottler

The label must name the person or company that has ultimate control over the content of the wine. This may be the bottler (loosely defined, since the wine may come in a box or other container) or, for foreign wines, the importer. In most cases, the bottler is the winery that made the wine; in others, it is a wine merchant or négociant who bought bulk wine for blending and bottling.

Phrases preceding the words "Bottled by" on the label can indicate what involvement the bottler had in making the wine. Maximum participation, from growing the grapes to making the wine, is indicated by the phrase "Grown, produced, and bottled by." Wines from a négociant might have a label that reads, "Blended, cellared, and bottled by."

Country of Origin

The label must always specify the wine's country of origin if the wine has been imported to the United States or if the label includes a vintage date. Sometimes, this will be clearly stated ("American Wine" or "Product of Chile"). Other times, it will be implied by reference to a more precise area ("Napa County" or "Brunello di Montalcino").

For wines identified by country of origin only (nothing more specific, such as a state or an appellation), US wine law requires only 75% content from the stated country; this means that "American Wine" may contain up to 25% foreign bulk wine. In the rare case of a wine with less than 75% content from any one country, the exact percentages from each country need to be stated. However, other countries may require a greater percentage of grapes to come from the stated place of origin, so these will likely exceed the 75% minimum.

Net Contents

The label's net contents statement lists the volume of wine contained in liters or milliliters; the equivalent in fluid ounces is optional. A standard bottle is 750 milliliters (25.4 fluid ounces), but several choices—both smaller and larger—are acceptable. Permitted variances are specified for each bottle size. No net contents figure is needed on the label if the bottles themselves have that information embossed on the glass.

Sulfite Statement

Wines containing 10 parts per million or more of sulfur dioxide, which actually encompasses nearly all wines, are required to carry a label statement, such as "Contains Sulfites." Some labels give the name of the actual chemical added, for example, "Contains Potassium Metabisulfite."

Health Warning

All alcoholic beverages sold in the United States, including wine, are required to display the following statements:

1. "GOVERNMENT WARNING: According to the Surgeon General, women should not drink alcoholic beverages during pregnancy because of the risk of birth defects."
2. "Consumption of alcoholic beverages impairs your ability to drive a car or operate machinery, and may cause health problems."

Wineries are not allowed to rebut or undermine these statements by adding anything to the label that would "suggest a relationship between the consumption of alcohol, wine, or any substance found within the wine, and health benefits." Nor can they refer consumers to "a third party or other source for information regarding the effects on health of wine or alcohol consumption."

Vintage Date

A vintage date is optional on a label, but if one is shown, the wine must meet the following criteria:

*   For wines from an AVA or a foreign equivalent appellation, a minimum of 95% of the wine in the bottle must have been made from grapes harvested in the stated year.
*   The minimum requirement is reduced to 85% if the place of origin is listed as a US state or county or as similar regions in other countries, such as a French IGP or Italian IGT.

Blending a small amount of wine from other years into a new wine allows winemakers to top up barrels or to average out the quality from year to year without significantly changing the character of the primary vintage.

Grape Variety

The basic rules for varietal labeling are as follows:

- If a single grape variety appears on the label, the wine must contain a minimum of 75% of that variety, grown in the appellation of origin cited on the label. Exceptions include the following:
  - The minimum is reduced to 51% for native North American grape varieties of the species *Vitis labrusca*.
  - Oregon has adopted a more stringent definition than federal law, requiring some of its iconic varietals, such as Pinot Noir, Pinot Gris, and Chardonnay, to have a minimum 90% content of the named variety.
- If no one grape variety constitutes 75% of a wine, it can be varietally labeled only if all the varieties are named, along with the percentage each one makes up.

In general, the minimum content for varietal labeling of wines imported into the European Union is 85%, but an agreement between the EU and the United States allows varietally labeled US wines to be exported to the EU with a minimum of only 75%. Nevertheless, some export-oriented wineries adhere to the EU minimum to avoid any possible difficulties.

Meritage

Meritage (rhymes with "heritage") is a term permitted for use with wines that are made in the style, and with the grape varieties, of the wines of Bordeaux.

The term *Meritage* was coined in 1988 by a group of vintners (the *Meritage Association*) in order to provide a recognizable name for blended wines to be used as an alternative to generic terms such as "table wine" or proprietary names (such as "Opus One" or "Elements"). Only members of the Meritage Alliance (as the group is now known) are entitled to use this term, and there are strict conditions for its use. For instance, a wine labeled as Meritage must be the winery's most expensive wine of its style, and production cannot exceed 25,000 cases.

A red Meritage must be made with the traditional red Bordeaux varieties and may contain Cabernet Sauvignon, Merlot, Cabernet Franc, Petit Verdot, Malbec, St. Macaire, Gros Verdot, and Carmenère. At least two of the grapes must be used, and no one grape can account for more than 90% of the blend. A white Meritage must be made using Sauvignon Blanc, Semillon, and Muscadelle, with at least two grape varieties in the blend, and a maximum of 90% of any single variety.

Figure 16-5: The famous sign welcoming visitors to Napa Valley

Appellation of Origin

While the majority of wines are required to indicate their country of origin, most are labeled with a more specific, and therefore theoretically higher-quality, place of origin. In the US, the places of origin for wines form the following idealized hierarchy based on size:

- Country
- State
- County
- AVA
- Vineyard

As in the case of vintage and variety, it is not essential that *all* of the grapes used in a particular wine be grown in the named place; a small proportion from outside the area can be used for blending. In general, for political units (country, state, county), it is sufficient that 75% of the grapes come from that location, although there are three exceptions: the states of California and Oregon both require wines carrying the state appellation to use 100% California or Oregon grapes, respectively; and those wines labeled as being from Washington State are required to use a minimum of 95% from that state. It is also possible to name two or three contiguous states or counties as the place of origin if the percentage from each one is stated. The standard is tighter for viticultural areas: for AVAs, the minimum content is 85%, and for a vineyard to be named on a label, the minimum is 95%. These rules are summarized in table 16–1.

"Estate Bottled"

The term *estate bottled* on a wine label evokes the château concept of Bordeaux, where a winery is situated in the middle of the vineyards and all of the wine is produced from grapes grown on-site. This may be the case for American estate-bottled wines, too, but sometimes the definition is stretched almost to the breaking point. In the US, the rules are as follows:

- The grapes must come from one or more vineyards owned or leased by the winery.
- The vineyard(s) must be within a single AVA.
- The winery must also be located in that AVA.

Because some AVAs are enormous, the winery and the vineyard could conceivably be separated by many miles. Nevertheless, when a winery is involved in the operation of the vineyards from which it sources its grapes, quality is often more evident.

Optional Terms that Are Not Legally Defined

Unregulated information may be included on a wine label at the discretion of the TTB. Examples include descriptors of the wine's sensory attributes, recommended serving temperatures, the history of the winery, and technical details about the wine or its production methods. However, the TTB routinely rejects labels that carry misleading information, health claims, or anything considered indecent.

Terms such as "Reserve," "Special Selection," and "Old Vines" may also be added. While these terms are generally associated with wines that are extraordinary in some way, and are often used to differentiate between a company's multiple product lines, they have no legal definition at the federal level.

GEOGRAPHY AND CLIMATE

The North American continent is essentially covered by three countries: Canada in the north, the United States in the center, and Mexico in the south, as well as a handful of small nations south of Mexico. The prime winegrowing latitudes of 30° to 50° north are almost entirely within US territory (on the

Table 16–1: Requirements for Use of Designations on US Wine Labels

REQUIREMENTS FOR USE OF DESIGNATIONS ON US WINE LABELS							
LABELING TERM	Grape Variety	Vintage	Appellation of Origin				
			Country	State	County	AVA	Specific Vineyard
Examples	Chardonnay	2009	Australia; France	New York; Michigan	Napa County; Yamhill County	Chalk Hill; Napa Valley	Bien Nacido Vineyard
MINIMUM CONTENT	75% (of named grape variety)*	95% (AVA) 85% (state or county)	75%	75%**	75%	85%***	95%

* Oregon requires a minimum of 90% for key varieties, e.g., Chardonnay and Pinot Noir.

**California and Oregon require 100%; Washington State requires 95%

***Oregon requires 95%

West Coast, the US ranges from 32° to 49°). The southernmost parts of Canada and northernmost parts of Mexico are also within the temperate climatic zone, where growing quality wine grapes is commercially feasible.

Because the entire country is within the favored latitudes for winegrowing, it might be expected that vineyards would be located all over the United States as they are in Italy and Greece. However, North America is a much larger landmass, and the central part of the country experiences a continental climate with weather extremes that make quality grape growing difficult. This situation is exacerbated in the mountainous West by high elevations.

Complex global air circulation patterns result in frequent rain in the exposed coastal areas of the Pacific Northwest, while down the coast the air gets progressively drier. The West Coast has a series of rugged mountain ranges that parallel the shoreline, including the Coast Range in California and Oregon, and the Cascades in Oregon and Washington. These mountains form a significant barrier to ocean air, producing a distinct line between the wetter coastal areas and the very dry interior zones. Furthermore, the same air circulation patterns cause ocean currents to move southward along the West Coast, bringing cold Arctic water down as far as Mexico and keeping the coastal areas much cooler than the interior of the country.

On the East Coast, the opposite air circulation flow has a tendency to push air and water northward from the subtropical Caribbean. This brings warm, very humid air and the warm waters of the Gulf Stream up from the south. With no mountains along the coast to provide a barrier, this humid air penetrates the Eastern Seaboard and produces ideal conditions for plant diseases and fungi to develop in the summertime, making viticulture much more challenging than it is on the West Coast. This problem limits the choices of grape varieties and raises the cost of grape growing on the East Coast.

US GRAPE VARIETIES

Native American Grape Varieties and Hybrids

When Norse explorers at the beginning of the eleventh century first visited North America, they named their discovery Vinland because of the wild grapevines they found growing there. However, these were not the vinifera wine grapes of Europe but various other species that had evolved somewhat different characteristics, making them far from ideal for wine production. Much later, when the English colonists tried making wine from these native American grapes, they found that there was a strong, unusual flavor component to the wine, which was unappealing to some. The grapes, of the species labrusca, were known as "fox grapes," and the flavor was described as "foxy." They were also extremely acidic.

Native American grapes continued to be used for winemaking since there was no alternative. The vinifera vines imported from Europe did not survive transplanting in America, primarily due to phylloxera and secondarily to disease, although these causes had not yet been identified. Various viticulturists investigated thousands of individual grapevines and helped to propagate the most satisfactory ones for winemaking.

These native American grapes included Catawba, Delaware, Niagara, and Concord. There is speculation that these may have had one or more vinifera ancestors, presumably from random propagation of native grapes with unsuccessful plants from an early vinifera vineyard, and so they are sometimes referred to as native American hybrids. Their overwhelming characteristics, however, are those of labrusca vines. Native American grapes of other species include Norton and the more distantly related muscadine grape Scuppernong. All of these varieties continue to be used to make wine today in the eastern and midwestern US, and most are also grown for use in grape juice and as table grapes.

Figure 16–6: Concord grapes

Once it was discovered that phylloxera was responsible for the destruction of the early American vinifera plants as well as those in vineyards throughout Europe, the native American species took on a new role as saviors of the world's vinifera vineyards. Native American species had evolved and adapted to coexist with phylloxera. Viticulturists used these resistant vines to combat the phylloxera blight in two ways. The first was to hybridize native American grapes and vinifera, with the goal of developing phylloxera-resistant vines that produced fruit with a vinifera flavor profile. That goal was never completely achieved, but botanists in France developed many varieties that came close, such as the white Seyval Blanc and Vidal Blanc, and the red Chambourcin. These French-American hybrids were a temporary solution to the phylloxera problem in France, but they became very popular in the eastern United States, where they represented a step up in quality from the native American varieties.

The second manner in which native North American grape varieties were used to neutralize the phylloxera threat was through grafting. It was discovered that the rootstock of an American grapevine could successfully be grafted with the upper end, or scion, of a vinifera vine. The graft would take root and grow into the lower trunk of the new vine, while everything above it, including the fruit, would remain 100% vinifera. This method proved to be the answer that viticulturists sought, and most vinifera vines the world over are grafted onto American rootstock today. The choice of exactly which native American vine is used for the rootstock allows the grape grower to control the vine's rate of growth and to pair the vine to the specific soil and climate to which it is best adapted.

Vinifera Grape Varieties

The majority of the wine made in the United States is produced using vinifera grape varieties originally brought into the country from Europe. For the most part, these are selected from among the dozen or so prominent international varieties, such as Chardonnay and Cabernet Sauvignon, that have been shown to produce excellent wine in many different locales. However, some vines were imported so long ago that it is not always clear what varieties they were.

For instance, research in recent years has determined that Zinfandel is identical to the native Croatian grape known as Crljenak Kaštelanski (Tribidrag), and that a Long Island grape grower named George Gibbs brought the variety to his nursery in the 1820s. By the year 1829, the name *Zinfardel* was being used, which later, after several permutations, morphed into *Zinfandel*. The meaning and etymology of the name remain a mystery. Likewise, Petite Sirah is now known to be the same grape as *Durif*, a natural Syrah × Peloursin cross that—in the 1860s—occurred by chance in the nursery of a French botanist by the name of Francois Durif.

As part of the wine labeling regulations in the US, the TTB maintains a list of grape varieties that are approved as type designations for American wine. The list currently includes more than 300 grape names, as well as 47 that are pending approval. Within this list, some grapes are considered identical, with the following grape names among those approved as synonyms:

- Fumé Blanc for Sauvignon Blanc
- Mataro and Monastrell for Mourvèdre
- Muscat Canelli for Muscat Blanc
- Pinot Grigio for Pinot Gris
- Shiraz for Syrah
- Valdepeñas for Tempranillo
- White Riesling for Riesling
- Durif for Petite Sirah
- Garnacha for Grenache
- Ugni Blanc for Trebbiano

Grape name synonyms that are no longer permitted for use on American wine labels include the following:

- Gamay Beaujolais (previously used for Pinot Noir or Valdiguié)
- Johannisberg Riesling (previously used for Riesling)
- Napa Gamay (previously used for Valdiguié or Gamay)

CALIFORNIA

California is by far the largest wine producer of the fifty US states. It contains about 80% of the vineyard acreage in the country and produces more than 81% of the wine. According to the California-based Wine Institute and the California Association of Winegrape Growers, the California wine industry has an annual impact of more than $61 billion on the state's economy and $121 billion nationally.

The state is ideally suited for viticulture with ample sunshine, mild winters, generally low humidity, and a Mediterranean climate that rarely brings any rainfall or even clouds in the summer or during harvest season.

Areas in the north and right along the coast can be too cool for significant grape growing, while sheltered interior valleys can get excessively hot during the summer, but there are many inland parts of the state that receive cooling sea breezes that moderate the heat and provide perfect growing conditions. In particular, high-quality wine regions are found between Santa Barbara and Mendocino Counties inland from breaks in the coastal mountain ranges.

MAJOR WINEGROWING AREAS OF CALIFORNIA

As of December 2021, California has 142 AVAs. Five of these are broad regional AVAs that collectively encompass most of the other smaller appellations. These AVAs are as follows:

- North Coast: encompasses all or part of Napa, Sonoma, Mendocino, Lake, Marin, and Solano counties—all of which are located north of San Francisco Bay

Main Wine Growing Regions of California

Copyright: The Society of Wine Educators 2016

Figure 16-7: California wine regions

- Sierra Foothills: in the Sierra Nevada Mountains east of Sacramento
- San Francisco Bay: covering the area from San Francisco and Oakland south to Santa Cruz (overlaps a portion of the Central Coast AVA)
- Central Coast: takes in the Pacific coast counties between Oakland and Santa Barbara
- South Coast: below Los Angeles

These five "super-AVAs" are defined only loosely by climate and geology; their primary purpose is to allow grapes from several distant quality wine regions to be blended and still qualify for AVA and estate bottled status.

Meanwhile, the majority of California's grapes, used mostly for table grapes, juice, and raisins, but also for a considerable amount of wine, are grown in the Central Valley, particularly the San Joaquin Valley south of Sacramento. Comprising nearly 300,000 acres (121,400 ha), this is the largest vineyard acreage in the state, yet it does not fall under any of the super-AVAs.

Napa County, in particular the Napa Valley AVA and its sub-appellations, is the best-known US wine region. For the most part, this reputation has been built on the strength of Napa Valley's powerful Cabernet Sauvignons and Cabernet-led Bordeaux-style blends. These outstanding wines are produced by large, well-established wineries as well as by numerous small boutique wineries that have achieved "cult" status, with demand far exceeding the supply, even at sky-high prices.

Grapes have been grown in Napa since the 1830s, and the first winery in the valley was established in the 1860s. There are now more than 400 wineries in the county. At 45,000 acres (18,200 ha), Napa is the third largest California county in terms of wine grape acreage planted, after San Joaquin and Sonoma. The area contains almost a tenth of the state's vineyards by acreage, but because vineyard yields are kept low, the county's wine production is just 4% of the state total by volume.

Geography and Climate

Napa County lies north of San Pablo Bay, an upper extension of San Francisco Bay, with the Napa River generally running north to south the length of the county. The Napa Valley itself is a very narrow valley, flanked by mountain ranges on either side that separate the valley from Solano County to the east and Sonoma County to the west. For the most part, these mountains protect the valley proper from the cold air coming off the Pacific Ocean, keeping the valley warm and sunny throughout most of the growing season. However, the Mediterranean climate does show some variation within the valley because of its geography.

In terms of climate, the most important feature in Napa is the air that works its way north off the chilly waters of San Pablo Bay. The high pressure and heat of California's interior pulls cool air off the bay, bringing frequent morning fogs and keeping the southern part of the county significantly cooler than the valley farther north.

During the morning, the valley floor is blanketed in fog (which burns off later in the day) while the hillsides are generally warmer, since they sit above

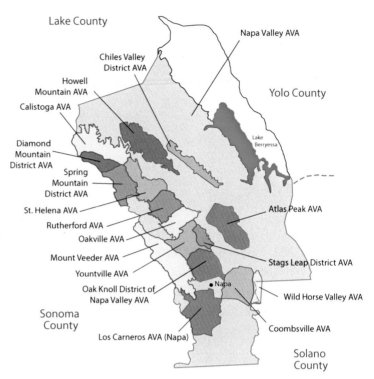

AVAs of Napa County

Copyright: The Society of Wine Educators 2016

Figure 16–8: Napa County Wine Regions

the fog. Once the fog has burned off, however, the hillsides are generally cooler than the valley floor due to their elevation. Similarly, high-elevation vineyards in the mountains generally have cooler days and warmer nights than those on the valley floor.

Napa also varies from the west to the east. The eastern side of the valley is drier and warmer because it is a farther distance from the ocean, while the western appellations are subject to cooler temperatures and greater oceanic influence.

Grape Varieties

About three-quarters of Napa County's total acreage is devoted to red varieties. Cabernet Sauvignon is by far the leading grape variety, followed by Merlot and Pinot Noir. Chardonnay and Sauvignon Blanc are the most widely planted white grapes. A wide range of well-known grapes—including Zinfandel, Cabernet France, Petite Sirah, and Malbec—are planted throughout the area, but all other varieties are minor players by comparison with the more than 22,000 acres (8,900 ha) dedicated to Cabernet

LEADING GRAPE VARIETIES OF NAPA VALLEY

Red Grapes	White Grapes
Cabernet Sauvignon	Chardonnay
Merlot	Sauvignon Blanc
Pinot Noir	Semillon
Zinfandel	Pinot Gris/Grigio
Cabernet Franc	Muscat
Petite Sirah	
Syrah	
Petit Verdot	
Malbec	

Figure 16-9: Leading Grape Varieties of Napa Valley

Sauvignon. The diversity of terroir, as discussed above, influences which grapes are grown where throughout the valley.

Napa Appellations

Napa County is one of the counties included in the North Coast AVA. Within the county itself, there are 17 AVAs, including the Napa Valley AVA, which itself covers the majority of the land in the county—aside from Lake Berryessa and some surrounding areas. The majority of Napa's vineyards are located in the western half of the county.

The heart of the Napa Valley, stretching north from the city of Napa, includes those appellations that are often referred to as the "valley floor appellations" of Napa. This is prime Cabernet Sauvignon territory and home to the majority of the county's most famous wineries, with vineyards planted along both sides of the Napa River and up into the hillsides. Appellations in this central part of Napa include the following:

- **Calistoga AVA:** Calistoga is one of the warmest (and northernmost) AVAs of Napa. Summertime temperatures can reach 100°F (38°C) in the summer—but the proximity to the Chalk Hill Gap can bring cooling breezes in the evenings. Principal varieties include Cabernet Sauvignon, Zinfandel, Syrah and Petite Sirah.
- **St. Helena AVA:** St. Helena is a warm area—summertime temperatures can reach the mid-90s°F (34–36°C). This area experiences less fog, less wind, and more heat retention due to the narrowing of the valley floor. In addition to its plantings of Cabernet Sauvignon, St. Helena is planted to Merlot, Cabernet Franc, Zinfandel, and several white varieties.
- **Rutherford AVA:** Rutherford, a moderately warm area known for its "Rutherford dust," is home to a unique soil type and climate, resulting in wines with firm tannins. This area is largely planted to Cabernet Sauvignon, Merlot, Cabernet Franc, and Sauvignon Blanc.
- **Oakville AVA:** Oakville is a fairly warm area with a good deal of moderating influence from the night and early morning fog. Leading grapes include Cabernet Sauvignon, Cabernet Franc, Merlot, and Sauvignon Blanc.
- **Yountville AVA:** Yountville is a moderate climate area influenced by morning fog and the strong breezes off of San Pablo Bay. Afternoons here are typically cooler than those located farther north in the valley.
- **Stags Leap District AVA:** Stags Leap District is a moderately warm area, somewhat cooled by afternoon winds. The bare rocks of Stags Leap itself and the surrounding hills radiate warmth, meaning that mid-summer temperatures can reach as high as 100°F (37.7°C), but typically remain in the mid-90s (34° to 36°C).
- **Chiles Valley AVA:** Chiles Valley is located somewhat to the east of the valley floor appellations and extends into the hillsides of the Vaca Mountains. Summer days are fairly warm, but the vineyards at the higher elevations (which go as high as 1,200 feet [366 m]) get quite chilly at night.

The southern section of the county, due in part to its proximity to San Pablo Bay, experiences a somewhat cooler climate. Appellations in this area include the following:

- **Oak Knoll District of Napa Valley AVA:** Oak Knoll has a cool, well-balanced climate with a good deal of marine influence and fog that often remains until late-morning. Chardonnay is a leading grape variety, as well as Merlot, Cabernet Sauvignon, Pinot Noir, and Riesling.
- **Coombsville AVA:** This is one of the cooler areas of Napa, located very close to San Pablo Bay. Daytime temperatures in the summer can be as many as ten degrees (F) lower than most other

Napa AVAs. Due to the morning fog and humidity, a portion of this area allows for the development of botrytis.

- **Carneros/Los Carneros AVA:** Carneros, shared with Sonoma County and located to the south (and extending to the east) of Oak Knoll, is one of the coolest regions of Napa. Carneros is planted mainly with Chardonnay and Pinot Noir, some of which go into the county's sparkling wines.
- **Wild Horse Valley AVA:** This region, located close to San Pablo Bay and shared with Solano County, is another of the coolest areas of Napa. Chardonnay and Pinot Noir are the main grape varieties.

Napa's higher-elevation appellations include those located in the Mayacamas Mountains to the west of the valley (along the border with Sonoma County), as well as a few located in the Vaca Mountains to the east. These include the following:

- **Mount Veeder AVA:** This is a cool-to-moderate climate area located along the border with Sonoma. Summertime highs average 85°F (29°C). Elevations range from 500 to 2,600 feet (152–192 m) with most vineyards above the fog line.
- **Diamond Mountain District AVA:** This is a moderately warm climate area, located along the border with Sonoma. Temperatures in the summer can reach as high as 90°F (32°C) and see less temperature fluctuation than those on the valley floor below. Elevation ranges from 400 to 2,200 feet (122 to 671 m).
- **Spring Mountain District AVA:** This region, located along the border with Sonoma, is cool-to-moderate, depending on elevation and aspect. Typical summertime highs reach 85°F (29°C), and elevation ranges from 600 to 2,600 feet (183–792 m).
- **Howell Mountain AVA:** Howell Mountain is located above the fog line on the eastern side of the valley. This is the only appellation in Napa that is elevation-specific, with the boundaries drawn at the 1,400 foot (425 m) contour, while central portions of the AVA reach up to 2,400 feet (730 m) in elevation. Principal grape varieties include Cabernet Sauvignon, Merlot, Zinfandel and Viognier

- **Atlas Peak AVA:** The Atlas Peak AVA is located on the eastern side of the county in the Vaca Range and with vineyards planted at 760–2,600 feet (232–792 m) above sea level. Summer temperatures rarely reaching above 90°F (32°C). Cabernet Sauvignon and Chardonnay are the main grape varieties planted in the Atlas Peak AVA.

SONOMA COUNTY

Sonoma County is somewhat less widely known internationally than Napa, but it is generally considered Napa's equal in terms of quality wine production. It is not as centralized as Napa and is more diverse in terms of terroir, which contributes to its less prominent identity and, many believe, to its charm.

Sonoma's commercial wine industry began in the 1850s, with quality vinifera grape varieties introduced to the area in the 1860s. It has remained at the forefront of wine production ever since, even during Prohibition, and now has about one-eighth of the state's acreage under vine.

Geography and Climate

As a county with 60 miles (96 km) of coastline, Sonoma is more strongly influenced by the ocean than are more inland areas like Napa, and the immediate coastal zone is a marginal winegrowing region. However, the coastal ridges that parallel the shoreline either block or channel the fog and keep a barrier between the cold ocean water and the majority of the vineyard areas of Sonoma. Areas where sea breezes penetrate—most notably, the gap where the Russian River breaks through the coastal range—are the coolest parts of the county, whereas the warmest climate is found in the northeast corner, furthest from these moderating influences.

Grape Varieties

About two-thirds of Sonoma's wines are red, with Pinot Noir and Cabernet Sauvignon as the leading red varieties. Merlot and Zinfandel are also important red grapes. The single most widely planted variety, however, is Chardonnay, which accounts for 80% of the county's white wines.

Sonoma Appellations

The AVAs of Sonoma cover a larger area than the AVAs of Napa, and there is no one single AVA covering the majority of the county. Sonoma's AVAs are more like overlapping pieces of a puzzle.

The Sonoma Coast AVA: This area covers a large swath of the county's coastline and is heavily influenced by the nearby ocean. The Sonoma Coast AVA has an exceptionally cool climate and a high degree of rainfall—even relative to other parts of Sonoma. The area runs parallel to the Pacific Ocean from San Pablo Bay to the border with Mendocino County. Pinot Noir, Chardonnay, and cool-climate Syrah are the leading grapes and wines produced here. At nearly 500,000 acres (202,300 ha), it makes sense that the Sonoma Coast AVA contains many microclimates, as defined by the numerous mountain ridges, hills, and valleys that make up the area. Two smaller AVAs are located within the boundaries of the Sonoma Coast AVA: the Fort Ross-Seaview AVA (a sub-appellation located in the northern, coastal area) and the Petaluma Gap AVA (an overlapping AVA shared between Sonoma and Marin Counties).

- **Fort Ross-Seaview:** In 2011, the Fort Ross–Seaview AVA was carved out within the northern portion of the Sonoma Coast AVA. Vineyards within this steep, mountainous region are generally planted at elevations of 800 to 1,800 feet (244 to 550 m) above sea level.
- **Petaluma Gap:** Approved in 2017, the Petaluma Gap AVA covers the southern portion of the Sonoma Coast AVA and extends into the northern part of Marin County. The namesake Petaluma Gap—a geological feature known as a *wind gap*—is actually a 15-mile-wide area of low-lying hills that creates something of an opening in the otherwise much taller coastal mountains. This feature allows for almost-daily, west-to-east afternoon breezes that range from 8 to 20 miles an hour and cool the area. The Petaluma Gap is largely planted to Pinot Noir, Chardonnay, and Syrah.

The Russian River Valley AVA: The Russian River Valley, located in the county's center (inland of the Russian River's cut through the coastal range) is another cool-climate region. Although warmer than the coast, these lower-temperature areas are influenced by the maritime air and morning fogs, making them ideal for Pinot Noir and Chardonnay—produced in both still and sparkling versions. Single-vineyard wines are also highly prized in these areas. This region has two sub-appellations:

LEADING GRAPE VARIETIES OF SONOMA COUNTY

Red Grapes	White Grapes
Pinot Noir	Chardonnay
Cabernet Sauvignon	Sauvignon Blanc
Zinfandel	Pinot Gris/Grigio
Merlot	Viognier
Syrah	Semillon
Petite Sirah	
Cabernet Franc	
Malbec	
Sangiovese	
Petit Verdot	

Figure 16–10: Leading Grape Varieties of Sonoma County

- **Green Valley of Russian River Valley:** The Green Valley of Russian River Valley sub-appellation is one of the smaller AVAs of Sonoma County and considered to be the most consistent in terms of its cool, foggy climate and sandy soils.
- **Chalk Hill:** The Chalk Hill AVA, also within the Russian River Valley AVA, takes its name from the chalky appearance of the area's volcanic white soils. The Chalk Hill AVA, which is slightly warmer than the surrounding areas, is well-known for robust Chardonnay and Sauvignon Blanc.

The Sonoma Valley AVA: The Sonoma Valley AVA covers a thin stretch of land located between the Sonoma Mountains to the west and the Mayacamas Mountains to the east. The mountains to the west block much of the cooling influence coming from the Pacific Ocean; however, the AVA lies in the watershed of Sonoma Creek—which drains into San Pablo Bay and allows for the cooling effects and fog of the bay to penetrate inland. The Sonoma Valley AVA has several sub-appellations:

AVAs of Sonoma County

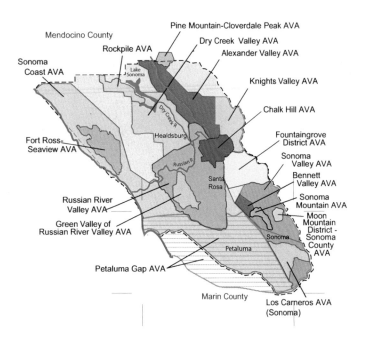

Copyright: The Society of Wine Educators 2021

Figure 16–11: Sonoma County wine regions

- **Sonoma Mountain AVA:** The Sonoma Mountain AVA is a small but diverse area located in the hills to the east of the Sonoma Valley. Many of the vineyards are planted above the fog line and on east-facing slopes, making for long days of full sun. Other vineyards are planted in the valleys with varying levels of sun—as such, this small area is planted to a wide range of grape varieties.
- **Bennett Valley AVA:** The tiny Bennett Valley AVA is located in a valley just to the north of the Sonoma Mountain AVA. Surrounded by hills, this is one of the cooler areas of the Sonoma Valley.
- **Moon Mountain District Sonoma County AVA:** This area is located along the western slopes of the Mayacamas Mountains, on the border between Napa and Sonoma. This mountainous area is unique due to its red, rocky, and iron-rich volcanic soils.
- **Carneros/Los Carneros AVA:** This cool-climate area, shared between Napa and Sonoma Counties, is influenced by both San Pablo Bay and the Petaluma Gap—both of which allow for coastal breezes to penetrate inland. The main products here are Chardonnay, Pinot Noir, and sparkling wines.

The inland areas: In the inland areas to the north of the Sonoma Valley AVA, the average temperatures steadily rise, and these regions typically experience much warmer climates than those closer to the waters. Sonoma's inland AVAs include the following:

- **Dry Creek Valley AVA:** The Dry Creek Valley AVA is considered to be one of the best areas in California for Zinfandel—which has been cultivated continuously in the region for over 100 years. Just two miles wide, Dry Creek Valley is located on the southern edge of Lake Sonoma and follows Dry Creek (a tributary of the Russian River). The area's signature wine—its rich, flavorful Zinfandel—is typically grown on the hillsides alongside Merlot and Cabernet Sauvignon; the slightly cooler valley floor is known for Sauvignon Blanc as well.
- **Rockpile AVA:** The Rockpile AVA, located on a high ridge above Lake Sonoma, is a sunny, mountainous area. Vineyards are planted at elevations up to of up to 1,900 feet (580 m). Like its neighbor-to-the-south, Dry Creek Valley, Rockpile is best known for rich, intensely colored Zinfandel.
- **Alexander Valley AVA:** The Alexander Valley AVA stretches along a southeasterly-flowing section of Russian River for close to 20 miles (33 km). Vineyards are planted on both sides of the river and into the foothills of the Mayacamas Mountains. This is one of the warmer parts of Sonoma and is well-known for vibrant, fruit-driven Cabernet Sauvignon.
- **Knights Valley AVA:** The Knights Valley AVA, located along the border with both Napa and Lake Counties, is planted mainly to Cabernet Sauvignon. This is a warm region consisting of several miles of mountainous terrain with well-drained soils and abundant sunshine.
- **Pine Mountain/Cloverdale Peak AVA:** The Pine Mountain-Cloverdale Peak AVA is shared between Sonoma and Mendocino Counties. Located in part on the slopes of Pine Mountain itself, it is one of the highest elevation grape-growing regions in California with vineyards ranging from 1,600 to 3,000 feet (488 to 914 m) above sea level.

- **Fountaingrove District AVA:** The Fountaingrove District AVA, approved in early 2015, lies just to the north of the Sonoma Valley AVA in the area between the Sonoma Coast AVA and the Napa Valley AVA. Most of the vineyards in the area are located in the foothills of the Mayacamas Mountains—some as high as 2,000 feet (700 m) above sea level.

The Northern Sonoma AVA: The large Northern Sonoma AVA encompasses most of the other Sonoma AVAs, with the exception of the area covered by the Sonoma Valley and Carneros AVAs in the far south/southeast of the county. This large AVA allows much of the wine grown and produced within the boundaries of Sonoma County to use an AVA as its place of origin, and in many cases also qualifies the wine to use the term "estate bottled" on the label.

MENDOCINO COUNTY

The area around Mendocino County, north of Sonoma, is mostly mountainous and forested, with much of the land not suitable for viticulture. The 17,000 acres (6,900 ha) of vineyards that do exist within the county are generally confined to river valleys, with 25% growing certified organic grapes.

Within the broad Mendocino AVA is the Anderson Valley AVA, one of the coolest winegrowing areas of California. This long, narrow valley in the south-central part of the county has a marginal climate that has proven excellent for Pinot Noir and sparkling wine production. Although planted in smaller quantities, aromatic white grapes such as Riesling, Gewürztraminer, and Pinot Gris also produce wines that are highly regarded.

The Mendocino Ridge AVA is unique in that it is noncontiguous, as only the areas at elevations of 1,200 feet (366 m) above sea level or higher are included. As such, this appellation is often referred to as "Islands in the Sky." Because of its location above the fog line, the vines receive plenty of cool-climate sunshine. Much of the area in this AVA is steep-sloped and covered with forests; currently just over 250 acres (101 ha) of the region's total 250,000 acres (101,170 ha) are planted to vines. New plantings are largely Pinot Noir, but the region maintains some

Figure 16–12: Smudge pots used to warm the vineyards in case of freeze

old vine Zinfandel, which creates some of the most distinctive Zinfandels in the state.

Most of the other vineyards of Mendocino lie along the eastern side of the county, connecting with adjacent Lake County. This relatively flat land in the watershed of the Russian River is well protected from maritime influence by the coastal mountains and therefore can get quite hot in midsummer, but it has cool nights. This wide diurnal variation permits grapes to reach full maturity while retaining vibrant acidity. Cabernet Sauvignon, Zinfandel, Petite Sirah, and Rhône varieties can be found here.

Mendocino County is home to the smallest AVA within the United States—the Cole Ranch AVA. Named after Ohio native John Cole, who planted the first vines in the area in the 1970s, the tiny appellation sits between the Russian River (to the east) and the Anderson Valley (to the west). The AVA's 60 acres (24 ha) of vines are largely planted to Cabernet Sauvignon, Merlot, Pinot Noir, and Riesling.

LAKE COUNTY

Located at the intersection of the Vaca and Mayacamas Mountains, Lake County is only 10 miles (16 km) from Calistoga, yet the drive along the winding roads takes an hour. The county contains one of the oldest geological lakes within the United States and is the largest geothermal field in North America. The presence of Clear Lake buffers the temperature, permitting grape growing despite the county's inland locale. Young volcanic soils provide extremely good drainage throughout the county.

The average elevation of Lake County's vineyards is 1,500 feet (460 m), with some areas reaching up to 3,000 feet (915 m) above sea level. The high elevation coupled with good air quality (the purest in California, according to the Environmental Protection Agency) maximizes the solar potential, resulting in higher levels of ultraviolet light. Consequently, the grapes develop thicker skins and higher levels of anthocyanins, polyphenols, and tannins, as well as lower levels of pyrazines. Moreover, there is low relative humidity and great diurnal swings, the latter of which prevent heat retention and promote good acid retention.

Cabernet Sauvignon is the most widely planted grape in Lake County, followed closely by Sauvignon Blanc. Merlot, Zinfandel, and Chardonnay are also represented. Lake County currently has seven designated AVAs:
- Benmore Valley
- Clear Lake
- High Valley
- Red Hills Lake County
- Big Valley District Lake County
- Kelsey Bench Lake County
- Guenoc Valley

THE CENTRAL COAST

Conceptually, the Central Coast is the cool-climate area along the Pacific coast between San Francisco and Santa Barbara, defined by the maritime influence of the Pacific Ocean. Prevailing winds blowing across the cold ocean currents create blankets of fog, cooling the coastal areas as far inland as they can penetrate until stopped by mountains. These areas are well-known for their Chardonnays, Pinot Noirs, and other well-structured, light- to medium-bodied wines.

California's Central Coast

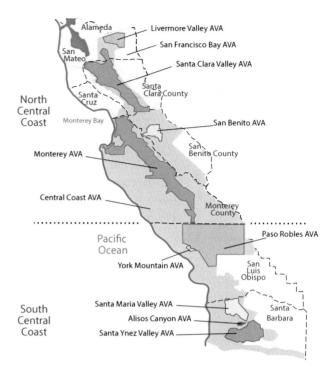

Copyright: The Society of Wine Educators 2020

Figure 16–13: California Central Coast wine regions

In reality, the Central Coast AVA covers a huge amount of ground, taking in almost the entire coast from San Francisco to Santa Barbara, but including some warmer, inland areas on the eastern side of the mountains as well. (Please note that while Santa Cruz County is part of the Central Coast AVA, the Santa Cruz Mountains AVA and its subregion, the Ben Lomond Mountain AVA, are specifically excluded.)

Many of the important wine regions of the Central Coast AVA are found within the counties of Monterey, San Luis Obispo, and Santa Barbara. These are discussed below.

Monterey County

Monterey County is one of the top five wine-producing California counties; nearly 20% of the state's Chardonnay is produced in Monterey. While logic might prompt one to think that Monterey's southerly locale would make it a warm region, this is not the case. At Monterey, there is a gap in the mountains where they begin to run east–west, or perpendicular rather than parallel to the ocean. This orientation plays a big role in the Monterey wine region, with the warmer air at the southwestern end of the valley creating a vacuum that pulls the cooler ocean air downstream. The primary appellation in this area is the Monterey AVA, along with several sub-AVAs:

- Cool-climate AVAs, located about midway down the valley, include Santa Lucia Highlands, Arroyo Seco, and Chalone. These areas are known for cool-climate grape varieties, including Pinot Noir, Chardonnay, Riesling, Pinot Blanc, and Pinot Grigio.
- The warmer areas of southern Monterey, including the San Lucas and Hames Valley AVAs, are known for Cabernet Sauvignon and Rhône varieties.

San Luis Obispo County

San Luis Obispo County is home to the following AVAs:

- The Paso Robles AVA covers roughly the entire northern half of San Luis Obispo County and extends across more than 666,500 acres (270,000 ha). This large AVA contains 11 AVAs (approved in November of 2014) within its boundaries; these sub-appellations showcase the diversity of the larger area in terms of its range of soils, varying levels of marine influence, and elevations—which range from 700 feet (213 m) to 2,400 feet (730 m) above sea level. Not surprisingly, a wide range of grapes are grown in the area. The leading varieties include Cabernet Sauvignon, Zinfandel, Merlot, Grenache, Syrah, and Mourvèdre; cooler areas are known for Pinot Noir and Chardonnay (among others). The sub-appellations of the Paso Robles AVA include: Adelaida District, Creston District, El Pomar District, Paso Robles Estrella District, Paso Robles Geneseo District, Paso Robles Highlands District, Paso Robles Willow Creek District, San Juan Creek, San Miguel District, Santa Margarita Ranch, and the Templeton Gap District.
- York Mountain is a small AVA that sits on the western edge of the much larger Paso Robles AVA. This is a mountainous region, very close to the ocean, that sits at the edge of the Templeton Gap—a channel in the Santa Lucia Mountains that draws the cool air inland towards Paso Robles.
- Edna Valley, a cool region located to the south of Paso Robles and close to the coast, features Chardonnay and Pinot Noir.
- Arroyo Grande Valley, another cool region, is located south of Edna Valley and close to the coast, also featuring Chardonnay and Pinot Noir.

Santa Barbara County

Santa Barbara County, located a 90-minute drive north of Los Angeles, is geologically unique in that it is one of the few places on the California coast where both the coastline and the mountain ranges run east–west as opposed to north–south. Seven AVAs are currently located within Santa Barbara County:

- Santa Maria Valley, an often foggy and windswept region, is the northernmost. It is known for cool-weather grapes, including Chardonnay and Pinot Noir.
- Santa Ynez Valley, a long east–west corridor with a diversity of climates, is the largest of the six and produces a wide range of wines.
- Ballard Canyon is a subregion somewhat centered within the larger Santa Ynez Valley AVA. The area has long been appreciated for spicy red wines produced from Syrah and Grenache.
- The Los Olivos District AVA is a subregion of the Santa Ynez Valley AVA, located just north of the Santa Ynez River, and just east of the Ballard Canyon AVA.
- Sta. Rita Hills, which sits mostly within the larger Santa Ynez Valley AVA, is located on its western border and therefore enjoys a much cooler climate than the inland areas.
- The Happy Canyon of Santa Barbara AVA, a subregion of the Santa Ynez Valley AVA located on its eastern side, is one of the warmer areas. Local lore suggests that the name of the region comes from the time of Prohibition, when bootleg alcohol was produced in the area, prompting folks to "take a trip to Happy Canyon."
- The Alisos Canyon AVA, approved in August of 2020, is a small region wedged between Santa Maria Valley (to the north), and the Santa Ynez Valley (to the south). The area has been described as a "Goldilocks Rhône Zone," referring to its climate as "not too hot, not too cold, but just right" for Rhône varieties such as Syrah, Grenache, and Viognier.

THE CENTRAL VALLEY

California's Central Valley is a huge expanse of fertile land between the Coast Range and the Sierra Nevada Mountains. Fifty-five percent of the state's total grape acreage is planted here, amid major plantings of other agricultural crops. Much of the grape crop goes into juice and raisin production, but a significant percentage is made into bulk wine. Wine grapes of the Central Valley include Chenin Blanc, French Colombard, Muscat, Chardonnay, Zinfandel, Cabernet Sauvignon, and Merlot.

Lodi

While much of the Central Valley is considered to be too hot for the production of quality wine, the area east of San Francisco Bay has, overall, a cooler climate. This is due to the presence of the largest gap in California's Coast Range, the Golden Gate entrance to San Francisco Bay. This gap provides access for the cool winds off the Pacific Ocean to penetrate inland, following the natural inlet of the San Joaquin/Sacramento River Delta to the foothills of the Sierra Nevada Mountains.

The principal appellation in this area is the Lodi AVA, with over 100,000 acres (40,500 ha) of vines and a surprisingly Mediterranean climate. During the growing season, the Lodi area is typically sunny, with warm daytime temperatures, cooling "delta breezes" in the afternoon, and a significant drop in temperatures at night. Diurnal temperature shifts can be as much as 45 degrees Fahrenheit and allow for the development of rich fruit flavors and bright, crisp acids in the grapes and the wines made from them.

The Lodi AVA, approved in 1986, currently has seven sub-appellations:
- Alta Mesa
- Borden Ranch
- Clements Hills
- Cosumnes River
- Jahant
- Mokelumne River
- Sloughhouse

Lodi and its sub-appellations grow over 70 different varieties of grapes, and have gained a reputation for old-vine Zinfandel, Petite Sirah, Cabernet Sauvignon, and Viognier, as well as other Rhône, Italian, and Spanish varieties. Lodi's Bechthold Vineyard, planted in 1886, is home to some of the world's oldest (and still productive, at 2 to 4 tons per acre) plantings of Cinsault.

AVAs of California's North Central Coast

Copyright: The Society of Wine Educators 2016

Figure 16–14: North Central Coast wine regions

THE SIERRA FOOTHILLS

The Sierra Foothills AVA covers a scattering of mostly high-elevation vineyards on the western slopes of the rugged Sierra Nevada range east of Sacramento and the Central Valley. Though geographically large, the area has just 5,700 acres (2,300 ha) planted to vines—just over 1% of California's total wine grape acreage. The vines are devoted overwhelmingly to red varieties, particularly Zinfandel. Comprised of eight counties, the area includes five sub-AVAs: North Yuba, Fiddletown, El Dorado, California Shenandoah Valley, and Fair Play.

SOUTHERN CALIFORNIA

Southern California might be more famous for sandy beaches than vineyards these days, but it is actually the birthplace of the California wine industry. Back in 1769, long before California was a state, Father Junípero Serra, a Spanish Franciscan missionary, founded the first Catholic mission in California on the site of present-day San Diego. This new outpost of Christianity, named San Diego de Alcalá, was the first of nine missions Serra would found, stretching from San Diego to modern-day San Francisco. Up and down the length of what is now the state of California,

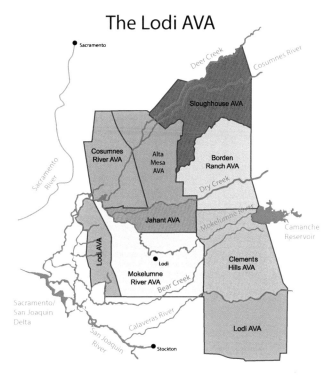

The Lodi AVA

Figure 16-15: The Lodi AVA and subregions

the Franciscan Fathers gave the area its humble viticultural beginnings by planting the Mission grape for use in sacramental wines.

While many Americans know the story of the California Missions, even dedicated wine lovers might be surprised to learn that commercial winemaking in California also had its origins in the southern end of the state. California's first commercial wineries were established in what is now Los Angeles as early as the 1820s. By 1833, the area was growing Bordeaux varieties brought to the area by Jean-Louis Vignes, a native of the Bordeaux region of France. Vignes named his estate "El Aliso," in honor of an ancient Sycamore tree growing near the entrance to his property. Known to his neighbors as "Don Luis del Aliso," Vignes was an adventurer who traveled the world before settling down, planting vineyards, and making wine in southern California.

Many producers followed in Vignes' footsteps, and the area of southern California soon became the largest grape-growing area in the state. However, winemaking in the region was decimated by both Prohibition and Pierce's disease. Soon, the land in southern California became more valuable to the makers of residential housing, parks, and office buildings than it was to the producers of wine.

However, winemaking still survives in the area today. The South Coast AVA, with over 3,000 acres (1,200 ha) under vine, includes parts of the counties of Los Angeles, San Bernardino, San Diego, Orange, and Riverside. The Temecula Valley AVA, located in Riverside County, currently has over 1,500 acres (610 ha) planted to vine. Smaller plantings are to be found in the Ramona Valley AVA and the San Pasqual Valley AVA (both in San Diego County). The area's most planted varieties include Zinfandel (including some very old vines), Cabernet Sauvignon, Merlot, and Syrah. The area is also becoming increasingly known for Petite Sirah and Viognier.

While not part of the South Coast AVA proper, the area just north of Los Angeles is home to one of California's newer AVAs, the Malibu Coast AVA, established in July of 2014. Upon its approval, the area's two existing AVAs, Saddle Rock–Malibu and Malibu–Newton Canyon, became sub-appellations of the new Malibu Coast AVA.

Warmer and drier inland AVAs in southern California include the Cucamonga Valley AVA (shared by Riverside and San Bernardino Counties), with just over 1,000 acres (405 ha) of vines. The large Antelope Valley of the High California Desert AVA and its tiny neighbors, the Sierra Pelona Valley and the Leona Valley AVAs, are located slightly to the north and east of Los Angeles.

WASHINGTON STATE

The state of Washington is the second largest producer of vinifera wine in the United States and, at more than 50,000 planted acres (20,200 ha), has the most vineyard acreage after California. State law requires that any wine using a Washington appellation contain a minimum of 95% Washington grapes.

Geography and Climate
Washington is divided by the high-altitude Cascade Mountain range into a cool and very rainy western part and a larger zone to the east that has desert-like conditions with hot summers, very cold winters, and very little precipitation.

Figure 16–16: Rain shadow diagram

The western section, near Puget Sound, is where the Washington wine industry began, but it has so little sunshine that ripening grapes can be quite difficult. For this reason, almost all of the state's vineyards are now located east of the Cascades, which form a rain shadow that creates the near-desert conditions. Despite the lack of rain, runoff from the snowy Cascades finds its way into the Columbia River and well water. This provides ample water for irrigation, without which viticulture would be impossible. The state's northerly latitude provides long days in midsummer and, in fact, offers more sunshine hours than California. The continental climate brings cold winters, making winterkill a very real threat to the vines.

Grape Varieties

Washington produces over 70 grape varieties, with nearly 60% of the state's vineyards planted to red grapes. Cabernet Sauvignon and Merlot are the most widely planted red varieties. Syrah is planted in less quantity; but is seen as an "up-and-coming" variety and draws some of the highest critical acclaim. While Chardonnay is the leading white variety by acreage, Washington State is considered a leading region for Riesling (the number two white grape).

WASHINGTON APPELLATIONS

As of December 2021, Washington has 19 AVAs — with all but one located in the rain shadow east of the Cascade Mountains.

The Puget Sound AVA, which is responsible for less than 1% of the state's wine production, is the only Washington State AVA located on the western side of the Cascade Mountains. This cooler, wetter part of the state is much better known as the home of the state's population centers of Seattle, Tacoma, and Olympia than as a wine region. However, because

LEADING GRAPE VARIETIES OF WASHINGTON STATE

Red Grapes	White Grapes
Cabernet Sauvignon	Chardonnay
Merlot	Riesling
Syrah	Pinot Gris/Grigio
Cabernet Franc	Sauvignon Blanc
Malbec	Gewürztraminer
Sangiovese	Viognier
Grenache	Semillon
Petit Verdot	Chenin Blanc

Figure 16–17: Leading Grape Varieties of Washington State

this AVA is close to residents and the tourist trade, many Washington State wineries maintain production facilities and tasting rooms here.

The remainder of Washington State's AVAs are located in the eastern section of the state, well within the rain shadow created by the high Cascade Mountains. The Columbia Valley AVA, one of the largest appellations in the country and the largest in Washington State, encompasses most of the state's vineyard land in eastern Washington, as well as a small section crossing into Oregon. The majority of the AVAs located in eastern Washington are contained within the borders of the Columbia Valley AVA. These include the following:

- **Lake Chelan AVA:** The Lake Chelan AVA sits at a higher elevation than the surrounding area and is significantly influenced by the "lake effect" that creates mild and favorable temperatures, resulting in a longer growing season and a reduced risk of frost.
- **Wahluke Slope AVA:** Comprising nearly 15% of Washington's total acreage, Wahluke Slope AVA is one of the driest and warmest AVAs in the state. It is planted to Merlot, Syrah, and Cabernet Sauvignon, along with some white varieties.
- **White Bluffs AVA:** The White Bluffs AVA — registered in July of 2021 — is situated atop an elevated plateau that averages 200 feet (60 m) higher than the surrounding area. This elevation provides a degree of protection against frosts and freezing temperatures. The area is named for a deep layer of lakebed sediment (the Ringold

Formation) that is whitish in color and visible in places alongside the Columbia River.

- **Naches Heights AVA:** The Naches Heights AVA was first planted in 2002 with Pinot Gris, Riesling, and Syrah. Elevations in the area range from 1,200 to 2,100 feet (366–640 m), making it considerably higher than the surrounding areas. Soils are mostly wind-blown loess with a significant amount of clay, which helps to retain water in this otherwise dry area.
- **Horse Heaven Hills AVA:** Located near the Columbia River, the Horse Heaven Hills AVA benefits from tempering winds and steep slopes. Some of the state's highest-rated wines hail from this appellation.
- **The Burn of Columbia Valley AVA:** The Burn of Columbia Valley AVA, registered in July of 2021, is a triangle-shaped appellation located alongside the north bank of the Columbia River. The topography of the area—comprised mainly of southeast-facing benchland sloping towards the river—makes it a bit warmer than much of the surrounding region. Cabernet Sauvignon is the leading variety.
- **Ancient Lakes of Columbia Valley AVA:** The Ancient Lakes of Columbia Valley AVA—defined on its western side by the Columbia River—is dominated by a gentle (4%) slope facing its eastern boundary. The area is named for a series of more than 30 pothole lakes—formed by the Missoula Floods more than 12,000 years ago—that dot the region.
- **Royal Slope AVA:** The Royal Slope AVA is almost entirely located on a series of gently rolling, south-facing slopes with elevations ranging from 610 feet (186 m) to 1,756 feet (535 m) above sea level. The area is particularly well-known for Washington State's first 100-point Syrah—Charles Smith's Royal City Syrah 2006, crafted using grapes sourced from Stoneridge Vineyard.
- **Walla Walla Valley AVA:** The Walla Walla Valley AVA spills over into Oregon and has been home to grape growing since the 1850s, when grapes were first planted by Italian immigrants. Although Cabernet Sauvignon is the leading grape, a wide range of varieties are currently planted here.

AVAs of Washington State

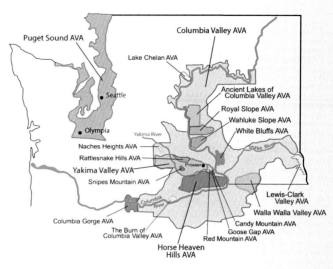

Copyright: The Society of Wine Educators 2022

Figure 16–18: Washington wine regions

- **Yakima Valley AVA:** The Yakima Valley AVA—with vineyards planted on either side of the winding Yakima River—was the state's first appellation and accounts for over one-third of the vineyards. This is one of the few areas in Washington State planted to a majority of white grapes, and its primary grape is Chardonnay. Other leading grape varieties include Cabernet Sauvignon, Merlot, Riesling, and Syrah. In recent years, several small sub-appellations have been approved within the confines of the Yakima Valley AVA. These include the following:
  - Rattlesnake Hills AVA
  - Red Mountain AVA
  - Snipes Mountain AVA
  - Candy Mountain AVA
  - Goose Gap AVA

Two more AVAs are located in eastern Washington but outside of the borders of the Columbia Valley AVA. These AVAs are described below:
- **Columbia Gorge AVA:** The Columbia Gorge AVA, which straddles the Columbia River, is partially located in the state of Oregon. Located where the Columbia River cuts a very narrow passage through the Cascade Mountains, this area encompasses a wide range of climates, soils, and geology.

- **Lewis-Clark Valley AVA:** The Lewis-Clark Valley AVA — the easternmost AVA in Washington State — roughly follows the contours of three rivers: the Snake, the Clearwater, and the Grande Ronde. Of the area's total 306,000 acres (124,000 ha), 72% are in Idaho, with the remaining 86,000 acres (35,000 ha) located in Washington State.

OREGON

The Oregon wine industry, dominated by small, often family-run vineyards, consistently ranks as one of the top four largest producers of wine in the United States. The wines of Oregon, particularly Pinot Noir, Pinot Gris, and sparkling wines, are highly acclaimed both in the United States and abroad.

From 1965 to 1968, UC Davis graduates David Lett, Charles Coury, and Dick Erath were separately determined to plant vineyards and make wine in Oregon's Willamette Valley. Seeing similarity between the terroir of Oregon and that of Burgundy, they set about crafting wines that emulated the Burgundian style of Pinot Noir, while at the same time respecting the valley's own unique soils and climate. Soon, the world noticed. Perhaps the most ringing endorsement of their success was the investment made by Maison Joseph Drouhin, a top Burgundy négociant and producer who established Domaine Drouhin in the Willamette Valley in 1988.

Geography and Climate

Most of Oregon's wineries are west of the Cascades, primarily located in the valley of the north-flowing Willamette River between the Coast Range and the Cascades. In the past, Oregon has not had much of a wine industry in the east, however, the areas close to and shared with Washington and Idaho are set for growth.

Many of Oregon's wine regions are well-suited to cool-climate viticulture. The growing season is typically long and dry, but there is always a concern that the grapes will not fully ripen before the approach of winter rains forces the growers to harvest.

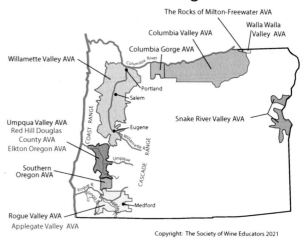

Figure 16–19: Oregon wine regions

There are additional vineyard areas in the southwest of the state, in the valleys of the Umpqua and Rogue Rivers. These warmer regions are better protected from the maritime effects and are able to ripen red grapes such as Cabernet Sauvignon, Merlot, and Syrah.

Grape Varieties

Oregon's premier grape variety is unquestionably Pinot Noir, which makes up close to 60% of the vineyard acreage. Other leading red grapes include Cabernet Sauvignon and Merlot. The top white variety is Pinot Gris, followed by Chardonnay, Riesling, and Pinot Blanc.

To a lesser extent, some producers are working with Syrah, Viognier, Tempranillo, and other Mediterranean varieties, many of which are sourced from the warmer areas in the southern reaches of the state.

Oregon wine law is unique in that it requires key varietal wines to contain a minimum of 90% of the grape variety stated on the label. Thus, many of Oregon's best known wines — including Pinot Noir and Pinot Gris — will contain a minimum of 90% of the named grape variety. In 2007, this regulation was loosened a bit to allow exceptions for the following 18 varieties: Cabernet Franc, Cabernet Sauvignon, Carmenère, Grenache, Malbec, Marsanne, Merlot, Mourvèdre, Petit Verdot, Petite Sirah, Roussanne, Sangiovese, Sauvignon Blanc, Semillon, Syrah, Tannat, Tempranillo, and Zinfandel.

LEADING GRAPE VARIETIES OF OREGON

Red Grapes	White Grapes
Pinot Noir	Pinot Gris
Syrah	Chardonnay
Cabernet Sauvignon	Riesling
Merlot	Pinot Blanc

Figure 16–20: Leading Grape Varieties of Oregon

Oregon Appellations

As of December 2021, there are 22 AVAs in Oregon. Nearly three-quarters of Oregon's vineyards fall within the large, cool-climate Willamette Valley AVA, situated approximately 50 miles (80 km) from the Pacific Ocean and about an hour's drive south of Portland. The Willamette Valley includes ten sub-appellations, as follows:

- Dundee Hills
- Ribbon Ridge
- Eola-Amity Hills
- Van Duzer Corridor
- McMinnville
- Yamhill-Carlton District
- Chehalem Mountains
- Laurelwood District
- Tualatin Hills
- Lower Long Tom

Extending from the southern tip of the Willamette Valley to the border of California, the Southern Oregon AVA combines the more precise Rogue Valley and Umpqua Valley AVAs. The Rogue Valley includes one sub-AVA, Applegate Valley, while the Umpqua Valley includes the sub-AVAs of Elkton Oregon and Red Hill Douglas County.

Three appellations straddle the Oregon–Washington border: Columbia Gorge, Columbia Valley, and Walla Walla Valley. The Rocks District of Milton-Freewater AVA—named after the cobblestone-rich soils that define its borders—lies entirely within the Oregon portion of the Walla Walla Valley AVA. "The Rocks" (as the district is often called) is a tiny area that covers just 3,770 acres (1,525 ha).

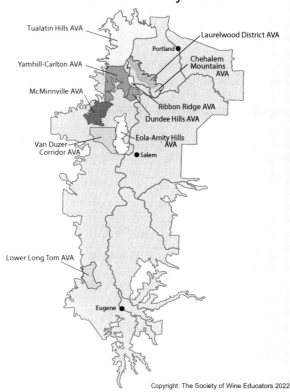

Willamette Valley AVAs

Tualatin Hills AVA
Laurelwood District AVA
Portland
Yamhill-Carlton AVA
Chehalem Mountains AVA
McMinnville AVA
Ribbon Ridge AVA
Dundee Hills AVA
Eola-Amity Hills AVA
Van Duzer Corridor AVA
Salem
Lower Long Tom AVA
Eugene

Copyright: The Society of Wine Educators 2022

Figure 16–21: AVAs of Oregon's Willamette Valley

The Snake River Valley AVA, located nearly 400 miles (645 km) inland of the Pacific Ocean, is located along the Oregon-Idaho border. The majority of the AVA's five million acres (two million ha) of land are located in the state of Idaho, where it follows the course of the Snake River for nearly 200 miles (322 km). While rather thinly populated with vineyards on the Oregon side, the Idaho side of the Snake River Valley AVA contains over 1,100 acres of commercial vines, accounting for nearly 85% of Idaho's commercial vine acreage. The Snake River Valley AVA is planted to a variety of grapes, including Cabernet Sauvignon, Merlot, Syrah, Chardonnay, and Riesling.

NEW YORK

Winegrowers in the eastern states face more difficult viticultural conditions than those in the west because of high summer humidity, which fosters mold and disease, and potentially harsh winters. Nevertheless, several states maintain flourishing wine industries.

New York played a significant role in the wine and grape industry of the United States before Prohibition, and in recent years the wine culture of the state has grown, evolved, and modernized considerably. The Finger Lakes AVA and its two sub-AVAs, Seneca Lake and Cayuga Lake, comprise the largest wine-producing region and account for 85% of New York's production. Here, with a climate akin to Germany's, Riesling and Cabernet Franc do well. The three main lakes of the region, Cayuga, Seneca, and Keuka, help to mitigate the region's temperature.

Originally, the Finger Lakes featured native and hybrid grapes exclusively. The region's embrace of vinifera in the early 1960s was due to the persistence of Dr. Konstantin Frank, a viticulturist from Russia who believed that European vines could survive the cold climate. Today, the area produces crisp, light-bodied wines using cool-climate vinifera varieties in addition to a good deal of labrusca varieties (particularly Concord, which thrives throughout the northeastern United States), and cold-hardy hybrids as well, including Vidal, Seyval Blanc, and Cayuga.

Downstate, the Long Island wine region is located just two hours east of New York City. With the first vines planted in 1973, the region is relatively young. This area is divided into the island's two "forks," including the North Fork of Long Island AVA and the Hamptons AVA in the South Fork. Home to a maritime climate, Long Island is significantly influenced by water, with the Atlantic Ocean to the south, Peconic Bay between the two forks, and the Long Island Sound to the north. Given these climatic conditions, Bordeaux-style blends abound, but single-variety wines are also prevalent, particularly Merlot and Chardonnay. Most of the wineries are located on the North Fork, where conditions are slightly more favorable and land is less expensive. Wines produced from a blend of grapes from both "forks" are labeled with the more general Long Island AVA.

AVAs of New York State

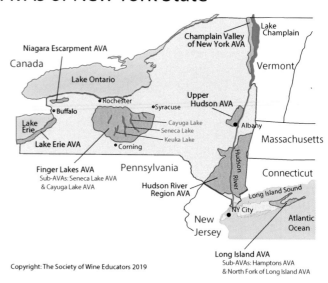

Figure 16-22: New York State wine regions

The Hudson River Region AVA, located north of New York City, is home to the Brotherhood Winery—established in 1839 and the oldest continuously operating winery in the United States. The region is also home to Benmarl Vineyards—originally planted with vines in the early 1800s and one of the oldest vineyards in the country. Despite its impressive history, the Hudson River Region AVA has seen much of its growth in the past few decades.

CANADA

Canada has a small modern wine industry that dates back to 1974, when the first winery license was granted following Canada's own version of Prohibition. Prohibition in Canada was enacted by the individual provinces beginning in 1918, with most provinces repealing by 1929. One lone holdout, Prince Edward Island, did not repeal Prohibition until 1948.

Canada's wine production is concentrated in Ontario and British Columbia, although small amounts of wine are made in Nova Scotia and Quebec, as well. Ontario and British Columbia are presently the only regions in Canada that produce a significant amount of wine that meets the standards of the country's appellation and quality control system, known as the Vintners Quality Alliance (VQA). The VQA began as a voluntary system in 1988, but has had the force of law in Ontario since 1999. As of 2005, British Columbia has its own appellation and quality system that includes standards for "BC VQA" wines as well as wines designated as "Wines of Marked Quality."

The majority of grapes are grown on the shores of the Great Lakes in the province of Ontario. This close proximity to water mitigates the seasonally cold weather and allows Canadian producers to grow a substantial quantity of vinifera grapes, including Chardonnay, Riesling, and Cabernet Franc. Of course, the winter cold plays an essential role in the making of icewine, one of Canada's specialties.

Approximately 85% of Ontario's vineyards lie in the Niagara Peninsula appellation, which radiates around Lake Ontario. Here, a wide range of microclimates is made possible by not only the maritime influence but also the Niagara Escarpment. The escarpment is a ridge of cliffs formed by millions of years of uneven erosion. It is responsible for the sheer drop of Niagara Falls. Due to the location of the ridge, the escarpment traps the warm air currents generated by Lake Ontario. This warm air hovers over the vineyard areas to the south of the escarpment, allowing grapes to ripen here despite the overall northern (and snowy) climate.

British Columbia is the other major source of Canadian wine. As in Washington State, the ideal conditions for winegrowing are found east of the Coast Range in the dry interior valleys. The premier growing area is the Okanagan Valley, which is planted almost exclusively with vinifera varieties led by Merlot, Pinot Gris, Chardonnay, and Pinot Noir.

Table 16-2: Geographical Indications of Ontario, Canada

GEOGRAPHICAL INDICATIONS OF ONTARIO, CANADA		
Viticultural Area	Regional Appellations	Sub-appellations
Lake Erie North Shore		South Islands (includes Pelee Island)
Niagara Peninsula	Niagara Escarpment	Beamsville Bench
		Short Hills Bench
		Twenty Mile Bench
	Niagara-on-the-Lake	Four Mile Creek
		Niagara Lakeshore
		Niagara River
		St. David's Bench
	(no regional appellation)	Creek Shores
		Lincoln Lakeshore
		Vinemount Ridge
Prince Edward County		

Source: Ontario Regulation 406/00: Rules of Vintners Quality Alliance Ontario relating to terms for VQA wine (September, 2021)

Table 16-3: Geographical Indications of British Columbia, Canada

GEOGRAPHICAL INDICATIONS OF BRITISH COLUMBIA, CANADA		
Province	Geographical Indication	Sub-appellations
British Columbia	Fraser Valley	
	Gulf Islands	
	Kootenays	
	Lillooet	
	Okanagan Valley	Golden Mile Bench
		Naramata Bench
		Okanagan Falls
		Skaha Bench
	Shuswap	
	Similkameen Valley	
	Thompson Valley	
	Vancouver Island	Cowichan Valley

Source: British Columbia Wine Authority (BCWA), 2021

MEXICO

Wine is vinified in at least seven Mexican states, with 90% of modern production centered in Baja California. The main wine region here is the Valle de Guadalupe near the city of Ensenada, where vines are planted at elevations ranging from 1,000 feet (305 m) to 1,250 feet (380 m), and where the area enjoys a Mediterranean climate. The city of Ensenada is considered a center of wine tourism in Mexico, and hosts an annual *Fiesta de la Vendimia* (Vintage Festival) every year in August. Ensenada is also a key point on the *Ruta del Vino* (Wine Route) that connects over 50 wineries as well as the cities of Tijuana and Tecate.

Mexico currently has nearly 6,200 acres (2,500 ha) planted to vinifera varieties. Principal white grape varieties include Chenin Blanc, Chardonnay, Sauvignon Blanc, and Viognier; principal red grapes include Cabernet Sauvignon, Merlot, Malbec, Grenache, Barbera, Syrah, and Tempranillo.

The Mexican state of Coahuila, located in northeastern Mexico adjacent to the US border, is the home of Casa Madero, one of the oldest wineries in the Americas. Casa Madero was founded by Don Lorenzo de Garcia in 1597 as Hacienda de San Lorenzo.

The estate was purchased by Don Evaristo Madero in 1893, and the name was changed to Casa Madero. The area, near the present-day city of Parras de la Fuente, enjoys a relatively cool climate due to the elevation provided by the Sierra Madre Oriental Mountains. These conditions make for well-balanced grapes and excellent wines, and Casa Madero continues to be one of the most important wine and brandy producers in Mexico.

SOUTH AMERICA

CHAPTER SEVENTEEN

LEARNING OBJECTIVES

After studying this chapter, the candidate should be able to:

- Recognize the importance of latitude and elevation for grape growing in South America.
- Describe the influences of the Andes on grape growing in Argentina and Chile.
- Discuss the major wine regions of Argentina and Chile.
- Recall the significant grape varieties grown in Argentina and Chile.
- Understand the general status of the wine industry in Brazil and Uruguay.

The majority of the South American continent lies in the tropics, but the Southern Cone at the bottom of the continent pushes south through the temperate winegrowing latitudes. Three major wine-producing countries are found here: Argentina, Chile, and Brazil. Argentina and Chile, moreover, are major wine exporters, sending bottled wine all over the world. Although its production is much smaller, Uruguay also produces wine for export. In this chapter, we take our first look at the wine producers of the Southern Hemisphere.

ARGENTINA

Argentina occupies the largest portion of suitable viticultural land in South America and makes the most wine. The huge cosmopolitan city of Buenos Aires is the primary market for Argentine wine, but the country's wine industry has become increasingly export-oriented. One of the keys to understanding Argentina's wine industry and culture in general is to know that the bulk of its population is of European origin. A large percentage of Argentina's population originated in Italy and Spain. As it is in those two countries, wine is an important part of Argentine culture and daily life.

GEOGRAPHY AND CLIMATE

Argentina is a wedge-shaped country lying between the long chain of the Andes Mountains to the west and the Atlantic Ocean to the east. The soaring Andean ridgeline, which also forms the border with Chile, creates a formidable barrier to the prevailing westerly winds and results in a significant rain shadow that keeps western Argentina very dry. The combination of dry air, plentiful irrigation water from Andean snowmelt, high elevations, and almost unlimited sunshine produces exceptional winegrowing conditions in Argentina's western foothills.

The climate in the Argentine wine regions is continental. Summers are hot, but the lack of humidity causes nighttime temperatures to drop rapidly, helping to retain acidity in the grapes. Winters are cold but not typically severe. However, the vineyards are often shaken by the fierce Zonda winds, which can damage leaves and fruit and, when followed by a cold front, bring the risk of frost damage. Around the time of the harvest, the greatest threat is posed by hailstorms, which can severely damage vineyard crops.

GRAPE VARIETIES

Historically, the wine industry of Argentina focused on a group of grape varieties—including the light red/pink-skinned grapes Criolla Grande, Criolla Chica, and Cereza—descended from the original vines (known as *País* or *Mission* grapes) brought into South America from Europe in the sixteenth century. As the wine industry of Argentina matured, many of these vines were replaced; however, they still account for nearly a third of all plantings in the country.

LEADING GRAPE VARIETIES OF ARGENTINA

Red Grapes	White Grapes
Malbec	Torrontés Riojano
Bonarda Argentina	Torrontés Mendocino
Cabernet Sauvignon	Torrontés Sanjuanino
Syrah	Chardonnay
Tempranillo	Moscatel de Alejandria
Merlot	Chenin Blanc
Pinot Noir	Sauvignon Blanc
Tannat	Viognier
Cabernet Franc	Pedro Giménez
Petit Verdot	

Pink-skinned Grapes: Cereza, Criolla Grande, Criolla Chica.

Figure 17-1: Leading Grape Varieties of Argentina

In decades past, the Criolla family of grapes was used primarily to produce inexpensive bulk wines; nonetheless, this too is evolving as the industry seeks to preserve the heritage of these vines and extend their use in higher-quality wines.

These days, Argentina is best known for two key grape varieties: Malbec and Torrontés. Malbec, a French grape from the area around Bordeaux, has become the country's signature red grape variety. Argentine Malbec tends to be deeply colored—often inky and opaque—and have corresponding fruit flavors of blackberry and plum.

The key white grape, Torrontés, produces a light-bodied wine with pronounced fruity and floral aromas. Torrontés has recently been determined to be at least three distinct varieties: Torrontés Mendocino, Torrontés Riojano, and Torrontés Sanjuanino. Of these, Torrontés Riojano is by far the most widely grown.

The remaining inventory of grape varieties planted in Argentina is long and diverse, with international varieties well represented. The leading reds include Bonarda Argentina (recently proven to be genetically identical to the grape known as *Douce Noire* in France and *Charbono* in California), Cabernet Sauvignon, and Syrah. Leading white grapes include Chardonnay, Moscatel de Alejandria, Sauvignon Blanc, Chenin Blanc, and Viognier. Pedro Giménez, while widely grown, is used primarily in the production of bulk wine, fortified wine, and blends.

ARGENTINE WINE LAWS

Argentina has a three-level appellation system that was enacted in 1999:

- *Denominación de origen controlada* (DOC), the highest level
- *Indicación geográfica* (IG), for quality wines below the DOC level
- *Indicación de procedencia* (IP), for table wines and regional wines

Argentina's DOC laws are European-style regulations, controlled and enforced by a local *consejo,* or council. The DOC regulations spell out geographic boundaries, permissible grape varieties, planting densities, and other requirements. However, only two DOC regions—Luján de Cuyo and San Rafael, both subregions of Mendoza—have been declared thus far; the system is still in its developmental stages.

The wine industry is also regulated by the Instituto Nacional de Vitivinicultura (INV). This regulating body places strict controls, including pricing requirements, on the best wines of Argentina. These wines, known as *vinos finos*, account for about 20% of all wine produced in the country. Vinos finos must be produced using premium grapes—a criterion that typically excludes wine produced from the Cereza or Criolla grape varieties. For vinos finos, the INV stipulates that all varietal wines must contain a minimum of 85% of the stated grape variety. New regulations that took effect with the 2011 vintage define the terms *Reserva* and *Gran Reserva*, and allow their use only on the labels of vinos finos. Reserva wines must have been aged a minimum of six months for white wines and one year for reds. The Gran Reserva designation requires a minimum aging period of one year for whites and two years for reds.

ARGENTINE WINE REGIONS

Jujuy: The Jujuy region, located in the extreme northwest of Argentina, is tucked deep into the Andes Mountains and as such contains some of highest-elevation vineyards in the world. One such vineyard—the Moya Vineyard at 10,922 feet (3,330 m) above sea level—has recently been named the highest vineyard in Argentina. The Jujuy region experiences very little rain, abundant sunshine, and a wide diurnal temperature swing. Commercial vine acreage is limited, totally a mere 65 acres (26 ha).

Salta: Salta—home to approximately 8,300 acres (3,365 ha) of vines—is known for its high-elevation vineyards which range from 5,000 to 10,200 feet (1,530 to 3,110 m) above sea level. The sub-region of Cafayate is home to a majority of the region's vineyards and is particularly well-known for high-altitude Torrontés Riojano in addition to Malbec and Cabernet Sauvignon. The Molinos subregion of Salta is home to another ultra-high elevation vineyard, *Altura Máxima* ("Maximum Height")—10,206 feet (3,111 m) high and planted to Malbec.

Tucumán: Tucumán—a sun-drenched, high-altitude, densely populated region—is home to just over 280 acres (113 ha) of vines. The area's vines are located primarily in the Calchaquí Valley (*Valles Calchaquíes*)—a geographic feature that stretches across parts of Catamarca and Salta as well. Cabernet Sauvignon, Merlot, and Torrontés Riojano make up the majority of the plantings.

Catamarca: Catamarca has nearly 6,200 acres (2,500 ha) planted to vine. Of these, nearly 40% are native Criolla grape varieties (some of which are used for bulk wine or table grapes). However, quality wine production—including unique wines based on Criolla varieties—is rapidly expanding. Torrontés Riojano is the leading export variety, followed by Cabernet Sauvignon, Malbec, and Syrah. The majority of the Catamarca's vineyards are located in a succession of high-elevation river valleys tucked between mountain ridges—where warm days, cool nights, and sunshine are abundant.

La Rioja: La Rioja, located south of Catamarca, is a relatively small producer known for warm days and cool nights, as well as a tendency for drought conditions. The majority of the vineyards are planted in the Famatina Valleys, located to either side of the Famatina mountain range. The region is planted 51% to red grapes, including Cabernet Sauvignon, Malbec, Bonarda, and Syrah. However, Torrontés Riojano is by far the single most widely-planted grape of the region and accounts for just over 32% of all plantings.

San Juan: San Juan, the next province to the south, is a warm and dry region. San Juan contains close to 17% of the country's vines, making it the second largest grape-producing province in the country (after Mendoza). San Juan's 82,200 acres (33, 250 ha) of vines are somewhat equally divided between red, white, and Criolla varieties. Syrah, Malbec, Bonarda, and Cabernet Sauvignon are the leading red varieties. A range of white grapes, led by Torrontés Sanjuanino, are planted; other white grapes important to San Juan include Torrontés Riojano, Chardonnay, Torrontés Mendocino, Chenin Blanc, Sauvignon Blanc, and Viognier.

Mendoza: Perfectly situated at the best latitude for wine production, Mendoza accounts for nearly 75% of Argentina's vineyard acreage and is home to many of the internationally renowned Argentine wineries. Mendoza takes advantage of the Andes, with most of its vineyards planted between 2,000 and 4,000 feet (610 to 1,220 m) above sea level. Over 61% of Mendoza's 372,500 acres (150,760 ha) of vines are planted to red grapes, led by Malbec, Bonarda, Cabernet Sauvignon, Syrah, and Tempranillo. Chardonnay, Torrontés Riojano, and Sauvignon Blanc are the leading white grapes. Mendoza is divided into five large sub-regions—Uco Valley, Primera Zona, Northern Oasis, East Mendoza, and South Mendoza. Both of Argentina's Denominación de Origen Controlada (DOC) wines—Luján de Cuyo DOC (Primera Zona) and San Rafael DOC (South Mendoza)—are located in the Mendoza Province.

Córdoba: The Argentina province of Córdoba—located almost in the geographic center of the country, to the east of La Rioja—has a long history of viticulture and wine production. Jesuit missionaries hailing from Spain settled in the province in the early 1600s and established several estancias (working ranches) complete with schools, churches, orchards, and vineyards. The Jesuits produced wine until 1767, when the Spanish crown expelled the Jesuits from Argentina. At this point most of the vineyards of Córdoba were abandoned, and wine production stagnated in the area until the 1870s when a strong wave of Italian immigration brought the industry back to life. Córdoba—located east of the Andes—contains a series of moderate-

Table 17–1: Wine Regions of Argentina

WINE REGIONS OF ARGENTINA			
Area	**Province**	**Subregions**	
North*	Catamarca	Belén, Pomán, Santa María, Tinogasta	
	Jujuy	Quebrada de Humahuaca, Tilcara*, Tumbaya*	
	Salta	Cachi, Cafayate/Cafayate Valley, Molinos, San Carlos	
	Tucumán	Amaicha del Valle*, Colalao del Valle*, Tafi	
Cuyo	Mendoza	Northern Oasis*	Guaymallén, Lavalle/Desierto de Lavalle, Las Heras
		Prima Zona*	Agrelo, Barrancas, Los Compuertas, El Paraiso, Godoy Cruz, Luján de Cuyo DOC, Luján de Cuyo, Lunlunta, Maipú, Russel
		Uco Valley	La Consulta, Los Chacayes, Pampa el Cepillo, Paraje Altamira, San Carlos, San Pablo, Tunuyán, Tupungato, Vista Flores
		East Mendoza*	Canota, Junín, La Paz, Santa Rosa
		South Mendoza*	General Alvear, San Rafael DOC, San Rafael
		Distrito Medrano	
	La Rioja*	Famatina	Valle de Chañarmuyo
		Arauco, Castelli*, Castro Barros, Chilecito, Felipe Varela, General Lamadrid, La Costa Riojana*, La Rioja Argentina, San Blas de los Sauces, Sanagasta, Vinchina	
	San Juan	25 de Mayo, 9 de Julio, Albardón, Angaco, Barreal, Calingasta, Caucete, Chimbas, Iglesia, Jáchal, Pedernal Valley, Pocito, Pozo de los Algarrobos, Rawson, Rivadavia, San Martín, Santa Lucia, Tulum Valley, Ullum, Valle Fértil, Zonda Valley, Zonda	
Valles Calchquíes (multi-region, multi-province GI)			
Valles del Famatina (multi-region, multi-province GI)			
Center*	Córdoba*	Colón, Colón Caroya, Córdoba Argentina, Cruz del Eje, San Javier	
	San Luis		
Patagonia	Chubut*	16 de Octubre Valley*, Los Altares*, Comarca Andina Paralelo 42*, Paso del Sapo*, Piedra Parada*, Río Chubut Lower Valley*, Río Pico Valley*, Sarmiento, Trevelin	
	La Pampa*	Río Colorado Upper Valley*	
	Neuquén	Añelo, Confluencia, Río Limay Valley*, San Patricio del Chañar*	
	Río Negro	Avellaneda, General Conesa, General Roca, Pichimahuida, Río Colorado Valley*, Upper Río Negro Valley	
Atlantic*	Buenos Aires*	Chapadmalal, Médanos*, Tandilia Hills*, Ventania Hills*, Villa Ventana	

*Indicates that as of December 2021, the area has not been officially declared a Geographical Indication; all other areas have been registered as official geographical indications by the INV

Source: Wines of Argentina (October 2021), *Instituto Nacional de Vitivinicultura (via Argentina.gob.ar)*

elevation mountain ranges in its western portion and an extensive plain covering much of the east. Leading grape varieties include Merlot, Pinot Noir, Malbec, Chardonnay, and Sauvignon Blanc.

Neuquén: The Neuquén Province is located south of Mendoza and considered part of Argentine Patagonia. The majority of the vineyards of Neuquén are located in the basins of the Limay and Neuquén rivers, in the southeastern part of the province. This is an area of moderate elevation—averaging between 886 feet (270 m) and 1,363 feet (415 m)—with a typically windy and dry climate. Days tend to be warm-to-hot, followed by brisk, desert-like cold nights. Nearly 85% of the vines in Neuquén are planted red grape varieties, led by Malbec, Cabernet Sauvignon, Merlot, and Pinot Noir. Nevertheless, the white wines of the region—led by Chardonnay, Sauvignon Blanc, and Semillon—enjoy an excellent reputation.

La Pampa: Located to the northeast of Neuquén and in the center of the country, La Pampa is a gently undulating plain—at an average elevation of 1,000 feet (305 m)—with 60-mile (96-km)-long fan-shaped valleys running from west to east. La Pampa experiences a moderate continental climate with mild autumns and springs, warm summers, and cold winters. Malbec accounts for nearly 50% of the region's 680 acres (275 ha) of vines. Other leading grapes varieties include Cabernet Sauvignon, Merlot, Cabernet Franc, Pinot Noir, and Chardonnay.

Río Negro: The vineyards of the Río Negro Province—planted across a series of west-east valleys located along the Colorado and Negro Rivers—are actually some of the *lowest* elevation vineyards in Argentina. Vine plantings stretch from the inland valleys in the western section of the province (where they top out at 1,214 feet/370 m in elevation) and continue to the east, almost to the point where the rivers meet the Atlantic Ocean (at 13 feet/4 m of elevation). Río Negro contains nearly 3,750 acres (1,515 ha) of vines; leading grapes include Malbec, Merlot, Pinot Noir, and all three versions of Torrontés.

Chubut: Chubut, located to the south of Río Negro, is currently the southernmost wine-producing province in Argentina. It also boasts one of the southernmost

Main Wine Areas of Argentina

Copyright: The Society of Wine Educators 2020

Figure 17-2: Argentine wine regions

vineyards in the world—Sarmiento—which sits below the 45th parallel (South). Many of the vineyards of Chubut are planted in the steppes (relatively flat, grassland areas) close to the Atlantic Coast. Nearly 60% of Chubut's 180 acres (73 ha) of vines are planted to red varieties. Pinot Noir is the leading grape, followed by Chardonnay, Merlot, Malbec, and Torrontés Riojano.

Buenos Aires: In recent years, as Argentine wine producers have begun to extend the limits of the country's viticulture to the east, the province of Buenos Aires has joined the ranks of emerging wine regions. The province currently contains less than 400 acres (160 ha) of vines in total, with Sauvignon Blanc and Chardonnay as the leading grape varieties; a diverse selection of red grapes, including Pinot Noir, are grown as well. In the southeast of the province, the Chapadmalal GI—located near the town of Mar del Plata and about 200 miles (320 km) south of the city of Buenos Aires—currently contains the easternmost vineyards in the country, some of which are planted just a few miles from the Atlantic Ocean. This ocean-influenced region is much cooler and receives more rainfall than many of Argentina's other vineyard areas.

CHILE

Chile stretches along South America's Pacific Coast for almost 2,700 miles (4,350 km), with viticulture involved in nearly 800 miles of that length (mostly between the latitudes of 30°S and 40°S). Like Australia and a few eastern European countries, Chile produces far more wine than its modest domestic market can absorb, and much of its wine is specifically intended for sale to consumers in other countries as a national revenue source. Two-thirds of Chile's total production is exported.

Figure 17–3: The Valley of the Moon in Chile's Atacama Desert

GEOGRAPHY AND CLIMATE

Located on the western edge of South America, Chile occupies more than half of the continent's Pacific coastline. The country is very narrow, rarely more than a hundred miles wide over most of its length, and squeezed between the ocean and the Andes. In the north is the Atacama Desert, one of earth's driest places, and in the south is the frozen archipelago of Tierra del Fuego. Thanks to these natural barriers and Chile's strict quarantine laws, the country holds the distinction of being considered phylloxera-free.

The capital city of Santiago and the majority of the vines are found in the long Central Valley that lies between low coastal mountains and the Andes. Here, the conditions are very similar to those of some of the prime winegrowing areas of California.

Stretched along the Pacific Ocean, Chile has a cold ocean current flowing along its shores from the polar seas, called the Humboldt Current. The prevailing westerly winds bring cool, moist air inland. Areas directly influenced by these breezes have low average temperatures and less sunshine. In most of the Central Valley, however, the coastal hills block the fog and chilly air, so the vineyards are warm, dry, and sunny throughout the growing season. The climate is Mediterranean, and most of the rain falls during the winter. Summer temperatures rarely exceed 90°F (32°C), and humidity is low.

The north–south Central Valley is cut longitudinally by several rivers running westward from the mountains to the ocean. These rivers, besides providing ample snowmelt water for irrigation, divide the long Central Valley into a series of smaller valley basins that get progressively cooler from north to south.

GRAPE VARIETIES

Many of Chile's vines were brought from Bordeaux during the mid-1800s, including Cabernet Sauvignon, Sauvignon Blanc, and Merlot. Cabernet Sauvignon is by far the most widely planted grape variety, and many people believe that Chile is ideally suited for the production of world-class, high-quality Cabernet Sauvignon. Other grapes from France, such as Syrah and Chardonnay, are also well represented.

Carmenère also arrived in Chile from Bordeaux in the 1800s. Pre-phylloxera, Carmenère was a regular ingredient in the typical Bordeaux red blend, but very little (if any) was used in the re-planting of France that followed the crisis. However, Carmenère thrived in Chile—so much so that it was often mistaken for a particular style of spicy Merlot—and referred to at times as *Merlot Chileno*. In 1994, however, Professor Jean-Michel Boursiquot of the Montpellier School of Oenology determined that much of what was considered to be Chilean Merlot was, in actuality, Carmenère.

In the vineyard, Carmenère is often the last grape to be picked, as it requires a lengthy season to reach full maturity. Therefore, it is not well suited to Bordeaux, but in the right areas it can produce great wines. Chilean Carmenère is rich in color, redolent of red fruits, spice, and berries, and has softer tannins than Cabernet Sauvignon.

The majority of Chile's wine grape acreage is devoted to red varieties, but plantings of Sauvignon Blanc and Chardonnay are notable. Although recent research had shown that much of Chile's Sauvignon Blanc vines were actually a less aromatic grape known as Sauvignon Vert (also known as Sauvignonasse or, in Italy, Friulano), most of these vines have since been replaced with true Sauvignon Blanc. However, the two varieties are still not always clearly differentiated, both being referred to simply as Sauvignon.

LEADING GRAPE VARIETIES OF CHILE

Red Grapes	White Grapes
Cabernet Sauvignon	Chardonnay
Merlot	Sauvignon Blanc
Carmenère	Viognier
Syrah	Semillon
Cabernet Franc	
Carignan	
Cinsault	
País (Listán Prieto)	
Pinot Noir	

Figure 17-4: Leading Grape Varieties of Chile

CHILEAN WINE LAWS

Chile's wine labeling system came into effect in 1995 and is largely similar to the system in the United States. Chile has a set of geographic place-of-origin laws, the *Denominación de Origen* (DO) system, which is essentially identical to the United States' system of American Viticultural Areas in that there are no subcategories for lower-quality wines as there are in Europe. Under Chilean wine law, the minimum requirements for place of origin, vintage, and variety on a wine label are all set at 75%. However, many export-oriented wineries use the higher 85% standard in order to be eligible to export their wines to the European Union.

CHILEAN APPELLATIONS

Chile defines its place-of-origin designations (DOs) based primarily on the progression of valleys southward through the middle of the country. The largest of the DOs are referred to as viticultural regions; these are further sub-divided into subregions, zones, and areas. In addition, geographical districts based on Chile's east–west geography—Costa (Coast), Entre Cordilleras (Between the Mountains), and Andes—have recently been approved for use on Chilean wine labels. These designations, designed to reflect the overwhelming influence of the Pacific Ocean and the Andes Mountains on Chilean viticulture, may be appended to existing DOs if a minimum of 85% of the grapes are grown in the stated district.

From north to south, the six main wine regions of Chile—known as Viticultural Regions or *Regiones Vitícolas*—are Atacama, Coquimbo, Aconcagua, the Central Valley, Del Sur (Southern Regions), and the Austral Region.

Atacama

Chile's northernmost viticultural region—the Atacama—sits on the border of one of the driest spots on earth: the Atacama Desert. This area can go years without rainfall and is unlikely to ever see more than 15 mm (0.6 inches) of rain per year. Despite this, irrigation makes agriculture possible in parts of the region, and two areas in particular—the Huasco and Copiapó Valleys, both named after rivers—have a history of grape growing and olive orchards. Typically, most of the grapes are used for table grapes or distilled into pisco; however, the area is seeing increasing interest in wine grape projects involving Chardonnay, Pinot Noir, and Sauvignon Blanc.

Coquimbo

Chile's northernmost fine wine region is the Coquimbo. The Elqui Valley subregion, located in the north, skirts the southern edge of the Atacama Desert. While the Elqui Valley has historically specialized in table grapes and other fruits, new high-altitude vineyards are producing Cabernet Sauvignon, Merlot, Carmenère, Chardonnay, and Sauvignon Blanc. In addition, the Elqui Valley is increasingly seen as one of the country's best producers of Syrah.

The subregion of the Limarí Valley was planted with vines as early as the mid-sixteenth century and has recently seen a renewed interest in high-quality viticulture. Cooling Pacific Ocean fogs and the influence of the Humboldt Current combine to make this an ideal location for mineral-driven whites, with

Wine Areas of Chile

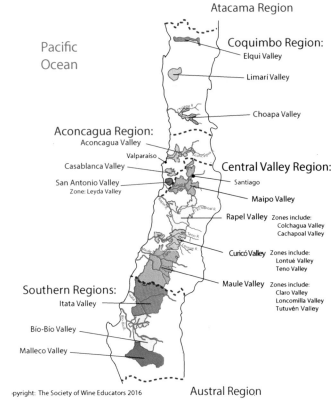

Figure 17-5: Chilean wine regions

white varieties, which make up 75% of all plantings, particularly Chardonnay and Sauvignon Blanc. The area is also gaining a reputation for its Pinot Noir.

Also close to the Pacific Ocean, the San Antonio Valley in Aconcagua's south possesses a cool climate, allowing a slow ripening of the grapes.

Pinot Noir, Chardonnay, Syrah, and Sauvignon Blanc are the leading varieties. The Leyda Valley, a zone located within the San Antonio Valley, is highly regarded for wines with minerality and complexity due to the granitic soils and very breezy climate.

The Central Valley (Valle Central)

The large Central Valley encompasses more than 80% of Chile's current winegrowing area and is the most general of the appellations. As demarcated viticulturally, it runs from the capital city of Santiago south about 230 miles (370 km). The Central Valley includes the following subregions, from north to south:

- Maipo Valley, surrounding Santiago, is the historical heart of the country and the center of Chile's winemaking culture. Not surprisingly, this area has some very old vines. The urban sprawl of the capital has pushed much of the winegrowing out of this area, but it is still an important source for well-balanced reds. Maipo's specialty is Cabernet Sauvignon, with lesser plantings of Merlot, Chardonnay, Carmenère, Sauvignon Blanc, and Syrah.
- Rapel Valley, comprising the Cachapoal and Colchagua Valleys, is overwhelmingly focused on red wine production. Cachapoal has a warm, but not hot, climate and is largely a producer of Cabernet Sauvignon, Merlot, Syrah, and Carmenère. To the south, Colchagua produces full-bodied, premium reds from Cabernet Sauvignon, Syrah, and Carmenère.
- Curicó Valley is located farther inland and thus has no maritime influence. Originally planted in the mid-1800s, the area experienced renewed interest and foreign investment during the 1970s. Curicó is more evenly planted with red and white varieties, particularly Sauvignon Blanc, Cabernet Sauvignon, and Carmenère.
- Maule Valley is located at the southern end of the Central Valley, where the valley floor broadens. This is one of Chile's largest subregions in terms

Chardonnay taking the lead. Another subregion, the Choapa Valley, is located at Chile's narrowest point, where there is virtually no distinction between the Andes and the Coastal Mountains. This small region has desert-like conditions, often receiving less than 5 inches (12.7 cm) of rain per year. The Choapa Valley is now producing small amounts of Cabernet Sauvignon and Syrah.

Aconcagua

The Aconcagua region, named after the river that runs through it, has three subregions: Aconcagua Valley, Casablanca Valley, and San Antonio Valley. The Aconcagua Valley subregion is the warmest region, with a distinctly Mediterranean climate. Coastal plantings feature white grapes, while the much hotter interior is home to Cabernet Sauvignon, Merlot, and Syrah.

Conversely, the Casablanca Valley is quite cool, as it is the most coastal wine area within Chile. Its proximity to the ocean provides it with the benefits of a maritime climate, including frequent morning fogs. Not surprisingly, Casablanca specializes in

Table 17-2: Appellations of Chile—Denominaciones de Origin

GEOGRAPHICAL INDICATIONS OF CHILE			
Viticultural Region	**Subregion**	**Zone**	**Area**
Atacama	Copiapó Valley		
	Huasco Valley		
Coquimbo	Elqui Valley		La Serena, Paiguano, Vicuña
	Limarí Valley		Ovalle, Punitaqui, Monte Patria, Río Hurtado
	Choapa Valley		Illapel, Salamanca
Aconcagua	Aconcagua Valley		Quillota, Zapallar, Hijuelas, Catemu, Panquehue, Llaillay, San Felipe, Santa María, Calle Larga, San Esteban
	Casablanca Valley		
	San Antonio Valley	(no zone)	Marga-Marga Valley
		Leyda Valley	San Juan, Santo Domingo, Cartagena, Algarrobo, Lo Abarca
Central Valley	Maipo Valley	(no zone)	Isla de Maipo, Talagante, Melipilla, Alhué, María Pinto, Colina, Calera de Tango, Til Til, Lampa, Santiago, Pirque, Puente Alto, Buin
	Rapel Valley	Cachapoal Valley	Rancagua, Peumo, Coltauco, Requínoa, Rengo, Machalí
		Colchagua Valley	Lolol, Litueche, Paredones, Pumanque, Apalta, Nancagua, Santa Cruz, Palmilla, Peralillo, Marchigüe, La Estrella, San Fernando, Chimbarongo, Los Lingues
	Curicó Valley	Teno Valley	Vichuquén, Licantén, Rauco, Romeral
		Lontué Valley	Sagrada Familia, Molina
	Maule Valley	Claro Valley	Curepto, Empedrado, Talca, Pencahue, San Rafael, San Clemente
		Loncomilla Valley	San Javier, Villa Alegre, Parral, Linares, Longaví , Retiro, Colbún
		Tutuvén Valley	Cauquenes
Southern Regions	Itata Valley		Coelemu, Portezuelo, Chillán, Quillón
	Bío-Bío Valley		Mulchén, Yumbel
	Malleco Valley		Traiguén
Austral Region	Cautin Valley		
	Osorno Valley		

Source: Wines of Chile (December 2021), *Diario Oficial de la Republica de Chile* (May 25, 2018)

of vineyard acreage and also one of its oldest. The Maule Valley enjoys a cooling ocean influence and the mild, dry climate permits many producers to practice organic viticulture. As is true in much of Chile, Cabernet Sauvignon is the leading grape variety of the Maule Valley; Malbec, Cabernet Franc, and Carmenère thrive here as well. The region is also developing a reputation for dry-farmed, old vine Carignan—as promoted by the dozen or so winery members of the *Vignadores de Carignan* (VIGNO) organization. Another specialty of the area is a rustic style of wine known as *pipeño*—often produced using the once-maligned País (Mission) grape variety—which by some accounts is the area's second most planted variety.

Del Sur (Southern Regions)

Chile's Southern Regions (Del Sur) viticultural region lies just south of the Central Valley. Here, the climate transitions from a warm and Mediterranean to cooler and rainier, reflecting the area's maritime influence. The region—long dedicated to País and Moscatel—represents just over 10% of total plantings of the country. However, as with other areas, the wine industry in the Southern Regions has begun to evolve.

The Itata Valley is the northernmost subregion of the Del Sur and borders the Maule Valley (to the north). País and Moscatel are still the most widely planted grapes in the area, however, Cabernet Sauvignon, Merlot, and Syrah are being planted next to restored vineyards of old-vine Carignan. To the south, the Bío-Bío Valley—with higher rainfall and humid, marine-inspired breezes—is being planted with Riesling, Chardonnay, and Sauvignon Blanc. The southernmost subregion, the Malleco Valley, has limited plantings (for now)—by some counts, the area has less than 50 acres/20 ha—planted mainly to Chardonnay and Pinot Noir.

Austral Region

The Austral Region—with its two subregions, the Cautín and Osorno Valleys—is at the southernmost extreme of winegrowing in Chile. The area is just beginning to be used for commercial viticulture and contains only a smattering of plantings (primarily Sauvignon Blanc, Chardonnay, and Pinot Noir). The

Austral area has far more rainfall most of Chile's other wine regions—up to 1,800 mm (70 inches) of rain a year—and is considered a marginal (if not experimental) location for viticulture. Nevertheless, several producers—some citing concerns of a future affected by climate change—are actively investing in the area.

Figure 17-6: Vineyards in Chile's Elqui Valley

BRAZIL

Brazil is the largest country in South America in terms of landmass, and currently ranks third in terms of wine production. Brazil has traditionally had hundreds of small, family-owned wineries producing light, fruit-driven wine for local consumption. However, in recent years, Brazilian wine has seen significant growth due predominantly to increasing investments in vinifera-based vineyards and modern winery facilities. As a result, more and more Brazilian wineries are producing high-quality wine for export.

Beginning in 2002, Brazil has awarded geographical indication status to certain wineproducing areas. There are currently only a few regions so designated, however, this is sure to change in the future. The classifications are as follows, starting with the highest:

• Denominação de Origem (DO)
• Indicação de Origem (IO)

Brazil has six main wine-producing regions. Four of these are located in the state of Río Grande do Sul, which is found in the southeastern portion of the country and considered to be Brazil's main wine-producing state. The major wine-producing regions of Brazil are as follows:

Serra Gaúcha: This area, located in the state of Río Grande do Sul, is considered to be the cradle of Brazilian wine production. It is responsible for over 85% of the country's wine. This area was settled, in large part, by Italian immigrants who brought the culture and industry of wine with them. While Serra Gaúcha is largely focused on red wines, its sparkling wines are increasing in quality and reputation. Leading vinifera grape varieties include Merlot, Cabernet Sauvignon, Cabernet Franc, and Tannat. Malvasia and Moscato are planted for use in Charmat method sparkling wines; grapes used for classic method sparkling wines include Chardonnay and Pinot Noir.

The Vale dos Vinhedos DO—Brazil's first (and to date, only) DO—is a subregion of Serra Gaúcha. The DO regulations require the use of vinifera grapes, with Merlot and Chardonnay specified as flagship varieties. Several regions with IO status—including Montes, Pinto Bandeira, Monte Belo do Sul, and Farroupilha—are also located within Serra Gaúcha.

Campanha: This small area, also located in the state of Río Grande do Sul, is situated on the southern border of the country, very close to Uruguay. These are some of the oldest vineyards in Brazil. The warm climate of the area combined with soils of mainly granite and limestone make this an ideal region for ripening sturdy red grapes such as Cabernet Sauvignon, Tempranillo, and Tannat.

Serra do Sudeste: Viticulture is fairly new to this area, being introduced in the 1970s but only seeing large-scale plantings since the early 2000s. Most grapes grown in this area are transported to wine producing facilities in Serra Gaúcha. Serra do Sudeste is located within the state of Río Grande do Sul.

Campos de Cima da Serra: This region, also within the state of Río Grande do Sul, is located directly to the north of Serra Gaúcha. The area, which has a relatively cool climate and long growing season, is planted mainly to Cabernet Sauvignon, Cabernet Franc, and Tannat, as well as aromatic white grapes such as Riesling, Pinot Gris, and Gewurztraminer.

Planalto Catarinense: This area is located to the north of Río Grande do Sul in the state of Santa Caterina. Planalto Catarinense currently contains just 741 acres (300 ha) dedicated to vinifera vines. At elevations of 2,900 to 4,600 feet (900 to 1,400 m) above sea level, these are the highest-elevation vineyards in the country. Leading grape varieties include Cabernet Sauvignon, Merlot, Pinot Noir, Chardonnay, and Sauvignon Blanc.

Vale do São Francisco: A sixth region, Vale do São Francisco (Valley of Saint Francis), is located in the northeastern part of Brazil in the state of Bahia. The vineyards in this region are located at 9° south latitude, with a climate classified as tropical semi-arid. This allows the vines to produce two harvests a year, making vine management quite challenging. The region produces single-variety wines and red blends, along with sparkling wines produced by both traditional and tank methods.

URUGUAY

Uruguay—located between Argentina and Brazil—is South America's fourth largest wine producer. The country falls just within the boundary edge of the temperate zone in terms of latitude, and much of the interior of the country experiences high humidity and subtropical temperatures, which makes winegrowing a challenge. While vineyards are found throughout the country, most are located in the southern part of the country (near the Río de la Plata estuary) or in the east, along the Atlantic coastline.

The Canelones District—located just north of the southern coastline and the capital city of Montevideo—is among the leaders. Over 60% of the country's commercial vineyards and a majority of the producers are located in this area. Other important areas include the up-and-coming Maldonado Region, located east of Montevideo on the Atlantic Coast and near the famous seaside resort town of Punta del Este. There are over a dozen producers in Maldonado, known for its rocky soils, cool climate, and a wine tourism route. The Colonia District, located in the southwest of the country along the Río de la Plata estuary, is considered one of the historic centers of wine production in Uruguay as well a leading region for Cabernet Sauvignon.

The majority of the wine grapes grown in Uruguay are vinifera, and the leading grape variety is Tannat—a hearty, tannic red grape first brought here from the French and Spanish Basque Country. It is estimated that Tannat accounts for nearly 25% of the total vineyard area of the country. Tannat is sometimes known here by the name *Harriague* in honor of Pascual Harriague (1819–1894), a Frenchman who helped to spread the grape throughout Uruguay.

Albariño was introduced to Uruguay in the early 2000s and is seen as having great potential, particularly in certain spots along the Atlantic Coast where the climate can be compared to that of Galicia. Other leading varieties include Cabernet Sauvignon, Cabernet Franc, Merlot, Chardonnay, Sauvignon Blanc, and Viognier. Black Muscat is widely grown and used to produce rosé, much of which is consumed domestically or exported to Brazil.

AUSTRALIA AND NEW ZEALAND

CHAPTER EIGHTEEN

LEARNING OBJECTIVES

After studying this chapter, the candidate should be able to:

- Discuss the general roles and positions of Australia and New Zealand in the global wine industry.
- Describe the basic elements of the Australian appellation system and wine labeling laws.
- Identify the physical locations and general climates of Australia's and New Zealand's major wine regions.
- Recall the significant grape varieties grown in Australia and New Zealand.

Among the nations of the Pacific collectively known as Oceania, the countries of Australia and New Zealand have developed a strong wine industry for production, consumption, and trade. These two countries have quickly gone from being the upstart newcomers on the world wine market to being well-established mainstream sources, and they now face the challenging transition from unbridled growth to market share maintenance.

AUSTRALIA

Australia has a relatively long history of winemaking; some areas have been making wine with traditional European grapes since the 1800s. Australia also has a well-deserved reputation for innovation, as evidenced by the positioning of Shiraz as a uniquely Australian style of Syrah, the use of nontraditional blends, and the widespread use of alternative labels and packaging.

Today, Australia is among the world's heavyweights in the wine industry, consistently ranking among the top ten countries for wine production. Wine is an important agricultural commodity in Australia, and a considerable amount of it is intended primarily for export markets.

Grapes are grown in all of Australia's states and territories, although commercial wine production is non-existent (or nearly so) in the Northern Territory. The majority of the country's vineyards and wineries are located in the southeastern quadrant and, to a lesser extent, along the southwestern coast.

GEOGRAPHY AND CLIMATE

Australia is a large country, roughly the size of the continental United States, situated in the South Pacific Ocean southeast of the Asian landmass. It extends well into the tropics, but the southern third of the country is within the temperate latitudes that begin at 30° south. This is where almost all of the vineyards are found, mainly in the states of South Australia, New South Wales, and Victoria, but also in Western Australia and the offshore state of Tasmania.

On average, the country is hot and dry and relatively inhospitable to grapes. Irrigation, especially in the areas surrounding the few large rivers, notably the Murray, Darling, and Murrumbidgee, provides the water necessary to turn barren stretches of the outback into lush, green vineyard land. In terms of the potentially excessive heat, location is the key to producing quality wine grapes. More moderate climatic conditions are found in the following areas:

- Along parts of the southern coast where vineyards are exposed to maritime cooling by the usual westerly winds, especially around Adelaide in South Australia, near Melbourne in Victoria, and south of Perth in Western Australia

- In Australia's primary mountain chain, the Great Dividing Range, which parallels the southeastern coast from Melbourne to Brisbane. Vineyards here benefit from cooler temperatures at higher elevations of up to 3,600 feet (1,100 m). Vineyards also line the western slopes of the mountains, where the range forces the westerly winds to drop much of their precipitation
- On the island of Tasmania—the southernmost part of Australia—which is surrounded by frigid ocean waters, making it the country's coolest winegrowing area

LEADING GRAPE VARIETIES OF AUSTRALIA

Red Grapes	White Grapes
Shiraz/Syrah	Chardonnay
Cabernet Sauvignon	Sauvignon Blanc
Merlot	Semillon
Pinot Noir	Pinot Gris
Grenache	Riesling
Mourvèdre	Muscat Gordo Blanco
Tempranillo	Colombard
	Verdelho
	Muscat Blanc à Petits Grains
	Viognier

Figure 18–1: Leading Grape Varieties of Australia

GRAPE VARIETIES

The grape variety for which Australia is best known is Shiraz. This is the same grape as the Syrah of the Rhône Valley in France, acquiring its alternative name in the eighteenth century when people mistakenly thought that the grape had originated in Shiraz, Persia. Australian Shiraz has proven very popular around the world, and it is the country's most widely planted grape, accounting for more than a quarter of vineyard acreage.

Among red grapes, the next most prominent are Cabernet Sauvignon and Merlot, both of which are frequently bottled as single-variety wines or blended with Shiraz. Although planted in much smaller quantities, Mourvèdre and Grenache are also frequently blended with Shiraz to create Rhône Valley-style wines, often referred to as GSM (Grenache-Shiraz-Mourvèdre).

Australia's white wines have also been in great demand in export markets. Chardonnay is the most prevalent white grape, accounting for more than half of all white wine production. Other leading white grape varieties include Sauvignon Blanc, Riesling, Semillon (an important product of the Hunter Valley), Viognier, and Pinot Gris.

Other varieties with significant plantings include Pinot Noir, Chenin Blanc, Gordo Blanco (Muscat of Alexandria) and Muscat Blanc à Petits Grains. In line with Australia's emphasis on innovation and diversity, a range of alternative varieties—including Vermentino, Fiano, Sangiovese, Barbera, Cabernet Franc, Touriga Nacional, and Grüner Veltliner (among others)—are being planted across the country.

AUSTRALIAN WINE LAWS

Australia's place-of-origin system is similar to that of the United States in that the appellations, officially known as *geographical indications* (GIs), are simply areas on a map. They place no restrictions on the viticultural or winemaking procedures of grape growers or winemakers within their boundaries.

As of December 2021, there are approximately 114 GIs in Australia. As in the American system, the place of origin for a wine can be the country as a whole or one or more states, such as Victoria or South Eastern Australia, even though these are political divisions and have no intrinsic viticultural meaning. Within the states are many more GIs: large ones called *zones,* most of which contain at least one smaller *region*—which may in turn contain *subregions.* It is in the smaller place-of-origin areas that some sort of homogeneity and distinctiveness, judging from a winegrowing standpoint, can be found. *Wine Australia* (previously known as the Australian Grape and Wine Authority) is the statutory agency in charge of the process.

In order to list a single GI on a wine label, at least 85% of the wine's grapes must have been grown in that appellation. If the proportion is less than 85%, then the winery has the option of either listing all of the GIs that apply or choosing a larger GI that meets the 85% prerequisite.

Vintage dates and single grape varieties on a wine label have the same minimum level requirement of 85%. If more than 15% of a blending grape is added, which is not unusual, the label can either forgo naming any grape varieties or list them all, in descending order of content. For example, a "Semillon-Chardonnay" contains 50% or more Semillon (but presumably less than 85%, or else it would simply say "Semillon") and 50% or less Chardonnay.

Aside from mandating the usual label information, Australia is the first country to require a "Best Before" date on some wines, as is typical on many other foodstuffs in all countries. The requirement applies only to wines that are not meant to have a shelf life of more than two years, and in practice it is usually only seen on bag-in-box products.

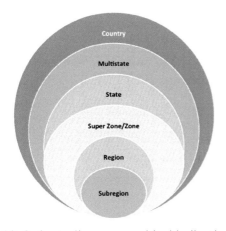

Figure 18–2: Australian geographical indications

AUSTRALIAN GEOGRAPHICAL INDICATIONS

Australia's place-name protection system was established in 1993. It has several levels that are nested one within another:

- *Multistate:* "South Eastern Australia" combines New South Wales, Victoria, Tasmania, the Australian Capital Territory, and parts of Queensland and South Australia into a single gigantic appellation.
- *State:* Leading wine-producing states include New South Wales, Victoria, South Australia, Western Australia, Tasmania, and Queensland.
- *Zone:* A zone is an area within a state, but is not necessarily delineated based on viticultural characteristics. The Adelaide zone itself contains three smaller zones and is therefore often called a *super-zone.*

- *Region:* A region is part of a zone that is defined by its viticulturally common features. A region must be a contiguous area that has "measurable homogeneity in grape growing attributes." Additional requirements ensure that regions have a respectable level of activity by multiple grape growers. Regions cannot overlap.
- *Subregion:* The requirements for a subregion are the same as those for a region, except that the viticultural homogeneity must be substantial.

AUSTRALIAN WINE STYLES

Australia is known primarily for its high-alcohol, fruit-driven, full-bodied wines. This is partly a natural result of the almost unlimited sunshine and warm-to-hot temperatures experienced in many areas of Australia, and partly a function of consumer demand for this style of wine. These wines range from simple, inexpensive, high-volume brands that have been very successful around the world to complex, handcrafted, pricier examples that are prized by aficionados of big, bold wines. Medium-alcohol wines with more natural acidity are also made in the cooler areas, but these represent only a small percentage of production. Overall, red wines are a bit more prevalent than white wines.

In addition to making table wines, Australia makes an array of sparkling wines and dessert wines. The sparkling wines, generally from the cooler regions, include not only the typical versions made from Chardonnay and Pinot Noir (either alone or blended), but also a considerable amount of sparkling red made from Shiraz. Dessert wines include botrytized Rieslings and Semillons as well as late-harvest Muscats. Port-style fortified wines are an Australian specialty, made from Muscat or various combinations of red grapes. Both dessert and fortified wines are known in Australia as "stickies."

Major Wine Areas of Australia

Figure 18-3: Australian Wine Regions

AUSTRALIAN APPELLATIONS

As noted earlier, Australia's place-of-origin designations include states, zones, and regions. Some of the renowned zones and regions in Australia include the following, listed generally from east to west:

New South Wales

- Hunter Valley: With a history dating back to the beginning of Australian viticulture, this area just north of Sydney is hot and humid, made suitable for winegrowing by the cooling effect of the afternoon sea breezes. The zone is known particularly for its Semillon, capable of long aging.
- Mudgee: Located on the west side of the Great Dividing Range with vineyards approaching 2,000 feet (610 m) in elevation, Mudgee has a reputation based on Cabernet Sauvignon and Shiraz.
- Riverina: This is physically the largest of Australia's regions, located in the fertile interior flatlands where irrigation makes it possible to produce about one-half of the country's wine. Although the main output is bulk table wine, some areas possess the humid, misty mornings and dry, warm afternoons conducive to the development of noble rot, so botrytis-affected Semillon is produced as well.

Tasmania

Located 150 miles (241 km) off the coast of Victoria, Tasmania has a very cool climate with a short growing season. The state's wine industry is still small, but it is growing based on its reputation for high-quality wines. It is especially known for Chardonnay, Pinot Noir, and sparkling wine.

Victoria

- Rutherglen: Rutherglen has a markedly continental climate that brings very hot summer days, while frosts are common in the spring and fall. It is known for fortified Muscat wines and big reds, especially from Shiraz.
- Yarra Valley and Mornington Peninsula: On the eastern outskirts of Melbourne, these two regions are cool growing areas with high humidity but little summer rain. Both are noted for Pinot Noir and Chardonnay, which are used in the production of still and sparkling wines.
- Heathcote: Lying between the Bendigo and Goulburn Valley regions, Heathcote has a distinctive climate influenced by cool winds that descend from the Mt. Camel Range and moderate the summer temperatures. It is primarily known for premium Shiraz.

Figure 18-4: Old-vine Grenache in Australia's Barossa Valley

Table 18-1: Australian Geographical Indications

AUSTRALIAN GEOGRAPHICAL INDICATIONS					
State/Zone	**Region**	**Subregion**	**State/Zone**	**Region**	**Subregion**
South Eastern Australia (Multi-state zone including New South Wales, Victoria, Tasmania, and parts of Queensland and South Australia)			**Western Australia**		
			Central Western Australia		
South Australia			Eastern Plains, inland and north of Western Australia		
Adelaide (Super-zone, includes Mount Lofty Ranges, Fleurieu, and Barossa)			Greater Perth	Peel	
				Perth Hills	
Barossa	Barossa Valley			Swan District	Swan Valley
	Eden Valley	High Eden	South West Australia	Blackwood Valley	
Far North	Southern Flinders Ranges			Geographe	
Fleurieu	Currency Creek			Great Southern	Albany
	Kangaroo Island				Denmark
	Langhorne Creek				Frankland River
	McLaren Vale				Mount Barker
	Southern Fleurieu				Porongurup
Limestone Coast	Coonawarra			Manjimup	
	Mount Benson			Margaret River	
	Mount Gambier			Pemberton	
	Padthaway		West Australian South East Coastal		
	Robe		**Queensland**		
	Wrattonbully			Granite Belt	
Lower Murray	Riverland			South Burnett	
Mount Lofty Ranges	Adelaide Hills	Lenswood	**Victoria**		
		Piccadilly Valley	Central Victoria	Bendigo	
	Adelaide Plains			Goulburn Valley	Nagambie Lakes
	Clare Valley			Heathcote	
The Peninsulas				Strathbogie Ranges	
New South Wales				Upper Goulburn	
Big Rivers	Murray Darling*		Gippsland		
	Perricoota		North East Victoria	Alpine Valleys	
	Riverina			Beechworth	
	Swan Hill*			Glenrowan	
Central Ranges	Cowra			King Valley	
	Mudgee			Rutherglen	
	Orange		North West Victoria	Murray Darling*	
Hunter Valley	Hunter	Broke Fordwich		Swan Hill*	
		Pokolbin	Port Phillip	Geelong	
		Upper Hunter Valley		Macedon Ranges	
Northern Rivers	Hastings River			Mornington Peninsula	
Northern Slopes	New England Australia			Sunbury	
South Coast	Shoalhaven Coast			Yarra Valley	
	Southern Highlands		Western Victoria	Grampians	Great Western
Southern New South Wales	Canberra District			Henty	
	Gundagai			Pyrenees	
	Hilltops		**Tasmania**		
	Tumbarumba		**Northern Territory**		
Western Plains			**Australian Capital Territory**		

* Partially in Big Rivers and partially in North West Victoria.
Source: Wine Australia

South Australia

- Coonawarra: This is the best known of the six regions of the Limestone Coast zone, due to its bright red soil called *terra rossa*, which rests over a free-draining limestone base. This region, thanks to its soil composition, is famous for its Cabernet Sauvignons.
- Barossa Valley and McLaren Vale: These are two of the regions surrounding Adelaide. The climate of this entire area is Mediterranean, generally warm and dry, becoming relatively cool in higher-elevation vineyards. Cool breezes regularly blow in from the ocean. McLaren Vale and the Barossa Valley are known for Shiraz.
- Clare Valley and Eden Valley: These two regions, both well-known for Riesling, surround Adelaide and feature similar climates, but they are cooler than most of the surrounding areas. The Clare Valley's cold nights and Eden Valley's high altitudes help to retain the much-needed acidity in the grapes of both areas.
- Riverland: This is a commercially important region with the second largest volume of wine production, just slightly behind Riverina.

Western Australia

- Margaret River: Located at Australia's southwestern extremity, Margaret River experiences constant sea breezes from the Indian and Southern Oceans that keep the area very cool in what would otherwise be an extremely warm Mediterranean climate. While both red and white grape varieties are planted here, Margaret River is especially prized for its white wines, including elegant Chardonnays and intense Sauvignon Blanc–Semillon blends.

NEW ZEALAND

Known as *Aotearoa*, "Land of the Long White Cloud," New Zealand was initially discovered by the Maori, who arrived from their native East Polynesia, in 1300. The Maori people account for 15% of the current population. The Dutchman Abel Tasman was the first European to see the country in 1642, but it wasn't until 1769 that explorer James Cook claimed New Zealand for Great Britain. The Treaty of Waitangi, signed in 1840, formally established a peaceful relationship between the Maori and the British. In 1947, New Zealand became an independent country.

The country's oldest winery—Mission Estate Winery, located in the Hawke's Bay region—was established in 1851 and still exists today. However, during the 1920s, phylloxera wiped out many of New Zealand's vines and it wasn't until the 1970s that the country began to once again establish a viable wine industry. With New Zealand's relatively recent entrance into the global wine industry and its limited landmass, its wine production is fairly small, but the country has quickly made a name for itself as a producer of high-quality wine.

Figure 18–5: New Zealand's Marlborough region

GEOGRAPHY AND CLIMATE

New Zealand is situated in the Pacific Ocean approximately 1,200 miles (1,930 km) east of Australia and a long way from any other large landmass. It is comprised of two main islands, the North Island and the South Island, and lies completely within the temperate winegrowing latitudes, spanning 36° to 45° south. However, its climate is cooler than might be expected for a place with its distance from the equator, since it is surrounded by cold ocean waters and few parts of the country are more than about 50 miles from the sea.

The primary topographic feature of New Zealand is the Southern Alps, a high mountain chain that runs the length of the South Island along the western coast. Given that the winds normally rise from the west, these mountains keep the eastern part of the island drier and sunnier than it would be otherwise. The North Island does not have the same mountain chain, but some shorter mountain systems and a few high volcanic mountains perform a similar function in places. As such, most of New Zealand's vineyards are found in the eastern part of the country—in the rain shadow of the Southern Alps or the North Island volcanoes—or in the warmer, northern part of the North Island.

LEADING GRAPE VARIETIES OF NEW ZEALAND

Red Grapes	White Grapes
Pinot Noir	Sauvignon Blanc
Merlot	Chardonnay
Syrah	Pinot Gris
Cabernet Sauvignon	Riesling
	Gewürztraminer
	Sauvignon Gris
	Viognier

Figure 18–6: Leading Grape Varieties of New Zealand

GRAPE VARIETIES

New Zealand's cool climate is tailor-made for white grape varieties, with over 80% of production focused on white wine. Sauvignon Blanc is the undisputed leader, accounting for close to 65% of all vines planted throughout the country. Sauvignon Blanc has an affinity for the terroir of New Zealand, producing wines that are considered to be both excellent in quality and quite unlike Sauvignon Blancs grown anywhere else. New Zealand Sauvignon Blanc typically shows a combination of tropical fruit flavors, stone fruit flavors (peach, nectarine, apricot), and grassiness that is both unique and very popular among consumers. Chardonnay and Pinot Gris are the other leading white grapes, while Riesling and Gewürztraminer are grown in smaller amounts.

Pinot Noir—currently planted to just over 14% of the country's total vineyard acreage—is concentrated in Marlborough, Central Otago, Canterbury, Wairarapa (Martinborough), and Nelson. Merlot is the second most widely plated red grape. Other red varieties such as Cabernet Sauvignon, Malbec, Cabernet Franc, and Syrah are planted in very small amounts, and are mostly found in the warmer areas such as Hawke's Bay, Gisborne, and Auckland.

NEW ZEALAND WINE LAWS

The Geographical Indications (Wine and Spirits) Registration Act of 2006 created a registration system for wine and spirit geographical indications in New Zealand; however, the act was never brought into force. In November of 2016, a revised bill— the Geographical Indications (Wine and Spirits) Registration Amendment Act—was passed and entered into force in July of 2017.

Soon thereafter, applications defining the specific boundaries of New Zealand's geographical indications began to be filed with the New Zealand Intellectual Property Office. Three geographical indications—New Zealand, South Island, and North Island—were immediately approved as "enduring geographical indications." Other applications for wine and spirit geographical indications (regions) and "local geographical indications" (subregions) have been submitted, and many of these have been accepted. (See table 18-2 for details, current as of December 2021.) New Zealand's geographical indications (excluding enduring indications) will need to be renewed after the first five years, and every ten years thereafter.

New Zealand wines are required to contain a minimum of 85% of a stated grape variety, vintage year, or region of origin—if such information is included on the label.

NEW ZEALAND APPELLATIONS

Marlborough

The Marlborough region on the South Island is home to over 68,700 acres (27,800 ha) of vineyards—accounting for roughly two-thirds of New Zealand's vines and grape production. The region is heavily planted to Sauvignon Blanc and has in many ways shaped the explosive growth in the New Zealand wine industry. Pinot Noir is the second most widely planted grape, and despite growth in other regions, Marlborough is still the largest grower of Pinot Noir in the country. Chardonnay, Pinot Gris, Riesling, Gewürztraminer, and Viognier are grown here as well. Production of high-quality traditional method sparkling wines—sometimes marketed under the Méthode Marlborough brand—is small, but critically renowned.

Cloudy Bay—which lent its name to the now-famous, ground-breaking producer of Sauvignon Blanc—and Clifford Bay are both situated along the coast of Marlborough. The Marlborough region can be considered to have three separate areas (considered unofficial subregions for the time being)—from the Wairau Valley in the north, to the Awatere Valley further south, and the Southern Valleys on the inland side.

- Wairau Valley: The Wairau Valley (known by the Maori as *Kei puta te Wairau*—the place with the hole in the cloud) is one of New Zealand's sunniest places. The region is known for stony, alluvial soils and a cool climate that tends to become drier as one heads inland.
- Awatere Valley: The Awatere Valley is located to the south of the Wairau Valley, stretching inland from the coast into the Kaikoura Ranges. This is one of the coolest, driest, and windiest areas of Marlborough—and many of the vineyards have some elevation.

- The Southern Valleys: Located inland, the vineyards of the Southern Valleys—consisting of the Omaka, Fairhall, Brancott, Ben Morvan and Waihopai Valleys—wind and wrap around the surrounding hills. The area has great diversity in terms of mesoclimates and soils, but it does tend to heavier, more clay-based soils than the areas closer to the coast.

Hawke's Bay

Hawke's Bay is the second largest of New Zealand's wine regions, in terms of both acreage and production. It is, however, in a distant second place (as compared to Marlborough) with just over 12,440 acres (5,034 ha) planted to vines. Located on the North Island—in one of the wider portions of the landmass—this is one of New Zealand's warmest regions as well as the country's leading producer of red wine other than Pinot Noir. Red grapes—primarily Pinot Noir, Cabernet Sauvignon, Merlot, and Syrah—account for just over one-third of the region's total planting. Hawke's Bay is also an important area for Sauvignon Blanc, Chardonnay, and Pinot Gris.

A key feature of the region is the Gimblett Gravels area. Gimblett Gravels, located 12 miles (19 km) inland, is a relatively warm area with unique soil made up of a mix of greywacke (a sedimentary sandstone) and a variety of mineral and rocky fragments (the gravels). Gimblett Gravels is primarily planted to red Bordeaux varieties and Syrah.

Gisborne

Located just to the north of Hawke's Bay—on the east coast of the North Island—Gisborne is heavily planted to white grapes. Nearly 50% of the region's vineyards are planted to Chardonnay—leading to the area's self-proclaimed nickname as the "Chardonnay capital of New Zealand." Other leading white grapes include Pinot Gris, Sauvignon Blanc, and Gewürztraminer. Sparkling wine is a specialty here, in addition to the more typical styles of dry varietal wines. Merlot accounts for much of the small amount of land planted to red grapes.

Gisborne benefits from its position at the widest part of the country, where the prevailing westerly winds are warmed as they cross the island. The region's vineyards stretch inland from Poverty Bay

Table 18-2: New Zealand Geographical Indications

NEW ZEALAND GEOGRAPHICAL INDICATIONS		
Enduring G.I.	Geographical Indications	Local Geographical Indications (sub-zones)
NORTH ISLAND	Auckland	Kumeu
		Matakana
		Waiheke Island
	Hawke's Bay	Central Hawke's Bay
		Gimblett Gravels**
	Gisborne	Manutuke**
		Ormond**
		Patutahi**
	Northland	
	Waikato/Bay of Plenty**	
	Wairarapa	Gladstone
		Martinborough
		Masterton
SOUTH ISLAND	Canterbury	Canterbury Plains**
		North Canterbury
		Waipara/Waipara Valley
		Waitaki Valley/Canterbury**
	Central Otago	Alexandra**
		Bannockburn*
		Bendigo**
		Cromwell/Lowburn/Pisa**
		Gibbston**
		Wanaka**
	Marlborough	Awatere Valley**
		Southern Valleys**
		Wairau Valley**
	Nelson	Moutere Hills**
		Waimea Plains**
	Waitaki Valley/North Otago	

*Indicates that as of December 2021, an application for official geographical indication status is on file with the New Zealand Intellectual Property Office.

**Indicates that an application has not yet been filed for official standing as a geographical indication; these areas continue to be considered "unofficial"

Source: New Zealand Wine (www.nzwine.com) and the New Zealand Intellectual Property Office, 2021

Note: No asterisk indicates that the geographical indication has been registered and is in force as of December 2021.

Major Wine Regions of New Zealand

Figure 18-7: New Zealand wine regions

on the eastern coast, with many vines planted on the rolling hillsides and along the interior valleys. As the easternmost wine region in a country located just west of the International Date Line, this is the first wine region in the world to greet each new day. Gisborne currently has three (currently unofficial) subregions—Manutuke, Ormond, and Patutahi.

Wairarapa

Wairarapa is small-producing wine region located on the southern end of New Zealand's North Island near the city of Wellington—and within the political region (province) also known as Wellington.

Slightly more than 50% of the vines are planted to Pinot Noir, and another large portion is planted to Sauvignon Blanc—Pinot Gris, Syrah, and Riesling make up most of the rest. The majority of the vineyards are planted about 18 miles (30 km) from the sea and as such, the area has a mostly maritime climate. However, some protection is provided by the Rimutaka and Tararua Mountain Ranges. Wairarapa has three sub-regions—Masterton, Martinborough and Gladstone.

Waitaki Valley/North Otago

The Waitaki Valley viticultural area follows the course of the Waitaki River for 46 miles (75 km) along its path between the foothills of the Southern Alps and the east coast of New Zealand's South Island. The wide bed of the Waitaki River is considered a traditional boundary between the states of Otago and Canterbury. Vines are planted on both sides of the river as well as up into the sloping hills surrounding the riverbed. The area on the north side of the river is located within the state of Canterbury and considered an unofficial sub-region of the Canterbury GI.

The portion located within the state of Otago (mainly to the south of the river) is a separate geographical indication known as Waitaki Valley/North Otago. The area has unique limestone-based soils—a reminder of its ancient past, when it was covered by the sea—as well as loess and alluvial deposits. Waitaki Valley/North Otago is a remote, cool-climate area planted mainly to Pinot Noir, Riesling, Pinot Gris, and Chardonnay.

Central Otago

Central Otago, situated near the southern end of New Zealand's South Island with vineyards located as far south as 45°S, is one of the southernmost wine producing regions in the world. This is an inland, mountainous region tucked into the eastern side of the Southern Alps, and the highest-elevation wine region in New Zealand. As such, the climate here, classified as moderate continental, is more extreme than other regions of New Zealand with hot, dry summers and cold winters. Many of the vineyards are planted on the area's steeply-angled mountain slopes; in the flatter areas, frost protection efforts are sometimes needed.

Central Otago is heavily focused on Pinot Noir and has established a positive reputation for its wines. Central Otago Pinot Noir typically has excellent structure, moderate to full tannins, and aromas associated with red fruits, raspberries, and herbs. Chardonnay, Pinot Gris, Sauvignon Blanc, and Riesling are produced here as well.

Central Otago currently has six (unofficial) subregions:

- Wanaka: Wanaka is the northernmost subregion, located about (80 km) north of Queenstown, tucked between the Crown Range and the Southern Alps. Lake Wanaka (the fourth largest lake in the country) helps to moderate the climate.
- Gibbston: Gibbston, located to the east of Queenstown in the Kawarau Gorge area, has the highest-elevation vineyards in Central Otago. This area has a cooler climate than some surrounding areas, assuaged in some spots by north-facing vineyards.
- Bannockburn: Bannockburn, located along the south bank of the Kawarau River, is one of the warmest and driest spots in Central Otago. The harvest here can be up to a month ahead of the rest of Central Otago.
- Alexandra: Alexandra is the most southerly subregion. The climate here is dry and the weather can tend to extremes.
- Bendigo: Bendigo, one of the warmest of the subregions, has a wealth of stony soils and vineyards planted on north-facing slopes.
- Cromwell/Lowburn/Pisa: This area covers the ground between Gibbston and Bannockburn with most vines planted on the lower terraces of the mountains as well as the valley floor.

Canterbury

The Canterbury region, extending along the South Island's eastern coastline, lies between the Southern Alps and the Pacific Ocean. This is a large region—the official geographical indication for wine production covers the entirety of the political region (province) of the same name—covering a total of more than 17,000 square miles (44,000 square km). However, only about 3,500 acres (1,419 ha) are planted to vineyards. This sunny, mild-climate region can have dry, warm summers—often punctuated by the area's dry *nor'wester* winds in addition to the cooling sea breezes. Pinot Noir and Sauvignon Blanc are the leading grape varieties of Canterbury, followed by Chardonnay, Riesling, and Pinot Gris.

The great majority of the area's vineyards are planted in the large (official) sub-region of North Canterbury. This area comprises the northern half of the region, bounded by the Rakia River to the south. The Waipara Valley—an official subregion situated within the boundaries of North Canterbury, located about 30 miles (48 km) north of the city of Christchurch—is of particular renown. It is centered on gravel and clay soils in the rolling hills surrounding the inland valley of the Waipara River.

Nelson

Nelson, located west of and adjacent to Marlborough on the South Island, is noted for Sauvignon Blanc, but Chardonnay, Pinot Noir, and Riesling are grown here as well. The town of Nelson, sitting on the edge of Tasman Bay, was established in 1841 as the South Island's first city.

This geographically small region is the only one that is situated west of the Southern Alps on New Zealand's South Island, yet it is surrounded on all sides by smaller mountain ranges. The protection of these mountains gives Nelson one of the sunniest climates in New Zealand (along with Marlborough), earning the area the nickname "Sunny Nelson."

Figure 18–8: Cabernet Sauvignon harvest in New Zealand's Hawke's Bay region

AFRICA

LEARNING OBJECTIVES

After studying this chapter, the candidate should be able to:

- Discuss the physical location and general climate of South Africa's major wine regions.
- Describe the significant grape varieties grown in South Africa.
- Recall South African synonyms for international grape varieties.
- Describe the basic elements of the South African appellation system and wine labeling laws.

In wine terms, "Africa" essentially means the nation of South Africa. Tropical climates, desert heat, and aridity combine to make the production of wine difficult to nearly impossible in most other countries on the continent. In northern Africa, a few locations, primarily those with a history of French occupation, produce some wine as well. For many reasons, consumption is low throughout Africa, although there are a few surprises, such as the fact that Angola (a former Portuguese colony) is Portugal's number-one destination for wine exports.

SOUTH AFRICA

South Africa has a long history of wine production that dates back to the seventeenth century, when travel and transport of goods between Europe and the colonies and trade markets of the East meant sailing around the entire continent of Africa. The harbor at Cape Town at the southern extremity of Africa was a mandatory stop for ships to replenish their supplies, and wine was one of the items that the cape could provide to passing ships. Vines from Europe were first planted in 1655, with the first wine made in 1659.

By 1709, there were 70,000 vineyard acres (28,300 ha) in Cape Town.

Concurrent with these developments, Simon van der Stel, the governor of Cape Town, planted 100,000 vines just outside the colony in an area known as Constantia. Thirty years later, South Africa's wine industry was further influenced when 150 French refugees, known as the Huguenots, settled in the Drakenstein Valley to escape religious persecution. The area became known as Franschhoek, which translates as "French Corner." By the mid-1700s, South African wines, including the renowned dessert wines of Constantia, were being exported to Europe, receiving great acclaim and developing an international reputation.

In the late 1800s, the opening of the Suez Canal, along with the arrival of phylloxera and oidium, dealt a severe blow to South Africa's wine industry. In 1918, after losing much of its export market, the wine industry was sustained by the creation of the Koöperatieve Wijnbouwers Vereniging van Zuid-Afrika Bpkt (KWV). This cooperative produced wine, made brandy, and stabilized grape prices. While the co-op saved the industry, it also established a quota system that, for a time, emphasized quantity over quality.

With political reform and the end of apartheid in the early 1990s, decades-long boycotts prohibiting much international trade with South Africa were lifted, and South Africa rejoined the international community. The country's wine industry soon found that, while it had a solid foundation in winemaking, it was technologically behind the times. In an effort to modernize, the KWV quotas were scrapped and South Africa embarked on an ambitious program of replanting vineyards, upgrading its winery technology, and focusing on improving the quality of its wines so as to reenter the export market.

Wine Areas of South Africa

Western Cape G.U.

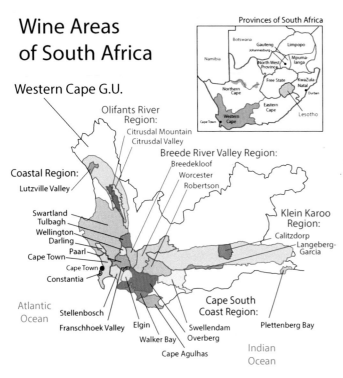

Figure 19–1: Wine areas of South Africa

GEOGRAPHY AND CLIMATE

South Africa is the only country in Africa that extends much beyond the 30° line marking the beginning of the winegrowing latitudes. The interior of the country has a semi-arid continental climate, and the eastern coast is subtropical and humid. However, the southwest around Cape Town enjoys a Mediterranean climate and is well suited to grape growing.

In general, the prime winegrowing areas are those influenced by the chilly waters of the South Atlantic and Southern Oceans. The Benguela Current, a cold ocean current that flows up the western coast from Antarctica, helps to generate moist fogs and cooling breezes as well the *Cape Doctor*. The Cape Doctor is a strong, often persistent southeasterly wind that helps to dry out the vineyards and minimize the risk of fungal diseases — but can also be ferocious enough to damage the vines. Geologically, South Africa is home to some of the oldest soils on earth, traceable to the first supercontinent one billion years ago. The range of soils includes sandstone, granite and shale, and clay.

GRAPE VARIETIES

The vineyards of South Africa are fairly evenly divided between white and red varieties; however, the leading grape remains Chenin Blanc. Chenin Blanc, sometimes referred to by the local name *Steen*, has long been the most widely planted variety and presently accounts for 18% of all grape production. South African Chenin Blanc is made into many styles of wine, including both oaked and unoaked table wines and sweet wines, as well as a range of sparkling wines. Chenin Blanc and Muscat Blanc à Petits Grains (sometimes archaically referred to as *Muscat de Frontignan*) are also used to produce late-harvest and botrytis-affected (*Noble Late Harvest*) dessert wines.

Chardonnay and Sauvignon Blanc are also widely planted and used in a range of wine styles. Muscat of Alexandria (traditionally referred to as Hanepoot) is often used in rich, flowery dessert wines, but produces complex dry wines as well. Other notable white grapes include Semillon, Viognier, Crouchen Blanc (formerly known as Cape Riesling), and Colombard (widely planted but often used in the production of brandy).

Cabernet Sauvignon is the leading red grape variety, followed closely by Shiraz (Syrah). Another popular red variety is Pinotage, an indigenous crossing of Pinot Noir and Cinsault that was developed almost a century ago at Stellenbosch University. In addition to showing up as a varietal wine, Pinotage is also used in a uniquely South African wine known as a Cape Blend. A Cape Blend is (unofficially) defined as containing between 30% and 70% Pinotage; the remainder being traditional Bordeaux red varieties. Other widely grown red grapes include Merlot, Cabernet Franc, Pinot Noir, Cinsault, and Ruby Cabernet.

SOUTH AFRICAN WINE LAWS

The appellation system in South Africa, known as the Wine of Origin (WO) Scheme, was introduced in 1973. The emphasis is on place-of-origin, with regulations defining differing sizes of geographical areas without any specific restrictions on the grape varieties used or types of wine produced. The various categories of areas, from largest to smallest, are the following:

LEADING GRAPE VARIETIES OF SOUTH AFRICA

Red Grapes	White Grapes
Cabernet Sauvignon	Chenin Blanc
Shiraz	Colombard
Pinotage	Sauvignon Blanc
Merlot	Chardonnay
Ruby Cabernet	Hanepoot (Muscat of Alexandria)
Cinsault	Semillon
Pinot Noir	Muscat Blanc à Petits Grains
Cabernet Franc	Viognier

Figure 19-2: Leading Grape Varieties of South African

- Geographical units
- Regions—larger encompassing areas
- Districts
- Wards—defined by soil, climate, and geological factors

The Wine of Origin Scheme is administered by the South African Wine and Spirit Board, which certifies all wines that list a specific place of origin, grape variety, or vintage date on the label. Wines that comply with the WO regulations receive a white paper seal affixed across the wine capsule. Certification requires that 100% of the wine come from the geographic area, estate, or vineyard listed on the label, or multiple areas adding up to 100%. If the vintage or grape variety is stated, 85% of the wine must be made from that year or variety. In addition, the wine must be sampled and approved by the board.

SOUTH AFRICAN APPELLATIONS

South Africa's primary geographical unit, the Western Cape, surrounds Cape Town and is home to most of the country's regions, districts, wards, and vineyards. Only about 5% of the vineyards land lies outside the Western Calpe, most of which is located well inland in the valley of the Orange River in the Northern Cape geographical unit.

The Coastal Region

Within the Western Cape, the Coastal Region is located along the western coast of the Cape and extends inland, encircling the original colony (and now city) of Cape Town. The Coastal Region is divided into nine districts: Stellenbosch, Cape Town, Paarl, Tulbagh, Darling, Franschhoek Valley, Wellington, Swartland, and Lutzville Valley (previously considered part of the Olifants River Region). Outstanding features of some of these districts are discussed below:

- The Stellenbosch District, located just east (and slightly south) of the city of Cape Town, is one of the oldest and most respected winegrowing areas of South Africa. Cabernet Sauvignon is the leading red wine of the area, which is also known for Chardonnay, Chenin Blanc, and Sauvignon Blanc.
- The Paarl District lies north of Stellenbosch and is a bit warmer, although it is still reasonably close to the ocean. This larger area is home to some of the more familiar South African brands and produces a full range of wines.
- The Franschhoek Valley District still shows its early French influence. The leading grapes include Chardonnay, Semillon, Syrah, and the red Bordeaux varieties.
- The Constantia Ward is located on the peninsula south of Cape Town, with a cool maritime climate and decomposed granite soils. The first vines in South Africa were planted here in the 1600s. Vin de Constance—the luscious, Muscat-based sweet white wine of the area—became quite famous in Europe during the 18th century and was for a while a leading export. However, the wine faded out of existence after phylloxera devastated the vineyards. Today, several wineries—including Groot Constantia and Klein Constantia—are once again producing the famous dessert wine. The region is also being revived as a wine growing site for dry white and red table wines.

Figure 19-3: Groot Constantia Winery

- The Swartland District is a very rugged area despite being only an hour's drive north of the city of Cape Town. Its Mediterranean climate provides intensive, dry summer heat and cooler nights. Soils vary, but they permit the vines to develop deep roots, enabling dry farming as well as the use of untrellised bush vines. A renaissance is taking place here, as growers and winemakers are reestablishing vineyards and gaining critical recognition for this new district, which is predominantly planted to Rhône varieties and Chenin Blanc.

The Cape South Coast Region

The Cape South Coast Region stretches some 250 miles (402 km) along the southwestern and southern coast of South Africa. This region contains 6 districts—Cape Agulhas, Elgin, Overberg, Plettenberg Bay, Swellendam, and Walker Bay— as well as a few stand-alone wards. The leading producers of the Cape South Coast Region include the following:

- The Elgin District is an up-and-coming area in the hills southeast of Stellenbosch, where the altitude provides cooler temperatures, which results in the slow ripening of grapes.
- The Walker Bay District is located in the southernmost part of the country, close to the shore and subject to winds off the Southern Ocean. Proximity to the sea near Hermanus and Cape Agulhas makes this one of the most maritime-influenced of all South African areas, and therefore one of the coolest winegrowing regions of the country. This zone is ideal for Pinot Noir and Chardonnay.

The Breede River Valley Region

About 100 miles (160 km) east of Cape Town, the Breede River provides irrigation to the warm interior wine regions of the Breede River Valley. The region was initially best known for its fortified wines and dessert wines and has recently distinguished itself with its Chardonnay and Sauvignon Blanc wines. The district of Robertson, known as the Valley of Vines and Roses, has undergone a dramatic wine evolution in the last few decades. A red wine project, started in the early 1990s, has brought the region's Shiraz and Cabernet Sauvignon to the attention of wine consumers both locally and internationally. Nearby, the vineyards of Worcester grow approximately 25% of the nation's wine and a good portion of the table grapes. They also produce a high-quality brandy.

Figure 19-4: South African vineyards with Table Mountain in the background

NORTHERN AFRICA

In the Northern Hemisphere, the entire North African coast on the Mediterranean Sea is above the 30th parallel, making wine production theoretically possible. However, there are additional challenges to winegrowing here, including the lack of water in these northern fringes of the Sahara Desert and the absence of significant maritime cooling, as the Mediterranean Sea does not get as cold as most ocean waters.

Despite these major hurdles, wine is produced in northern Africa. The most active wine industries are found in Morocco, Algeria, and Tunisia—areas that were under French control during the nineteenth or early twentieth century.

Algeria, a French overseas département until its independence in 1962, was once a major source of blending wine and basic table wine for France, producing well over 200 million cases of wine a year.

Today, that industry has declined, although Algeria remains the second largest wine producer in Africa. Most of the vineyard land is located in the foothills of the Atlas Mountains, and the vines are planted in sandy soils.

With the Sahara and the forbidding Atlas Mountains inland, grape growing in Algeria and the rest of northern Africa is largely confined to the Mediterranean coast and northern mountain slopes, where the coolest climatic conditions are found.

Algeria, Morocco, and Tunisia all have appellation systems (appellation d'origine garantie/AOG, or appellation d'origine contrôlée/AOC) modeled after the French system, with several designated regions. Carignan, Grenache, Cinsaut, and Muscat are among the top grape varieties grown.

Table 19-1: South African Appellations

SOUTH AFRICA: GEOGRAPHICAL INDICATIONS		
Western Cape Geographical Unit		
Region	**District**	**Wards**
Cape South Coast	Cape Agulhas	Elim
	Elgin	
	Lower Duivenhoks River	
	Overberg	Elandskloof/Kaaimansgat, Greyton, Klein River, Theewater
	Plettenberg Bay	
	Swellendam	Buffeljags, Malgas, Stormsvlei
	Walker Bay	Bot River, Hemel-en-Aarde Ridge, Hemel-en-Aarde Valley, Sunday's Glen, Springfontein Rim, Stanford Foothills, Upper Hemel-en-Aarde-Valley
	(no district)	Herbertsdale, Napier, Still Bay East
Coastal Region	Cape Town	Constantia, Durbanville, Hout Bay, Philadelphia
	Darling	Groenekloof
	Franshhoek (Valley)	
	Lutzville Valley	Koekenaap
	Paarl	Agter-Paarl, Simonsberg-Paarl, Voor-Paardeberg
	Stellenbosch	Banghoek, Bottelary, Devon Valley, Jonkershoek Valley, Papegaaiberg, Polkadraai Hills, Simonsberg-Stellenbosch, Vlottenburg
	Swartland	Malmesbury, Paardeberg/Perdeberg, Paardeberg South, Riebeekberg, Riebeeksrivier, St. Helena Bay
	Tulbagh	
	Wellington	Blouvlei, Bovlei, Groenberg, Limietberg, Mid-Berg River
	(no district)	Bamboes Bay, Lamberts Bay

Table 19–1: South African Appellations, *continued*

SOUTH AFRICA: GEOGRAPHICAL INDICATIONS		
Western Cape Geographical Unit		
Region	**District**	**Wards**
Breede River Valley	Breedekloof	Goudini, Slanghoek
	Robertson	Agterkliphoogte, Ashton, Boesmansrivier, Bonnievale, Eilandia, Goedemoed, Goree, Goudmyn, Hoopsrivier, Klaasvoogds, Le Chasseur, McGregor, Vinkrivier, Zandrivier
	Worcester	Hex River Valley, Nuy, Scherpenheuvel, Stettyn
Klein Karoo	Calitzdorp	
	Langeberg-Garcia	
	(no district)	Cango Valley, Koo Plateau, Montagu, Outeniqua, Tradouw, Tradouw Highlands, Upper Langkloof
Olifants River	Citrusdal Mountain	Piekenierskloof
	Citrusdal Valley	
	(no district)	Spruitdrift, Vredendal
(No region)	Ceres Plateau	Ceres
	(no district)	Cederberg, Leipoldtville-Sandveld, Nieuwoudtville, Prince Albert Valley, Swatberg
Northern Cape Geographical Unit		
(No region)	Douglas	
	Sutherland-Karoo	
	Central Orange River	Groblershoop, Grootdrink, Kakamas, Kelmoes, Upington
	(no district)	Hartswater, Prieska
Eastern Cape Geographical Unit		
(No region)	(no district)	St. Francis Bay
Kwazulu-Natal Geographical Unit		
(No region)	Central Drakensberg	
	Lions River	
Limpopo Geographical Unit		
Free State Geographical Unit		
(No region)	(No district)	Rietrivier FS

Source: Wines of South Africa (WOSA), December 2021

ASIA

LEARNING OBJECTIVES

After studying this chapter, the candidate should be able to:

- Describe the recent growth of the culture and business of wine in China.
- Discuss the physical location and general attributes of the wine-producing regions of China.
- Recall the main grape varieties used in Chinese wine.
- Describe the grape-based wine industry in Japan.

Wine—particularly grape-based wine—has generally not been given the cultural importance in Asia that it enjoys in much of the rest of the world. In addition, portions of the Asian continent are given over to geological and climatic obstacles—in terms of extreme mountains, deserts, and monsoons—not seen in much of the rest of the world. Despite these natural limitations, parts of Asia have their own long history with viticulture and winemaking. In addition, many parts of this vast continent are developing (or renewing) an interest in the culture and business of wine.

China in particular is an emerging wine powerhouse, and Japan—despite its small size—has a developing wine industry. Other areas of Asia, even those that push the boundaries of latitude and climate such as Vietnam, India, Indonesia, and Thailand, are producing wine in increasing, if minute, amounts. These wines are evolving in quality as well.

CHINA

While China has a long history of wine production reaching back several thousand years, it is only recently that the consumption of fine wine has become widespread among portions of the population. Beginning with the economic reforms of the 1980s and a more recent influx of investors from international wine- and spirit-producing powerhouses, domestic wine production increased steadily until 2016; since then, growth has leveled off or even slowed in some parts of the industry.

However, the numbers remain impressive, and with approximately 1,940,000 acres (785,000 ha) under vine, China is now considered one of the world leaders in grape and wine production. The country has over 500 wineries along with an estimated 52 million wine drinkers (Wine Intelligence). Domestically-produced wine—including a large majority made by Changyu Pioneer Wine Company and the China Great Wall Wine Company, the country's largest producers—accounts for nearly half of the wine consumed in the country. Dry red wines are the dominant style produced in China, comprising four-fifths of the total volume.

HISTORY

China, specifically the settlement of Jiahu, located in the central portion of the country south of the Yellow River Valley, is the site of what may be the world's first fermented beverage produced using grapes. In the 1980s, clay jars described as having "high necks, flaring rims and handles" were discovered in the area and dated from the early Neolithic period, estimated to be 7000–6600 BCE. Noted beverage historians Dr. Patrick McGovern and Professor Fang Hui and their team describe this ancient beverage as a

"Neolithic grog." The team was able to confirm via chemical analysis of the porous clay that the jars once contained a fermented beverage made using rice, honey, hawthorn fruit, and wild grapes.

Other important archeological finds in the area of Jiahu include the discovery, in 2011, of a tightly sealed bronze vessel containing liquid at a burial ground. The vessel was dated to more than 3,000 years ago, belonging to the era of the Shang and Western Zhou Dynasties. Chemical analysis of the contents revealed the liquid to be a fermented, alcoholic beverage produced using hawthorn fruit, wild grapes, rice, and beeswax. These discoveries have confirmed that grape-related winemaking has been present in Chinese culture for thousands of years.

The modern era of wine production in China is said to have begun around 1892, when Zhang Bishi, a Qing Dynasty diplomat, imported more than 100 European grape varieties for use in modern China's first winemaking facility, the Changyu Winemaking Company, located in the Shandong province. The company exists to this day and—now known as Changyu Pioneer Wine Company, Inc.—is one of the largest wine-producing companies in the world, yet remains essentially unknown outside of China.

Upon the founding of the People's Republic of China in 1949, the communist government became heavily involved in the country's wine industry. Under its command, the wine industry was expanded greatly, and it became common practice to blend grape-based wine with ferments produced from other fruits as well as grains. In 2004, new regulations mandated that wine be made strictly from grapes or grape juice.

Main Winegrowing Regions of China

Figure 20-1: Map of the major winegrowing regions of China

China's wine industry has experienced some exponential growth spurts in the last few decades, beginning with the economic reforms of the 1980s and a more recent influx of investors from international wine- and spirit-producing powerhouses. Examples of international companies with interests in the Chinese wine industry include Pernod Ricard, Torres, LVMH, Rémy Cointreau, and Domaines Barons de Rothschild.

Advances in quality have accelerated since the mid-2000s, and new wines from joint ventures and other enterprises are being released and will multiply in the years ahead. The profile of these wines and the image of Chinese wines in general will likely continue to evolve in unpredictable ways.

GEOGRAPHY AND CLIMATE

China is the fourth largest country in the world (by geographic area) and is somewhat comparable to the size of the United States (the US ranks third after Russia and Canada). Much of this land is taken up by deserts, particularly the Gobi Desert in the north and the Takla Makan Desert in the northwest. The far north of the country, located to the east of Mongolia, is isolated and mountainous, as is the far west of the country, which is dominated by the mountains and plateaus of the Kunlun Shan Mountain Range. To the southwest, the landscape consists of the immense Plateau of Tibet—which, at an average elevation of nearly 15,000 feet (4,500 m), covers one-fourth of China's surface—and the dramatic Himalayas.

Broadly speaking, China has a continental monsoon climate differentiated by region and characterized by dry, cold winters and rainy, hot summers. A good portion of the country is located within the temperate latitude zone considered ideal for viticulture, with only the portion extending from the city of Hangzhou down to Macau reaching farther south than 30° north latitude. Thus, most of China's grape growing and winemaking is focused in the northern portion of the country. The only exception to this is the Yunnan region, which borders Myanmar (Burma), Vietnam, and Laos.

As is to be expected in a country of such large scale, China's climate varies widely across the whole of the landmass. Precipitation ranges from an average of fewer than 2 inches (5 cm) per year in the Takla Makan Desert in the inland northwest, to 28 inches (71 cm) per year in the coastal sections of the northeast, with precipitation overall increasing as one travels farther south. Annual rainfall as high as 50 inches (127 cm) is often experienced in the areas around Macau.

GRAPE VARIETIES

The varieties that dominate plantings are Red Globe, Kyoho, Thompson Seedless, and Muscat, reflecting the substantial production of table grapes. Of the dozens of different species of the *Vitis* genus, many are native to China and the surrounding areas of Asia. For much of China's long grape growing history, these native grapes—now known by such names as *Vitis amurensis* (the Amur grape), *Vitis armata*, and *Vitis sinocinerea*—were the only grapes known.

Several hundred varieties of *Vitis vinifera* were imported into China beginning in 1892. As occurred in many other regions at the time, many of these initial vinifera vines did not survive—although some have lasted over the decades—and many were

used, along with local species, to create hybrids that are still in use today. As technical knowledge and understanding of climatic and geological suitability increases, vinifera grapes are becoming more widely grown and, in many cases, preferred for the production of wine.

Grape breeding programs, beginning in the 1950s, have led to over 50 new grape varieties considered to be native to China. These crosses and hybrids were created particularly for their resistance to the destructive low temperatures of northern Chinese winters and for their disease resistance in the areas with hot, humid summers. One of the most successful crosses is known as Yan 73, a Muscat Hamburg X Alicante Bouschet cross used to strengthen color in red wine owing to its pigmented pulp. Gongniang No. 1, a Muscat Hamburg X *Vitis amurensis* hybrid, is widely used in wine production for its extreme cold resistance; it can safely overwinter, without being buried for protection, in conditions as low as -7°F (-22°C), and has produced award-winning wines as well.

It is not currently known what the exact acreage is by grape variety in China. Cabernet Sauvignon is, by all estimates, the most widely planted wine grape, believed to account for half of all plantings. This is

Figure 20-2: Marselan grapes

followed by Cabernet Gernischt (the local name for what has recently been confirmed to be Carmenère), Merlot, Chardonnay (the leading white grape), Cabernet Franc, Shiraz, Gamay, Grenache, Marselan (a French-created Cabernet Sauvignon X Grenache cross), and Pinot Noir, among others.

Among the assorted grapes somewhat unique to China, the vinifera variety Longyan appears to have been planted in China for several hundred years. No one seems to know just how it arrived in Asia, but it has long been appreciated as a table grape, known by the name Dragon Eyes. Longyan is a high-yielding grape variety with a reddish-pink skin that produces wines often described as having a Gewürztraminer-like aroma and flavors of flowers, peaches, and lychee fruit.

WINE LAWS AND REGULATIONS IN CHINA

National regulations governing wine production and sales in China are still largely in their infancy. The first geographical indication protection regulation was put in place in 2005, requiring both local and foreign regions to be registered for protection with the General Administration of Quality Supervision, Inspection, and Quarantine (AQSIQ).

Other laws and regulations are now beginning to be enacted. For instance, in December 2012, the Shandong Bureau of Quality and Technical Supervision (SBQTS) approved and announced a set of standards concerning the use of the term "estate wine." The regulations require the producing estate to own all the vines, produce and bottle the wine within the estate, and only use grapes from vines that are more than three years old, among other requirements.

Also in December 2012, the Eastern Foot of Helan Mountain wine region, located within the Ningxia Hui Autonomous Region, became the first legally regulated and geographically defined wine region in China by vote of the People's Congress Standing Committee. These regulations set standards for viticulture and winemaking and limit the use of the regional name to wines produced 75% from grapes grown within the geographic confines of the area. In addition, two geographical indications in Xinjiang, Hoxud and Turpan, are pending approval.

As Chinese wineries begin to export, both local and regional laws such as these will take on greater importance and are likely to become more widespread.

CHINESE WINE REGIONS

Hebei

The Chinese province of Hebei is located in the northeast of the country between 36° and 42° north latitude, surrounding the municipalities of Beijing and Tianjin. Hebei, whose name can be literally translated as "north of the river," is located entirely north of the Yellow River, on the coast of the Bohai Sea. It is estimated that Hebei, together with neighboring Tianjin, has over 50 wineries and is responsible for up to half of China's total wine volume.

Despite its proximity to the ocean, coastal Hebei has a warm monsoon climate, experiencing hot, humid, and wet summers and autumns, followed by cold, dry winters. Winter temperatures are low enough to require vines to be buried. Portions of the northern section of the area situated at up to 3,300 feet (1,000 m) are well-suited for viticulture and enjoy a much cooler climate—as well as higher levels of sunshine—than the city of Beijing and the coastal areas. Here, as in China's other northern vineyards, viticulture is dependent upon irrigation.

The large population of the city of Beijing provides a ready market for much of the wine produced in Hebei. The Great Wall of China cuts through the area and, in many cases, vineyards are planted in its shadow. This area is home to several large producers of Chinese wine, including the China Great Wall Wine Company, which is currently China's largest producer by volume.

Hebei is also home to the Sino-French Demonstration Vineyard, planted in the late 1990s as a joint venture between the French and Chinese governments. The Sino-French Demonstration Vineyard, whose wines are marketed under the name Domaine Franco Chinois, grows a wide array of vinifera varieties, including Cabernet Sauvignon, Riesling, Viognier, Merlot, Marselan, and Petit Manseng.

Ningxia

The Ningxia Hui Autonomous Region is located about 500 miles (805 km) west of Beijing. The area is basically an alluvial plain of the Yellow River, situated on the eastern edge of the Gobi Desert. Due to centuries of agriculture, the soil here has been depleted to a fine type of loess soil, highly susceptible to wind and water erosion. Viticulture is encouraged in this area due to its affinity for such marginal conditions and to help prevent further erosion.

Thoroughly landlocked, Ningxia has a true continental climate, with significant day/night and summer/winter temperature variations. Summertime temperatures into the 80s F (upper 20s C) are assuaged by the altitude of the vineyards, which typically approach 4,000 feet (1,200 m) above sea level. The winters are long and very cold, however, which means that many vines must be buried under an insulating layer of dirt in order to survive. The months of December through February also see negligible precipitation; rainfall is concentrated in summer months, reaching only 8 inches (20 cm) annually. Irrigation is necessary for agriculture, and early methods to divert water from the Yellow River were developed during the Xia Dynasty (2100–1600 BC) and expanded in later periods.

The Ningxia region has proved to be one of China's most promising vineyard areas and is the focus of significant investment. The area has experienced significant growth and, by some counts, is home to over 200 wineries. These wineries produce a wide range of wines—using Cabernet Sauvignon, Cabernet Gernischt, Chardonnay, Riesling, and Syrah as well as other varieties—that include some high-quality wines that have won medals at international competitions. China's first official appellation, the Eastern Foot of Helan Mountain wine region, is located here, and several international companies have interests in this zone.

Figure 20-3: Vineyards in the Eastern Foot of Helan Mountain wine region

Shandong

The province of Shandong, located on the shores of the Yellow Sea somewhat equidistant between the cities of Beijing and Shanghai, is home to many of China's most prosperous wine producers. The majority of the viticulture in the area surrounds the Shandong Peninsula, located just south of the mouth of the Yellow River and extending 164 miles (264 km) eastward toward Korea.

Shandong's location on the ocean, with a coastline 1,800 miles (3,000 km) long, yields a temperate climate with maritime influences and significant humidity. The area is influenced by warm summer and autumn rains resulting from the East Asian Monsoon; this may lead to waterlogged soil and fungal issues. Heat and precipitation are both at their highest levels in July and August, an unusual coincidence not found in many leading wine regions and contrary to the pattern in Mediterranean climates. Winters are mild enough that vines do not need to be buried, a significant advantage and cost savings compared to China's northern regions.

Shandong is home to the Changyu Pioneer Wine Company, considered the first "modern" Chinese winery and credited with importing many vinifera varieties into China beginning in the 1890s. Cabernet Sauvignon, Cabernet Gernischt, Riesling, and Chardonnay are among the most important grape varieties grown in the province, supplemented by Marselan, Petit Manseng, and Petit Verdot.

Shanxi

The province of Shanxi, located about 250 miles (402 km) west of Beijing and adjoining Hebei, sits on a high loess plateau between the Gobi Desert and the coastal plains. The area experiences a continental climate featuring cold winters requiring over-winter vine protection, yet the vines have a high rate of survival compared to those in regions farther west. Summers are generally dry, but inconsistent summer rains of the East Asia Monsoon may cause problems with humidity. These issues are countered by the area's high altitude vineyards, which receive ample sunshine and possess excellent vine drainage. However, the rains vary from year to year, and the best vintages are typically those that experience a minimal amount of rain. The area devoted to wine grapes is relatively small, roughly 3,000 acres (1,200 ha).

Shanxi is the home of Grace Vineyards, founded in 1997 and considered to be one of China's most renowned wineries in terms of quality, reputation, and world-class facilities for tasting and tourism. The estate, with 148 acres (60 ha) under vine, produces approximately 400,000 bottles of wine a year (including some made with fruit sourced from Ningxia).

Xinjiang

The Xinjiang Uyghur Autonomous Region lies in the extreme west of the country, neighboring the central Asian countries of Kazakhstan, Tajikistan, and Afghanistan. The exact origins of viticulture in the area are uncertain, but vestiges of vineyard plots outside dwellings and the remains of a vinifera vine have been discovered dating from the 4th century BCE. In the 13th century, the famous explorer Marco Polo described his journey down the Silk Road, mentioning the fine grape wines of Xinjiang.

Figure 20-4: Vineyards in the Ningxia Autonomous Region

Xinjiang has the greatest surface area of China's autonomous regions and is considerably larger than the states of California and Texas combined. It is divided roughly in two by the Tien Shan Mountains. The dominant geographic feature is the formidable Takla Makan Desert covering nearly 130,000 square miles (337,000 km). The wine grape areas are to the north of the Tien Shan Mountains and to the south around the perimeter of the Takla Makan Desert. Xinjiang's Heshuo/Hoxud region obtained Geographical Indication status in 2015.

Yunnan

The Yunnan province lies mostly south of the Yangtze River and shares a border with Vietnam, Laos, and Myanmar. The region lies between 21° and 29° north latitude, well outside the temperate zone typically considered ideal for viticulture. However, as is the case in some other areas of the world, the tropical climate of the low latitudes is moderated by higher elevations, which average almost 5,000 feet (1,500 m) above sea level. In Yunnan, there is no need to bury vines as in northern China. The region also has the advantage of a long growing season; on the other hand, harvest coincides with the arrival of the rainy period.

The area is believed to have a 200-year history of wine production, which began—according to legend—when a French missionary traveled from India to Yunnan via the Ancient Tea Horse Trail. The missionary was given a plot of land in order to build a church. He planted a vineyard with grapevines that included a variety brought from France known as Rose Honey. Rose Honey is still grown in the area today, although it has since become extinct in France. Other distinctive varieties of uncertain origins— including some non-vinifera species and hybrids such as Crystal and French Wild—are also present in the region, along with more typical grapes such as Cabernet Sauvignon. All of these varieties are grown and sold by the Yunnan Red Wine Company, one of the largest of Yunnan's producers.

The newest project in Yunnan is the Shangri-La Winery Company Limited. Situated in the northwest corner of the province in Deqin at 28° north latitude, the company sources grapes from vineyards located on the steep slopes of the Mekong River. These vineyards are among the highest in the world at 8,200 feet (2,500 m).

JAPAN

The densely populated island country of Japan has traditionally been more closely associated with the production and consumption of rice wine (sake) than grape-based wine; however, Japan has its own history and tradition of viticulture and grape wine production. Japan has been making wine from the Koshu grape, considered to be its own native variety, since the 8th century. Vineyards are estimated to cover 44,500 acres (18,000 ha), yet a mere 5,000 acres (2,000 ha) are dedicated to wine grapes. Japan currently has about 200 (grape-based) wineries.

HISTORY

Wine has a little-known but long history in Japan. According to the most widely repeated legend, viticulture and wine production began in 718 CE when a Buddhist Monk by the name of Gyoki had a vision of the Yakushi Buddha (the Buddha of medicine and healing) holding a bunch of grapes. In honor of the vision, Gyoki planted the first vineyards in Japan at the Daizenji Temple, located in present-day Yamanashi Prefecture about 65 miles (105 km) west of Tokyo.

The appreciation of European wine in Japan dates back to the 16th century, when Portuguese missionaries arrived in Japan bearing gifts of Portuguese wine for the feudal lords of Kyūshū. This wine became known as *chintashu* (a phonetic equivalent of the Portuguese word "red" [*tinta*] and the Japanese word for "liquor" [*shu*]). The gifts were well accepted, and the locals, who developed a taste for the wine, continued to import it. This practice all but ceased, however, during the 17th and 18th centuries as the sakoku policy of imperial isolationism applied strict regulations to commerce, trade, and travel.

Beginning in the 1870s, with the opening of the country during the Meiji Restoration, viticulture and wine production was once again attempted in parts of Japan, using North American and European grape varieties.

The first modern Japanese wines were produced in 1874 in the city of Kōfu (Yamanashi Prefecture, on the island of Honshu). The endeavors had some minor success, but it was not until after World War II that winemaking in Japan began in earnest. The interest in wine saw another increase in the 1970s and beyond, as many western products and fashions found their way to Japan, and Japanese tourism to the west increased in turn. In the last few decades, wine consumption in Japan has grown exponentially, yet remains less than 3 liters per capita (the highest in Asia). While the majority of the wine consumed continues to be imported, domestic production has increased as well.

GEOGRAPHY AND CLIMATE

Located in the Pacific Ocean, Japan is an archipelago of 6,852 islands. Four of these islands (from north to south—Hokkaido, Honshu, Shikoku, and Kyushu) make up about 97% of the country's land area and support most of the country's 126 million people. This long, narrow nation stretches from 24° to 46° north latitude. The climate is primarily temperate but varies from north to south and includes some extremes, such as the heavy winter snowfall experienced in the north, and the hot, downward-sloping winds sometimes experienced on the Honshu west coast.

While there are vineyards from the far north to the south, the majority of Japanese wine is produced on Honshu (the main island), primarily in Nagano, Yamagata, and Yamanashi. These three prefectures produce almost half of the nation's grapes and an even larger percentage of the wine. Other regions known for viticulture and winemaking include Hokkaido, despite its location in the frigid north, and Miyazaki Prefecture on the southern island of Kyushu. In Kyushu, humidity is a serious challenge, and vines here are often trained on overhead trellises or pergolas known as *tanazukuri*. These tanazukuri encourage air circulation beneath the vine canopies, thus reducing the risk of fungal disease.

Figure 20-5: Koshu grapevines trained on tanazukuri

GRAPE VARIETIES

There are relatively few grape varieties that are commercially grown for use in winemaking in Japan; these include Koshu, considered to be native to Japan, Europe's Muscat of Alexandria, and Muscat Bailey-A, a Japanese hybrid. However, there are fragmented plantings of many other varieties, including Merlot, Chardonnay, Cabernet Sauvignon, Kerner, and Zweigelt.

The story of Japan's native variety, Koshu, begins with the original grapes planted by the monk Gyoki. According to legend, they were found "growing wild." However, it is now believed that they were brought from Europe by travelers, as modern DNA mapping has proven them to be of *Vitis vinifera* origin with 90% of the vinifera footprint still intact. The original European grapes apparently modified themselves over the generations so that the contemporary descendant is in fact a hybrid, now known as Koshu and considered to be a variety indigenous to Japan. Koshu is a pink-skinned grape variety known for producing light-bodied white wines with delicate fruit and floral flavors. Sparkling versions are produced as well. Officially recognized by the International Organization of Vine and Wine (OIV) in 2010 as a wine grape, plantings of Koshu are found primarily in Katsunuma (a town in Yamanashi Prefecture).

The Muscat Bailey-A grape is a red hybrid grape created in 1927 by Zenbei Kawakami at the Iwanohara Winery in Japan's Niigata Prefecture. Kawakami set out to create a red wine grape variety that would thrive in Japan's climate. The result is a hybrid between the Bailey variety (already a complicated vinifera/rupestris hybrid) and Muscat Hamburg (Black Muscat). Muscat Bailey-A produces wines with a very grape juice-like flavor and, on its own, is generally used to produce sweet wine. However, it is sometimes blended with vinifera grapes to create a sturdier red blend.

Wine Laws and Regulations in Japan

In 2005, Japan introduced its first meaningful regulations requiring that a product marketed as a "Wine of Japan" be produced entirely with grapes grown in Japan. Previously, wines produced in the country, regardless of the origin of the grapes or other base materials, were sold as "Japanese Wine."

In October of 2018, the Japanese National Tax Agency confirmed a new set of wine regulations that require varietal wines to be produced using a minimum of 85% grapes of the named variety. Additionally, the new laws limit the use of geographical indications and other stated places-of-origin to wines that are comprised of a minimum of 85% grapes grown in the named place.

In 2013, the Yamanashi Prefecture (located on the island of Honshu) was awarded the first Japanese Geographical Indication for wine. The Yamanashi GI is approved for wines produced using a range of grape varieties, including Koshu and Muscat Bailey-A. The island of Hokkaido was awarded Japan's second geographical indication in October of 2018. Hokkaido GI wines are produced using Koshu, Muscat Bailey-A, and several other grapes—including the unique, cool-climate Pinot Noir grown on the island. Independent municipal bodies in Japan are also beginning to create their own systems of regional standards and appellations, such as the Nagano Prefecture's *Wine Domain of Origin Certification Regulation* (known as "NAC").

WINE
CONSUMPTION
AND SERVICE

UNIT FOUR

UNIT FOUR WINE CONSUMPTION AND SERVICE

THE SENSORY EVALUATION OF WINE

CHAPTER TWENTY-ONE

LEARNING OBJECTIVES

After studying this chapter, the candidate should be able to:

- Describe the physiological processes of sight, smell, and taste.
- Identify visual clues concerning a wine's characteristics.
- Recognize the differences between detection threshold and recognition threshold.
- Discuss the differences between aromas, flavors, and taste sensations.
- Recall general procedures for setting up a wine tasting.
- Understand the techniques used in evaluating wine.

Wine tasting, and indeed the tasting of any food or beverage, is actually a complex interplay of sight, aromas, tactile sensations, tastes, and other perceptions, both psychological and physiological. This chapter begins by discussing the physiology of taste, explaining just what happens in our bodies as we "taste" a glass of wine, and finishes with a discussion on how best to set up a formal tasting session.

UNDERSTANDING THE SENSES

Wine tasting involves sensations and perceptions. *Sensation* refers to an organism's neurological response to a stimulus in the environment, while *perception* involves the brain's interpretation of the information gathered by the senses. A *sensory stimulus* in wine is any chemical, physical, or thermal activator that can produce a response in a sense receptor.

An individual's *detection threshold* indicates the smallest amount of stimulus necessary to trigger an *unidentifiable* sensation; *recognition threshold* refers to the smallest amount of stimulus required to trigger an *identifiable* sensation. Whereas the detection threshold for most people is genetically determined, a person's recognition threshold can be lowered through practice and by focusing while tasting.

SIGHT

The first sense used to examine a wine is that of sight. Sight receptors are located in the retina, which lines the eye. Millions of receptor cells respond to the stimuli of light waves, which enter through the cornea and are then focused by the lens onto the retina. Nerve cells in the retina then convert the light into electrical impulses that travel to the brain for interpretation. There are three kinds of color receptor cells in the retina, each specializing in receiving stimuli from a different part of the color spectrum. By integrating the information received from these specialized cells, the brain makes it possible to discriminate among several hundred different hues.

A wine taster can distinguish a wide range of colors, from yellow-greens to reds and purples. An experienced taster can derive valuable clues from the visual aspects of a wine, and these will alert him or her to what smells and tastes might follow.

Look for the following:
- **Very pale yellow-greens** in young white table wines from cool growing regions and in whites made from grapes that have not reached optimal ripeness and maturity
- **Yellow**, which can range from straw yellow to lemon yellow, the standard hue for most young dry white wines
- **Deep golden yellow** in older whites, in young whites from warm growing regions, and in white wines that have spent some time in barrel
- **Amber gold**, which may be a sign of a maderized or oxidized white wine
- **Inky purples** in young reds
- **Brick-red** tones in older, mature reds
- **Ruby-orange** highlights in high-acid reds
- **Black-blue** highlights in low-acid reds
- **Rust**, which may be an indicator of an oxidized red wine

In addition to evaluating hue, the wine taster is interested in the intensity of the color, which may be described as pale, medium or deep (opaque). Other visual clues for the taster include the development of legs or tears, sediment or other deposits, and a visible rim variation (particularly in red wines). In the case of sparkling wines, the presence, formation, lasting power, and size of the bubbles (sometimes referred to as the "bead") should be noted.

Figure 21–1: Sensory evaluation – sight

The sense of sight is the most familiar and most often used sense. Because they are comfortable with their sense of sight, beginning wine tasters often spend a lot of time contemplating the color and appearance of a wine. However, in reality, the sense of sight, as compared to the other senses, offers the taster the least amount of information.

SMELL

Our appreciation of wine is due mainly to its scent. The sense of smell is our most important, sensitive, and versatile sensory evaluation tool. It is used both when actively inhaling the aromas of a wine and when holding wine in the mouth to taste it. This is because the flavors that are experienced are primarily from aromas that reach the nose when the wine is held in the mouth.

The sensitivity of an individual's sense of smell to some molecules is astonishing. Humans can recognize the off-odor of hydrogen sulfide (which is responsible for the characteristic smell of hard-boiled egg yolks) in concentrations of 3 parts per billion. Even smaller amounts of the compound that accounts for the bell pepper aroma in Cabernet Sauvignon, 1 to 5 parts per *trillion*, can be perceived.

The versatile sense of smell can detect an enormous range of scents, up to an estimated ten thousand different odors. A typical taster can be trained to identify about a thousand specific aromas, and with some of these, several different intensities or concentrations can be discerned. Wines are estimated to contain at least two hundred odorous compounds.

The sensory organ for the sense of smell is a small patch of special tissue called the *olfactory epithelium*.

In humans, this patch of cells is located on the roof and wall of the inside of the nose. The olfactory epithelium is about the size of a dime and contains millions of nerve cells. More specifically, olfactory receptor neurons will become stimulated by chemicals in the air that diffuse across the mucous membrane and trigger the cilia in the nose. Once stimulated, these send the message along axons, where it terminates in the olfactory area of the brain.

In normal breathing, not much air reaches the olfactory epithelium, only an estimated 5% to 10% of what is possible. Therefore, when tasting wine, it is necessary to sniff deeply in order to direct more air, along with aroma molecules, up into the olfactory epithelium. About a tenfold amplification of stimulant at the receptor site is possible with deep, deliberate sniffing.

Air gets to the olfactory epithelium via two routes:
- Directly through the nostrils
- Indirectly through the mouth and rear nasal passages as the wine is held in the mouth and after the wine has been swallowed

Figure 21–2: Sensory evaluation – smell

Odorous molecules can only be delivered to the olfactory epithelium by air; thus, only the ones that can evaporate from the surface of a wine at the temperature at which it is served can be smelled. The molecules that are able to become airborne are called *volatile components*. The greater the surface area or the higher the temperature of a wine sample, the more its volatile molecules will evaporate.

Wine is known to contain a complex range of aromas that may be categorized as primary, secondary, and tertiary aromas (although not all wines will contain all three types). These aroma categories are defined as follows:
- Primary aromas: Primary aromas are derived from the grape variety (or varieties)—as influenced by terroir, climate, and other factors in the vineyard—and the initial fermentation. Fruity and floral notes are often considered to be primary aromas.
- Secondary aromas: Secondary aromas are created via post-fermentation winemaking processes and procedures, such as lees contact, oak aging, post-fermentation oxidation, and/or malolactic fermentation. Some examples of (possible) secondary aromas include buttery notes, vanilla, clove, wood-derived aromas, and the scent of "bread dough" often detected in Champagne.
- Tertiary aromas: Tertiary aromas are the result of the aging process. Examples of tertiary aromas that may arise as a result of extensive bottle aging include leather, mushroom, toffee, or forest floor (among others); sweet white wines may also develop aromas of honey or dried fruit. Wine that undergoes extensive barrel aging, such as Tawny Port, may also develop tertiary aromas (including coffee, toffee, or caramel). Tertiary aromas may be referred to as a wine's *bouquet*.

The following wine tasting techniques may help the taster in detecting and recognizing a wine's aromas:
- Wine tasters may hold the bowl of a glass of cold wine in their hands (rather than by the stem) to warm the wine and release more aromatic molecules.
- Wine tasters swirl wine in the glass to increase its surface area so that the concentration of volatile molecules in the air above the wine will be higher when they put their noses into the glass to sniff.
- Wine aromas often seem more intense when the wines are in the mouth than when one is sniffing them. This is because wines in the mouth have been warmed up, possibly to 98°F (37°C), as compared to serving temperatures of 45°F to 68°F (5°C to 20°C), and therefore release more volatile components.
- When wine tasters draw air through the wine as they hold it in their mouths, they increase the surface area of the warmed wine and enable more odor-saturated air to reach the olfactory epithelium through the back of the mouth and the nasal cavities.

TASTE

As noted above, most of what is commonly called the "taste" of a wine is, strictly speaking, a result of the complex aromas and resulting flavors that are actually perceived by the sense of smell. Smell and taste are often confused. Most people use the word *taste* to describe all of the sensations, including tastes, aromas, and thermal/tactile sensations, that come from a comestible in the mouth. Wine tasters must distinguish among these sensory experiences.

In this regard, the actual taste components to be found in wine are typically acidity, bitterness, and, perhaps, some level of sweetness. It is also possible, although not particularly typical, for wine to contain saltiness and umami. Concerning saltiness, it is also important to note that certain flavors—often referred to as "minerality" or by other such terms—may be mistaken for true saltiness, and that the topics of saltiness and minerality in wine remain open for debate.

In order for solids to be tasted, they must dissolve. Without saliva or another fluid such as wine to dissolve the substances that produce taste stimuli, only touch sensations could be experienced in the mouth. Because saliva coats the entire oral cavity, it efficiently delivers taste stimuli to the ten thousand or so taste buds located on the tongue, the roof of the mouth, the back of the epiglottis, and the tonsils.

Taste buds are located in the papillae found on the tip, along the side edges, and on the back of the tongue. While research concerning the number and types of taste components perceptible to the human tongue continues, it is generally accepted that the sense of taste can supply information about the following five sensory properties:

- sweet
- sour
- bitter
- salty
- umami

Humans are most sensitive to bitterness and least sensitive to sweetness. The threshold for the bitterness of quinine sulfate is an estimated one thousand to ten thousand times lower than the threshold for the sweetness of table sugar. In comparison, human sensitivities to sourness and saltiness are intermediate.

The average recognition threshold for sugar is around 1%. Thus, very few people will notice the sweetness of a wine with a residual sugar level of 0.5% or below; at 1%, about one-half of tasters will detect the sugar, although it can sometimes be masked by acidity or tannin.

Acidity will be perceived as a mouthwatering sensation similar to that experienced when eating tart foods such as citrus fruits. Acidity and sugar balance each other; therefore, wines with higher acidity will appear to be less sweet, while wines with higher sugar will be perceived as less acidic.

The word *umami*, which stems from the Japanese term for "savory" or "delicious," refers to "the protein taste." Defined as the taste of the salts of glutamic acid, an amino acid, umami compounds are derived from glutamates that are formed when proteins degrade. Umami provides the savory tastes in meats, seafood, poultry, dairy products, ripe tomatoes, cheeses, cured foods, stocks, and sauces. Umami is found in many types of food, especially those that have gone through aging, fermentation, or extended ripening. Umami is considered to be somewhat rare in wine, although it has been reported by tasters in certain well-aged wines, particularly red wines. In addition, wines that have undergone sur lie aging long enough to allow the expired yeast cells to decompose—for instance, Champagne, certain styles of Muscadet, and fino Sherries—may contain recognizable levels of umami.

As mentioned earlier, true saltiness is rare in wines, although some tasters report a distinct salty sensation when evaluating certain high-acid, dry wines and wines such as Manzanilla Sherry. As such, the sensory evaluation of a wine primarily yields information about its concentrations of sweetness, acidity, and bitterness. In some instances, saltiness and/or umami taste components may also be noted. The brain then interprets the information and determines how well balanced a wine is for these tastes.

TACTILE SENSATION (TOUCH)

There are sensors in the mouth and nose that allow people to respond to the tactile stimuli in wines. These stimuli include viscosity, texture, dissolved gas, serving temperatures, astringency, heat from alcohol, and sulfur dioxide content.

Wine tasters refer to the thickness or viscosity of the wine as *body*. For example, wines with relatively high sugar concentrations or high alcohol content have more body and seem more mouth-filling.

The bubbles of carbon dioxide in a sparkling wine bounce around in the mouth and tickle the touch receptors there and in the nose. A "prickly" sensation can even be detected with wines that have only a small amount of dissolved carbon dioxide from being bottled shortly after a cold fermentation.

Astringency is a tasting term most often associated with young, powerful red wines. Often related to tannins, astringency is a textural, drying sensation felt on the palate as a result of the shrinking, puckering, or contraction of the tissues of the mouth. Moderate astringency can nicely offset the richness of a fatty meal, but higher levels can make a wine seem unpalatable, and may signal that a wine could benefit from further aging.

A wine with high alcoholic content will produce a hot tactile sensation as well as a sweet taste for most people, while hypersensitive tasters may perceive alcohol as a bitter sensation. In fact, alcohol is unique among sensory stimulants—it is a pure substance that can stimulate three sensory systems: the tactile (hot sensation), gustatory (sweet or bitter sensation), and olfactory (a penetrating, pungent odor).

Touch sensors in the nose may trigger a sneeze in response to a wine that has too much sulfur dioxide. If the smell of sulfur dioxide can be perceived in wine, it is considered a flaw.

TASTING PROCEDURES

This section describes how to properly perform a wine tasting—otherwise known as the sensory evaluation of wine. The basic process includes the following basic steps: appearance, aroma, palate, and overall impressions. These steps will be discussed in detail in the remainder of this chapter. It is also helpful to keep in mind the following best practices:

- When tasting several wines, evaluate the color and appearance of all the wines first, and then quickly smell them all to get a fresh impression.
- Next, smell each wine in detail, making notes.
- Finally, begin the process of actually tasting the wines by taking a sip of the first wine and noting its tastes, flavors, and textures before moving on to the next.
- Be sure to rest as needed during the process in order to avoid sensory adaptation and palate fatigue. Have plenty of water available for hydration. Unsalted crackers or (unseasoned) bread for palate cleansing are also useful.

When practicing your tasting skills, it is helpful to use a systematic approach to tasting and to make notes of your tasting experiences. As such, a standardized tasting form—The Society of Wine Educators' Logical Tasting Rationale to Accompany the Certified Specialist of Wine Study Guide—is provided in appendix C.

GLASSWARE AND WINES

Ideally, tasting glasses should be:

- tulip-shaped, to trap the wine's aromas
- thin, so that the wine can be warmed if necessary
- clear, to show color accurately
- large, so a 2-ounce (59-ml) serving can be swirled and splashed about with impunity.

The standard International Standards Organization (ISO) glass is 6.5 ounces (192 ml) and is very effective for tasting. However, 8- or 10-ounce (238- or 296-ml) glasses are acceptable alternatives. Glasses should have been washed with an unscented detergent, rinsed thoroughly, drained, optimally polished dry, and stored so as not to pick up odors.

Figure 21-3: Room set up for a formal tasting

Wines are often tasted in related groups, known as *flights*, whenever possible. For many purposes, wines are ideally tasted blind, identified by code only. Wines should be presented at approximately the same temperatures at which they would be served with a meal:

- Sweet white wines: 43°F–47°F (6°C–8°C)
- Dry Sherry: 43°F–47°F (6°C–8°C)
- Sparkling wines: 43°F–50°F (6°C–10°C)
- Light white wines and rosés: 45°F–50°F (7°C–10°C)
- Medium- to full-bodied, dry white wines: 50°F–55°F (10°C–13°C)
- Light-bodied red wines: 50°F–55°F (10°C–13°C)
- Tawny Port and sweet Sherry: 54°F–61°F (12°C–16°C)
- Medium-bodied red wines: 55°F (13°C)
- Full-bodied and aged red wines: 59°F–64°F (15°C–18°C)
- Vintage Port: 64°F–68°F (18°C–20°C)

APPEARANCE

This first stage of wine evaluation involves a visual inspection of the wine for clarity, color, and legs (or tears). Other items to note may include deposits (sediment), a rim variation, and in some cases, the bubble display.

Clarity: To inspect for clarity, hold the wine up to a bright source of light such as a clear light bulb or candle. Modern-day technology allows for most wines to be made clear and bright, if that is the style the winemaker intends. Some unfiltered, unfined, or similarly styled wines may be somewhat cloudy or turbid by design. While not necessarily a fault, any sign of cloudiness or haziness should be investigated.

- Terms used to describe clarity include (in order of increasing clarity) dull, clear, and brilliant.

Color: To evaluate a wine's color, begin by holding the wine glass over a white surface. Tip the glass at an angle to view the edge of the wine, observing both color and hue. To compare the colors of several wines, place the glasses on a white surface, fill them to equal depths, and inspect the wines from above.

- Terms used to describe the color of red wines include purple, ruby, and garnet. Purple indicates a touch of blue, ruby indicates mostly red, and garnet implies a hint of orange or brown. Older red wines with a noticeable brown hue may be described as tawny, amber, or brown.
- Terms used to describe rosé include pink (the most common term), to salmon (if the wine shows a hint of orange) to orange (which is quite rare).
- The most common term used to describe the color of young white wines is yellow. However, white wines made from under-ripe grapes or from a cool climate (or year) may have a hint of green resulting in a yellow/green color. An aged white wine, or one produced from grapes grown in a warmer climate (or year), may have a hint of orange or brown in the hue and might be described as gold, amber, or (in the extreme) brown.

Bubbles: Evaluating the bubble display of sparkling wines requires keen attention to the stream of bubbles and the size of the bubbles. Although there are other benchmarks of quality in sparkling wine, all other things being equal, the smaller the bead (bubble) and the more continuous and persistent the bubble streams, the higher the quality.

Legs or tears: The rivulets known as legs or tears may be indicators of a wine's alcohol content. Because water and alcohol evaporate at different rates, tears will form on the inside of the glass after the wine is swirled (or the glass is tilted) due to the change in surface tension. Wines with higher levels of alcohol tend to show slow-moving, well-defined tears. Dessert wines and other wines with high levels of residual sugar will also have higher viscosity and may show thick, slow-forming tears. The presence of such tears is taken as an indicator of the body or weight of a wine; however, it should be noted other factors such as ambient temperature and (potential) soapy residue on the inside of glass may also affect the appearance and character of the tears.

Rim Variation: Red wines may exhibit a variation in color around the rim; this can be observed upon tilting the glass and looking through the edge of the wine in the glass. A visible rim variation could be an indication of variety, age, or maturation. This feature is not visibly obvious in most white wines. In a red wine, however, the oxidation that occurs due to aging will first show as a color gradation—often described as vaguely orange, brick, or garnet in color—around the edge of the glass. As the age of the wine increases, the color variation will morph into a wider band approaching (but rarely reaching) the wine's core.

Young red wines are often dark purple-red in color and opaque; such wines may show a thin circle of pink or fuchsia around the edge of the glass. In addition, some varieties (such as Sangiovese or Grenache) are often observed to show an orange hue around the rim even while young.

Deposits: Wine may have deposits of visible particles (sediment) in the glass. Such deposits do not otherwise affect the overall clarity (or turbidity) of the wine. Tartrate crystals—which may be found in many types of wine at any age—are one of the more common types of visible sediment and typically indicate that the wine was not cold-stabilized. Older red wines may show sediment due to the polymerization of tannins and other solids that fall out of suspension in the wine with time. Some young red wines may throw sediment as well, so it is advisable to look for other indications of age (or youth) in such wines.

AROMA

For many, the aromatic evaluation of wine proves to be the most difficult step in the process. Therefore, a high level of concentration may be needed for this part of the sensory analysis. You may find it helpful to look at a wine aroma checklist, such as is provided in appendix D, for a list of descriptive terms often used in the process of wine evaluation.

Figure 21–4: Two-year-old (left) and six-year-old (right) Cabernet Sauvignon

Follow these steps to perform a thorough aromatic analysis of a wine:

- Before swirling the wine, put your nose into the glass above the wine and sniff quickly and deeply.
- Next, reflect on the aromas, and note your impressions on paper. Refer to the wine aroma checklist found in appendix D for help with the terminology that may be used to identify specific aromas in your wine. (Do not, however, feel that you need to limit yourself to the categories or terms found on the checklist—or any other type of wine aroma identification tool.)
- Hold the glass by the stem (unless the wine in it has been served too cold and you want to warm it). Swirl the wine in the glass for several quick revolutions. Put your nose back into the glass and take one or two quick, deep sniffs. Record your impressions, and note any associations you make with the wine's aromas. These will help you file and recall the aromas of this wine and others like it. Each time you taste, you are adding a mental "reference library" of standards with which to compare other wines of this type when you taste them.
- Rest 15 to 45 seconds as you reflect and record your impressions.
- Swirl the glass briefly and sniff again. Once again, note your impressions.

ON THE PALATE

Once you have taken a sip of the wine, you can begin to evaluate the tastes, flavors, and tactile sensations of the wine. These characteristics are often referred to as "in-mouth impressions."

To begin this stage of wine evaluation, use the following steps:

- Place a small amount of wine (about a tablespoon) in your mouth. Move the wine all over your tongue and the inside of your mouth with a chewing motion so that all your taste buds come into contact with the wine and the tactile receptors in your mouth can sense it.
- Next, allow the wine to warm in your mouth so that more of the volatile compounds can escape. If you hold the wine in your mouth a little longer, you will be able to appreciate more of its flavors.
- Draw some air into your mouth and through the wine to extract the volatile components and force them up to your olfactory epithelium through the opening in the back of your mouth. This will cause some "slurping noises" so this step may not be appropriate for all occasions, but it should be acceptable in a serious wine tasting.
- Using a paper cup or a designated spittoon, spit out the wine. Consuming alcohol will alter your abilities of perception, and you want to keep them sharp.
- Repeat these four steps and if the situation is appropriate, swallow a small amount of wine.

Water, crackers, or bread may be offered as a palate-cleansing option between wines. However, cheese, fruit, salty items, or other foods should be avoided, as their aromas, tastes, and composition will greatly impact the way the wines are perceived.

While using the steps outlined above, you can draw your attention to the taste components (sweetness, acidity, and bitterness) of a wine as well as its level of tannin, level of alcohol, body, and flavors. The following guidelines offer some terms that may be used when describing these aspects of wine or when writing tasting notes.

Sweetness: Sweetness in wine typically relates to the remaining sugar left over after fermentation; such sugar is referred to a "residual sugar" (RS).

Sweetness in a wine may be described using the following terms: dry, off-dry, or sweet.
- Dry: Use this term if the wine has no discernible residual sugar.
- Off-dry: Use this term if a wine has a barely or slightly discernible level of sweetness.
- Sweet: Use this term for any wine that is obviously sweet, including all true dessert wines.

Acidity: In evaluating acidity, pay attention to the sensations that are both tasted and felt on the palate—acidity is often accompanied by a "zing" or "tingling" effect felt on the tongue as well as the mouthwatering effect of the acidity.

Acidity in a wine may be described using the following terms: low, medium, or high.
- Low: Use this term if the wine has a "just barely detectable" level of acidity.
- Medium: Use this term if the level of acidity reminds you of the acidity of a fresh red apple.
- High: Use this term if the wine is very acidic; almost seeming (but not quite) sour; such as you might experience when eating fresh green table grapes.

Bitterness: For many people, bitterness is perceived on the back of the palate and will be one of the last taste sensations to be perceived. Bitter taste sensations also have great longevity and will typically be the last of the taste sensations to fade away after the wine has been swallowed (or spit). It is important to learn to differentiate between the taste components of acidity and bitterness; both tastes may contribute to the "edge" or "bite" experienced by a taster, but they may play different roles in the overall balance of the wine and are especially divergent in terms of the interactions concerning wine and food.

Bitter tastes in red wines are often the result of tannins. This statement, however, must be viewed with caution as a variety of different tannins (such as those derived from grapes and those derived from oak) may be found in red wine, and tannins obviously evolve in character over the life of the wine. White wines—even those without any perceptible tannin or oak contact—may also contain bitter taste components. White wines that are typically low-acid—such as certain examples of Viognier and Gewürztraminer—are likely to demonstrate some degree of bitterness. Bitter tastes in wine that are derived from phenolic compounds are often referred to as *phenolic bitterness*.

The levels of bitterness in a wine may be described using the following terms: none, low, medium, or high; and may be defined as follows:

- None: Use this term if the wine contains no discernible bitterness.
- Low: Use this term if you detect just a slight "tingle" of bitterness on the back of the tongue or throat, particularly on the finish.
- Medium: Use this term if the wine has a noticeable bitter sensation, yet it is pleasant and in balance with the other taste components of the wine.
- High: Use this term if the wine has a noticeable level of bitterness that is the leading taste component of the wine.

Tannin: Tannins are mostly found in red wine, although it is possible for white wines made with oak influence or skin contact to show some tannin as well. Tannins are a major contributor to the weight of red wines and are also responsible for the textural drying sensation of many red wines. When evaluating a wine for tannin, it may help to use the formalized tasting technique of drawing some air into the mouth or before swallowing or spitting. The level of tannin in a wine may be described using the following terms: none, low, medium, or high.

- None: Most white and rosé wines will show no evidence of tannin.
- Low: Use this term if, after tasting the wine and drawing some air into the mouth, you detect just a slight drying sensation on the palate, and/or if the drying sensation is confined to the back of your mouth.
- Medium: Use this term if the drying sensation from the tannin is easily detectable not just on the back of the mouth or the tongue, but also closer to the middle of your tongue or on the gums.

- High: Use this term if the tannins are easily detectable with both texture and dryness all over the tongue and on the sides of the mouth. In some cases, you may even be able to detect dryness on the roof of your mouth.

Level of Alcohol: Alcohol affects the flavor of a wine as well as body, aroma, and texture. The other components of flavor must be in balance with the alcohol, or the wine will have a "hot" (burning) taste or feel. High-alcohol wines, all other things being equal, will seem viscous and full-bodied, while low-alcohol wines may seem a bit lean or even watery (unless there is a bit of residual sugar to enhance the mouthfeel).

The level of alcohol in a wine may be described using the following terms: low, medium, or high.

- Low: Use this term for wines that have up to 11% alcohol by volume.
- Medium: Use this term for wines that have between 11.5% and 13.5% alcohol by volume.
- High: Use this term for wines that have 14% alcohol by volume or higher.

Body: Body, sometimes referred to as "mouthfeel" or "weight" is the textural or tactile sensation of a wine. Alcohol, residual sugar, and tannin are the main components of mouthfeel for most wines.

Conversely, high levels of acidity can make a wine seem lighter in body.

The body of a wine may be described using the following terms: light, medium, or full.

- Light: A light-bodied wine will seem just slightly more viscous than water, and is most likely low alcohol, medium-to-high in acidity, and delicately flavored. Many young, fruity, and/or unoaked white wines will fall into this category.
- Medium: The medium-bodied indicator is often appropriate for wines moderate in alcohol, tannin, and/or acidity. Flavorful white wines such as Viognier or oaked Chardonnay, as well as the lighter styles of red wines such as some Pinot Noir and Beaujolais are likely to be medium-bodied.

- Full: A wine that is medium-to-high in alcohol and/ or tannin, and bold in flavor may be described as full-bodied. Red wines are more likely than white wines to be full-bodied (although there certainly are some full-bodied white wines). Very sweet dessert wines (of any color) are also likely to be full-bodied.

Flavors: Flavors in wine may be described using the same terminology used in the description of aromas. However, you may find that the flavors experienced on the palate are quite different than the aromas you previously recognized, and you may find that the flavors present themselves at different levels of intensity than the aromas did.

Figure 21–5: Taking notes can help you describe your overall impressions of a wine

OVERALL IMPRESSIONS

After you have analyzed the wine for its separate components, you will want to take a step back and consider the wine as a whole. This stage of wine evaluation may include an assessment of the wine's balance, finish, complexity, and intensity; and by considering these four characteristics, you can reach a conclusion about the overall quality of the wine.

Balance: One of the most desired traits in a wine is good balance, where the concentration of fruit and sugar is in harmony with the levels of acidity and tannin. In a balanced wine, all of these components seem to be in proportion and appropriate to the style of the wine.

Finish: A wine's finish includes its aftertaste (the tastes, aromas, and flavors that linger on the palate after the wine has been spit out or swallowed) and its length (how long those sensations last). A wine's finish may be lean, cleansing, mouth-filling, or warm (among other possible descriptors), but, above all else, it should be pleasant.

The finish of a wine is typically described by its length using the following terms: short, medium, or long.
- Short: Use this term if the finish lasts for five seconds or less.
- Medium: Use this term if the finish lasts for between six and thirty seconds.
- Long: Use this term if the finish lasts for longer than thirty seconds; a finish lasting for a minute or longer may also be described as "lengthy" or "persistent."

Complexity: Complexity is one of the most subjective descriptions used in wine evaluation. Complexity in wine typically comes from "layers" of scents and flavors, and is often derived from a mix of primary, secondary, and (sometimes) tertiary characteristics—many of which may be revealed only as the wine evolves in the glass. Complexity—along with its ability to hold one's interest—is a desirable component of many high-quality wines.

Intensity: A wine's aromas and flavors may be described in terms of their intensity (sometimes referred to as "concentration"). If a wine's aromas or flavors seem to leap out of the glass and take no effort to notice or recognize, the wine could be described as having a high level of intensity. If the aromas need to be coaxed out the glass or the flavors are somewhat hard to describe, the wine may have a light or medium level of intensity. Wines of marked quality are typically expected to have a high level of intensity of aroma and/or flavor.

Quality: The concept of "quality" in wine is subjective at best, and even the most revered wine critics will often disagree on the quality level of any given wine. Adding to the confusion is the fact that price should—but does not always—reflect quality, and that even within a specific batch of wine the quality of an individual bottle (or serving) may vary based on the care taken and conditions found in the transportation, storage, and service of the wine. However, there is a standard vocabulary used to describe the favorable attributes of wine. It is expected that a high-quality wine will be well balanced, have an appropriate level of intensity of flavors (concentration), have a long and pleasant finish, and be high in interest and complexity.

Quality in wine can be described, in a simplified manner, by using the following terms: poor, acceptable, good, very good, or excellent. In order to be described as "excellent," a wine should demonstrate good balance, a long and pleasant finish, a high level of complexity, and an intensity of aroma, taste, and/or flavor.

- Poor: Use this term if a wine does not show any of the features of quality (balance, finish, complexity or intensity).
- Acceptable: Use this term if a wine shows one out of the four possible features of quality.
- Good: Use this term if a wine shows two out of the four possible features of quality.
- Very good: Use this term if a wine shows three out of the four possible features of quality.
- Excellent: Use this term for a wine that demonstrates all four possible features of quality, and is described as having (as noted above) good balance, a long and pleasant finish, a high level of complexity, and an intensity of aroma, taste, and/or flavor.

On a final note, we should not leave the topic of wine quality without mentioning sheer physical pleasure. In other words, did you (or your customer) enjoy it? Many would argue that this is the most important aspect of a wine's character.

THE IMPACT OF ALCOHOL ON HEALTH

CHAPTER TWENTY-TWO

LEARNING OBJECTIVES

After studying this chapter, the candidate should be able to:

- Recognize the potential negative consequences of excessive alcohol consumption.
- Discuss the potential health benefits of the moderate intake of alcohol.
- Recall what resveratrol is and how it impacts one's health.
- Understand how to achieve a healthy balance between the risks and benefits associated with alcohol consumption.

The appreciation and consumption of wine is on the rise in many countries around the world, presenting numerous opportunities for the wine professional. However, it also presents a unique set of challenges. Almost every aspect of the wine and spirits professional's job involves the ingestion of alcohol to some degree, including during training, sales, wine dinners, and trade tastings. Even when expectorating, some absorption of alcohol occurs.

The effects of alcohol can have dangerous consequences for both the professional and the consumer. However, there appear to be some health benefits associated with a moderate daily intake of alcohol. This chapter will examine the current research on the risks and potential benefits of alcohol consumption.

Please note that nothing contained in this chapter or in the Study Guide as a whole constitutes medical advice. Such advice should only be obtained from a licensed medical professional.

HARMFUL EFFECTS OF ALCOHOL

Humans have been enjoying alcohol for thousands of years, and it is more widely available now than ever before. It is becoming prevalent in cultures with no prior history of alcohol consumption, and its use is increasing in many cultures that have a long tradition of imbibing.

Alcohol has properties that can act as a depressant, aid in relaxation, encourage social interaction, relieve feelings of anxiety, and enhance a meal. Studies demonstrate that restaurant visits accompanied by an alcoholic beverage are perceived to be more enjoyable and worthwhile experiences than those that are not.

When ethanol, the main chemical in alcoholic beverages, is absorbed into the bloodstream, it enters the brain, where it induces feelings of pleasure. A moderate intake of ethanol at the appropriate time may be pleasurable; however, some of the effects of ethanol, particularly at higher doses, may be unwanted and have serious consequences.

The dangers of the abusive consumption of alcohol are well-known and publicized:

- Intoxication: When alcohol is absorbed, it affects the brain's ability to further regulate its intake. This can lead to intoxication as the buildup of acetaldehyde in the bloodstream occurs. Acetaldehyde is a by-product of the metabolic process of ethanol in the liver and is more toxic than ethanol itself. When one becomes intoxicated, motor skills, speech, judgment, and the ability to drive become greatly impaired. In some cases, intoxication can lead a person to commit violent acts and exhibit socially inappropriate behavior.

- Alcohol-Related Diseases: Consumption of alcohol can increase the risk of serious diseases such as cirrhosis, a potentially fatal liver condition. Additionally, studies have shown that 100 ml of ethanol a day (equivalent to just over a bottle of wine) causes a condition known as fatty liver, in which fat accumulates within the cells of the liver. If alcohol consumption ceases, the condition can be reversed. Cirrhosis, however, cannot be reversed and may result from continued alcohol abuse. Alcohol consumption may also increase the risk of developing many types of cancer, especially cancers of the mouth, esophagus, stomach, and breast. Other risks include stroke, high blood pressure, and heart attack.

- Alcohol Abuse: Individuals who abuse alcohol for extended periods of time often develop a tolerance. When this occurs, more and more alcohol is required to achieve past effects, and the likelihood of addiction greatly increases. Addiction can lead to severe problems with health, finances, relationships, and career. Prolonged, excessive drinking also contributes to several psychiatric conditions, such as depression.

- Binge Drinking: In developed countries, alcohol ranks third among risks to health and is the largest cause of premature death in people between the ages of 15 and 29. This is largely because young adults may "save up" their drinking for one big night out a week, a practice known as binge drinking. Binge drinking may result in a rapid rise of alcohol in the bloodstream and may also contribute to a host of alcohol-related incidents, such as motor vehicle accidents and fatal alcohol poisoning.

BENEFITS OF MODERATE CONSUMPTION

There is strong evidence to support the claim that some degree of alcohol consumption may be beneficial to human health; however, there is no universally accepted "safe" level of consumption. The USDA recommends up to one drink per day for women and up to two drinks per day for men as a definition of *moderate* consumption. The definition of *one drink* is as follows:

- Wine (12%-14% abv) – 5 ounces (148 ml)
- Beer (5% abv) – 12 ounces (355 ml)
- Spirits (40% abv) – 1.5 ounces (44 ml)

Studies have shown that the overall lowest mortality rates occur at this level of alcohol consumption, while the highest rates occur in heavy drinkers. Moderate alcohol intake has been shown to reduce the risk of dementia and Alzheimer's disease, osteoporosis, certain types of cancer, and stroke. Extensive studies indicate that moderate drinkers tend to have lower mortality rates than those who abstain or drink very rarely.

Perhaps the most widely publicized potential benefit is the decreased risk of developing coronary heart disease, due to ethanol's reported clot- and plaque-reducing properties. However, this effect is only significant in people who are at risk of developing coronary heart disease.

Another important point to consider is that alcohol increases blood pressure, so a generalization cannot be made that a moderate amount of alcohol is beneficial for every individual. Furthermore, some individuals may be more prone to addictive behavior than others and should abstain from alcohol, as potential health risks far outweigh any possible benefits.

RESERVERATROL

Wine drinkers tend to be better protected against coronary heart disease, dementia, Alzheimer's disease, stroke, osteoporosis, peptic ulcers, and many types of cancers than those who drink beer or spirits. Many studies attribute this to resveratrol, a potent phenolic compound present in grape skins and seeds, and therefore often present in significant levels in red wine. There are many phenolic compounds present in wine that are responsible for color and tannin content, and they are all powerful antioxidants that help to protect cells from free-radical damage. However, it is resveratrol that has received the most attention for its anti-aging, disease-preventing, and cancer-fighting properties. It may even be an effective treatment in those with type 2 diabetes, helping the body to overcome insulin resistance.

When weighing the potential health benefits associated with alcohol consumption, it is important to remember that these benefits occur only in certain doses and in certain individuals. There are many factors to consider, including gender, weight, medical history, and genetic makeup. More specifically, a healthy limit of alcohol for women is generally lower than that for men because women's bodies tend to metabolize ethanol more slowly. Additionally, some individuals are unable to tolerate even a moderate level of consumption due to the lack of a specific genetic enzyme needed to metabolize alcohol effectively.

Figure 22-1: Wine with food...in moderation!

THE DECISION TO IMBIBE

The decision to imbibe, and how much, should depend on one's specific situation. It would, of course, be ill-advised to consume alcohol to protect from one disease while putting oneself at greater risk for another. For example, alcohol has been shown to increase the risk of breast cancer in women. The risk may be lessened if the alcohol is red wine, consumed at a moderate level (1 to 1.5 glasses per day); however, at higher levels of consumption, this effect is nullified.

The greatest benefits of alcohol consumption to health have been shown to occur when alcohol is consumed with meals, preferably at the same time each day, and not in excess of the recommended servings. Consuming alcohol with food slows down its absorption, which is healthier for the liver, kidneys, heart, and nervous system.

282

UNIT FOUR WINE CONSUMPTION AND SERVICE

WINE ETIQUETTE AND SERVICE

CHAPTER TWENTY-THREE

LEARNING OBJECTIVES

After studying this chapter, the candidate should be able to:

- Describe the factors involved in professional wine service, including set-up, glassware, opening a bottle, and order of service.
- Understand how temperature, decanting, and storage impact the perceived qualities of a wine.
- Recall the elements of best practices in food and wine pairing.
- Recognize how fat, salt, sweetness, acidity, and bitterness in foods impact the flavors of wine.
- Describe the key actions wine professionals can take to ensure the responsible service of alcohol.

A wine professional should always be conscious of his or her behavior in any social or business setting. All wine professionals should protect their reputation and that of the industry by consuming alcohol in moderation, and avoiding attitudes and behaviors such as arrogance, condescension, and public bashing of any wine or wine style. Wine, after all, is meant to be enjoyed and shared with others.

WINE SERVICE

The primary goals of wine service in the on-premise environment are to enhance the customer's experience by assisting with the selection and service of wine that delights the guest, enhances the food and occasion, and proves profitable for the establishment. In this regard, knowledge of the various styles of wine made throughout the world and an understanding of food and wine pairing principles are essential. While the details of service and the level of formality will vary from establishment to establishment, solid knowledge and

practiced skills in the procedures that follow should be part of every wine professional's repertoire.

The On-Premise/Restaurant Set-up

To prepare for service, it is necessary to gather the required tools and equipment in advance. The glassware should be free of soap and spots. This is particularly important for flutes, as a flute with soap residue will deaden the bubbles in a sparkling wine. After being washed, glassware should be rinsed or steamed with clean, hot water and polished free of streaks, residue, and fingerprints with a clean, dry, lint-free cloth. Handling the glassware by the stem will eliminate finger smudges.

Depending on the restaurant's policies and facilities, there are two different options for serving chilled wine—using a wine chiller that maintains the service temperature, or using an ice bucket to further chill a wine. When white or rosé wines are stored under refrigeration, it is best to ask the guests whether they prefer the wine served in an ice bucket or chiller. Chillers must be stored under refrigeration prior to service, and there needs to be sufficient storage space available. If ice buckets are used, they should be prepared in advance on busy nights by filling them two-thirds full with ice. When needed, water should be added to the bucket. The ice and water combination chills wine more quickly than ice alone. Serviettes (napkins, towels, or small linens) should be neatly folded and ready to be placed on top of each bucket to wipe the bottles after they have been submerged.

Sufficient quantities of each wine offered on the list should be available and accessible to supply the day's needs. Reds should be served at cool room temperature; whites and rosés should be chilled. Note, however, that some people prefer high-acid reds such as Beaujolais, Barbera, and Chianti to be slightly chilled as well.

As mentioned in the section on setting up a wine tasting, the suggested serving temperature ranges are as follows:

WINE STYLE/TEMPERATURE
Sweet white wines: 43°F–47°F (6°C–8°C)
Dry Sherry: 43°F–47°F (6°C–8°C)
Sparkling wines: 43°F–50°F (6°C–10°C)
Light white wines and rosés: 45°F–50°F (7°C–10°C)
Medium- to full-bodied, dry white wines: 50°F–55°F (10°C–13°C)
Light-bodied red wines: 50°F–55°F (10°C–13°C)
Tawny Port and sweet Sherry: 54°F–61°F (12°C–16°C)
Medium-bodied red wines: 55°F (13°C)
Full-bodied and aged red wines: 59°F–64°F (15°C–18°C)
Vintage Port: 64°F–68°F (18°C–20°C)

Avoid prolonged cold box storage of the white wines by ensuring that stock is rotated. Also, do not serve the white wines too cold. A wine's volatile aromas are not readily released when the temperature is too cold. A wine served too cold will display fewer aromatics and less flavor than its more temperate counterpart. In general, the higher quality, more complex, and older a white wine is, the less it should be chilled. Conversely, the higher the acidity, the cooler it should be served.

ORDER TAKING

To begin the process of wine service, the server should determine who will be responsible for ordering the wine for the table. In the context of wine service, this person is referred to as the host. If it is not immediately apparent who at the table is to assume this function, the server should politely ask. While taking the order and sampling the wine, the server should, whenever possible, stand to the right of the host.

While some guests may be very comfortable with wine and know precisely what they wish to order without the need for assistance, many will need some guidance. Accordingly, the server should be familiar with the restaurant's wine list, including details concerning each wine on the list and how those

wines pair with the items on the food menu. The server should also ask the guest about which wines he or she has enjoyed in the past (and which ones he or she hasn't) to get a better understanding of what wine the patron may like. Throughout the process, the server should develop a dialogue with the guest to build trust and confidence.

Once a wine selection has been made, the server should repeat the selection back to the customer, along with the vintage, to confirm the order. It is also important to ensure that the correct information is relayed to the bartender or other on-premise colleagues who may be responsible for obtaining the specific bottle of wine.

Figure 23–1: Presenting the wine

SERVICE

Once the wine is ordered, the server should select the appropriate glasses and carry them to the table on a beverage tray. The glasses should be set to the right of the water glass, above the knife on the right side of each place setting. Presuming that the table is freestanding, the glasses should be placed on the table from the right-hand side of the customer, with the server walking around the table in a clockwise direction.

Figure 23-2: Cutting the capsule

After the glasses have been set, the wine should be brought to the table. The bottle is presented to the host from the right side by holding it at an angle, label facing up, so that the selection can be confirmed. The brand name of the wine, its appellation, and the vintage should be repeated back to the guest, and the bottle should not be opened until the guest has accepted the wine.

During the process of removing the cork, the bottle may be held in one hand or placed on a table. While service standards vary, many experts suggest placing the bottle on a table whenever possible for better leverage and to minimize shaking—which could dislodge sediment in older wines.

To begin the process, the server should use the knife of the corkscrew to cut around the capsule below the raised lip or bulge of the bottle's neck. If using a wine opener that has a foil cutter, a clean cut can be made above the raised lip.

The top of the capsule should be removed and placed in an apron or pocket (never in the ice bucket or on the table). If the foil tears while cutting it, the entire capsule should be removed. If the wine is sealed with a screw cap, the server simply unscrews the cap and places it in his or her pocket or out of sight of the guest and proceeds with service.

The label of the bottle should, whenever possible, face the guest while the wine is being opened and served. The server inserts the tip of the corkscrew's

Figure 23-3: Removing the cork

spiral into the center of the cork from a 45° angle and twists it into an upright position. While holding the bottle with one hand, the server turns the corkscrew until the entire spiral—save for one turn—has entered the cork. The corkscrew lever is then placed on the lip of the bottle and held in place with a finger of one hand, while the other hand slowly and gently pulls the handle of the corkscrew upward in order to extract the cork. Corks should be removed from the bottle as quietly as possible. A server should never allow his or her fingers to touch the mouth of the bottle.

Once removed from the bottle, the cork should be taken off the corkscrew and placed to the right of the host, without placing the bottle on the table, if it hasn't already been. In formal service, a side plate or tray is used to present the cork. This tradition dates back to the days when the winery's seal, emblazoned on the cork, was a guarantee of authenticity.

Taking a clean napkin, the server wipes the rim of the bottle and, holding the bottle approximately 2 inches (5 cm) above the glass, pours the host a sample (1 to 2 ounces [30 to 59 ml]) so he or she can evaluate and accept the beverage.

If a customer is dissatisfied with the wine, the server should, without confrontation, determine the cause, such as cork taint or a sulfur-based fault. Whatever the cause, if the wine in question is indeed faulty, the guest's glass should immediately be replaced with a new one, and a fresh bottle of the same wine should be presented, with service beginning again. Restaurants and retailers are often able to obtain a credit from their distributor when returning faulty bottles.

However, if the guest simply doesn't like the wine, the server should follow the restaurant's policies and possibly suggest that the customer try a different wine. If possible, the server should find out what the guest doesn't like about the wine so that an appropriate substitute can be recommended. A hostile attitude should never be taken. Bottles that have been returned and are in good condition may be used in by-the-glass programs.

Presuming that the wine is sound and has been accepted by the guest, the server should then fill the glasses, moving clockwise around the table (when possible) and finishing with the host. If a guest of honor is present, this person may be served first regardless of seat position.

Wine is poured from the customer's right unless at a booth or otherwise unreachable. The glasses should not be lifted from the table, and they should be filled only one-third to one-half full, depending on the size of the wine glass. As there are five 5-ounce (148-ml) glasses of wine in a wine bottle, a table of up to five people will be adequately served in this fashion. With large tables of six or more, the pour should be adjusted appropriately to ensure that all guests get an equal amount of wine.

In order to avoid dripping wine at the completion of each pour, the bottle is given a slight twist when lifting it from the glass and the rim of the bottle is wiped with a serviette to catch any drips. If there is wine left in the bottle when the server is finished pouring, he or she should place the wine bottle on the table to the right of the host or, in the case of white wines, in an ice bucket to the right of the host. In formal service, the wine may be placed on a coaster instead of directly on the table, or at a side table or station.

Figure 23–4: Pouring the wine

If a second bottle of the same wine is ordered, the host should be brought a fresh glass for tasting the new bottle. Upon approval, the table is served. If the second bottle of wine ordered is different from the first, fresh glasses are needed for everyone. If a second set of glasses is required, the second glass is placed directly behind the first. Any dirty glasses remaining on the table should be removed.

Serving older red wines requires careful handling, as these wines can have quite a bit of sediment in the bottle. The usual practice is to stand these wines upright for a while, and then remove the cork and decant the wine off the sediment.

If the cork breaks off in the neck of the bottle, the corkscrew should be gently reinserted to try to salvage the remaining section. If it can be extracted cleanly from the bottle, the wine continues to be served as described above. If it is unsalvageable, the server should ask the guest if it is acceptable to decant through a cheesecloth or a specifically designed decorative wine funnel that has a filtering screen to catch any bits of cork that have fallen into the wine.

Service of Sparkling Wine

Bottles of sparkling wine take a little extra care when opening, and proper service has as much to do with safety as ceremony. First, it is important to be sure that the bottle has not been shaken or roughly handled en route to the table. Next, the server should make sure that it is properly chilled, as cold reduces the pressure inside the bottle and allows for more control of the cork. Finally, the server should ensure that the bottle and his or her hands are dry; wet bottles are slippery and difficult to control.

Figure 23-6: Serving sparkling wine

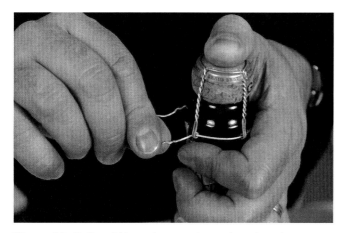

Figure 23-5: Sparkling wine—unfastening the wire cage

Care must be taken when opening such bottles, as a Champagne cork is capable of flying across a room at 65 mph. Many injuries have resulted from lack of attention when opening a bottle of sparkling wine. In addition, the bottle can slip from one's hands if it isn't held tightly. During the process of opening a sparkling wine, the bottle may be held in one hand or may be placed in the ice bucket.

To begin the process of opening a bottle of sparkling wine, the small tab is pulled to allow a clean tear along the perforation of the capsule. Alternatively, a cut may be made by cutting the foil beneath the wire cage. The foil is removed from the top of the cork and placed in the server's pocket. A cloth napkin is placed over the bottle, and, with one hand, the server grips the neck of the bottle and places a thumb on top of the cork. With the other hand, the wire cage is unfastened by untwisting it in a counterclockwise fashion, usually for six twists. Removing the cage can allow the cork to be suddenly expelled, so it is best not to remove the cage—or one's thumb—from the cork.

Holding the bottle at a 45° angle, the server rotates the bottle while tightly holding onto the cork. The cork is not twisted or turned, as the top section of the cork may break off. It is important to ensure that the cork is not pointing at anyone or at anything breakable. After a few turns of the bottle, the cork should slide gently into the napkin with a soft hiss. If the wine is not quite as cold as it should be, the server should try to hold in the cork so that the escaping CO_2 can be released from the side of the cork as it is being expelled. A loud pop, although festive, allows too much carbon dioxide to escape and deflates the bead.

If the sparkling wine begins to foam out of the bottle after the cork is popped, it is possible that it was not properly chilled. To prevent the loss of good wine, the bottle should be returned to a 45° angle for a few seconds. It should stop foaming immediately. The entire cork, including the cage, is presented to the guest, and the server proceeds with service.

SERVICE TIPS

TEMPERATURE

Most sparkling and white wines are served far too cold. "Chilled" and "ice-cold" are not the same. As there are five glasses of wine in a wine bottle, a four-top will usually finish the first bottle of wine long before it warms enough to require the use of an ice bucket. Accordingly, an ice bucket should not automatically be brought to the table for still white wine. The server should ask first.

As a demonstration, purposely overchill a bottle of high-quality white wine. Sniff and sip it immediately, and then continue to do this every few minutes thereafter. Notice that as the wine slowly warms up, more and more volatile aromas and flavors are released.

Many red wines served at room temperature in this day and age are served too warm, and the taste of alcohol becomes predominant, resulting in the perception of a dull and hot wine. The room-temperature rule for red wines was written in the days before central heating.

Figure 23-7: Decanting wine

BREATHING AND DECANTING

Most fine red wines improve if allowed to breathe for a while, although just how long the process should be allowed to last is a hotly debated issue. The preferred method to allow a wine to breathe is to aerate the wine by carefully pouring it into a decanter or carafe.

The purpose of decanting is to allow the wine's aromas and flavors to develop by exposing the wine to oxygen. For those wines that are not overly delicate, vigorously splashing the wine as it is poured into the decanter further aerates the wine. The few moments it takes to decant a wine is roughly equivalent to hours of time spent simply letting the wine stand opened.

Decanting may be appropriate in the following cases:

- *Young, robust red wines:* Many wines are released into the market so quickly after bottling that they are still heavily tannic. This can mask the fruit and coat the mouth with astringency. Decanting softens and mellows these tannins through exposure to air; this same exposure allows the fruit flavors to emerge more fully.
- *Complex wines with moderate aging:* Some wines, such as Nebbiolo-based reds and various Cabernet Sauvignons, are dense, compact, and complex, able to age for decades. Wines of this type with limited age may be improved by being decanted for an hour or so, which allows the aromas to open and expand.
- *Fully aged and mature wines:* These older wines may be fragile, and too much splashing may dry out the fruit and tannins. It might be helpful to use a stoppered decanter and consume the wine immediately after decanting, before the delicate aromas dissipate.
- *Wines with sediment:* Certain wines may have sediment in the bottle. Ideally, these wines should be stored in a decanting cradle or placed upright for an hour or so to allow the sediment to sink to the bottom of the bottle before service. The wine can then be carefully decanted over a lit candle to allow the server to see when sediment reaches the shoulders of the bottle. If this is not an option, the wine may be decanted through a wine funnel with a filter screen. The wine should be poured slowly so the sediment is caught in the filter, leaving the last ounce or so of sediment-concentrated wine in the bottle.

- *Biodynamic white wines:* Many producers of white wines such as Domaine Zind-Humbrecht and Pascal Jolivet insist their younger-vintage white wines improve with aeration. This is to remedy any potential reductive nature in the wine that may be due to the minimal exposure to oxygen the wines receive during production and storage.

STORAGE

Proper wine storage can be either very expensive (wine cellars or wine cabinets) or inexpensive (closets and basements). Regardless of which option is chosen, there are a few basic guidelines that should be followed.

A wine cellar should provide the following:
- Cool temperatures (50°F–60°F/10°C–15°C)
- A moderately humid environment (65%–75%)
- Constant temperature or minimal temperature fluctuations
- An environment with no vibrations
- No light, especially sunlight
- Storage for wine bottles on their sides or at an angle, so that the cork remains moist and does not dry out. Wine may be stored with the labels face-up to prevent scuffing or staining, although some people recommend storing the labels face-down to prevent them from getting dusty.

The vast majority of wines are meant to be consumed in their youth. The fresh acidity and fruit character of these wines will be enjoyed best during the first few years after their release. With time, wines lose some of these favorable attributes as chemical and phenolic reactions occur within the bottle. Thus, only a small percentage of wines should be laid down to age for any considerable period of time.

Figure 23–8: Well-equipped wine cellar

FOOD AND WINE

Wine is most often enjoyed with food, and such pairings are often a topic of much discussion and difference of opinion. There have been many approaches to food and wine pairing, from the classically elaborate French systems of the nineteenth century, where each specific variation of a dish needed to be paired with a specific wine, to the more modern proposition that any wine can be paired with any food based on the customer's preference. In between those two extremes are several approaches that provide some general guidelines as to what elements will enhance the pairing of food and wine.

In general, a good food and wine pairing has been achieved when both the food and the wine remain unchanged or seem more enjoyable when consumed together. However, in some cases, the food or the wine (or occasionally both) are enhanced and transformed— creating a wonderful symbiotic relationship. Some classic examples include Sauternes with foie gras, ruby Port with Stilton cheese, rack of lamb with St.-Émilion, and fresh oysters with Chablis. While these pairings are matters of personal taste, there are also reasons why they do work well for most diners.

In most cases, the key to a successful pairing of wine and food is an understanding of how the different components of one affect the other. As has been discussed previously, a given wine will contain varying levels of several possible taste components— to include sweetness, acidity, bitterness, tannin, umami and (in rare cases) saltiness. Food can also be described in these terms, and may contain fat and aspects of chemesthesis (such as perceived "heat" from chili peppers) as well. When choosing wine to accompany a specific dish, it helps to consider the components of both the food and the wine, and to understand how these components—as well as other factors such as flavor intensity—are likely to interplay.

One caveat: as in all things related to food and wine, people will vary in their abilities to notice, recognize, and enjoy certain aspects of any given wine-and-food pairing. As such, it is always recommended to keep individual preferences—the *delight of the diner*— in mind.

Figure 23–9: Classic pairing—Cabernet Sauvignon and filet mignon

INTENSITY

In many successful wine and food pairings, neither one overpowers the other in intensity. Many refer to this as matching the intensity of the wine to the food. Along these lines, a light fish, such as trout or perch, would probably pair well with Muscadet (a light-bodied white wine), but it would most likely be overwhelmed by Barolo (a full-bodied red wine). Conversely, the medium weight of a salmon preparation is a perfect foil for a medium-bodied Pinot Noir.

In the case of very rich food, such as blue cheese, roasted meats, or rich desserts, it may also work to contrast the heaviness of the food with a lighter wine. In this case, the wine serves as a refreshing break from the heaviness of the food and acts as a palate cleanser. For instance, a rich dessert, such as apricot cheesecake, can pair delightfully with a similarly rich and heavy dessert wine such as Sauternes. However, it could also make a successful pairing, albeit in a different way, with a lighter dessert wine such as Moscato d'Asti.

ACIDITY

The acidity in wine is one of the key elements that makes wine an outstanding partner for food. This acidity increases salivation, which can actually cause a lifting effect that enhances the flavors of food.

While it may seem counterintuitive, acidity in food will actually decrease the perception of acidity in wine. Therefore, foods high in acid will not pair well with anything but correspondingly high-acid wines; otherwise, the wine will seem flat. For this reason, many of the most food-loving wines in the world are high in acid. Pairings that take excellent advantage of this interaction include goat cheese with Sauvignon Blanc, in which the wine becomes softer and the fruit flavors more detectable, and a tomato-based sauce served with a high-acid red wine such as Barbera. In the case of very acidic foods such as ceviche (fish or shellfish marinated in lime juice or other high-acid liquid) and salads dressed with vinaigrette, it is best to choose a high-acid wine such as Riesling, Prosecco, or cool-climate Sauvignon Blanc.

In addition to reducing the perception of acidity in a wine, moderate-to-high acid foods can *increase* the perception of sweetness and fruitiness in a wine, and may cause the wine to seem richer or fuller in body.

SWEETNESS

Sweetness in food can diminish the perception of sweetness, body, and fruitiness in a wine. This can be an advantage when serving ultra-sweet wines, such as certain ice wines or late-harvest wines that may seem overly sweet when tasted on their own. Served with sweet foods, such wines are often perceived as less sweet, less rich, and—to some people—more balanced. However, this same effect can have a negative impact on the flavors of a dry wine, making it seem overly thin and unpleasantly acidic to some diners.

Wines with a slight sweetness, such as an off-dry Riesling, can balance spicy flavors in food. At a certain point, spicy "heat" will not only make it impossible to detect the flavors in wine but may also increase the perception of any bitterness or tannin. The one taste that will diminish the perception of spicy "heat" on the palate is sweetness. A dish with a moderate amount of spiciness is best paired with an acidic but slightly sweet wine, such as an off-dry version of Riesling or Chenin Blanc.

BITTERNESS

In contrast to the taste dynamics of sweetness and acidity, where the components tend to cancel each other out, bitterness in food enhances the bitter tastes in wine. Unless this is desirable, one should try to pair bitter tastes in food with wines that are low in bitterness. Wines that are medium-to-high in acidity and those with some residual sugar typically pair well with bitter tastes in food. Keep in mind that oak-aged wines have a bitter component to them. Overly bitter foods are not necessarily appreciated by the American palate, but foods such as spinach, broccoli, asparagus, and eggplant have an element of bitterness to them. The bitterness in chocolate is the main reason why this delightful food is so difficult to pair with wine, but it does tend to work well with sweet, intensely flavored wines such as ruby Port or late-harvest Zinfandel.

FATS

A bit (or a lot) of fat can give a dish amplitude and richness, provide satiety, and even cause the release of endorphins. Fats also have the ability to coat the tongue, sometimes to the point where it is difficult for the diner to discern flavors. This fact is the basis for the often-successful pairing of acidic wines—especially white wines such as Albariño or Sauvignon Blanc and/or sparkling wines—with fatty or oily foods. In such a pairing, the acidic wine can have the effect of "cutting through the richness" and cleansing the palate after a bite of rich foods (such as those in cream or butter sauces) or fatty foods—be it a juicy burger or fried potatoes.

SALT

Moderately salty foods made with a good-quality salt product can pair well with a wide range of wines. In general, salt in food can made a wine seem richer in body and fruitiness, while toning down any bitterness or astringency. In particular, the cooling, refreshing acidity of wines such as Sauvignon Blanc or Champagne can pair well with moderately salty foods—the combination of salt and acidity can lend a pleasant accent to the flavors of both the wine and the food. Salt-and-sweet is another classic culinary combination, and salty foods tend to pair well with sweet wines—as seen in the pairing of sweet wines with salty blue cheese.

Salt is one component of food that is not typically found in wine and therefore generally presents a contrast. Salt in food can be tough on wine if taken to extremes, so overly salty foods should be avoided

Figure 23-10: Classic pairing: Riesling and sushi

with fine wines. Many people believe that wines with alcohol levels in the 14%-16% abv range or those with overtly oaky flavors should be used with caution in combination with salty foods, as these pairings create a bitter sensation on the palate for some people. It is also best to avoid iodized salt when preparing food to be paired with wine, as many people perceive such products to be bitter—which can be problematic when combined with any bitter tastes in the wine.

UMAMI

The pairing of umami-rich foods and wine can be difficult to comprehend, in part because the taste component of umami can be tricky to isolate, recognize, and even understand. However, it is an important concept to grasp, as many food that are considered to be difficult to pair with wine—such as asparagus and eggs—may have earned the reputation based on their level of umami. In simple terms, umami-rich foods may increase the perception of bitterness and astringency in wine, while at the same time diminishing the perception of the wine's sweetness, fruitiness, and richness (from viscosity or body). Some of these interactions can be assuaged by the use of salt, as discussed above.

FLAVORS

Much attention has been paid to matching and contrasting flavors in wine and food. For example, it can be argued that smoked foods do well with the floral flavors of Riesling (based on a flavor contrast), or that the use of herbs enhances the varietal character of an herbaceous Sauvignon Blanc (based on a flavor match). Many aficionados take it a step further and consider *flavor synergy*—the sometimes surprising combining of flavors that creates a pleasant, new flavor not experienced in the wine or the food alone—to be one of the ultimate goals of food and wine pairing. Yet this is an area where it becomes even more difficult to draw universal conclusions, as the effect of a certain flavor combination is very difficult to predict. Thankfully, most flavor interactions are pleasant, and as long as a wine pairing is predicted to be successful based on taste components, the flavors will most likely be harmonious as well.

THE IMPORTANCE OF PREPARATION

When it comes to the successful pairing of food and wine, many people tend to concentrate on the main ingredient, such as chicken, beef, or fish. However, the basic building blocks of a meal typically provide very little by way of tastes (particularly sweetness, saltiness, and acidity) or flavors before they are prepared. In this sense, the preparation matters just as much as the ingredient. If chicken is the main dish of a meal, we have a clue as to what the meal may entail, but we really need to know the specifics: is it smoked chicken served with spicy apricot chutney, poached chicken with lemon-herb vinaigrette, or sautéed chicken with crispy onions and shallot cream sauce? All of these dishes bring a unique combination of taste and flavor components—to potentially include elements of sweetness, saltiness, bitterness, acidity, umami, chemesthesis, fat, and intensity—to the table, and each has its own set of ideal wine pairings that would bring out the best in the dish and the meal.

RESPONSIBLE BEVERAGE ALCOHOL SERVICE

In the United States, third-party liability and negligence laws affect anyone who serves beverage alcohol, whether in a food and beverage establishment, at a wine tasting event, or in one's own home. There are a number of states that now require all servers of beverage alcohol to show proof of having successfully completed an acceptable responsible service training program. While some states require any public server of alcohol to have completed their own programs, most states recognize the validity of two programs that are offered throughout the United States and internationally: the National Restaurant Association's ServSafe Alcohol® and TIPS® (Training for Intervention ProcedureS).

Regardless of state requirements, having such certification can reduce liability insurance premiums for any server or employer. In EU countries, laws tend to be even more stringent than the laws in the United States, and there is a concerted effort to counter alcohol abuse. The Society of Wine Educators regards this to be a significant issue and encourages all who take the Certified Specialist of Wine (CSW) Exam to be properly trained and certified. It also requires all Certified Wine Educators (CWEs) to be certified in responsible beverage alcohol service at the time they earn the CWE certification.

Although the food and beverage industry cannot be responsible for all of the problems associated with excess alcohol consumption, servers of beverage alcohol, including members of the wine trade and educators who conduct wine tastings, can ensure that their behavior promotes responsible consumption of alcoholic beverages by doing the following things:

- Checking identification as a matter of routine in every case in which there is doubt about a taster's age.
- Recognizing the signs of intoxication and refraining from serving anyone who has consumed too much alcohol or exhibits signs of intoxication.
- Declining to serve any customer who appears to have consumed excess alcohol elsewhere.
- Encouraging impaired customers to call for a cab or contact a friend to get a ride home, or offering to make the call oneself.
- Persuading the customer to surrender the car keys when warranted.
- Observing responsible standards in serving and consuming alcohol so as to set a good example for colleagues, students, and friends.

ADDITIONAL
RESOURCES

GLOSSARY OF WINE TERMS

Abfüller: German. A labeling term that indicates a wine produced at a commercial winery that buys grapes from other sources

Acetaldehyde: The most common aldehyde in wine, formed by the oxidation of ethanol

Acetic acid: An acid that may be created in wine by a specific bacteria when the wine is oxidized or exposed to air, generally considered a fault when above the recognition threshold; see also acetobacter

Acetobacter: The type of bacteria that may cause wine spoilage in the presence of oxygen by producing acetic acid; see also acetic acid

Acid: The class of chemical compounds that produce a tart, sharp, or biting character in wine; see also lactic acid; malic acid; tartaric acid; citric acid; total acidity

Acidification: Adding acid to grape must or wine for the purpose of creating a balanced wine

Alcohol: The by-product of yeast and sugar; the intoxicating element of wine; see also ethanol

Aldehyde: Any of several chemical compounds caused by the oxidation of alcohol

American Viticultural Area: An officially recognized wine region (appellation) in the United States

Amtliche Prüfungsnummer: German. AP number; a certificate number on the label that is unique to that bottling, issued after government approval

Anbaugebiet: German. A specified winegrowing region (plural *Anbaugebiete*)

Ancestral Method: A traditional method of making sparkling wine that calls for bottling an incompletely fermented wine and allowing fermentation to continue in the bottle; also known as *méthode rurale*

Anthocyanin: A type of pigment found in plants that gives grapes and wine a blue, purple, or red coloration

Appellation: A specific name, based on geography, under which a wine grower is authorized to identify and market wine; the area designated by such a name; see also Denomination of Origin; Geographical Indication

Appellation d'origine contrôlée (AOC): French. The highest category of quality wine or wine region in France; a protected designation of origin (PDO)

Appellation d'origine protégée (AOP): French. Term used to designate the highest category of quality wine or wine region in France within the EU's overarching labeling protocol (equal to appellation d'origine contrôlée [AOC]); a protected designation of origin (PDO)

Aroma: A sensory characteristic of a wine detectable by the olfactory senses of the nose; the scent of a wine deriving from a specific grape variety

Ascensence: The resulting state of a wine when acetic acid and ethyl acetate combine; generally considered a wine fault

Aspect: The relationship of the slope of a vineyard to the sun or compass; e.g., a vineyard with a southern aspect slopes downward to the south

Assemblage: French. The process or stage of blending wines

Astringency: A textural, drying sensation felt on the palate resulting from the shrinking, puckering, or contraction of the tissues of the mouth; often related to tannins

Ausbruch: German. A term used to describe a high-quality, botrytis-affected sweet wine produced in the area surrounding the Austrian town of Rust

Auslese: German. A category of the Prädikat that represents wine made from selected fully ripe bunches of grapes

Autochthonous: Native or indigenous, specifically referring to grapes that are the result of natural crossbreeding or natural mutation in a specific area

Autolysis: The disintegration of dead yeast cells in wine due to the action of their own enzymes

Balthazar: A traditional large bottle for sparkling wine that holds 12 liters, equivalent to 16 standard bottles

Barrique: French. A standard wine barrel of approximately 225-liter (60-gallon) capacity

Base wine: Wine after the initial fermentation, prior to further handling such as blending, fortification, or addition of liqueur de tirage

Bâtonnage: French. Stirring, especially the winemaking practice of stirring up the lees from the bottom of a barrel or tank during aging

Baumé: French. A measure of the sugar level in grapes or juice used in France; represents the potential level of alcohol in the finished wine

Beerenauslese (BA): German. A category of the Prädikat that represents sweet dessert wines made from individually harvested overripe berries possibly also affected by botrytis

Beneficio: Portuguese. The volume of Port a vineyard is allowed to produce in a given year, based on the vineyard ranking and harvest conditions

Bereich: German. A regional or district appellation (plural *Bereiche*)

Bergwein: German. A term used in Austria to denote a wine produced using grapes that are grown on extraordinarily steep mountain slopes with at least a 26% gradient.

Berry set: The transition of fertilized grapevine flowers into grapes (berries); also known as *fruit set*

Bianco: Italian. White

Biodynamic viticulture: A system of grape growing based on metaphysical principles

Blanc: French. White

Blanc de blancs: French. 1. Literally, white from whites; 2. A white wine made entirely from white grapes, usually used to describe sparkling wines

Blanc de noirs: French. 1. Literally, white from blacks; 2. A white wine made entirely from red (black) grapes, usually used to describe sparkling wines

Blanco: Spanish. White

Blush: Pink, typically referring to a rosé wine that is off-dry to sweet

Bodega: Spanish. 1. Winery. 2. Wine cellar. 3. Wine shop or market

Botrytis (*Botrytis cinerea*)**:** Noble rot; a fungus that, under appropriate conditions, draws water out of grapes and thereby concentrates the sugar content (while simultaneously adding distinctive flavor elements)

Bouquet: The complex range of aromas that evolve in a wine following fermentation and aging, particularly bottle aging; see also tertiary aromas

Brettanomyces: Several members of a yeast family that can infect a winery and some or all of the wines; often associated with various scents including a "sweaty" or "horsy" odor

Brix: A measure of the sugar level in grapes or juice

Brut: A sweetness category of sparkling wine with little or no perceptible sugar

Bud break: The initial appearance of green shoots growing out of dormant buds each spring

Butt: Spanish. A type of oak barrel used in the production of Sherry

Cadastro: Portuguese. A vineyard ranking system used in the Douro that assesses twelve factors (including altitude, yield, and locality), awarding or subtracting points to arrive at a total score and classification (from A [high] to F [low])

Cane: A one-year-old grapevine branch that will support new growth in the current year

Canopy: 1. The upper part of a grapevine, including the leaves, fruit, shoots, cordons, and canes; 2. The part of a grapevine above the ground (to include the trunk)

Canopy management: A variety of techniques used to alter the position or number of shoots, leaves, and grape clusters in a vine's canopy

Canopy microclimate: The environment within and directly surrounding a single vine's canopy (or, at most, a small section of a single row)

Canteiros: Portuguese. Rafters in the warehouses where Madeira is stored and aged

Cap: The floating mass of grape skins and other solids formed during fermentation, typically seen in red wine production

Capsule: The wrapping that covers the neck and cork of a wine bottle

Carbonic maceration: An intracellular fermentation process that may occur in whole, unbroken grapes in the absence of oxygen and without the use of yeast

Chaptalization: Adding sugar to grape juice before fermentation to increase the alcohol content of the finished wine

Charmat: A method used in the making of sparkling wines that involves the use of large pressurized tanks at all stages of production; see also cuve close

Château: French. A wine estate, particularly in Bordeaux (plural *châteaux*)

Chemesthesis: A chemically-based sensory reaction distinct from taste or smell—such as the "heat" from chili peppers or the "coolness" derived from peppermint—that may contribute to the overall perception of a specific flavor

Citric acid: A minor acid found in grapes in very small amounts and sometimes used for acidification (but not considered appropriate for use in most quality wines)

Clairet: A light red style of wine; a specialty of the Bordeaux region of France

Claret: 1. An English term that was historically used to refer to the red wines of Bordeaux; 2. A generic term for dry red wine, most often used to describe a Bordeaux-style red wine

Clarification: The process of removing haze and particulate matter from wine

Classico: Italian. From the historic, central, or traditional part of a wine region

Climat: French. In Burgundy, a single vineyard site

Clone: 1. A grapevine grown by rooting or grafting a cutting from another vine, which is therefore genetically identical to the original plant; 2. A grape variety that has mutated to be slightly different from its parent

Cloning: The process of producing vines from a single parent by cultivating cuttings of the original

Clos: French. 1. "Walled" or "enclosed." 2. A walled or enclosed vineyard; may be used to describe a vineyard that was historically enclosed even if the walls no longer exist

Cold soak: A period of aqueous (as opposed to alcoholic) extraction prior to fermentation that is accomplished by maintaining a temperature low enough to prevent the start of fermentation

Cold stabilization: The process of removing excess tartaric acid from a wine by chilling the wine to a very low temperature (25°F to 30°F)

Continental climate: A climate typical of the interior sections of large landmasses, characterized by hot summers, cold winters, and precipitation throughout the year

Control state: A US state in which the state government performs the role of wine (or liquor) distributor and/or retailer

Cordon: 1. An arm or branch of a grapevine, from which fruit-producing shoots grow; 2. The wire of a trellis on which a vine cordon is trained

Cork taint: A characteristic undesirable aroma sometimes found in wine contaminated by TCA

Corked: 1. Affected by cork taint; 2. Sealed with a cork

Cosecha: Spanish. 1. Harvest; 2. Vintage; see also vendimia

Côte: French. 1. Slope; 2. Coast

Coulure: French. A vine malady where many flowers fail to become fully developed berries, also known as *shatter*

Crémant: French. Literally "creaming"; a term used specifically for French sparkling wines made by the classic method outside of the Champagne region

Criadera: Spanish. Literally "nursery"; a row or set of barrels in a solera system that contain Sherry

Crianza: Spanish. A term used for Spanish DO and DOCa wines that have gone through minimum periods of barrel and/or bottle aging as defined by an area's regulating council; see also reserva and gran reserva

Cross, crossing: The offspring produced via the sexual reproduction of different subspecies within the same species, e.g., a variety produced by the cross-fertilization of one vinifera grape variety with another

Cru: French. 1. A vineyard or vineyard site, also translated as "growth" (e.g., premier cru = first growth); 2. A wine-producing village

Cru bourgeois: French. A consortium of top châteaux in the Médoc from among those that were not included in the Bordeaux Classification of 1855

Cru classé: French. "Classified growth"; a château or wine estate listed on one of the official classifications (e.g., the Bordeaux Classification of 1855)

Crusher-destemmer: A machine that breaks open harvested grapes to begin the extraction of juice for fermentation and removes the stems from grape bunches

Cryoextraction: Freezing grapes post-harvest in a commercial freezer; a method of producing very sweet juice for the production of dessert wines

Cultivar: A grape variety produced through selective breeding

Cuve close: French. 1. "Closed vessel"; a pressurized tank; 2. The tank method of sparkling wine production; see also Charmat

Cuvée: French. 1. A blend of many different wines; 2. The first juice to emerge from the press in the production of traditional method sparkling wine

Débourbage: French. Juice settling

Decanting: Moving wine from a bottle into another container (decanter) for the purposes of aeration and/or separating the wine from sediment

Dégorgement: French. Disgorging

Délestage: French. A type of pumping over in which the fermenting juice is drained into a separate holding tank before it is returned to the original tank by spraying it over the now sunken cap; see also rack and return

Denominação de origem controlada (DOC): Portuguese. The highest category of wine or wine region in Portugal; a protected designation of origin (PDO)

Denominación de origen (DO): Spanish. The second highest category of wine or wine region in Spain; a protected designation of origin (PDO); see also vino de pago

Denominación de origen calificada (DOCa): Spanish. The highest category of wine or wine region in Spain; a protected designation of origin (PDO); see also vino de pago

Denomination of origin: 1. The name of an officially recognized quality wine region; 2. The region itself; see also appellation; geographical indication

Denominazione di origine controllata (DOC): Italian. The second highest category of wine or wine region in Italy; a protected designation of origin (PDO)

Denominazione di origine controllata e garantita (DOCG): Italian. The highest category of wine or wine region in Italy; a protected designation of origin (PDO)

Dessert wine: 1. A wine intended for consumption after a meal; 2. Any sweet wine; 3. A legal classification used in the United States for any wine with more than 14% alcohol

Detection threshold: The smallest amount of a stimulus (e.g., sugar on the tongue) necessary to be noticed but not identified

Deutscher: German. Literally, "German"

Deutscher Wein: German. Basic table wine made from 100% German grapes

Disgorging: The process of removing dead yeast cells from bottle-fermented sparkling wine after the second fermentation; see also dégorgement

Distillation: The separation and concentration of the alcohol from a fermented liquid by a series of evaporation and condensation processes

Districtus Austriae Controllatus (DAC): The highest category of quality wine in Austria

Diurnal: Daily, e.g., the diurnal temperature range is the difference between the high and low temperatures in a single day

Dolce: Italian. Sweet

Dosage: The addition of sugar, juice, and/or wine to sparkling wine after disgorging in order to top the bottle off and achieve the desired sweetness level

Doux: French. Sweet

Downy mildew: A serious fungal disease of grapevines; also known as *peronospora*

Dry: Not sweet; lacking perceptible sugar

Dulce: Spanish. Sweet

Edelfäule: German. Botrytis

Einzellage: German. A single, officially designated vineyard (plural *Einzellagen*)

Eiswein: German. Ice wine, a dessert wine produced by crushing frozen grapes and discarding the ice prior to fermentation; see also ice wine

En primeur: French. The system of selling wine as futures

Enology: The science of wine and winemaking

Erste lage: German. "First site," often compared to the use of *premier cru* in Burgundy; a VDP term

Erzeugerabfüllung: German. "Producer-bottled"; the labeling term for wines bottled by cooperatives of growers

Estate: Typically, a winery that owns and makes wine from the vineyards that surround it

Ester: Any of various chemical compounds that result from the joining of an acid and an alcohol

Estufa: Portuguese. 1. "Oven"; a hot warehouse for storing and aging Madeira (plural *estufagem*); 2. A method of producing Madeira

Ethanol: The principal alcohol found in wine

Ethyl acetate: A common ester formed through a reaction of ethanol and acetic acid; associated with the odor of fingernail polish remover

Extended maceration: A winemaking technique that keeps a newly fermented batch of red wine in contact with the skins and seeds after fermentation is complete; prolonged skin contact

Extra dry: A sweetness category of sparkling wine that is off-dry

Feinherb: German. Off-dry

Fermentation: A complex biochemical process by which yeast cells convert sugar to alcohol and other chemical compounds with carbon dioxide and heat as by-products; see also carbonic maceration; malolactic fermentation

Field blend: More than one different grape variety grown together in the same vineyard

Fining: A clarification procedure in which a nonreactive material such as gelatin or bentonite clay is added to wine to attract suspended and electrically charged particles in order to draw them out of the liquid

Flavone (or flavonol): A phenolic compound found in plants that gives grapes a yellow coloration

Flavor: A sensory characteristic of a wine detectable as a combination of taste, aroma, and tactile sensations

Flight: A selection of wines presented together for purposes such as sensory evaluation and comparison

Flor: A film-forming, floating yeast most commonly associated with southwestern Spain; responsible for the character of fino Sherry

Flying winemaker: A winemaker who makes wine in multiple, widely spaced locations, especially in both the Northern and Southern Hemispheres

Fortification: The addition of distilled spirits to a base wine

Fortified wine: Wine to which distilled spirits have been added to raise the final alcohol level, generally to 15% or higher

Foxy: A descriptor commonly used to describe an aroma characteristic of some native North American grape varieties, particularly *Vitis labrusca*

Franchise state: A US state in which state laws grant distributors exclusive relationships with suppliers' brands, often giving them considerable leverage over wineries and importers

Frizzante: Italian. Slightly sparkling

Fructose: One of the two most prevalent sugars (along with glucose) in grapes

Fruit set: The transition of fertilized grapevine flowers into grapes; also known as *berry set*

Futures: Wine offered for sale prior to bottling

Galet: French. A type of large rounded stone found in the southern Rhône and elsewhere

Generoso: Spanish. Fortified

Geographical indication: 1. The name of an officially recognized wine region; 2. The region itself; see also appellation; denomination of origin; protected geographical indication

Glucose: One of the two most prevalent sugars (along with fructose) in grapes

Grafting: Inserting a cutting from one grapevine into an incision on another so that they will fuse together and grow as one plant

Gran reserva: Spanish. 1. A term used for Spanish DO and DOCa wines that have gone through extended periods of barrel and/or bottle aging as defined by an area's regulating council; 2. A term used for vinos finos in Argentina that have undergone a specified period of aging; see also crianza and reserva

Grand cru: French. "Great growth"; the highest classification level in Burgundy and Champagne, and a superior appellation in St.-Émilion and Alsace

Grappa: Italian. A spirit distilled from pomace

Grosse lage: German. "Great site," often compared to the use of *grand cru* in Burgundy; a VDP term

Grosses Gewächs: German. A label term used to denote dry wines produced in Erste Lage sites; a VDP term

Grosslage: German. An officially designated group of vineyards/einzellagen (plural *grosslagen*)

Gutsabfüllung: German. Estate-bottled

Gutswein: German. Estate wine; often compared to the use of *Bourgogne régional* in Burgundy; a VDP term

Gyropalette: A fully automated device to replace hand riddling of sparkling wine bottles

Halbsüss: German. Half-sweet

Halbtrocken: German. Literally, half-dry; the labeling term for a wine that is off-dry

Half-bottle: A wine bottle containing 375 milliliters

Hang time: The period between the earliest possible harvest date for a specific vineyard and the actual harvest date, allowing for additional ripening of the fruit

Hectare: A metric unit of surface area, equal to 2.47 acres

Hybrid: The offspring of sexual reproduction of different but closely related species, e.g., a grape produced by cross-fertilizing vinifera with another grape species such as *labrusca* or *riparia*

Hydrogen sulfide (H$_2$S): A colorless gas formed by sulfur compounds in the complete absence of oxygen, often has the odor of rotten eggs

Ice wine, icewine: A dessert wine produced by crushing frozen grapes and discarding the ice prior to fermentation; see also Eiswein

Indicazione geografica tipica (IGT): Italian. The higher category of basic wine in Italy, from a protected geographical indication (PGI)

Indigenous (varieties): Native to the area; not imported

Inert: Not readily reactive with other elements or compounds

Inoculation: A winemaking procedure in which an active yeast culture (or other agent) is added to juice, must, or wine in order to initiate fermentation

Integrated Pest Management (IPM): An approach to vineyard pest control that utilizes a variety of different methods in an attempt to solve pest problems while minimizing risk to the environment

International varieties: Grape varieties that have been widely transplanted to winegrowing areas in many parts of the world

Jeroboam: A traditional large bottle for sparkling wine that holds 3 liters, equivalent to four standard bottles

Kabinett: German. A category of the Prädikat that represents wine made from minimally ripe bunches of grapes

Kimmeridgian marl: A type of clay- or limestone-based soil derived from a seabed of the late Jurassic era

Klosterneuburger Mostwaage (KMW): A measure of the sugar level in grapes or juice used in Austria

Kosher: Wine (or other foods) made under strict rabbinical supervision and therefore suitable for consumption by Orthodox Jews

Labrusca (*Vitis labrusca*): A species of wine grape native to North America

Lactic acid: A mild acid that is not found in grapes but is created in wine via malolactic fermentation

Lagar: Portuguese. An open trough, often made of granite or concrete, traditionally used in the Douro for treading grapes and fermentation

Lees: Sediment found in wine during and after fermentation, consisting primarily of dead yeast cells and grape solids

Legs: Streaks produced by viscous droplets of liquid that run slowly down the interior of a glass of wine after swirling; see also tears

Lieblich: German. Half-sweet

Liquoroso: Italian. Fortified

Liqueur de tirage: French. A mixture of yeast and sugar added to a base wine to initiate a second fermentation and create a sparkling wine

Maceration: The soaking of grape skins and other solids in grape juice or newly made wine in order to extract color, tannin, and other phenolics from the skins and into the liquid; may occur before, during, and/or after fermentation

Macroclimate: The climatic conditions of the overall region, roughly synonymous with climate

Maderization: The process a wine undergoes when subjected to heat and oxidation; see also maderized

Maderized: Term used for a wine that has taken on the cooked character of Madeira or that has otherwise been subject to heat and oxidation; see also maderization

Magnum: A wine bottle with double the capacity of a standard bottle, i.e., 1.5 liters, especially when referring to sparkling wine

Malic acid: A moderately strong acid that is found in abundance in unripe grapes but that decreases as the grapes ripen; the primary input to malolactic fermentation

Malolactic fermentation: A biochemical process by which lactic acid bacteria convert malic acid to lactic acid, thereby reducing a wine's acidity and altering the flavor profile; often referred to as malolactic conversion

Marc: French. 1. Grape pomace; 2. A spirit distilled from pomace; 3. In Champagne, a traditional measure of grape quantity equivalent to about 4,000 kilograms

Marginal climate: A climate type that has such cool temperatures or such a short growing season that grapes are at times just barely able to achieve an acceptable degree of ripeness

Maritime climate: A climate typical of coastal sections of large landmasses, characterized by warm summers and cool winters, with considerable precipitation and humidity throughout the year

Martinotti method: An Italian term for the Charmat (bulk) method of sparkling wine production; named in honor of Federico Martinotti (1860-1924)

Mediterranean climate: A climate typical of the southwestern quadrants of large landmasses in the temperate zone, characterized by hot, dry summers and mild, rainy winters

Mercaptan: A sulfurous compound that is very malodorous and generally ruins a wine if it develops, often described as smelling of onions, garlic, or cabbage

Mesoclimate: The climate of a relatively small area, such as a vineyard

Methuselah: A traditional large bottle for sparkling wine that holds 6 liters, equivalent to eight standard bottles

Mevushal (wine): Kosher wine that has been flash-pasteurized and is therefore permanently kosher

Microclimate: The climate of a small, very specific area, such as a section of a vineyard row or a single vine

Micro-oxygenation: A controversial procedure that involves the introduction of minuscule amounts of oxygen into a tank of young wine, intended to simulate the natural conditions in a wooden barrel

Millerandage: Abnormal fruit set, a vine condition that results in grape bunches that have a high proportion of small seedless berries mixed in with the normal, larger, seed-bearing grapes.

Millésime: French. Vintage-dated

Mistelle: French. A sweet fortified wine made by adding grape spirits to grape must that may or may not have begun fermentation; a specific type of vin de liqueur

Mousse: French. 1. Literally, foam; 2. The bubbles in sparkling wine; 3. The foam that develops on top of vigorously fermenting wine

Muselet: A wire cage used to secure the cork in a bottle of sparkling wine

Must: Unfermented grape juice, may also include skins, seeds, and stems

Must weight: The density or specific gravity of unfermented grape juice, which roughly equates to the juice's sugar content and therefore the potential alcohol in the finished wine; measures of must weight include the widely used Brix scale, as well as Baumé, sometimes used in France, Oechsle in Germany, and KMW in Austria

Mutage: A winemaking process of stopping (or "muting") fermentation, usually by the addition of distilled spirits; may also involve the use of sulfur dioxide

Mutation: A genetic change; a natural but random alteration to the DNA of a grapevine that results in traits unlike those of the plant's parents or clone source

Nebuchadnezzar: A traditional large bottle for sparkling wine that holds 15 liters, equivalent to twenty standard bottles

Negociant/négociant: An intermediary who buys grapes or finished wine for resale and who may also ferment, age, blend, and/or bottle the wine

Noble rot: A term used in France and elsewhere to refer to the beneficial form of botrytis; see also pourriture noble

Node: A protuberance (thickened section) of a cane that will develop into a bud, leaves, shoots, tendrils, and/or flowers

Oechsle: German. A measure of the sugar level in grapes or must used in Germany

Oenophile: Literally, wine lover

Off-dry: Having a small amount of perceptible sugar

Off-odor: An unpleasant or atypical aroma in a wine

Off-premise: Away from the place of business; specifically, the segment of the wine industry that sells wine for consumption elsewhere, such as wine shops and supermarkets; cf. on-premise

Oidium: Powdery mildew

Olfactory epithelium: A patch of specialized cells located inside the nasal cavity; a sensory receptor for smell

On-premise: At the place of business; specifically, the segment of the wine industry that sells wine for consumption on-site, such as restaurants and wine bars; cf. off-premise

Organic viticulture: A practice of grape growing based on the avoidance of non-natural, manufactured chemicals such as pesticides and fertilizers

Organoleptic: Those properties of wine (or food) that are perceived by the senses; often used in relation to the sensory evaluation of wine, e.g., the organoleptic evaluation of wine

Ortswein: German. "Classified site wine"; often compared to the *village* wine classification of Burgundy; a VDP term

Oxidation: Chemical changes that take place in the presence of oxygen

Oxidized: A wine that has undergone oxidation; such a wine may show discoloration as well as a stale, flat aroma and flavor

Peronospora: Downy mildew

Pétillant: French. Slightly sparkling

Pétillant Naturel: French. 1. Literally, sparkling natural/naturally sparkling; 2. Unofficial term used to describe certain lightly sparkling wines produced using some version of the ancestral method; often abbreviated as "Pét-Nat"

pH: A measure of the strength of an acid or of an acidic solution such as wine; cf. total acidity

Phenolics: A class of complex carbohydrate molecules often responsible for certain organoleptic properties and other aspects of wine; also known as polyphenolics or polyphenols

Phenolic maturity: The point at which a grape reaches its ideal level of phenolic compounds such as tannins, anthocyanins, flavones, and other compounds that enhance the color, flavor, and aromas of the resulting wine

Photosynthesis: A biochemical process by which green plants convert carbon dioxide and water into simple sugar and oxygen

Phylloxera (*Daktulosphaira vitifoliae*): An insect (root louse) that sucks sap from grapevines, reducing their productivity and eventually killing them; one of the most serious pests in viticulture

Physical maturity: The point at which a grape attains its optimal level of sugar ripeness

Piccolo: Italian. 1. Literally, small; 2. A wine bottle holding 187.5 milliliters; see also split

Pierce's disease: One of the most serious vine diseases threatening vineyards today, caused by bacteria spread by the glassy-winged sharpshooter and other insects

Pigéage: French. The form of cap management known as "punching down"

Pipe: Portuguese. An oak barrel used in the production of Port

Polymerize: To join together two molecules, e.g., phenolics, to create a larger one

Polyphenolics: Long-chain phenolic molecules

Pomace: The residue left after grapes are pressed, consisting of skins, seeds, stems, and other solids

Pourriture noble: French. "Noble rot"; botrytis

Powdery mildew: A serious fungal disease of grapevines; also known as oidium

Prädikat: German. One of the subdivisions used to categorize Prädikatswein based on sugar level at harvest (plural *Prädikate*)

Prädikatswein: German. The highest category of wine in Germany, from a protected designation of origin (PDO); also used in Austria

Premier cru: French. "First growth"; the highest classification level in Bordeaux and the second highest classification level in Burgundy and Champagne

Press: 1. To squeeze grapes in order to extract the juice from the solids; 2. The machine used to press grapes, must, or finished wine

Primary aromas: Those aromas in a wine considered to be derived from the grape itself; see also secondary aromas, tertiary aromas

Protected designation of origin (PDO): The legal category of officially recognized quality wine regions used throughout the European Union

Protected geographical indication (PGI): The legal category of officially recognized wine regions below the quality wine level used throughout the European Union

Pruning: The removal of unwanted canes, shoots, and leaves from grapevines

Pumping over: A method of cap management that involves drawing liquid from the bottom of a tank of fermenting juice and pouring it over the top of the floating solids to wet and break up the cap

Punching down: A method of cap management that involves physically pushing the floating solids down into the tank of fermenting juice

Pupitre: French. A wooden rack traditionally used to hold bottles of sparkling wine during the process of riddling

Qualitätswein: German. The second highest category of wine in Germany (PDO)

Quality wine: Wine with superior characteristics; a legal category of wine with specific requirements used throughout the European Union

Quality Wine Produced in a Specified Region (QWPSR): Formerly, the general legal category of officially recognized quality wine regions in the European Union; has now been replaced by "protected designation of origin (PDO)"

Quinta: Portuguese. Wine estate

Rack and return: A type of cap management that involves draining the fermenting juice into a separate holding tank before it is returned to the original tank by spraying it over the now sunken cap; see also délestage

Racking: A clarification process that involves moving wine from one vessel (tank, barrel) to another in order to separate the wine from sediment

Rebêche: French. In Champagne production, juice from the flesh nearest to the pips or skins that is extracted by more powerful pressing after the taille; may be used for still wines, vinegars, or distillation

Recioto: Italian. A style of sweet wine made from dried grapes

Recognition threshold: The smallest amount of a stimulus (e.g., sugar on the tongue) necessary to be noticed and identified

Reduction: The chemical opposite of oxidation in which oxygen is scavenged from various molecules

Refractometer: A device that measures the refraction of light through a liquid, used to measure the sugar level of grape juice in Brix

Rehoboam: A traditional large bottle for sparkling wine that holds 4.5 liters, equivalent to six standard bottles

Remontage: French. The form of cap management known as "pumping over"

Remuage: French. Riddling

Reserva: Spanish. 1. A term used for Spanish DO and DOCa wines that have gone through moderate periods of barrel and/or bottle aging as defined by an area's regulating council; 2. A term used for vinos finos in Argentina that have undergone a specified period of aging; 3. A somewhat undefined term when used in Spanish-speaking wine areas such as Chile; see also crianza and gran reserva

Reserve: 1. Wine with superior characteristics compared to a winery's other wines; may or may not be legally defined; 2. To hold back for future use

Residual sugar: Sugar that remains in a wine after fermentation, usually measured in grams per liter (g/L) or percent

Respiration: The biological process of breaking down chemicals such as sugar in order to release stored energy

Resveratrol: A phenolic compound found in grapes that is believed to have beneficial health effects for humans

Riddling: Shaking and repositioning bottles of sparkling wine in order to move dead yeast cells to the neck of the bottle for disgorging; see also remuage

Ripasso: Italian. A style of wine made from combining the pomace left over from the production of Amarone or recioto with a batch of freshly fermented wine

Rootstock: The portion of a grafted grapevine that is rooted in the soil; cf. scion

Rosado: Spanish. Rosé

Rosato: Italian. Rosé

Rosé: French. Pink-hued wine made from red grapes that have had limited contact with the grape skins

Rosso: Italian. Red

Rot: German. Red

Rouge: French. Red

Saccharomyces cerevisiae: The species of yeast most widely used in winemaking

Saignée: French. Literally, bled; a process used for the production of rosé wine in which a portion of the juice is run off from a batch of macerating or fermenting must; may also result in the production of deeply hued red wines

Salmanazar: A traditional large bottle for sparkling wine that holds 9 liters, equivalent to twelve standard bottles

Schaumwein: German. Aerated sparkling wine produced via carbonation

Schilfwein: German. A term used in Austria to denote a wine produced from grapes dried post-harvest; may refer to grapes dried on mats of reeds (*Schilf*); see also Strohwein

Scion: The portion of a grafted grapevine that produces shoots, leaves, and fruit; cf. rootstock

Sec: French. 1. Dry; 2. A sweetness category of sparkling wine that is moderately sweet

Secco: Italian. Dry

Seco: Spanish. Dry

Secondary aromas: Those aromas in a wine considered to be derived from the winemaking process; see also primary aromas, tertiary aromas

Sekt: German. Sparkling wine typically produced using the tank method

Sélection de grains nobles: French. A wine made from selected grapes affected by botrytis

Solera: Spanish. 1. A system of aging and fractional blending of wines traditionally used for Sherry; 2. The lowest (oldest) set of barrels in a solera system

Sparkling wine: Wine that contains dissolved carbon dioxide under pressure so that it produces bubbles spontaneously when its bottle is opened

Spätlese: German. A category of the Prädikat that represents wine made from ripe bunches of grapes

Species: A grouping of grapevines that are genetically similar, have broad characteristics in common, and can produce viable offspring through sexual reproduction; see also labrusca; subspecies; variety; vinifera

Split: A wine bottle containing 187.5 milliliters; see also piccolo

Spumante: Italian. Fully sparkling

Spur: The shortened stub of a grapevine cane created via pruning

Still: 1. Not sparkling; 2. A piece of equipment used for distillation

Stomata: Openings on the underside of a vine's leaves

Strohwine: German. A term used in Austria to denote a wine produced from grapes dried post-harvest; may refer to grapes dried on mats of straw (*Stroh*); see also Schilfwein

Stuck fermentation: A situation in which the fermentation of wine stops on its own before the desired level of alcohol is produced

Subspecies: A grouping of grapevines within a species that have considerable genetic and qualitative similarity; more or less synonymous with variety

Succinic acid: An acid that is a minor component in grapes and a by-product of normal alcoholic fermentation

Sulfite: A category of sulfur-containing chemical compounds

Sulfur dioxide: The most common form of sulfur in wine; a preservative

Sur lie: French. "On the lees," referring to wine that has had extended time in contact with dead yeast cells

Sur pointe: French. An upside-down vertical positioning of a bottle, sometimes used in the riddling stage of sparkling wine

Süss: German. Sweet

Süssreserve: German. Grape juice held in reserve to be added to wine as a sweetening agent after fermentation

Sustainability: A philosophy of agriculture that focuses on maintaining the viability of the land, the crops, agricultural businesses, and the agricultural workforce

Table wine: 1. A wine intended for consumption during a meal; 2. Any nonsparkling, unfortified, and relatively dry wine; 3. In the United States, any wine with 14% alcohol or less; 4. The former general legal category for wines with minimal restrictions on production in the European Union, now simply referred to as "wine"

Taille: French. In Champagne production, fractions of juice from specific pressings

Tannic: Containing high levels of tannin

Tannin: A phenolic compound found in grapes that gives wine a somewhat bitter taste and a distinctive mouth-drying feel

Tartaric acid: The most common acid in grapes and wine

Tartrate: A crystalline compound that is formed when wine contains more tartaric acid than it can retain in a dissolved state, particularly when the wine is chilled

Taste: A sensory characteristic of a wine detectable by the taste buds of the tongue and mouth

TCA: 2,4,6-trichloroanisole, the primary chemical responsible for cork taint

Tears: Streaks produced by viscous droplets of liquid that run slowly down the interior of a glass of wine after swirling; see also legs

Teinturier: A red wine grape with dark (red/blue/purple) flesh in addition to dark skin

Terroir: French. The all-inclusive physical environment of a vineyard

Tertiary aromas: The complex range of aromas that evolve in a wine following fermentation and aging, particularly bottle aging; also known as bouquet; see also primary aromas; secondary aromas

Tête de cuvée: French. The finest sparkling wine made by a given winery

Three-tier system: A regulatory system in the United States and some other countries that requires separation among businesses involved in (1) making, (2) distributing, and (3) retailing wine

Tinto: Spanish. Red; red wine

Tirage: French. Bottling

Tonne: A metric ton, equal to 1,000 kilograms or about 2,200 pounds (compared to a standard English ton of 2,000 pounds)

Total acidity: A measure of the quantity of all the acids in a wine, usually in grams per liter (g/L); cf. pH

Training system: A method of positioning and shaping grapevines to improve the quality of the fruit and/or the ease of harvesting

Transfer method: A method of sparkling wine production that follows the traditional method through the second fermentation and lees aging, then begins the clarification stage with the wine emptied into a pressurized tank

Translocation: The movement of sugar and other compounds from one part of a plant to another, especially from leaves to fruit

Transpiration: The evaporation of water through openings on the underside of plants' leaves (stomata)

Trellis: A physical structure to support grapevines as part of a training system

Trocken: German. Dry

Trockenbeerenauslese (TBA): German. A category of the Prädikat that represents very sweet dessert wines made from individually harvested, extremely overripe berries that are often affected by botrytis

Turbid: Cloudy, having sediment or foreign particles

Umami: One of the generally accepted five basic taste components; represents the taste sensation of certain amino acids

Vanillin: A phenolic compound found in oak that gives barrel-aged wines a vanilla aroma or flavor

Varietal: Relating to a grape variety

Varietal wine: A wine made primarily with a single grape variety and named for a single grape variety

Variety: A named type of grapevine with recognizable characteristics; more or less synonymous with *subspecies*

Vendange: French. The grape harvest

Vendange tardive: French. "Late harvest"; wine made from overripe grapes

Vendemmia: Italian. The grape harvest

Vendimia: Spanish. 1. Harvest; 2. Vintage; see also cosecha

Veraison: A biochemical change in grapes when color (other than green) first appears in the grapes, sugar and other flavor components are stored in the grapes, and the berries begin to enlarge and soften

Verband Deutscher Prädikatsweingüter (VDP): German. The organization of Germany's leading wine estates

Vin de France: French. Basic wine ("table wine") made from 100% French grapes

Vin de liqueur: French. Sweet fortified wine

Vin de pays: French. "Country wine"; the higher category of basic wine in France, from a protected geographical indication (PGI)

Vin doux naturel: French. A sweet fortified wine made by adding grape spirits to partially fermented grape must

Vinho regional: Portuguese. "Regional wine"; the higher category of basic wine in Portugal, from a protected geographical indication (PGI)

Vinifera (*Vitis vinifera*): The species of wine grape native to the Middle East and Europe that is used to produce most quality wine

Vinification: The process of winemaking

Vino de calidad con indicación geográfica (VCIG): Spanish. One of the subcategories of quality wine used in Spain; a protected designation of origin (PDO)

Vino de la tierra (VdlT): Spanish. "Country wine"; the higher category of basic wine in Spain, from a protected geographical indication (PGI)

Vino de pago: Spanish. "Estate wine"; a PDO-level wine category granted to individual wine estates of distinction

Vintage: 1. The year in which grapes were harvested; 2. A style of wine, generally used in reference to sparkling or fortified wine

Viticulture: The science and practice of grape growing, sometimes known as *winegrowing*

Volatile: Prone to evaporation

Weiss: German. White

Weissherbst: German. A single-variety rosé of Qualitätswein quality or higher

Yeast: Single-celled organisms responsible for the primary alcoholic fermentation of wine; see also Saccharomyces cerevisiae

The following works include sources used in the preparation of this guide and additional references that may be useful to candidates.

GENERAL

Bird, David. *Understanding Wine Technology, 3rd ed.* Newark: DBQA Publishing, 2011.

Clarke, Oz. *Oz Clarke's World of Wine: A Grand Tour of the Great Wine Regions.* New York: Sterling Epicure, 2017.

Clarke, Oz, and Margaret Rand. *Grapes & Wines: A Comprehensive Guide to Varieties and Flavours, Revised and Expanded Edition.* New York: Sterling Epicure, 2015.

Goode, Jamie. *The Science of Wine: From Vine to Glass, 2nd ed.* Berkeley: University of California Press, 2014.

Goode, Jamie. *Flawless: Understanding Faults in Wine.* Berkeley: University of California Press, 2018.

Hudelson, John. *Wine Faults—Causes, Effects, Cures.* San Francisco: Wine Appreciation Guild, 2011.

Jackson. Nick. *Beyond Flavour: The Indispensable Handbook to Blind Wine Tasting.* New York, 2020.

Johnson, Hugh, and Jancis Robinson. *The World Atlas of Wine, 8th ed.* London: Mitchell Beazley, 2019.

MacNeil, Karen. *The Wine Bible, 2nd ed.* New York: Workman, 2015.

Robinson, Jancis, Julia Harding, and José Vouillamoz. *Wine Grapes.* New York: Harper Collins Publishers, 2012.

Robinson, Jancis, ed. *The Oxford Companion to Wine, 4th ed.* New York: Oxford University Press, 2015.

Skelton, Stephen. Viticulture: *An Introduction to Commercial Grape Growing for Wine Production, 2nd ed.* London: S.P. Skelton Ltd, 2001.

Smith, Clark. *Postmodern Winemaking: Rethinking the Modern Science of an Ancient Craft.* Berkeley: University of California Press, 2014.

Taber, George. *Judgment of Paris: California vs. France and the Historic 1976 Paris Tasting That Revolutionized Wine.* New York: Scribner, 2005.

Zraly, Kevin. *The Windows on the World Complete Wine Course, 35th Anniversary Edition.* New York: Sterling Publishing, 2020.

WINES OF EUROPE AND THE MEDITERRANEAN

Anson, Jane. *Inside Bordeaux: The Châteaux, their Wines and the Terroir.* BB&R Press, London, 2020

Baiocchi, Talia. *Sherry: A Modern Guide to the Wine World's Best-Kept Secret, with Cocktails and Recipes.* Berkeley: Ten Speed Press, 2014.

Brook, Stephen. *The Wines of Austria.* Oxford: Infinite Ideas Publishing, 2019.

D'Agata, Ian. *Italy's Native Wine Grape Terroirs.* Oakland: University of California Press, 2019.

D'Agata, Ian. *Native Wine Grapes of Italy.* Oakland: University of California Press, 2014.

Evans, Sarah Jane. *The Wines of Northern Spain: From Galicia to the Pyrenees and Rioja to the Basque Country.* Oxford: Infinite Ideas Ltd, 2018

Krebiehl, Anne. *The Wines of Germany.* Oxford: Infinite Ideas Publishing, 2019.

Lazarakis, Konstantinos. *The Wines of Greece.* Oxford: Infinite Ideas Ltd, 2018.

Lewin, Benjamin. *Wines of France: A Guide to 500 Leading Vineyards.* Dover: Vendange Press, 2015.

Liem, Peter. *Champagne: The Essential Guide to the Wines, Producers, and Terroirs of the Iconic Region.* Berkeley: Ten Speed Press, 2017.

Mayson, Richard. *Port and the Douro, 4th ed.* London: Mitchell Beazley, 2018.

Rogov, Daniel. *The Ultimate Rogov's Guide to Israeli Wines.* San Francisco: Wine Appreciation Guild, 2011.

WINES OF NORTH AMERICA

Bonne, Jon. *The New California Wine: A Guide to the Producers and Wines Behind a Revolution in Taste*. Berkeley: Ten Speed Press, 2013.

Gregutt, Paul. *Washington Wines and Wineries: The Essential Guide*. Berkeley: University of California Press, 2011.

Perry, Vivian. *Winemakers of the Willamette Valley: Pioneering Vintners from Oregon's Wine Country*. London: The History Press, 2013.

Philips, Rod. *The Wines of Canada*. Oxford: Infinite Ideas Ltd, 2017.

Robinson, Jancis, and Linda Murphy. *American Wine: The Ultimate Companion to the Wines and Wineries of the United States*. Berkeley: University of California Press, 2012.

WINES OF SOUTH AMERICA

Desimone, Mike, and Jeff Jenssen. *Wines of the Southern Hemisphere*. New York: Sterling Epicure, 2012.

Goldstein, Evan. *Wines of South America: The Essential Guide*. Oakland: University of California Press, 2014.

WINES OF OCEANIA, AFRICA, AND ASIA

Clark, Jim. *The Wines of South Africa*. Oxford: Infinite Ideas Ltd, 2020.

Gibb, Rebecca. *The Wines of New Zealand*. Oxford: Infinite Ideas Ltd, 2018.

Halliday, James. *Wine Atlas of Australia*. London: Hardie Grant. 2014.

Moran, Warren. *New Zealand Wine: The Land, the Vines, the People*. Auckland: Auckland University Press, 2016.

Rose, Anthony. *Sake and the Wines of Japan*. Oxford: Infinite Ideas Ltd, 2018.

THE SOCIETY OF WINE EDUCATORS' LOGICAL TASTING RATIONALE

Below you will find a copy of the Society of Wine Educators' Logical Tasting Rationale to accompany the Certified Specialist of Wine Study Guide. The Logical Tasting Rationale categorizes the wine tasting process into five steps: Appearance, Aroma, Palate, Finish, and Quality. Instructions on the use of this form may be found in chapter 21 of this Study Guide. A template for writing a simplified wine tasting note using the same terminology may be found in the CSW Workbook.

THE SOCIETY OF WINE EDUCATORS' LOGICAL TASTING RATIONALE TO ACCOMPANY THE CERTIFIED SPECIALIST OF WINE STUDY GUIDE					
Wine:					
Glass number:					
Notes about this wine:					
Appearance					
Clarity:	Brilliant	Clear	Dull		
Depth:	Pale	Medium	Deep	Opaque	
Hue: White:	Platinum	Yellow/Green	Yellow	Gold	Amber	Brown
Rosé:	Pink	Salmon	Orange		
Red:	Purple	Ruby	Garnet	Tawny	Brown
Other Observations:	Bubbles	Legs	Rim Variation	Deposits	None
Aromas					
Aromas: See appendix D (Wine Aroma Checklist) for suggested terminology.					
Palate					
Sweetness:	Dry	Off-dry	Sweet		
Acidity:	Low	Medium	High		
Bitterness:	None	Low	Medium	High	
Tannin:	None	Low	Medium	High	
Alcohol:	Low	Medium	High		
Body: Light	Medium	Full			
Flavors: See appendix D (Wine Aroma Checklist) for suggested terminology.					
Finish					
Finish:	Short	Medium	Long		
Quality					
Quality:	Poor	Acceptable	Good	Very Good	Excellent
Further Notes:					

WINE AROMA CHECKLIST

The following wine aroma checklist presents many of the most common wine aromas and classifies them for ease of detection and recognition. The categories on the checklist are not mutually exclusive and are not intended to represent an absolute or a standard; checklists such as this are merely meant to be a tool to help the student understand the many aromas that may be recognized in wine.

AROMA CATEGORY	SPECIFIC AROMAS
Tree Fruit	Apricot, nectarine, peach, yellow pear, red apple, white peach, red plum, quince
Citrus Fruit	Grapefruit, lemon, lemon curd, lemonade, lime, orange, mandarin orange, orange peel, orange zest, tangerine
Green Fruit	Gooseberry, green grape, green apple, green pear, green plum
Tropical Fruit	Papaya, mango, pineapple, guava, banana, kiwi, lychee, melon, passion fruit
Red Fruit	Red cherry, sour cherry, raspberry, strawberry, pomegranate, red plum, red currant, rhubarb, grape, grape juice
Black Fruit	Blackberry, black cherry, black currant (cassis), black plum, blueberry, boysenberry, mulberry
Dried Fruit	Dried cherry, fig, raisin, golden raisin, prune, jam, fruit cake, baked apple, apricot jam
Floral	Acacia, chamomile, dried flowers, jasmine, honeysuckle, lavender, orange blossom, perfume, rose, rose petal, violet, wildflower, elderflower, geranium, potpourri
Vegetal	Green bell pepper, eucalyptus, fennel, menthol, fresh tobacco leaf, tomato leaf, green olive, black olive, asparagus, celery
Fresh herbs	Dill, lemon grass, mint, rosemary, bay leaf, thyme, sage
Dry Herbs	Hay, straw, dried herbs, herbs de Provence, dried tobacco
Grassy	Green grass, freshly cut grass
Minerality	Flint, graphite (pencil lead), salt air, gunpowder, steel, slate, wet concrete, wet stone, chalk, wet chalk, fresh rain, gravel, granite
Butter	Butter, buttered popcorn, butterscotch
Yeast	Yeast, bread dough, brioche
Toast	Toast, burnt toast
Nuts	Almond, hazelnut, marzipan, walnut
Oak	Oak, fresh-cut lumber, cedar, cigar box, pine, sandalwood, smoke
Vanilla	Vanilla, vanilla cookies
Coconut	Coconut
Honey	Honey
Botrytis	Musty, moldy, honey, honeysuckle, beeswax, apricot
Earthy	Barnyard, bramble, smoke, dirt, wet dirt, wet leaves, dusty, forest floor, musk, garrigue
Mushroom	Mushroom, truffles

AROMA CATEGORY	SPECIFIC AROMAS
Tea	Black tea
Coffee	Coffee, espresso, burnt coffee, mocha
Leather	Leather, leathery, wet saddle
Spice	Anise, baking spices, black pepper, cinnamon, clove, ginger, nutmeg, white pepper, incense
Chemical	Petrol (gasoline), diesel, kerosene, nail polish remover (acetone), cosmetic, rubber bands, varnish, tar, ammonia, "pipi du chat"
Other	Chocolate, cocoa, cola, smoke, soy sauce, balsamic, maple, smoked meat, bacon, wet dog, wet wool, game (gamey), wax (waxy, beeswax), lanolin

Made in United States
North Haven, CT
17 January 2024

47585971R00175